FOUNDATIONS OF THE
FRANKFURT SCHOOL
OF SOCIAL RESEARCH

FOUNDATIONS OF THE FRANKFURT SCHOOL OF SOCIAL RESEARCH

Edited by
Judith Marcus *and* **Zoltán Tar**

Transaction Books
New Brunswick (U.S.A.) and London (U.K.)

Second Printing, 1988.
Copyright © 1984 by Transaction, Inc.
New Brunswick, New Jersey 08903

Library of Congress Catalog Number: 84-8610
ISBN: 0-87855-963-9 (paper)
Printed in the United States of America

Library of Congress Cataloging in Publication Data
Main entry under title:
Foundations of the Frankfurt School of Social Research.
   Includes index.
   1. Frankfurt school of sociology—Addresses, essays, lectures.
2. Frankfurt school of sociology—History—Addresses, essays, lectures.
I. Marcus, Judith. II. Tar, Zoltán.
HM24.F6785   1984   301'.01   84-8610
ISBN 0-87855-963-9 (pbk.)

Contents

Preface

Our greatest debt goes to Professor Joseph B. Maier, who advised and participated at every stage of this project. As its chairman, he invited Zoltán Tar to his Columbia University seminar on Content and Method and suggested the title for the talk: "The Frankfurt School Revisited"; thus the idea for the present volume was born. As the discussant of the ASA session on Critical Theory in 1980, he contributed further to a more correct evaluation of Frankfurt thought. Four of the papers presented at that session (Kreckel, Kurzweil, Löwy, and Heydebrand-Burris) are incorporated here. The editors also wish to thank Alice Maier, long-time secretary to Max Horkheimer and one of the executors of his estate, for generously sharing with us her recollection of her years with the institute and its director.

Most of the arguments set out in the "Introduction" were first presented in lectures and seminars given at various times in New York City (Columbia University and New School for Social Research) and at the universities of Munich and Zagreb. Grateful acknowledgment is given to teachers and students at these institutions, especially to Drs. Dirk Käsler and Helmut Dubiel in Munich and Ivan Kuvacic and Gajo Petrovic in Zagreb.

Thanks are due to Mrs. Hope McAloon for her prompt and careful technical assistance. At Transaction thanks are due to Dalia Buzin.

Needless to say that the chief responsibility lies with the editors for the selection, editing, and in many cases for the translation of the material, and with Zoltán Tar alone for the "Introduction."

Judith Marcus
Zoltán Tar

Acknowledgments

The editors gratefully acknowledge the following authors, publishers, and publications for permission to use previously published material:

Joseph B. Maier, "Contribution to a Critique of Critical Theory," *The New Social Sciences,* Baidya Nath Varma, ed. (Westport, Conn.: Greenwood Press, 1976), pp. 73–101. Reprinted by permission of the publisher, Greenwood Press, a Division of Congressional Information Service, Inc.

Jürgen Habermas, "The Frankfurt School in New York," *Süddeutsche Zeitung* (Munich, August 2–3, 1980), pp. 1–2. Translated by Judith Marcus. Translated and reprinted by permission of the author.

Alfred Schmidt, "The Idea of Critical Theory," was originally published in Max Horkheimer, *Kritische Theorie,* vol. 2 (Frankfurt am Main: S. Fischer Verlag, 1968), pp. 333–58. Translated—by permission of the author—in an abridged form by Judith Marcus. Reprinted by permission of the publisher.

Heinz Lubasz, "Review Essay of Martin Jay, *The Dialectical Imagination,*" was first published in *History and Theory,* vol. xiv, no. 2 (1975):200–212. Reprinted by permission of the author and of the copyright holder, Wesleyan University. Copyright © 1975.

Leszek Kolakowski, "The Frankfurt School and Critical Theory," is an excerpt from his book *Main Currents of Marxism,* vol. 3, translated by P.S. Falla (Oxford: Clarendon Press, 1978), pp. 357–80, 395. Copyright © 1978 by Oxford University Press. Reprinted by permission of Oxford University Press.

Michael Landmann, "Critique of Reason from Max Weber to Jürgen Habermas," is reprinted from his book *Alienatory Reason* (Normal, Ill.: Applied Literature Press, 1978), pp. 105–19, by permission of the author.

Arnold Künzli, "Left Irrationalism," is an excerpt from his book *Aufklärung und Dialektik* (Freiburg: Verlag Rombach, 1971), pp. 123–56. Translated by Zoltán Tar and Judith Marcus. Reprinted by permission of the author.

Karl R. Popper, "Reason or Revolution?" was first published in *Archives Européennes de Sociologie 11* (1970):252–62, and reprinted in Theodor

W. Adorno et al., *The Positivist Dispute in German Sociology* (London: Heinemann Educational Books, 1976), pp. 288–300. Reprinted by permission of the author.

Georg Lukács, "On Walter Benjamin," was originally published in his book *Ästhetik* (Neuwied-Berlin: Luchterhand, 1963), vol. 2, pp. 759–66. Translated version first appeared in *New Left Review* 110 (July–August 1978):83–88. Reprinted by permission of NLR.

István Hermann, "Lukács and Horkheimer: The Place of Aesthetics in Horkheimer's Thought," is taken from his book *A szfinx rejtvénye* (Budapest: Gondolat, 1973), pp. 151–67. Translated by Judith Marcus. Reprinted by permission of the author.

Ferenc Fehér, "Negative Philosophy of Music—Positive Results," *New German Critique* 4 (Winter 1975):99–111. Reprinted by permission of NGC.

Peter Uwe Hohendahl, "Autonomy of Art: Looking Back at Adorno's *Aesthetische Theorie,*" *The German Quarterly* 54 (March 1981):133–49. Reprinted by permission of GQ.

Paul F. Lazarsfeld, "Critical Theory and Dialectics," is reprinted from his book *Qualitative Analysis: Historical and Critical Essays* (Boston: Allyn and Bacon, 1972), pp. 168–80. This essay was originally published in *Main Trends of Research in the Social and Human Sciences* (Paris: Mouton, UNESCO, 1970), pp. 111–17.

Franco Ferrarotti, "The Struggle of Reason against Total Bureaucratization," is an excerpt from his book *Il Pensiero Sociologico da Auguste Comte a Max Horkheimer* (Milan: Mondadori, 1974). Translated by Judith Marcus. Reprinted and translated by permission of the author.

Hans-Jürgen Krahl, "The Political Contradictions in Adorno's Critical Theory," was originally published in *Frankfurter Rundschau* (August 20, 1969). English translation first appeared in *Sociological Review* 23 (1975):831–34. Reprinted by permission of the publisher and of the copyrights holder of Krahl's writings. © Verlag Neue Kritik, Frankfurt am Main.

Ehrhard Bahr, "The Anti-Semitism Studies of the Frankfurt School: The Failure of Critical Theory," *The German Studies Review,* vol. 1, no. 2 (May 1978):125–38. Reprinted by permission of GSR.

Giacomo Marramao, "Political Economy and Critical Theory," is an excerpt from his book *Teoria e prassi dell'economia di piano* (Bari: De

Donato, 1973), pp. 11–47. Edited and translated by Zoltán Tar and Judith Marcus. Reprinted by permission of the author.

Göran Therborn, "The Frankfurt School," *New Left Review* 63 (September–October 1970):75–96. Reprinted by permission of NLR.

Lucio Colletti, "From Hegel to Marcuse," is an excerpt from his book *From Rousseau to Lenin: Studies in Ideology and Society* (London: New Left Books, 1972), pp. 128–40. Reprinted by permission of NLB of the *Monthly Review Press*. Copyright © 1972 by NLB.

Lucien Goldmann, "Understanding Marcuse," *Partisan Review,* vol. 38, no. 3 (1971):247–62. Copyright © 1971 by Partisan Review. Reprinted by permission of PR.

Introduction

Zoltán Tar

"A specter is haunting the sociological enterprise—the specter of the Frankfurt School." So began my introduction to a study of the Critical Theories of the Frankfurt thinkers Max Horkheimer and Theodor W. Adorno.[1] In the years since passed, a considerable part of the "cloud of myth, ambiguity, and confusion" I then thought surrounded the school has been dispelled—and not only in the sociological enterprise. While I choose to direct my attention exclusively toward the sociological aspect and implications of Frankfurt thought, I am keenly aware of the truly interdisciplinary endeavor of the school ranging from philosophy and sociology to economics, political science, and literary scholarship—institutionally anchored in the Institute for Social Research since its establishment in Frankfurt am Main in 1923. Accordingly, the reception, perception, and dissection of the intellectual heritage of the school cut through a cross-section of academic disciplines.

The images and perception of the school in their diversity extend well beyond academia. For example, one of the popular images of the Frankfurt School perpetuated in the media is that of a breeding ground for the West German—even worldwide—student protest movement of the 1960s and the terrorist movement of the Baader-Meinhof kind in the 1970s. The first accusation was made and persisted despite Adorno's dissociation from the radical students in his famous *Spiegel* interview: "I had set up a theoretical model but could not expect that it would be put into practice with Molotov cocktails."[2] Even Jürgen Habermas's denunciation of the radical students as "left-fascists"[3] could not quite erase that image. During the 1970s at the height of West German terrorist activities, conservative and right-wing West German politicians[4] stated publicly that the Frankfurt School was directly responsible for them. Those views were reported widely, as exemplified by Flora Lewis's article in *The New York Times*.[5] The American echo of such outrageous assertions is undoubtedly due to its unfamiliarity with the content of the original Frankfurt studies; this assumption is partly confirmed by John Leonard's recent complaint in his review of a Brecht biography that "we are not told what the Frankfurt School was all about."[6] I will come back later to the American

1

perception of "what the school was about" in my brief discussion of the reception of the Frankfurt School in the United States.

Almost a decade ago it was still possible to assert that "the impact of the Frankfurt School on the American academic community and intellectual circles . . . was minimal."[7] This is obviously no longer the case for several reasons. First, many admirers and advocates of Frankfurt thought, graduate students of the late 1960s and early 1970s, became part of the junior and middle-level echelons of the academic establishment and contributed to the dissemination of Critical Theory. Another factor in the increasing impact of the school is the availability of English translations of most of the major works of Horkheimer, Adorno, et al., often brought out in inexpensive paperback editions. The secondary literature has in the meantime grown to such an extent that its compilation would be an almost insurmountable task. These factors not only help to preserve the intellectual heritage of the Frankfurt School but also contribute to a marked divergence in its image and perception and to the often acrimonious tone of the discussion about its nature and impact. Therein lies at least in part the answer to the queston: Why add a volume of two dozen essays to the already voluminous literature published on the Frankfurt School and Critical Theory?

The first and most obvious reason for such an essay collection is to make easily available scattered articles and a critical assessment to those interested in Frankfurt thought. Quite a few of the essays included have never before been translated into English. Others have, but either in a pirated or incorrectly rendered version[8] which does not contribute to a better understanding of what "the school is all about." These essays are now available for the first time translated from the original German, Hungarian, or Italian texts. The ongoing intellectual battle over the Frankfurt School and/or Critical Theory also inspired a collection of representative articles that deal with different aspects of the work of major writers of the school and at the same time reflect their *polarized* perception and reception both in Europe and the United States. Some of the contributions were written exclusively for this volume, and their themes were first tentatively explored in the framework of the Critical Theory session at the 1980 annual meeting of the American Sociological Association in New York City, with myself as organizer, Judith Marcus as presider, and Joseph B. Maier as discussant. At least in one case— that of Sir Karl Popper's "autobiographical musings" on the Frankfurt School—the contribution was an unexpected but very welcome "bonus" to an already published article by the same author. In other cases—such as the short excursion of Lukács on Benjamin or Kolakowski's assessment of Adorno's philosophical contribution—the critical reflections on Frankfurt thought were buried in large-scale works which made it unlikely that they would have been easily discovered by those in search of literature on the Frankfurt School only.

Just as the original Institute for Social Research assembled outstanding representatives of many disciplines, the selection and organization of this collection mirrors that interdisciplinary endeavor. Since, for better or worse, the traditional division of labor manifests itself also within academia in the form of the departmentalization of knowledge, the essays are grouped under six topical headings. Reflecting the worldwide reception of the Frankfurt School, the selection includes Western and Eastern European scholarship as well as their American counterparts. The same is true for the ideological outlook for the authors, ranging from conservative to liberal to neo-Marxist. In short, the objective was to provide a comprehensive reevaluation of Frankfurt thought on the basis of disciplinary breakdown—cutting the Frankfurt School into pieces, so to speak—by outstanding representatives of individual academic disciplines, who often assessed the achievements and shortcomings of the Frankfurt School from opposite intellectual and political positions.

Only one aspect is missing that would have deserved a separate heading: the Frankfurt School and Judaism. In my book *The Frankfurt School*, I judged the impact of Judaism as latent throughout the 50-year history of Frankfurt thought and gave the topic "Frankfurt School and Judaic thought" a rather sketchy treatment.[9] Although I may have simplified the connection between the Judaic heritage and Frankfurt thought— and would treat the whole question a bit differently today—I still believe that I was on the right track. Thus, I read with great interest and a certain satisfaction Gershom Scholem's cryptic remark in his book *From Berlin to Jerusalem*[10] that the Institute for Social Research of Max Horkheimer was one of the most remarkable "Jewish sects" that German Jewry produced. I am also glad that I stimulated at least some interest in the subject among those members of the New Left interested in the Frankfurt School. While Martin Jay in his *Dialectical Imagination* almost dismissed the "meaningfulness of Jewishness" and its role in Frankfurt thought and considered Judaism's impact "negligible," he seems to have reconsidered his position as his recent article demonstrates.[11] There are others who move along this line and even try to discover their own Jewish roots that had been buried in their suburban upbringing and "radical" politics.[12] George Steiner perceptively remarks that the "Scarsdale experience" (where things just "do not happen" as they did in Europe) may give only a limited, purely intellectual understanding without any "personal relevance"[13] of what the Jewish experience was in Europe; it does not quite suffice to understand the more complex historical-sociological experience in European Jewish intellectuals like Horkheimer, Benjamin, Adorno, or Lukács. The Bolshevik Jew, Georg Lukács, whose brother was murdered in Mauthausen by the Nazis, could only sympathize with Semprun's Jewish hero who in the French resistance did not wish to die a "Jewish death," meaning that in the Marxist-Trotskyist tradition he wanted not the limited Jewish emancipation but the emancipation of all the oppressed, as Heinrich Heine so eloquently put it: "What is the great assignment of our times? It is the emancipation, not only of the people of Ireland, of the Greeks, the Jews of Frankfurt, the blacks of West India and similar depressed people, but of the whole world."[14]

If I were to approach this issue today, I would start with Milton Friedman's reflections on the subject (without feeling obliged to embrace his politics and/or economics), that is, with the existence historically of two Jewish traditions. Before leaving for Israel on a fact-finding and consulting trip in 1977, Friedman expressed his views on capitalism, socialism, and the Jews: "My first visit to Israel was made about 15 years ago, and after I left Israel I summarized my impressions by saying that I thought . . . [that] two Jewish traditions were at war with one another in Israel. One of them was a very recent tradition—a tradition 100 or 150 years old. That is the tradition of socialism. . . . Jewish intellectuals have been strongly prosocialist and have contributed disproportionally to the socialist literature. The other tradition, I said was at least 2,000 years old. . . . Here was a tradition of how you get around government regulations. How you find chinks in controls, how you find those areas in which the free market operates and make the most of it."[15] I think Friedman was simplifying things when assuming that the socialist tradition in Judaism is only 100 to 150 years old; both traditions are as old as Judaism itself and often work side by side.

The uninitiated or those who would first encounter the Frankfurt heritage through this collection may be slightly taken aback by the references at one time to the Institute for Social Research, and then to the Frankfurt School or Critical Theory. The complaint may seem justified that they should be told what the "Frankfurt School is all about." It is a generally acknowledged fact that "for any analysis of the sixties and seventies it is crucial to understand the role of the Frankfurt School."[16] The Frankfurt School story has three different sociopolitical contexts in which the intellectual work of the school underwent changes; in addition, historical events even forced the school to change its geographic setting. "There is an interesting story to be told about the transformation of a Marxist institute . . . into a center of critical sociophilosophical theory," as Heinz Lubasz remarks in his contribution to this volume.

The Story of the Frankfurt School

The institutional origins of the Frankfurt School and its Critical Theory go back to 1923 when the Institut für Sozialforschung was established in Frankfurt am Main, privately endowed and affiliated with the Johann Wolfgang Goethe University at Frankfurt. As Bertolt Brecht, the acid-tongued German playwright described it: "A rich old man, the grain speculator Weil, dies, disturbed by the miseries on earth. In his will he leaves a large sum for the establishment of an institute to investigate the sources of that misery, which is, of course, he himself."[17] Brecht may have taken some poetic liberty with the facts but he was not quite off the mark. Martin Jay's work on the history of the Frankfurt School and the Institute of Social Research has little to say about the genesis of the institute and its philosophy, as promised on the book's jacket.[18] Dissatisfied with a "court history" that relied mainly on the account and materials retrospectively given by institute members, Ulrika Migdal[19] recently published the result of her longstanding and painstaking research of that genesis and philosophy. We learn that the gifts of the founder, Hermann Weil, were indeed substantial. Migdal traces Weil's life and dealings from the time when he was an economic advisor to the German Imperial Army to his efforts to establish business connections with the new state, Soviet Russia, in the form of grain imports from the Ukraine. She convincingly argues that the coproduction of MEGA (*Marx-Engels Historisch Kritische Gesamtausgabe*) by the Frankfurt Institute and the Marx-Engels Institute of Moscow and the exclusive grain imports to war-ravaged Austria and Germany in 1921–22 were not accidental.

Be that as it may, 1923 was decisive in many ways. It represents a watershed for the European labor movement, for theory and praxis. Three historical events, interrelated in many ways, stand out: First, the defeat of the October 1923 Communist uprising in Hamburg; second, publication of Georg Lukács's *History and Class Consciousness*; and third, foundation of the Frankfurt Institute by Hermann Weil, after he had once before, in 1920, attempted to establish such an institute.

The defeat of the Hamburg insurrection marked the very end of a wave of East and Central European revolutionary movements that began in Petrograd and swept through Budapest, Munich, and Berlin. The Hamburg failure was the last link in the chain of events that shook the old political and social structure of Czarist Russia, the Austro-Hungarian Monarchy, and imperial Germany. There began a period of transition leading up to the emergence of new types of political and socioeconomic structures: Stalinism in Russia, nazism in Germany, semifascist states in some other European countries, and reformed capitalism in the West. The establishment of the Frankfurt Institute marks the beginnings of the postrevolutionary epoch; it began with a Marxist orientation but moved away from it gradually.

History and Class Consciousness provides a connecting link between the first and third event. While Lukács's essays, written in Budapest and Vienna, were clearly inspired by the six years of revolutionary upheavals, they expressed messianic hopes and looked forward to the long period of academization of important Marxist themes such as alienation and reification, which were most poignantly discussed in the now famous reification essay.[20] These themes were first picked up by the Frankfurt thinkers, then by postwar French intellectuals, and revived more recently in the 1960s worldwide. (Another theme, that of totality, had its revival in the "world-system perspective" of Immanuel Wallerstein.) The coincidence of the establishment of the Frankfurt Institute and the publication of the Lukács volume led some people to conclude that Lukács was the founder of so-called Western Marxism. Such a conclusion can only be made on the basis of unfamiliarity with European intellectual history and the meaning of Lukács's work. Lukács himself refrained from using the term and vehemently protested any such linkage.

The almost 50-year history of the Frankfurt Institute may conveniently be divided into three distinct periods, each named after a director who not only put his indelible mark on the philosophy and politics of the institute but also led the school's fortunes through different historical settings and geographic locations.

The first period from 1924 to 1930 is usually called the "Grünberg era." (The first director, Kurt Albrecht Gerlach never assumed his post as he died unexpectedly at the age of thirty-six.) Carl Grünberg, labor historian at the University of Vienna, gave the institute an orthodox Marxist orientation. He gave notice in his opening address that he was for the "dictatorship of the director" (a policy which its second director, Max Horkheimer, equally adhered to); consequently, a "sharing of the direction of the institute with those who have a different *Weltanschauung* or methodological approach is entirely inconceivable."[21] The relatively short "Grünberg era" was dominated by such politically committed Marxists as Henryk Grossmann and Karl August Wittfogel and by institutional contacts with the Marx-Engels Institute of Moscow, and was characterized by a vehement antimetaphysical stance. Although Ulrike Migdal's meticulously researched *Frühgeschichte* takes a significant step in this direction, the "Grünberg era" as an integral part of the history of the Frankfurt School is still awaiting a chronicler. Very few American students of Frankfurt thought are aware of this so-called positivist Marxist phase of the Frankfurt School.

Carl Grünberg considered Marxism both as a *Weltanschauung* and as a research method. He stated in his inaugural address that Marxism as an economic and social theory, until then the stepchild of German universities, was to have a home in the new institute. He perceived his time as a transitional period "from capitalism to socialism." His Marxist interpretation was vehemently antiphilosophical: "Philosophical and historical materialism have conceptually nothing to do with each other," he declared. To him, the task of historical materialism was the investigation of "the given concrete world in its becoming and change."[22]

Among the first members of the institute were sociologists, economists, philosophers, psychologists, historians, sinologists, and literary scholars. Most of the members had a Jewish middle- or upper-middle-class background; some were members of the Communist Party (such as Karl August Wittfogel, Richard Sorge, and Henryk Grossmann); and most of them were in some way active in the left-wing politics of Weimar Germany. The journal Grünberg began editing while still in Vienna, generally called the *Grünberg Archiv*, became the main outlet for the early Frankfurt Institute and emphasized labor history in accordance with Grünberg's leanings. Among the theoretical achievements of this first phase of the Frankfurt School was the publication in 1929 of Henryk Grossmann's *The Law of Accumulation and Collapse in the Capitalist System*, Friedrich Pollock's *Die planwirtschaftlichen Versuche in der Sowietunion, 1917–1927*, and Karl August Wittfogel's *Wirtschaft und Gesellschaft Chinas*, published in 1931.

After illness forced Grünberg to give up his directorship in 1928 and the short interim period with Friedrich Pollock at the helm ended, the second phase of the Frankfurt Institute commenced in 1931 with Max Horkheimer's leadership. The "Horkheimer era" lasted until the early 1950s, and it took the institute from Weimar Germany to New York City and exile in the United States. It meant a gradual turning away from Marxism, even of a "professorial Marxism" type, toward a more pessimistic philosophy of culture culminating in such works as *Dialectic of Enlightenment* and *Eclipse of Reason*. Horkheimer outlined as the main task of the institute the examination of the interrelationship between the economic substructure of society, the psychic development of the individual, and cultural phenomena, in search of a comprehensive and general theory of contemporary capitalist society. The order of the day was to establish a close and fruitful cooperation between philosophy and the individual disciplines. Social philosophy was conceived as a "materialist theory of history," combined with and supported by empirical research results. The organization of research based on philosophical formulations of problems was seen as the immediate task. In such research endeavors, philosophers, sociologists, economists, historians, and psychologists were to become permanently formed research teams aimed at grasping societal processes in their totality.

Horkheimer's personality clearly was a factor in the shift of the institute's direction, especially in terms of political commitment. The contemporaneous historical events mentioned earlier—the withering away of revolutionary ferment and the emergence of totalitarian regimes—also had their impact. Horkheimer's autobiograpical remarks reveal him weighing the available alternatives, those of a revolutionary and the more secure and smooth academic lifestyle with the foreseeable outcome: "The revolutionary career is not a series of banquets . . . , nor does it hold the promise of interesting research or . . . salaries." Thus, it is chosen "rarely" by people who are "merely talented" but do not possess "superhuman faith."[23] Horkheimer clearly thought himself to be "merely talented," unlike Marx, Trotsky, and Lukács who chose the revolutionary career. He was guided by his own political maxim: "The man of means . . . can permit himself leftist leanings, provided he goes abroad in time."[24] After Hitler rose to power in 1933, the institute was forced out of Germany; Horkheimer and most of its members moved via Switzerland, France, and England to the United States, settling at first in New York City.

The institute entered into a loose affiliation with Columbia University. The exact circumstances of this affiliation became more fully known in 1980 when Lewis S. Feuer published his account of how "the only Marxist research institute in the Western world . . . was offered a building by Columbia University," whose president, Nicholas Murray Butler, was "an austere conservative."[25] After having found only a "pleasant naiveté" in Martin Jay's brief account, Feuer presented *his* version of the story, based on the correspondence in the Presidential Archives of Columbia University. As it turned out, the Department of Sociology, especially its chairman, Robert M. McIver, and one of its members, Robert M. Lynd, were instrumental in bringing the institute to Columbia. One of the main reasons why the affiliation went smoothly was the abundance of funds the institute had at its disposal and was transferring to these shores. Feuer cites Friedrich Pollock's letter outlining the *exact* financial background of the institute. We learn that *one* of the endowments had the 1934 value of 5 million Swiss francs, not a negligible sum in the years of deepest depression. The institute's budget for 1935 was $100,000, according to Pollock. Should one day the *definitive* history of the institute and the Frankfurt School be written, the results of both Ulrike Migdal's and Lewis S. Feuer's research, though not their political speculations, would have to be incorporated.

It was during the institute's sojourn in New York City that the term *Critical Theory* was coined by Max Horkheimer in an 1937 essay[26] and then seconded in another one by Herbert Marcuse.[27] Critical Theory is not a theory in the ordinary meaning of the term, any more than Durkheim's *Rules of Sociological Method* constitute easy-to-follow, step-by-step research instructions. Critical Theory's implications concerning theory and attitude may be summarized as follows: There is a historical continuity between Critical Theory and the critical philosophy of German idealism, on one hand, and Marx's critique of political economy and of capitalist society, on the other. Critical Theory as an attitude means that the critical theorist is guided by the maxim that "the thrust toward a rational society is innate in every man."

Although no mention is made of Lukács, there is a definite linkage as far as the ethical bent is concerned, albeit without the organizational commitment as in the case of Lukács. There is a tendency in America to disregard the existence and overriding importance of the ethical commitment in the case of Lukács,[28] mainly due to ignorance. This ethical aspect is best expressed in Horkheimer's statement that "Critical Theory of society is, in its totality, the unfolding of a single existential judgment."[29]

As for the theoretical output of the Frankfurt Institute, the second phase just as the other phases can best be illuminated by paraphrasing Hegel's dictum that social philosophy is nothing but its own time apprehended in thought to which is added the supplemental (Engelsian) proposition that it is and remains limited objectively by the historical conditions and subjectively by the physical and mental constitution of its creator. An analysis of Horkheimer's works and those of his friend, Theodor W. Adorno, since the early 1940s confirms this.

As a consequence of historical events during the second phase of the Frankfurt Institute such as the rise of totalitarian regimes, World War II with its mass killings on the battlefields, the murder of millions of innocent civilians, and the extermination of European Jewry in death camps, there was a shift of interest in Frankfurt thought. The shift was away from a general theory of capitalist society and its concerns and in the direction of specific problems such as the attempt to formulate a theory of fascism: to provide an explanation for the rise and nature of fascism in Germany and Europe; reveal the economic base and political superstructure of the same; and delineate the social psychology or personality of the fascist individual. At first, Horkheimer argued that fascism was the natural and logical outcome of late capitalist society in its stage of permanent crisis; and in stating that "he who will not speak of capitalism should keep silent about fascism too," Horkheimer came perilously close to adopting the classical orthodox Marxist definition of Dimitrov.[30] To be sure, the much more complex phenomenon of fascism deserves a more sophisticated explanatory scheme, taking into account the economic, political, and psychological factors and their interrelation. (Ehrhard Bahr's essay in this volume addresses that issue.) A perusal of the institute's publications yields no critical assessment of or reflections on the atrocities of the Stalinist period, such as the purge trials, the liquidation of the kulaks, the camps, although there may have been ample internal discussion and debates on this subject.

This is not the place to enter into a critical discussion of the theoretical accomplishments and shortcomings, or even to summarize the major works of the second phase of the Frankfurt Institute; for that the interested reader ought to scrutinize existing studies and the original works of institute members as well as the contributions presented in this volume. A few remarks may be in order about the main task, the shifts of emphasis of the Frankfurt thinkers during that period. As late as 1937, the critical theorist's task was still to contribute to the change toward a rational and just society. Earlier hopes for such an achievement had given way to despair, to a deeply pessimistic appraisal of the chances for a betterment of mankind's affairs. This change in attitude was the result of a deeper knowledge of and insight into American late capitalist society, on one hand, and of the commencement of the final solution of the Jewish question in Hitler's Germany. The joint product of Horkheimer and Adorno's perceptions of the time was the *Dialectic of Enlightenment*. Western civilization was looked upon as in the process of decomposition and collapse; the world was conceived of as the decay of one's own existence. The authors sought to explain why "mankind, instead of entering into a truly human condition is sinking into a new kind of barbarism."[31] The volume was intended to be a metatheoretical treatise on sociology, psychology, and above all, science. Science and technology's transformation from an instrument of liberation into a medium of total reification in capitalist society, and its diabolical use by the Nazis made the authors conclude that "terror and civilization are inseparable."[32] In a parallel study, entitled *Eclipse of Reason*, Horkheimer duly attacked positivism, pragmatism, and scientism. His criticism falls back on a long line of antiscience tradition inherent in German intellectual currents since German idealism. The "eclipse of reason" (*Vernunft*) and the triumph of *Verstand* characterize for Horkheimer and Adorno the *Zeitgeist*, the universal feeling of fear and disillusion in the face of the diminishing hope that the "subject" will ever be able to assert itself and resist all-powerful manipulation in a society of total bureaucratization. We find here echoes of Max Weber, who exclaimed that "the great question is . . . what can we oppose to this machinery [of bureaucracy] in order to keep a portion of mankind free from this parcelling-out of the soul."[33]

The second phase of Frankfurt thought saw the gradual incorporation of Freudian psychoanalytic theory and conceptualization which culminated in the study *The Authoritarian Personality* by Adorno et al. This study has been hailed by some as "the union of German theory and American empiricism" and sharply criticized by others such as David Riesman who wrote that "if there exists a danger of international repression in America today, it ensues more . . . from the threat of totalitarian Soviet expansion than from sources in American 'authoritarian personality.'"[34]

The third phase began in 1950 when Horkheimer and Adorno returned to Germany. Other members of the institute had already drifted into academic, government, or private jobs. The return of the two chief theorists of the institute was motivated by the usual push and pull factors in migrational movements and aided by both the changing political climate in the United States (rising McCarthyism, Cold War atmosphere) and Adorno's unwillingness and inability to express himself in any other language than German and his failure to get a teaching position.[35] After their return to Frankfurt am Main, the institute was formally reestablished in 1951. The same year, Horkheimer became rector of the University of Frankfurt, a post he held until 1953. Horkheimer and Adorno's collaboration continued in Frankfurt in the 1950s and 1960s until Horkheimer's official retirement in 1958 and Adorno's death in 1969, which marked the end of the Frankfurt School. It should be noted that after a short and transitory codirectorship of Horkheimer and Adorno, Adorno was perhaps more fully responsible for what later became known as the Frankfurt School. Thus this third and final period may properly be called the "Adorno era." The term itself, *Frankfurt School*, was never used by anyone during the first two periods of the Frankfurt Institute; it was invented by critics of Frankfurt thought well after 1950. Horkheimer and Adorno accepted the term reluctantly and rarely used it.

Within the framework of the reestablished institute, Horkheimer and Adorno represented the loyal opposition to the restored West German capitalist system. They became highly visible figures in West Germany's cultural life; they took it upon themselves to reeducate the public and educate a new generation of German intellectuals. In this sense alone it can be said that they helped bring about the oppositional movement of the late 1960s. Students then took literally the anticapitalism of early Critical Theory, disseminated partly through pirated editions of out of

print writings; confrontation between the Frankfurt School and demonstrating students ensued. Leaflets proclaiming "Adorno als Institution
ist tot!" ("Adorno as an institution is dead!") were distributed. Adorno
had to cancel his lectures and in a seminar on dialectics, female revolutionary students bared their breasts to him. The love affair between
the Frankfurt School and radicalized students had run its course.[36]

As to the theoretical content of the third phase, Horkheimer and
Adorno's collaboration that had begun in California continued in Frankfurt
in the 1950s and early 1960s. Emphasizing the identity of their thought,
they coauthored several volumes on philosophy and sociology, most
notably *Soziologische Exkurse* (1956) and *Sociologica II* (1962). These
two volumes come closest to what could be called systematic statements
on the Frankfurt School of sociology. However, the lion's share of the
critique of positivist and empirical sociology belongs to Adorno. Adorno
is also mainly responsible for the codification of the theory of society,
culminating in *Negative Dialectics*. "Theory of society" is a label for the
attempted codification of Critical Theory as sociology. This is not the
place to elaborate on the Frankfurt criticism of positivist and empirical
sociological traditions nor to present theory of society's theoretical and
methodological positions at any length.[37] Suffice it to say that dialectical
theory of society deals with societal totality, with the laws of motion of
society as a whole, and it aims at gaining insight into societal intercon-
nections from basic structural conditions such as relations of exchange.
(Totality is understood here as a dialectical category of reciprocal relationships.) Theory of society is thus macrosociology with conceptualization and terminology such as *totality, essence,* and *appearance,* which
are Hegelian. I once characterized theory of society as an "amalgamation
of artistic reflections (*Kulturkritik*), combined with Marxian categories
and elements, and a pessimistic philosophy of history," and see no reason
to revise my assessment.[38] A major part of the Frankfurt School's critique
of positivist sociology was carried out in the so-called *Positivismusstreit*
(positivism dispute), which has since been published in both German
and English.

The question of what is the legacy of the school is important and
legitimate. My tentative and general answer is that it will continue to
exert influence on a significant segment of younger sociologists, especially
those with a humanist concern and a critical bent. As to its particular
concerns and problems, the legacy of the Frankfurt School may be
summed up under four headings.

First, the *humanist concern*. This continued throughout the school's
history and served as an antidote to quantifying sociology, which, if

pushed to the extreme, plays a part in the dehumanization of the individual who either gets lost behind the numbers or is left to individual psychology.

Second, *sensitivity* to the real problems of the age, such as the crisis of European societies combined with the rise of totalitarian regimes. Today, this sensitivity can be applied to the crisis of Western civilization. More specifically, there are issues discussed today that derive from the following ideas of the Frankfurt thinkers: the *domination of nature*, which characterizes the dominant tendency in Western capitalist-industrial civilizations that could lead to a "revenge of nature," in other words, the possibility that "progress" results in such regressions as diminishing resources (energy), destruction of the environment, etc. Further, the idea of a *legitimation crisis*, meaning a loss of trust in governments, the existence of a "credibility gap" referred to by many social philosophers, sociologists, and political scientists. Here Jürgen Habermas, the second-generation Frankfurt thinker, comes to mind.[39] Related to this problem is that of *authority* or lack of it. A recent book by Richard Sennett entitled *Authority* (1981) demonstrates the continuing impact of the ideas of the Frankfurt thinkers, as does Christopher Lasch's work *The Culture of Narcissism* (1978). Finally, the concept and growing significance of the Third World, first registered by Karl August Wittfogel, an early member of the institute, and outlined in his study *China Awakening* (1926) and elaborated in his monumental work *Economy and Society of China* (1931).

Third, the Frankfurt Institute pioneered the concept of *interdisciplinary research* to deal with the problems of the age long before the idea became part—under the label "think-tank"—of the American research scene. At the Institut für Sozialforschung a research team was assembled representing all the major disciplines from philosophy to economics and psychology; the work of the organization was interrupted in 1933 and the scholars dispersed. Later there was a renewed attempt in the *Zeitschrift für Sozialforschung* to deal in an interdisciplinary fashion with contemporary phenomena.[40]

Lastly, there should be a mention of Adorno's writings, almost ten volumes on the sociology of literature, art, and music, and of his posthumously published *Aesthetics* which provides a theoretical summation of his views.

Assessments of the relevance and legacy of the Frankfurt School will continue and certainly undergo changes as more translations followed by interpretations and debates are forthcoming. Moreover, there are many areas and subareas of sociology, such as social psychology, the study of mass media, political institutions, religion, art and literature, and prejudice, that is, elements of the "superstructure," whereby the contribution of the Critical Theory of the Frankfurt School will remain a source of inspiration for a long time to come. One thinks of Georg Simmel's statement when assessing the legacy of the Frankfurt School: "I know that I shall die without intellectual heirs, and that is as it should be. My legacy will be like cash, distributed to many heirs, each transforming his part into use according to his nature—a use which will no longer reveal its indebtedness to this heritage."[41]

Reception and Perception of the Frankfurt School

As mentioned at the beginning of this introduction, the impact of the Frankfurt School on the American academic and intellectual scene was minimal, especially during its sojourn in the United States, until the late 1940s. First, there was the language barrier consciously maintained on both sides. As those who are well versed in Frankfurt thought know, the inaccessibility is only partly due to language barriers; it is also intrinsic in Frankfurt thought. Adorno himself pointed out that the matter of language goes beyond one's being able to express oneself in a newly acquired language; in his case it meant that the German language he wrote in "obviously has an elective affinity to philosophy, particularly to its speculative moment."[42] What little response there was, consisted of three kinds: First, the Frankfurt contribution to social science, such as *The Authoritarian Personality*, was sharply criticized on methodological grounds. Second, the rejection on political grounds was based on "native" resentment of those "left-wing" and "highbrow" intellectuals who dared to meddle in American political matters; finally, there were those who praised Frankfurt thought uncritically mainly because they were not really acquainted with its ideas.

Today we can no longer speak of negligible impact nor inaccessibility as a major problem since the most important works of the Frankfurt theorists are available in English translation (however badly done in many cases). Beginning with the 1960s, the Frankfurt School found its way into textbooks, encyclopedias, and curricula. I cannot summarize here even rudimentarily the reception of the school in Western and Eastern Europe, but will limit myself to a short assessment of the American perception, reception, and influence of the Frankfurt School. The latter appealed most to a certain segment of the New Left at least partly because of parallel existential conditions and sociopolitical factors. Just as in the case of Frankfurt School members, many New Left students of the 1960s and 1970s were born into middle- or upper-middle-class (mostly Jewish) homes with an egalitarian-liberal atmosphere that later stood in sharp contrast with the realities of the societal totality they encountered, such as discrimination and racism in late capitalist American society and the ongoing Vietnam war. The similarity extends to the impossibility of following up the revolutionary excitement with a lasting commitment, with praxis; thus in both cases there followed a *Versöhnung mit der Wirklichkeit* (making one's peace with reality) and what Frank Parkin called "the academization of Marxism" to which I may add, of Critical Theory. If there existed a dissimilarity, it can be perceived in the missing serious theoretical anchorage of the New Left, unlike their Frankfurt ascendants.

The New Left had a deep sympathy and great understanding for the Frankfurt theorists' antiempiricist and antipositivist stance. The link between positivism and capitalism has often been given as the main justification for this stance. Since Kolakowski's treatment of Adorno admirably discusses this issue, I will not go into it in any detail.

It is probably not by accident that since the 1960s and 1970s, Frankfurt thought with its speculative content mainly influenced those young students who empathized with it and had an aversion to more systematic thinking as well as to empirically grounded critical scholarship. Beyond them, however, there is a continuing interest in and indebtedness to certain Frankfurt ideas and critical positions within the Anglo-Saxon world and a still growing preoccupation in Continental scholarship.[43]

Notes on the Contributions

If it is true that the heritage of the Frankfurt School had for long eluded both its birthplace, Europe, and the English-speaking world, and provoked little reaction from the scholarly world during its heyday, it is also true that since its rediscovery in the late 1960s Frankfurt thought has spawned a wealth of debate and discussion on both its representatives and ideas. The resulting literature is a good indication of the complexity, controversial nature, and even contradictions in the ideas of the Frankfurt School. There has been much discussion about the validity and even the value of Frankfurt thought, including the debate about its most influential and direction-giving contribution to twentieth-century social sciences: Critical Theory or theory of society as it was called in the latter period of the school.

The discussion is undoubtedly due to the fact that the modes of presentation characteristic of Critical Theory ensnare and/or confuse many would-be students of the school. As Paul Connerton aptly put it: "Two lines of least resistance immediately offer themselves when confronted with the problem" of the writings of the Frankfurt theorists. "They may incite either to dismissal or to monumentalization."[44] The debate with Frankfurt thought represented by the essays in this volume does not belong to either of these two categories. The writers accepted the challenge of the serious intent of the Frankfurt ideas and undertook the equally serious task of critical assessment. The Frankfurt Institute represented a prestigous, diverse group with an impressive array of talents. Since the Grünberg era there was a multitude of topics discussed in its journal, first called the *Grünberg Archiv* and later *Zeitschrift für Sozialforschung*. The selections in this volume reflect a wide range of topics; aspects of Frankfurt thought are dissected and examined by an array of distinguished contemporary scholars representing a cross-section of academic disciplines. Moving from the general to the particular, the essays are arranged from history and history of ideas to Marxism; their diversity encompasses all the social sciences and philosophy and literary scholarship. It is to be regretted that many valuable and interesting contributions were omitted only because of space limitations. However, the guiding principle of the selection was adhered to: to collect important and many hitherto untranslated or little-known critical contributions in one easily accessible English-language volume. Some contributions have appeared before but were either pirated (and therefore could not be considered for this volume) or so inadequately translated that their meaning was distorted in many cases.[45]

In Part One, "History and History of Ideas," Joseph Maier recounts the intellectual career of Horkheimer, Adorno, and Marcuse, all of whom had been his one-time teachers, later his "fatherly friends," and with whom he closely collaborated since their arrival in the United States and their sojourn at Columbia University. Horkheimer's thought is analyzed as an "amalgam of Marxism, psychoanalysis, and patriarchal disdain for mass society." The Frankfurt thinkers are described as romantic critics of industrial society, living in splendid isolation on Morningside Heights in New York City.[46] Although Maier was intimately acquainted with the Frankfurt thinkers, especially Horkheimer, whose papers he is today in charge of (together with Alfred Schmidt of Frankfurt University), he is nevertheless able to deliver an unusually objective critical assessment of Frankfurt thought. Joseph Maier and Alfred Schmidt represent two successive generations of students of the Frankfurt School: Maier the small contingent of 1940s America and Schmidt the sizable group of followers of Germany of the 1960s. Mannheim's thesis that "the problem of generations . . . is one of the indispensable guides to an understanding of the structure of social and intellectual movements"[47] seems to be borne out by the two "friendly" critics, Maier and Schmidt. While Maier follows the career of the school, Schmidt in his "Postscript" to Horkheimer's selected 1930s essays in two volumes, presents the essence of

Horkheimer's reflections focusing on three key themes: the structure of history (problems of historical social science), Horkheimer's reinterpretation of the age-old epistemological issue of idealism versus materialism, and the position of traditional and Critical Theory on the theory of science.

In his magnificent review essay of Martin Jay's *The Dialectical Imagination*, Heinz Lubasz gives in broad outlines the real problems and issues of leftist intellectuals of twentieth-century Europe that Jay's book purported to tell about. In Lubasz's view, the issues centered around the theory/practice relationship. He also maintains that Jay's book is not *the* history of the Frankfurt School but rather a chronicle that uncritically accepts reminiscences and tends to ignore the real social and historical forces which shaped the fate of the school as well as the question of its place in European intellectual history. In Lubasz's opinion the true history of Frankfurt thought can only be accomplished by the research and presentation ("Forschung und Darstellung") of the history of the Frankfurt Institute in its totality from 1923 until at least 1969, the year of Adorno's death.

Jürgen Habermas, considered by many as belonging to the second-generation Frankfurt School, assesses the journal of the Horkheimer era, *Zeitschrift für Sozialforschung*, on the occasion of its German-language publication in paperback. His discussion centers around four themes: Horkheimer; Erich Fromm; the theory of culture represented by Löwenthal, Adorno, and Benjamin; and the political economy writings in the *Zeitschrift*. Habermas forcefully demonstrates the unique character of the *Zeitschrift* as a remarkable document of European *Geistesgeschichte*.

Part Two, "Philosophy," begins with Leszek Kolakowski's comprehensive analysis of Adorno's philosophical masterpiece, *Negative Dialectics*. Castigating the "pretentious obscurity" of Adorno's style, he judges it as a philosophical counterpart to the abandonment of form in modern art, music, and literature—surely a harsh judgment. He calls *Negative Dialectics* a doctrine of scepticism, consisting of uncritical borrowings from Marx, Hegel, Nietzsche, Lukács, Bergson, and Bloch. (Lucio Colletti goes farther by accusing Horkheimer and Adorno of intellectual theft ["geistiger Diebstahl"].)[48] Kolakowski also dissects the alleged link between positivism, conservatism, and totalitarianism.

Arnold Künzli provides a different textual exegesis of Adorno's *Negative Dialectics* and combines it with a psychological interpretation of some of its themes. He argues convincingly against and finally rejects Adorno's nihilistic picture of a post-Auschwitz world, analyzing it—albeit speculatively—as Adorno's guilt-ridden relationship to his own Jewishness. This pessimism of the post-Auschwitzian world in Adorno's later philosophy is considered most objectionable not only by Künzli but also by many fellow–Jewish refugees from European fascism. Ernst Bloch, for example, who was living in exile in America under comparatively harsher circumstances, found it possible to work on his masterpiece, *Das Prinzip Hoffnung* (The Principle of Hope), even though he could not sustain his guiding principle, "ubi Lenin ibi Jerusalem," after his return to East Germany.

Michael Landmann takes up the much-discussed topic of reason/unreason and guides us with admirable ease through the treatment of this issue in the work of Max Weber, who initiated the modern debate with his "Occidental rationalism" thesis. He then discusses Lukács, who deals with the problem of synthesizing the Marxist treatment of alienation with Weber's rationalization. Horkheimer and Adorno contributed absolute despair to the ideas of their precursors. Landmann concludes with a presentation of Habermas's reformulation of the problems of reason and shows the complex relationship between alienation and reason: Increased rationalization and the concomitantly increased alienation are dual aspects of the same historical process which culminated in Western capitalist-industrial civilization.

Karl Popper's two short essays—one kindly offered and published here for the first time, and adding an autobiographical note to his assessment of the Frankfurt School—are related to the now famous positivism dispute of German sociology in 1961 of which he was a key participant. Agreeing in one respect with Joseph Maier, Popper castigates Adorno for his views on culture, finding them pure snobbery. Regarding matters of epistemology and philosophy in general, his verdict is again—not unexpectedly—extremely negative. He simply terms much of what has been written by the Frankfurt thinkers as mumbo jumbo, and backs up his statement by translating some of Adorno's "bombastic" statements into plain language. Popper too objects strenuously to Adorno's post-Auschwitzian expression of anxiety and despair, regardless of his own experiences in exile. Popper forcefully rejects the label "positivist," and gives a clear overview of the basics of his own epistemology of the social sciences, contrasting it with those of Horkheimer and Adorno.

Part Three, "Aesthetics," begins with a short piece by Georg Lukács on one aspect of Benjamin's work: the concept of allegory. The old Lukács laboring on his last magnum opus, *Aesthetics*, pays high praise to Walter Benjamin, *the* aesthetician of the Frankfurt School, however loose and tenuous the connection may actually have been. Lukács tried to build Benjamin's ideas into his own aesthetic edifice. Although they never met, there was a mutual respect and a certain influence. Benjamin spoke of Lukács's *History and Class Consciousness* as the "event" of

1923 (along with Thomas Mann's *Der Zauberberg*) in one of his letters. Lukács in an interview called Benjamin "extraordinarily gifted" and highly perceptive of many "quite new problems" of aesthetics.[49]

István Hermann, one of Lukács's early students at Budapest University, compares Lukács's and Horkheimer's positions on the aesthetic education of man, a significant theme of German idealism. From a Marxist standpoint, Hermann rejects Horkheimer's pessimistic assessment of the possibilities of modern man in an age of mass culture and total manipulation and contrasts it, not surprisingly, with Lukács's more optimistic standpoint.

Peter Uwe Hohendahl's contribution is a welcome discussion of Adorno's posthumous *Ästhetische Theorie*, thus far untranslated into English. Adorno's work is considered by many as *the* legacy of Critical Theory. Strangely enough, it was coolly received by West Germany's Left audience, who by the time it was published, had moved well beyond Adorno toward a more organized and orthodox version of Marxism. Hohendahl's intriguing treatment explains why it was no accident that Adorno's last work deals with aesthetic rather than social and political problems. Hohendahl pinpoints Adorno's thesis on the autonomy of art in the idealist tradition of Kant, Schiller, and Hegel. He concludes with a discussion of *Ästhetische Theorie* as the product of the 1960s and its relevance for the 1980s is established.

Ferenc Fehér, presently of Australia, sees Adorno as the theorist of avant-garde music and as "the major opponent of the reflection theory and the critic who has done most to 'loosen up' the causal relationship between art and society." He examines Adorno's problem in the framework of the Adorno/Lukács controversy and argues for trying to find the common elements in their works rather than their bitter disagreements. Both Adorno and Lukács, for example, shared an admiration for the golden age of bourgeois art, the autonomous subject, the bourgeois individual, and held in reverence the artistic microcosm of totality created by that autonomous subject.

Part Four, "Sociology and Social Psychology," begins with Paul Lazarsfeld who has had a lifelong lively intellectual exchange with members of the Frankfurt School, especially Adorno. (Both men reported on their professional and intellectual contacts and disagreements in *The Intellectual Migration*.)[50] His brief essay offers a remarkably concise evaluation of his colleagues from the same geographic location but diametrically opposite intellectual landscape. Lazarsfeld discusses Critical Theory as "Marxism without proletariat" and has high praise for Adorno's sociology of music. On the other hand, he thinks that Adorno and his followers did much harm to the sociological enterprise. He talks of the "hypnotic effect" of

Adorno's language and attributes Critical Theory's attraction for young German students to it.

Franco Ferrarotti of Rome University, a self-styled critical sociologist, centers his argumentation on the three theoretical essays of *Autorität und Familie* (1936) and considers this work the key to understanding the Frankfurt School. He recaps Horkheimer's tracing of the role of authority in history; the family is regarded as the essential instrument for reproducing authoritarianism—a view clearly rooted in the author's German experience. Ferrarotti is equally critical of the American traditional tendency to lean toward the psychological, avoiding both the economic and political dimensions—not to mention the historical dimension—and the Frankfurt School's tendency to sidestep particular historical and political situations in favor of a speculative analysis of a wide category of "domination" as such.

Reinhard Kreckel revisits the famous positivism dispute of 1961 that did not resolve any issues. The question of course arises: Why revisit it then? Well, sociologists still argue about the *Methodenstreit* of 1905 that did not resolve anything either. Kreckel's contribution offers a fresh look by someone who was not involved in the original events. The critique of positivism is important in the sense that it has been the central issue of Frankfurt Critical Theory since its inception. Kreckel traces the history and development of this critique from Horkheimer's 1937 attack on a vaguely defined "traditional theory," a critique that replaced Marx's critique of political economy. Kreckel outlines the "falsificationist" conception of science of Critical Rationalism of the Popper School, and argues that any attempt to apply Critical Rationalism to sociology seems to lead to the conclusion that, by its own standards, the results are highly unsatisfactory. Kreckel hopes to overcome this stalemate and "to prepare the ground for a partial joining of forces" between Critical Theory and Critical Rationalism.

Edith Kurzweil compares the uses of psychoanalysis by Critical Theory and structuralism of France. She outlines and analyzes both their similarities and differences which are partly due to native historical and societal conditions and context. She shows that the increasingly vigorous dialogue with psychoanalysis commenced as the school's focus shifted from Marx's political economy to the themes of domination, alienation, and reification. Kurzweil critically dissects Marcuse's linking of Schiller and Freud which led to ideas that were to become a major tool for liberation. She concludes that psychoanalytically informed criticism, whether in its Frankfurt or in its Parisian incarnation, continues to search for improved methods; and this is the main merit of both schools.

Michael Löwy analyzes how knowledge and social classes are related in Critical Theory. In his *Auseinandersetzung* with Mannheim in the 1930s, Horkheimer seemed to recognize that the knowledge of truth corresponds to a certain social positioning, argues Löwy, but he failed to state clearly which classes are supposed to be the social bearers of Critical Theory. Marcuse's writings of the same period show more the influence of Lukács, states Löwy, in that he considers truth intimately related to the struggle of oppressed groups. He concludes that after 1945 all three of the Frankfurt School thinkers (Horkheimer, Adorno, and Marcuse) moved toward a conception that gives some (critical) sectors of the intelligentsia the privilege of bearers of true knowledge. Löwy's essay is a Marxist sociology of knowledge-type critique of Horkheimer's and Marcuse's views of knowledge and truth.

Part Five, "Political Science and Political Economy," opens with Hans Jürgen Krahl's extremely brief and sharp criticism of his one-time teacher and mentor Adorno. Krahl, as one of the leaders of the student Left, expresses the sentiments of his movement. Together with Rudi Dutschke, Krahl was the most articulate voice of his generation on theory.

Ehrhard Bahr examines and critically evaluates the Frankfurt School's major preoccupation during its middle period: the theoretical confrontation with fascism and anti-Semitism. The fact that the Frankfurt School was a relative latecomer to the study of these two phenomena can be explained partly, in Bahr's view, by its effort to minimize the overwhelmingly Jewish membership of the institute. Be that as it may, Horkheimer's 1939 essay "The Jews and Europe" was the first attempt to come to terms with the problem. The more scholarly and systematic treatment of the problem by Franz Neumann in *Behemoth* (1942) did not receive the support of the leadership of the institute mainly because it was too Marxist for its taste. Bahr politely avoids Adorno's naive propositions about the causal link between the "falling rate of profit" and the rise of fascism in *Minima Moralia*. A philosophical explanation was attempted by Horkheimer and Adorno in the "Elements of Anti-Semitism" chapter of *Dialectic of Enlightenment*, and Bahr reproaches the two for omitting concrete historical analysis and data and for discussing "anti-Semitism as paranoia," thereby reducing the sociological and historical analysis to the level of individual psychology.

Giacomo Marramao sets out to refute the idea that the Frankfurt School completely abandoned political economy which was the kernel of Marx's critical theory. To do that he investigates the political economy of Friedrich Pollock. Marramao claims that Pollock's political economy and the ideas of the philosophers of the *Zeitschrift für Sozialforschung* are in a "reciprocal relation." He also provides a sketch of the more complex Pollock-Adorno and Pollock-Horkheimer relationships.

Part Six, "Marxism," begins with Göran Therborn, a Danish-born Marxist sociologist, who was probably the first to subject the theories of Horkheimer and Adorno—and to a lesser degree Marcuse's—to a thorough systematic critical Marxist analysis. He attempts to situate and systematize Critical Theory in three respects: its relationship to traditional theory, to science, and to politics. Therborn ultimately finds Critical Theory to be reductionist: He asserts that Horkheimer's Critical Theory involves a double reduction of science and of politics to philosophy. As a consequence, Marxism's value as a theory of social formations and as a guide to political praxis is abolished.

Lucio Colletti, an Italian Marxist philosopher, offers a critique of the Frankfurt School from the position of scientific-philosophical Marxism. He states that in Marcuse's interpretation of Hegel "we are dealing with familiar romantic themes" blended with Heideggerian elements. He discusses the modern variations on "idealist reaction against science" from Heidegger to Horkheimer and Adorno's *Dialectic of Enlightenment.* Instead of seeing the "evil" in the determinate organization of society, in a certain system of social relations, they locate it in industry, technology, and science. Thus, he judges Heidegger, Husserl, Jaspers, Horkheimer, and Adorno as having this one thing in common in spite of their differences.

The late Lucien Goldmann attempts to "understand" Marcuse and states unequivocally that the relation of radical students of the 1960s to Marcuse is "based on misunderstanding." He sketches Marcuse's career from his first, Heideggerian phase, to his "critical pessimism" and contrasts it with the career of Ernst Bloch. Goldmann believes that Marcuse merely uses "Hegel and Hegelian language to return to a Kantian and Fichtean position." Even so Goldmann gives a sympathetic though critical evaluation of Marcuse, whose shifting responses are said to have finally culminated in a "limited optimism" with regard to social change under the impact of the social movements of students and minorities in the 1960s.

Wolf Heydebrand and Beverly Burris attempt to illuminate one aspect of the Frankfurt School: its relation to praxis with particular focus on the work of Jürgen Habermas. The school had been preoccupied with developing a "theory of praxis" since the 1930s, but this interest turned increasingly into a pessimistic appraisal of the chances for concrete political action. The authors discuss Habermas's turn to the analysis of the phenomena of "work and interaction" as two aspects of praxis, then to "communicative competence" as a first step of praxis, and lastly,

Habermas's concern with developing a "universal pragmatics." In this contribution, Habermas is criticized from a Marxist position. In the last analysis, Habermas's "vision" of political emancipation is said to remain at the level of political emancipation as visualized "by the young Hegelians and does not take the last step toward human emancipation" as proposed by Marx.

Notes

1. See Zoltán Tar, *The Frankfurt School: The Critical Theories of Max Hork-heimer and Theodor W. Adorno* (New York: Wiley, 1977).
2. "Keine Angst vor dem Elfenbeinturm: Spiegel Gespräch mit dem Frankfurter Sozialphilosophen Professor Theodor W. Adorno," *Der Spiegel* 23 (May 5, 1969):204.
3. Jürgen Habermas, *Protestbewegung und Hochschulreform* (Frankfurt: Suhr-kamp, 1969), p. 148.
4. See Rolf Wiggershaus, "Die Geschichte der Frankfurter Schule: Gibt es bei uns öffentlich geehrte Verursacher des Terrors?" *Neue Rundschau* 89 (no. 4, 1978):571–87.
5. Flora Lewis, "German Students Sympathize with Causes, but Not Terrorism," *New York Times*, Week in Review (November 13, 1977):3.
6. John Leonard, review of *Brecht: A Biography*, by Klaus Völker, *New York Times* (December 7, 1978).
7. Tar, *Frankfurt School*, p. 2.
8. See I.H. (Irving Howe), "The Piracy of *Telos*," *Dissent* (Winter 1981):86.
9. Tar, *Frankfurt School*, pp. 55–60, 78–79, 181–89, 205.
10. Gershom Scholem, *Von Berlin nach Jerusalem* (Frankfurt: Suhrkamp, 1977), p. 167.
11. Martin Jay, "The Jews and the Frankfurt School," *New German Critique* (Winter 1980):137–49.
12. Cf. Paul Breines, "Germans, Journals, and Jews/Madison, Men, Marxism, and Mosse: A Tale of Jewish-Leftist Identity Confusion in America," *New German Critique* (Spring-Summer 1980):81–103.
13. For a discussion of this problem see George Steiner, *Language and Silence* (New York: Atheneum, 1972), pp. 143–44.
14. In *Conversations with Lukács*, ed. Theo Pinkus et al. (Cambridge, Mass.: MIT Press, 1975), pp. 69–70. Lukács refers to Jorge Semprun's *The Long Voyage*, trans. Richard Seaver (New York: Grove, 1964). See also Leon Trotsky, *On the Jewish Question* (New York: Pathfinder, 1970). Heinrich Heine's reflections on assimilation can be found only in German, vol. 4 of *Heines Sämtliche Werke* (Leipzig: Insel, 1912).
15. See "Friedman's Crusade," *Wall Street Journal* (June 28, 1977).
16. Peter Uwe Hohendahl, *The Institution of Criticism* (Ithaca and London: Cornell University Press, 1982), p. 29.
17. Bertolt Brecht, *Arbeitsjournal, 1938–1942*, ed. Werner Hecht, vol. 1 (Frankfurt: Suhrkamp, 1973), p. 443.
18. Martin Jay, *The Dialectical Imagination: A History of the Frankfurt School and the Institute of Social Research, 1923–1950* (Boston: Little, Brown, 1973).

19. Ulrike Migdal, *Die Frühgeschichte des Frankfurter Instituts für Sozialforschung* (Frankfurt and New York: Campus, 1981). G.L. Ulmen already stressed the significance of the *Frühgeschichte* by noting: "While I do not dispute Jay's point regarding the orientation for the Institute's late and post-Weimar period, it has led him to interpret the origin and early and middle years of the Institute wholly on the basis of what came later, thus giving an unclear and inconsistent picture of the Institute's aim in the 1920s. This can only be done by a close study of the Institute under Carl Grünberg and Wittfogel's writings. Concerning Grünberg's Institute and Horkheimer's, one cannot speak of a development but only of a change in direction. Clearly it is essential to distinguish carefully between the Institute of Social Research and the 'Frankfurt School' and Jay has not done so." *The Science of Society: Toward an Understanding of the Life and Work of Karl August Wittfogel* (The Hague, Paris, and New York: Mouton, 1978), p. 548.

20. Georg Lukács, *History and Class Consciousness*, trans. Rodney Livingstone (London: Merlin, 1971).

21. Quoted in Tar, p. 17.

22. Ibid., pp. 16–17.

23. Ibid., p. 50.

24. Max Horkheimer, *Dawn and Decline: Notes, 1926–1931 and 1950–1969*, trans. Michael Shaw (New York: Seabury, 1978), p. 45.

25. Lewis S. Feuer, "The Frankfurt Marxists and the Columbia Liberals," *Survey* 25 (Summer 1980):156–76.

26. Max Horkheimer, "Traditionelle und kritische Theorie," *Zeitschrift für Sozialforschung* 6 (1937):245–92.

27. Herbert Marcuse, "Philosophie und kritische Theorie," *Zeitschrift für Sozialforschung* 6 (1937):635–47.

28. Martin Jay writes: "To make Lukács into an ethical Marxist is to misunderstand the depth of his repudiation of Bernstein and the Revisionists." Martin Jay, "Critical Theory Criticized: Zoltán Tar and the Frankfurt School," *Central European History* 12 (March 1979):93, n. 10. For a more detailed discussion of Lukács and ethics see Judith Marcus: *Georg Lukács and Thomas Mann* (Amherst, Mass.: University of Massachussetts Press, 1985). For a criticism of Jay's confusion see Zoltán Tar, "The Weber-Lukács Encounter," in *Max Weber's Political Sociology*, ed. Ronald Glassman and Vatro Murvar (Westport, Conn.: Greenwood, 1984), pp. 109–35.

29. Max Horkheimer, *Critical Theory*, trans. Matthew J. O'Connell et al. (New York: Herder and Herder, 1972), p. 277.

30. See Tar, *Frankfurt School*, pp. 74–77.

31. Max Horkheimer and Theodor W. Adorno, *Dialectic of Enlightenment* (New York: Herder and Herder, 1972), p. xi.

32. Horkheimer and Adorno, *Dialectic*, p. 217.

33. Quoted in J.P. Mayer, *Max Weber and German Politics* (London: Faber and Faber, 1944), p. 128.

34. David Riesman, "Some Observations on Social Science Research," *Antioch Review* 1 (1951):259–78.

35. Adorno summarized his American experiences in *Minima Moralia*, significantly subtitled *Reflections from a Damaged Life*, a beautiful confession on problems of intellectual existence in exile, a work which remained without echo because only few people, who shared similar experience and injuries,

can really understand it. Adorno was never able to secure a teaching position in spite of his publication record and letters of recommendation such as by Thomas Mann. To be sure, there were intellectuals in exile even more damaged than Adorno. In a collection of interviews with social scientists whose careers were interrupted by the Nazis and the war, one of the interviewees, Hans Gerth, concluded his story with the exclamation: "Adorno referred to the 'damaged life.' My God, he had no idea just how damaged it can be." Gerth, a refugee from Nazi Germany, was shunned by fellow exiles because he left Germany only in 1937; later he was denounced by his American colleagues at the University of Illinois. See Matthias Greffrath, *Die Zerstörung einer Zukunft: Gespräche mit emigrierten Sozialwissenschaftlern* (Reinbeck bei Hamburg: Rowohlt, 1979), p. 95.

36. "Of Barricades and Ivory Towers: An Interview with T.W. Adorno," *Encounter* 33 (September 1969):65.

37. For more detailed discussion see Tar, *Frankfurt School*, ch. 3.

38. Tar, *Frankfurt School*, p. 170ff.

39. Jürgen Habermas, *Legitimation Crisis* (Boston, Mass.: Beacon, 1975).

40. See Habermas's contribution in this volume (ch. 2).

41. Georg Simmel, *On Individuality and Social Forms*, ed. with intro. by Donald N. Levine (Chicago, Ill.: University of Chicago Press, 1971), p. xiii.

42. Quoted in Tar, *Frankfurt School*, p. 173.

43. See Paul Connerton, *The Tragedy of Enlightenment: An Essay on the Frankfurt School* (Cambridge: Cambridge University Press, 1980); Klaus Hansen (ed.), *Frankfurter Schule und Liberalismus* (Baden-Baden: Nomos, 1981); J.N. Davydov, *Kritika social'no-filosofkix vozzreni j Frankfurtsko j skoly* (Moscow: Nauka, 1977); Richard Kilminster, *Praxis and Method: A Sociological Dialogue with Lukacs, Gramsci, and the Early Frankfurt School* (London: Routledge & Kegan Paul, 1979); and Tom Bottomore, *The Frankfurt School* (London: Tavistock, 1984).

44. Paul Connerton (ed.), *Critical Sociology* (New York: Penguin, 1976), p. 15.

45. Jürgen Habermas complained in his letter relating to his article reprinted in this volume that appeared in *Telos* (by his permission!) that it was "butchered" in the process. He requested in a subsequent letter addressed to Dr. Marcus that a new translation be undertaken. After checking the *Telos* version, the editors of this volume decided on a new translation as the preceding one was full of inaccuracies, and often change of meaning possibly due to an inadequate knowledge of German.

46. As Leo Löwenthal remembered, the Frankfurt Institute came to America during its most difficult period: "Those were depression times in America. Let's face it: we hardly noticed what went on all around us. We were so intent on establishing our own little German island here that we almost forgot about the terrible experience that America had to cope with." *Mitmachen wollte ich nie: Ein autobiographisches Gespräch mit Helmut Dubiel* (Frankfurt: Suhrkamp, 1980), p. 74.

47. Karl Mannheim, "The Problem of Generations," in *Essays on the Sociology of Knowledge* (London: Routledge & Kegan Paul, 1968), pp. 286–87.

48. Lucio Colletti, "Marx, Hegel, und die Frankfurter Schule," in *Marxismus als Soziologie* (Berlin: Merve, 1973), p. 81.

49. Georg Lukács, "An Unofficial Interview," *New Left Review* (July-August 1971):56.
50. Paul F. Lazarsfeld, "An Episode in the History of Social Research: A Memoir," and T. W. Adorno, "Scientific Experiences of a European Scholar in America," in *The Intellectual Migration: Europe and America, 1930-1960* (Cambridge, Mass.: Harvard University Press, 1969), pp. 270–337, 338–70.

Part One
HISTORY AND HISTORY OF IDEAS

1

Contribution to a
Critique of Critical Theory

Joseph B. Maier

"History," writes C.V. Wedgwood in her biography of William the Silent, "is lived forwards but it is written in retrospect. We know the end before we consider the beginning and we can never wholly recapture what it was to know the beginning only."[1] In a way, the following observations are an attempt to do just that; for those who were the principal architects of Critical Theory did not know the end. It would betray a serious deficiency in one's sense of humor, as well as a lack of philosophic piety, were one to undertake a systematic exposition and criticism of Critical Theory in the narrow compass of these pages. The difficulty of such a task is intensified by the fact that although I agree with Edward Shils that "Horkheimer is in a certain sense one of the most influential of social thinkers,"[2] I do not believe his greatness nor the importance of the Frankfurt School, which he founded and guided for more than a generation, to lie either in the uniqueness of their viewpoint—an amalgam of Marxism, psychoanalysis, and patrician disdain for mass society—in the rigor of their deductions, or in the adequacy of their organic determinism to the facts of experience they sought to explain.

To tell parts of a tale of great conceptions and failures seems no less important today than an attempt at complete detachment and objectivity. The protagonists of that tale were men of rare intellect. Two of them, Max Horkheimer and Herbert Marcuse, I had the great fortune to count among my special teachers and fatherly friends. It is in the first place with their thought, and in the second place with the work of Jürgen Habermas, the product of a later generation of Frankfurt School writers, that I propose to deal here. Their writings were parts of a tale, whose end is not yet written, of the repudiation by radical academics, especially in the social sciences, of the ancient Western ideal of dispassionate reason, of objective inquiry, in the study of man and society. They were also parts of a tale of men of good will. "Three passions simple but overwhelmingly strong, have governed my life," wrote Bertrand Russell in the prologue to his autobiography, "the longing for love, the search for knowledge, and unbearable pity for the suffering of mankind."[3] Such were indeed the passions that governed the lives of all members of the Frankfurt School. Almost all of them were, like Horkheimer and Marcuse, sons of the *haute bourgeoisie,* born and burdened with a deep sense of justice.

Promise and Reality

Horkheimer's Critical Theory was meant to be a critical theory of bourgeois society, its structure and its history. It was born out of the conviction that in the bourgeois era both the true notion of existing society and the utopian notion of a just and truly human society must perforce assume the form of a theoretical critique of existing conditions as a precondition of practical transformation. This does not mean that the goals of the bourgeoisie were simply to be denied and the bourgeoisie's political emancipation critically cancelled. History since the eighteenth century was not simply a history of the decline of the ideas of liberty, equality, and justice. "What is untenable," said Horkheimer, "is not the ideas and ideals of the bourgeoisie, but the conditions of reality that fail to correspond to them. The watchwords of the Enlightenment and of the French Revolution have lost none of their validity. To demonstrate their relevance in the face of a contradictory reality, is precisely the undertaking of the dialectical critique of the reality hiding behind the slogans. These ideas are but the particular features of the rational society advanced as the necessary demands of morality."[4]

This, according to Horkheimer, was the meaning of the bourgeois revolution—to realize the idea of liberty, equality, and justice in its indivisibility, "the establishment of the right order of things among men, the kind of social order which would satisfy the inalienable right of all to a decent life."[5] The course of the French Revolution was soon to disclose the bourgeois limitations of the struggle to remake the world. "It became evident that the political emancipation of the bourgeoisie and the unfettered growth of unequal economic forces in unchecked competition were one thing, the enthusiastically proclaimed aim and purpose of the struggle quite another."

Here was the negative historical experience on which Horkheimer grounded his critical theory. Convinced of the destructive dynamics inherent in bourgeois society, he planted his own critical thought in the tradition of Marx: "The present order of society is fully comprehended in the critique of political economy."[6] It is a doomed order. It is, in fact, seen as "perishing because of an obsolete principle of economic organization. The decay of culture is related thereto."[7]

"Ruthless Criticism of Everything Existing"

In the most emphatic sense imaginable, the watchword of the young Horkheimer, as of the young Marx some eighty years earlier, was *Kritik*— criticism. Like the young Marx before him, Horkheimer refrained from raising a dogmatic flag. He did not wish to create a new ideology or modify an old one. He had no design of the future, no program, no ready-made solutions for all time. He possessed no blueprint of a brave new world. His concern was the liberation of man. What he did consider as his principal task and mission to the last day of his life, was, in Marx's words, the "ruthless criticism of everything existing."[8] Reason, he argued in the young Hegelian manner, has always existed, only hitherto not always in a reasonable form. Like Marx, he felt that the critic could start out by taking "any form of theoretical and practical consciousness and develop from the unique forms of existing society the true reality as its norm."[9] The point and pride of Horkheimer's critical theory—or science of freedom, as he might also have called it—was the considered denunciation of, and implicit invitation to change, all those conditions in which a sizable number of men, if not all mankind, were alienated, abased, enslaved, and made pitiful.

The earliest formulations of Horkheimer's critical theory were written in the 1920s. While the Marxist elements were unmistakable, the very language revealed an aristocratic aloofness from sacred writ, at odds with both the reformist versions of the Social Democrats and the rigid dogmatism of the Communists. In 1930, when Horkheimer became professor of social philosophy and director of the Institute of Social Research at the University of Frankfurt, his principal intellectual interests were still focused on the philosophy of Hegel. It was one of the essential ingredients of critical theory. It was to Hegel, he believed, that our insight into the structures of collective life was owed. It was Hegel who sought to comprehend the faculties of men in the context of history. It was he who discovered reason to be at work in the inevitable historical progression from "low" and "false" to "higher" and "truer" forms of existence.

Horkheimer was truly Hegelian in regard to objectivity of outlook. But he shied away from blindly trusting the course of history to produce the right and righteous state of things. This notion, he thought, was an error of a dubious idealism: it metaphysically "elevated" the victims of the historical process into necessary elements of a universal plan of salvation. History, he said, "testifies to the fact that a better society has been brought forth by a lesser one, and that a still better one could yet be realized. It is another fact, however, that the price paid for this course is the suffering and misery of individuals. Between these two facts there are a number of explanatory connections; but no justifying meaning relates one to the other."[10]

For all of Horkheimer's affinities with Hegel and Marx, such statements reveal subtle differences from their basic thought and from the early influence of Schopenhauer's compassionate pessimism. From the very beginning, his theory was "critical" in the sense that his own historical materialism was not a positive *Weltanschauung,* not another "ideology," but a critique and denunciation of existing miseries. It was "critical" also in that it never concealed his profound sense of the tragic. Even under the most favorable circumstances, in the best of societies, man was destined to remain a finite and wanting creature. The influence of Schopenhauer prevented Horkheimer, unlike Georg Lukács and other rediscoverers of the dialectic, from becoming a dogmatic devotee of another "knowledge of the whole" or gospel of salvation, in the service of which all means were justified. To him, the dialectic, like all knowledge, was "incomplete" and finite, itself a transitory aspect of the interaction and strife of men with nature and one another.

The Frankfurt School in New York

Horkheimer's real fame was founded on the nine volumes of the *Zeitschrift für Sozialforschung,* which he edited from 1932 to 1940. The first volume was published in Leipzig. Upon Hitler's ascent to power, the Institute of Social Research moved to Paris, then Geneva, and ultimately New York. The subsequent volumes were written and edited in its New York headquarters at Columbia University under the imprint of the Librarie Félix Alcan in Paris. In a series of lead essays Horkheimer developed the categorical apparatus of critical theory and firmly set the tone of the *Zeitschrift.* The journal unambiguously exhibited its character of "house organ" of the institute. Its principal authors—among them T. W. Adorno, Erich Fromm, Herbert Marcuse, Leo Lowenthal, Friedrich Pollock, Walter Benjamin, Karl August Wittfogel, Henryk Grossmann, Franz Neumann, and Otto Kirchheimer—constituted a group of *engagé* intellectuals, each of whom made his contribution to a common theory of the social whole from the vantage point of his particular interest and competency.

In the foreword to the first issue of the *Zeitschrift* to appear in exile, Horkheimer reaffirmed his own and his collaborators' view of theory as "a factor of change." Even in New York, the *Zeitschrift* was to continue to appear in German. For the moment, Horkheimer seemed optimistic enough to suggest that the theory propounded under his direction might yet become "a material force" for "progressive forces of mankind" in their effort to usher in the "realm of freedom." That optimism was not, however, wholehearted. After World War I, no man as sensitive to changes in the political atmosphere as Horkheimer could fully persuade himself that the German proletariat was a revolutionary force. In the end the experiences of exile, fascism, and war extinguished even the remnants of Horkheimer's tenuous optimism; and thirty years later, when his critical theory surfaced as a *Flaschenpost,* it became a "material force" in the hands of a generation of philosophical and psychological parricides.

In the United States until recently, relatively little was known about the background and history of the Institute of Social Research and its members. To be sure, the names of Herbert Marcuse, Erich Fromm, Franz Neumann, and Max Horkheimer have come to wider attention since the appearance of *Reason and Revolution* (1941), *Escape from Freedom* (1941), *Behemoth* (1942), and *Eclipse of Reason* (1947), re-spectively their first major publications in English in this country. Now we have a thoroughgoing study that will serve as *the* source on the subject for a long time to come—Martin Jay's *The Dialectical Imagination: A History of the Frankfurt School and the Institute of Social Research, 1923-1950.* Several American publishers have issued translations of major works by the key members of the institute, among them Horkheimer's *Critical Theory,* Horkheimer and Adorno's *Dialectic of Enlightenment,* Adorno's *Negative Dialectic,* and Marcuse's *Studies in Critical Philosophy.*

During the turmoil of the 1960s, when a new generation of radicals adopted Marx as God and Marcuse as his principal prophet, it seemed for a moment that the message of the mid-1930s had been received, a new *Methodenstreit* had erupted, and the institute's historic hour finally come. Now, as the New Left is fading away, some scattered survivals among American college students and faculty appear to have regained or retained an academic interest in the intellectual traditions of the Frankfurt School. For the most part, however, Max Horkheimer and his colleagues remained outsiders. *Volens nolens,* they never became integral parts of Columbia or the American intellectual scene. The calculated decision to write in German ruled out the possibility of a large American following; the *Zeitschrift* reached no appreciable American audience, even though it carried an occasional article in English by a prominent American social scientist. It was conceived and born in splendid isolation. Its contribution to America, Horkheimer would say time and again, would be greater if he and his group preserved in this country the last island of German culture. In spite of the institute's excellent relations with

Columbia and with the American Jewish Committee, therefore, no real "Frankfurt School" took root on these shores.

Yet the presence of the institute on American soil did make a difference. There was, of course, always a group of intellectuals, however small in number, who did mine the gold in the pages of the *Zeitschrift*. There was, above all, the institute's participation in the conception and direction of the famous series "Studies in Prejudice" sponsored by the American Jewish Committee. *The Authoritarian Personality* (1950), more particularly, was a major intellectual event and caused a veritable flood of social science publications in this country and abroad. And there had been, earlier, Horkheimer's *Eclipse of Reason,* the first simplified version of critical theory in English. It foreshadowed much of Marcuse's work of the mid-1950s and 1960s, especially in *Eros and Civilization* (1955) and *One-Dimensional Man* (1964). It was largely in the ideas formulated in the *Zeitschrift* essays and in *Eclipse of Reason* that the American theory of mass culture had its origin.

The Theory of Mass Culture

Grossly oversimplified, the ideas themselves may be quickly summarized. Modern society has become increasingly destructive of individuality as authority has become more concentrated and as organization has become more inclusive and more depersonalized. Man has become a pawn for manipulation by others. The units of the older societies were also totalities, in the sense that they had grown into hierarchically organized entities. There is a crucial difference, however, between the social units of the modern industrial era and those of earlier epochs. In Horkheimer's words:

> The earlier societies, which were supposed to conform to an abstract spiritual model, contained an element that is lacking in the purely pragmatistic totalities of industrialism. The latter likewise have a hierarchical structure; but they are thoroughly and despotically integrated. For example, promotion of their functionaries to higher rank is not based on qualifications related to any spiritual ideals. Almost exclusively it is a matter of their ability to manipulate people; here purely administrative and technical skills determine the selection of governing personnel. Such capacities were by no means lacking in the hierarchical leadership of former societies; but the dissolution of relation between leadership capacities and an objectivized framework of spiritual ideals is what gives the modern totalities their distinctive character.[11]

The instinctual drives of man, repressed by modern industrialism, are manipulated by those who control the economy and the cultural media in the interest of their private profit and for the purpose of maintaining and expanding their political and economic dominion. The individual's capacity for and his use of reason declines. The essential tendency of mass culture is precisely this—to "sell" the people "the way of life in which they are fixed and which they unconsciously abhor but overtly acclaim."

The function of social theory under the conditions of modern industrialism, Horkheimer declared, can be none other than to be "negative," to offer a critical analysis of reality, "including the workers' own warped thoughts." Yet it was precisely this negative, or critical, function of theory that was being abandoned or stifled in the modern bourgeois world. Under the title "The Revolt of Nature," Horkheimer devoted an entire chapter in *Eclipse of Reason* to tracing the decline and degeneracy of "traditional" theory and philosophy. What passes for reason in the present, he argued, can better be named unreason. Instrumental, subjective, formal, manipulative reason was the handmaiden of technological domination. The new objectivism, descriptivism, pragmatism and positivism, in which all rational goals were abandoned and reason itself was gutted of its original content, merely reflected the misery of existing conditions. Such was indeed the dialectic of the Enlightenment: Bourgeois theory in the guise of instrumental reason not only failed to provide a basis for criticizing the status quo, failed to become what it once set out to be—a science of freedom—but had itself become a powerful means for the ever more subtle and efficient repression and domination of man.

Whatever the proverbial grain of truth in this romantic critique of industrial society, it will be forever impossible to explain satisfactorily how a group of formidable and generous minds like Horkheimer and his collaborators came to identify Charles Peirce, William James, John Dewey, Sidney Hook, and Ernest Nagel with the abasement of reason, "the anti-philosophical spirit that is inseparable from the subjective concept of reason, and that in Europe culminated in the totalitarian persecution of intellectuals, whether or not they were its pioneers." Was it because these men wrote in English instead of German, that they insisted on intelligence rather than *Geist?* Was it that *Geist* or reason was capable of grasping relationships, while lesser mental qualities like intelligence or warranted knowledge could only pry into things or manipulate sets of symbols and concept in a schizoid way? But that would make Horkheimer seem more parochial then he really was. To his dying day he considered himself a loyal American. True, his analyses were all too frequently permeated by the worst sort of European intellectual snobbery. His characterizations of American pragmatism were gross caricatures. Did he think less of Dewey because Dewey was not a Marxist?

But for Horkheimer Marxism was never a body of received truths either, and he would have been among the first to exclaim, like Marx himself, "Moi, je ne suis pas marxiste!" Could it be that Dewey and Hook were ignorant and unappreciative of the European philosophic tradition and of Hegel, or that they were in the least inclined to compromise the cause of reason and freedom? That would have been false on the face of it!

If the problem was to know what kind of culture is so free in itself that it "conceives and begets political freedom as its accompaniment and consequence," these Americans had always known, in Dewey's words, that "the relations which exist between persons, outside of political institutions, relations of industry, of communication, of science, art and religion, affect daily associations, and thereby deeply affect the attitudes and habits expressed in government and rules of law. If it is true that the political and legal react to shape the other things, it is even more true that political institutions are an effect, not a cause."[12] And if Horkheimer's objection to American pragmatism was that it is a "success philosophy," that there is no appreciation for the poignant value of the lost cause, it must be countered that Hegelianism and Marxism are far more "defective" in this regard, linking themselves to the decisive events of world history, as one idea and one national spirit triumphs over the other.

The profoundness of Horkheimer's misunderstanding was probably a matter of language, after all. He felt uncomfortable with "the treacherous lucidity of style" of American philosophy. His tongue was German, not English or American. And this was so, "not merely because one can never express as exactly in a new language what one means, with all the nuances and the rhythms of the train of thought, as in one's own. Rather, the German language has a special elective affinity [*Wahlverwandtschaft*] to philosophy, and, to be sure, to its speculative moment."[13] American and English were not just different codes for the same message. Each language expresses a group's sense of what is important and true, each edits the universe, as it were.

It is true, the theory of mass culture did not lack articulate critics. There were *The Future as Nightmare* by Mark R. Hillegas and "Technophobia on the Left: Are British Intellectuals Anti-Science?" by Gerald Leach in England; and "Anti-Progress: A Study in the Romantic Roots of German Sociology" by Arthur Mitzman and "Daydreams and Nightmares: Reflections on the Criticism of Mass Culture" by Edward Shils in America. But what made the theory of mass culture so appealing to a segment of Anglo-American intellectuals to begin with? Part of the answer is that it seemed, first, to explain why the rise of the masses had not led to the liberation of the mind and body promised by Marx.

The theory was especially congenial to intellectuals who, because of the particular conditions of their work and training, were more status-conscious than others; more thoroughly convinced of the superior value of some ideas and ways of doing things, particularly their own; more individualistic in their personal attitudes and more inclined to "do their own thing," while at the time vaguely more liberal and radical in their political preferences. The theory of mass culture permitted them to attack modern industrial society for forcing them into bureaucratic bondage and for cheapening their cultural norms. And it allowed them, simultaneously, to reaffirm their solidarity with the deprived and depraved masses undergoing "terroristic annihilation . . . unconsciously through the social process." In short, mass society was evil because it had man's alienation from himself and nature writ large all over it; man's mind was duped, his instincts perverted, his freedom and identity increasingly threatened by the prevailing "productive relationships," the overt and covert manipulations of those in power.

Marxism and Phenomenology

The immediate impact of Herbert Marcuse on public consciousness has been far greater than that of any other member of the institute. None ever earned quite the same reputation of angel of the apocalypse and chart maker of the royal road to the new society. Like his institute colleagues, he was a man of great culture and erudition, but he was always more straightforward and elemental in the style and manner with which he stressed the importance of "negative thinking." In his pre-1964 writings Marcuse was apparently convinced that modern American capitalism, through its ability to sustain abundance and popular culture, had eliminated all but the slightest possibility for significant antisystem protest and violence. It was utterly unlikely, he argued, even for the "outsider" group, like the Blacks, to break with middle-class norms.[14] So convinced he was of their basic docility that in a symposium at Rutgers University in 1965, he went "out on a limb" saying that he preferred that the "brain-washed" Blacks "not have the right to choose wrongly," that is, to vote. After 1965 he tried to account for the upheavals in terms of some newly discovered structural trends that generated large groups of people alienated from the system and impelled them to demonstrate or fulminate against it, on the campuses or in the streets. By the time Horkheimer and Adorno had given up their belief in any social group as a vehicle of social salvation, Marcuse was widely acclaimed by radicals for discovering in the "marginals"—students, Blacks, the Third World—a new, vital revolutionary force.

From the outset, Marcuse had differed from Horkheimer and Adorno. It is true, he was a Marxist when he joined the group. But he was also strongly influenced by existentialism and phenomenology. He had studied Heidegger and had been an assistant to him. His affinity with Heidegger, and later with Sartre, was a basic element of his thought. Marcuse's was the earliest among heroic attempts to synthesize Heidegger and Marx. It was certainly avant-gardist and "advanced" to fuse these two global perspectives on man. Was not each concerned with man in the totality of his situation? What was decisive for Marcuse was that each showed the same preoccupation with *crises*—existentialism, with the crisis that threatened the existence of modern man, and Marxism, with the crisis that threatened the existence of modern society.

In an essay entitled "Contributions to a Phenomenology of Historical Materialism," Marcuse greeted Heidegger's *Being and Time* as a "turning point at which bourgeois philosophy dissolves from within and opens the way to a new 'concrete' science."[15] Heidegger had accomplished this amazing feat, Marcuse argued, by demonstrating, "in its whole radical gravity," the ontological importance of history and of being-in-the-world (*In-der-Welt-sein*) as a world of human interaction. He had raised the question of what was involved in existence at an "unauthentic" as well as an "authentic" level in the context of an analysis of man's profound concern or care (*Sorge*) about his "thrownness" *(Geworfenheit),* abandonment, in a limited here-and-now set of possibilities. And he had shown that the "facticity" or realness of the being of man was not of the same order as that of other entities—that man could achieve authentic being by projecting (*entwerfen*) his possibilities outward, through "resoluteness" *(Entschlossenheit),* through decisive action in the world.

According to Marcuse, Heidegger in his radical quest had taken bourgeois philosophy to its very limits—the threshold of praxis. It was Marxism, however, that in a concrete and specific manner pointed to the "authentic deed" and answered Heidegger's question about the possibility of authentic existence in a concrete way. For all its seeming concreteness, Heidegger's philosophy was not concrete enough. It was still primarily concerned with a new approach to the traditional problems of the *philosophia perennis.* Marxism, on the other hand—"a dialectical phenomenology, a method of persistent and utmost concreteness"—clearly recognized that in this class society and at this point in history, there was only one class capable of decisive action, of historical concreteness, of acting as the identical subject-object of the real history of mankind. "The historical deed," Marcuse explained, "is possible today only as the deed of the proletariat, because it is the only *Dasein* (the only being that is here and now, that realizes the presence of Being), with whose existence the deed is necessarily given."[16] Because of its central role in the process of production, the proletariat was a really revolutionary class, the class that held the future in its hands. And only through revolution could the emancipation of man beyond the proletariat be realized.

Once Marcuse had moved into the charmed circle of the institute, the influence of Horkheimer on his work became dominant, and the existentialist outlook and vocabulary were temporarily submerged. Marcuse's *Zeitschrift* essays throughout the 1930s were genuine complements to Horkheimer's own formulations of critical theory. In contrast to traditional philosophy, Marcuse wrote in one of his programmatic essays, critical theory was not absorbed in the search for permanent answers to the age-old questions of man's essence and conditions. Rather, it "means to show only the specific social conditions at the root of philosophy's inability to pose the problem in a more comprehensive way, and to indicate that any other solution [lies] beyond that philosophy's boundaries. The untruth inherent in all transcendental treatment of the problem thus comes into philosophy 'from the outside'; hence it can be overcome only outside philosophy."[17] As for scientific objectivity, critical theory made no fetish of it. "Scientific objectivity as such," Marcuse declared, "is never a sufficient guarantee of truth, especially in a situation where the truth speaks as strongly against the facts and is as well hidden behind them as today. Scientific predictability does not coincide with the futuristic mode in which truth exists."[18] Quite deliberately, therefore, critical theory would always contain a strongly utopian strain, which transcended the here and now: "Without fantasy, all philosophical knowledge remains in the grip of the present or the past and severed from the future, which is the only link between philosophy and the real history of mankind."[19]

Reason and Revolution

With Horkheimer and the other members of the institute, Marcuse shared the belief, however uncertain and fragile, in the possibility of a transformed future toward which praxis-oriented critical theory might make a contribution. His *Reason and Revolution,* published in 1941 and dedicated to Max Horkheimer and the Institute of Social Research, still exuded a good deal of that belief, although it was a belief in the victory of "progressive ideas and movements" rather than of the proletariat. Marcuse's book was a reinterpretation of Hegel's philosophy, offered in the hope of demonstrating that Hegel's basic concepts were "hostile to the tendencies that have led into Fascist theory and practice." While Marcuse extolled Hegel's critical and rational standards, he tried to go beyond a mere restatement and elucidate the implications of Hegel's ideas that closely identified them with Marxist theory. Noting Hegel's "keen insight into the locale of progressive ideas and movements," Marcuse in a show of patriotic emotion even echoed Hegel's belief that "the American rational spirit [has] a decisive role in the struggle for an adequate order of life." He quoted Hegel's reference to the victory of some future and intensely vital rationality of the American nation and recalled that the great German philosopher, knowing far better than his critics the forces that threatened freedom and reason, and recognizing these forces to have been bound up with the social system Europe has acquired, once looked beyond that continent to this as the only "land of the future."[20]

Observing that *Reason and Revolution* was a fitting valedictory for Marcuse, whose association with the institute was to lessen in the 1940s as his involvement with governmental service grew, Martin Jay commented:

> Working with the OSS and the State Department was not precisely what the Frankfurt School had meant when it advocated revolutionary *praxis,* a point that its detractors on the left were to make in subsequent years. Still, like other members of the Institute, who worked with the government during the war, Marcuse was faithful to the observation that the unity of theory and practice was only a utopian hope. In the light of the existing alternatives, aiding the war effort against Hitler while maintaining the purity of one's theoretical commitment can scarcely be called a dishonorable compromise.[21]

By 1960, when Marcuse wrote a new preface entitled "A Note on Dialectic" to the reissue of *Reason and Revolution,* the mood of guarded optimism that had enveloped the original edition of the book was gone. There was no more reference to "the American national spirit" or to America as the only "land of the future." Following an approach more fully developed earlier in his *Eros and Civilization* and later in his *One-Dimensional Man,* Marcuse placed instead a renewed emphasis on fantasy and poetry, on negation, on the inner link between dialectical thought and the effort of avant-garde literature—"the effort to break the power of facts over the word, and to speak a language which is not the language of those who establish, enforce, and benefit from the facts."[22] Mallarmé, Maurice Blanchot, and Valéry—with these men Marcuse shared, he claimed, "the search for an 'authentic language'—the language of negotiation as the Great Refusal to accept the rules of a game in which the dice are loaded. The absent must be made present because the greater part of the truth is in that which is absent." To the interpretation of that-which-is in terms of that-which-is-not, to the employment of dialectical logic, the kind of logic that "reveals modes and contents of thought which transcend the codified pattern of use and validation" and "recovers tabooed meaning and thus appears almost as a return, or rather a conscious liberation, of the repressed"—to such an undertaking, the study of Hegel, of Marx's materialistic "subversion" of Hegel, and of Freud was recommended as an excellent guide.

One must of course remember, Marcuse cautioned, that whatever the experience of liberation as a result of engaging in such strenuous intellectual exercise, it would be a liberation in thought, in theory, only; that the divorce of thought from action, of theory from practice, was itself part of the unfree world, which no thought and no theory could undo; but that dialectic theory "may help to prepare the ground for their possible reunion, and the ability of thought to develop a logic and language of contradiction is a prerequisite for this task."[23] To remove any doubt as to what he meant by dialectical contradiction and to distinguish this "determinate negation" from all "pseudo and crackpot opposition, beatnik and hipsterism," Marcuse made it clear that what he had in mind was "ultimately a *political* negation." It was a negation to be enacted by "historical factors and forces." But precisely at this point Marcuse saw himself compelled to admit his inability to identify the revolutionary partners who would effect the essential "reunion" of theory and practice. There were none, he confessed, because "those social groups which dialectical theory identified as the forces of negation are either defeated or reconciled with the established system. Before the power of the given facts, the power of negative thinking stands condemned."[24]

The Role of the Students

At the height of his fame in 1968, Marcuse was asked how he saw his position in relation to the student uprisings all over the world. He replied: "The answer is very simple. I am deeply committed to the movement of 'angry students,' but I am certainly not their spokesman. It is the press and publicity that have given me this title." He particularly objected to the juxtaposition of his name and photograph with those of Che Guevara and Régis Debray, because "these men have truly risked . . . their lives in the battle for a more human society, whereas I participate in this battle only through my words and my ideas." To the extent that his words preceded the students' action, it was, Marcuse said, "more a case of encounter than of direct influence." He went on to explain:

In my books, I have tried to make a critique of society . . . I have tried to show that contemporary society is a repressive society in all its aspects, that even the comfort, the prosperity, the alleged political and moral freedom are utilized for oppressive ends. I have tried to show that any change would require a total rejection or, to speak the language of the students, a perpetual confrontation of this society. And that is not merely a question of changing the institutions but rather, and this is more important, of totally changing human beings in their attitudes, their instincts, their goals, and their values. This, I think, is the point of contact between my books and the worldwide student movement.[25]

To some observers it appeared as if Marcuse had at last identified the student *enragés* as the "historical forces" of revolutionary change. They thought that Marcuse, for all his professed attachment to Marx, had all too easily dismissed Marx's judgment in *The Eighteenth Brumaire* on the value of bohemianism in the revolutionary struggle and the harebrained idea of an alliance between the *Lumpenproletariat* and the *Lumpenintelligenz*. A closer examination of Marcuse's views, however, revealed that this was not quite so. The "angry students," he explained, were only "militant minorities who can articulate the needs and aspirations of the silent masses, but by themselves they are not revolutionaries." And as if to avoid being accused of having completely broken with orthodox Marxism, he added: "In spite of everything that has been said, I still cannot imagine a revolution without the working class."[26]

Whatever the precise role in the historical drama Marcuse assigned to the student rebels, he did make it clear that he saw something new in the movement—"a very strong element of anarchy. . . . In the revolutionary movement of the twentieth century, I believe it is new. At least on this scale, it is new." By the same token one could say that what made Marcuse so attractive to the student activists was also something new—the profoundly anarchist-existentialist element in his own philosophy which was submerged in the 1930s and 1940s but surfaced again with renewed vigor and a strong French accent in the 1960s. True, Marcuse did not cause the youth revolt. In the United States, it was sparked by Vietnam, by racial conflict, and later on by what has been called the crisis of the university. But he did provide the imagery, the visions, the natural law conceptions—in short, the ideological justifications of the movement. The tryst that he arranged between Marxism on the one hand and Sartre and Maurice Merleau-Ponty on the other opened up new and exciting possibilities—the chance to connect the useless passion of the self with the hated other in an orgasmic rendezvous with truth, that perfect moment of communal violence which is revolution. There was the spectacle of intellectuals lusting for an apocalypse in order to resolve their abstract paradoxes, of Sartre trying to convince Thorez that a dialogue with nothingness was superior to dialectical materialism as a philosophical basis for revolution. And there was the vision of esthetes, Luddites, and leftists on the barricades engaged in an "existential" free-for-all.

On the concrete issues of the day, whether Vietnam, the race conflict, or the university crisis, at any point along the line Marcuse and those who "articulate the needs and aspirations of the silent masses" could have formulated and pressed for rational alternatives. They might have followed the advice of Raymond Aron, who found himself in an analogous situation in France: "When all is said and done at times I am tempted to turn Boetian and state that every society is subject to the constraints of fact—the need for organization, for a technical hierarchy, the need for a techno-bureaucracy and so on. French intellectuals are so subtle that they end up by forgetting the obvious."[27] More pristine in their views and values, Marcuse and the movement preferred instead the course of total rejection. Hailing the coming together of Marx and André Breton as an attempt to "translate into reality the most advanced ideas and values of the imagination," Marcuse felt the student rebellion likewise taught us the lesson "that truth is not only in rationality, but just as much and perhaps more in the imagery." Adventurism, romanticism, imagination—call it what you will; but to Marcuse "it is an element necessary to all revolution." In sum, he believed that the student riots, whatever their immediate results and costs, were "a real turning point in the development of contemporary society."[28]

Marcuse thus leaves us with the impression that, although the student *enragés* may not be *the* "chosen people" of universal salvation, he most assuredly considered them an indispensable element. Recently, however, this belief appears to have suffered some modification in Marcuse's constant effort at reserving all options. Writing about the Watergate affair, Marcuse presents a characteristic argument: The violation of law and morality by high government officials was nothing out of the ordinary, not an aberration; it was, on the contrary, quite ordinary, just the sort of thing one would expect of American capitalism in the 1970s. In the early days of the system, Marcuse continued, the rule of law and the political morality associated with it facilitated the growth of the productive forces; now they have become fetters on it. In the 1970s American capitalism just cannot function without the use of illegal and violent means. There are no obvious villains and heroes. The whole system is sick and done for.

Since Marcuse as an *homme engagé* never aimed at balanced presentations, one should perhaps not reproach him for his failure to point to the courts, the Congress, and the press as live and functioning parts of the system; for his failure to appreciate the stability of the rule of law in a system which, for all its precariousness, has proved itself more enduring than any we have known in history. But how is one to interpret his amazing observation that the opposition to Watergate "does not come from the left, it comes from those conservative and liberal forces which are still committed to the progressive ideas of the Republic"?[29]

Unlike Marcuse, Horkheimer and Adorno were never willing to take seriously the antics of the ultra-Left. They probably would have been more charitable toward those they considered "real radicals." Even before the end of the 1960s, Horkheimer warned against the dangers of "pseudorevolutionary" acts on the Left as well as "pseudoconservative" acts on the Right. "A true conservatism that takes man's spiritual heritage seriously," he said, "is more closely related to the revolutionary mentality, which does not simply reject that heritage but absorbs it into a new synthesis, than it is to the radicalism of the Right which seeks to eliminate them both."[30] Would it be utterly mistaken to regard the above reference to "the progressive ideas of the Republic" as indicative of Marcuse's adoption of a like stance? A man of good will should have no difficulty in recognizing the justification in futuristic terms of present, sometimes very awful, actions as a very dubious undertaking at best. What matters in any case is not the nobility of our intentions but the sum of our acts. If we were prepared to be the sum of our acts and prepared to accept the consequences of those acts, there would be hope. As Raymond Aron, Marcuse's old friend and adversary, said: "For history to be comparable to a dialogue in which Reason has the last word, it is necessary that the questions be as reasonable as the answers, that the situations created by past answers or the things themselves be as reasonable as the questions."[31]

Return to Frankfurt

Referring to the opportunity he had "to enter into the lives of the Institute's members and appreciate in a more immediate way the impact of their personal experiences as intellectuals in exile," Martin Jay states in the introduction of his book: "In many ways, both for good and for ill, they were the unique experiences of an extraordinary generation whose historical moment has now irrevocably passed."[32] It is difficult to disagree with this evaluation of the situation. There is, however, some cunning of history, if not of reason, in the fact that much of the recent attention paid to Critical Theory was aroused by the appearance of work done in the relative obscurity of the 1920s and 1930s. "Already near the end of the twenties," said Horkheimer two years before his death in July 1973, certainly by the beginning of the thirties, we were convinced of the probabilities of a National Socialist victory, as well as of the fact that it could be met only through revolutionary actions. That it needed a world war we did not yet envisage at that time. We thought of an uprising in our own country and because of that, Marxism won its decisive meaning for our thought. After our emigration to America via Geneva, the Marxist interpretation of social events remained, to be sure, dominant, which did not mean in any way, however, that a dogmatic materialism had become the decisive theme of our position. Reflecting on political systems taught us rather that it was necessary, as Adorno has expressed it, "not to think of claims to the Absolute as certain and yet, not to deduct anything from the appeal to the emphatic concept of the truth."[33]

The notion of a specific Frankfurt School did not develop until after the institute had been forced by the Nazis to leave Frankfurt, and the term itself gained currency only after the institute's return to Germany in 1950. The audience for which Horkheimer and his colleagues had for so many years insisted on writing in German had come into being, the *Flaschenpost* had arrived at its destination. There was a new generation of German students willing, nay, eager and anxious to learn the gospel of Critical Theory. The Frankfurt School became more of an "insider" in the Federal Republic than it had ever been during the heydays of Weimar. Now it was one of the major currents of German sociological and philosophical thought. In 1968, *Der Spiegel* celebrated Horkheimer as "one of the few philosophical *Herrscherfiguren* of our time." Horkheimer and Adorno realized, of course, that Bonn was not Weimar, and that the present *Rechtsstaat,* the freest state the Germans have ever had in their history, was radically different from the hell that was Germany under Hitler. Their critical theory turned against *die verwaltete Welt,* called attention to the seeming rewards and real dangers of an increasingly administered world. In the face of this worldwide trend, theory was the only form of praxis still open to honest men. That meant that no party and no movement, neither the Old Left nor the New, indeed no collectivity of any sort was on the side of truth; and that the residue of the forces of true change was located in the critical individual alone.

For years Horkheimer has refused to yield to the clamor for republication of his essays from the *Zeitschrift für Sozialforschung.* Pirated editions had begun to circulate among an impatient German student body. Finally, in 1967 *Zur Kritik der Instrumentellen Vernunft,* a German version of *Eclipse of Reason,* appeared; it was followed in 1968 by *Kritische Theorie,* a 2-volume collection of Horkheimer's early writings. In the respective forewords to these books Horkheimer explained that he had been reluctant to reissue his earlier work because he was afraid that the unsophisticated student of Critical Theory might easily overlook the historical context of his reflections and mistake the past for the present. His detached appraisal of the present situation, his detachment and skepticism toward even the possibility of actualizing the Marxian vision of the realm of freedom, had the anticipated result.

The criticism leveled by the orthodox Marxists was relatively measured. Georg Lukács expressed his disdain for the entire Frankfurt School by dubbing it the "Grand Hotel *Abgrund* [Abyss]." But the fury of the New Left, which had drawn so much of its original inspiration from Horkheimer, Adorno, and Marcuse, was boundless. The disciples turned on the masters. They had once welcomed Marcuse with flowers when he came from America to visit their campuses; now they booed him. Horkheimer and Adorno became the targets of personal scorn and abuse, if not physical violence. The students' hostility turned against everything their erstwhile idols might at any time have been connected with. It became stridently, even riotously, antiestablishment, anti-American, and anti-Semitic (in the guise of being "merely" anti-Zionist and anti-Israel, to be sure). With a sharp eye for both social irrationalities and the images and contexts to express them, Jürgen Habermas, who, together with Alfred Schmidt, belongs to the most gifted and promising scions of the latter-day Frankfurt School, felt constrained to identify the demonstrators as "left Fascists." If that seems too harsh a political judgment, it was certainly an accurate psychological evaluation; the self-righteous *Systemüberwinder* and *Chaoten* who taunted and tormented Horkheimer and Adorno in the 1960s were, psychologically, not far removed from the troopers who yelled for their blood in the 1930s.

The Latter-Day Frankfurt School

Throughout the Western world during the late 1960s, university faculties were torn into factions. For some academics, student radicals could do no wrong; for others this was an opportunity to realize their own vision of a new university and a just society. Some thought now was the time to advance their careers and gain power; for others the chance to become a hero to the students was too great a temptation to be resisted. What it added up to was, in the words of Raymond Aron, an "ideological debauchery" and a "psychodrama." "Every one of us," he wrote, "indulged in role playing. . . . I have told you that I played the part of Tocqueville, which is not without a touch of the ridiculous, but others played Saint-Just, Robespierre or Lenin, which all things considered was even more ridiculous."[34] While most of the gurus remained silent and many "led" their disciples by psychologically following them, Jürgen Habermas was one of the few important exceptions to the general rule. An early supporter of student politics calling for the "democratization" of the principal institutions, especially those of higher learning, Habermas did not hesitate to raise his voice against "The Pseudo-Revolution and Its Children." He denounced "the ritualized forms of blackmail" practiced by a movement, which required "not an economic, but a socialpsychological explanation." The theories with which the rioters identified themselves were, he said, "either vague or demonstrably false" and in any case incapable of serving as guides to proper political action. What was worse, he said, was this: "From a false assessment of the situation is drawn a fatal strategy, which will not only permanently isolate students in universities and schools, but will weaken all social and political forces that demand democratization."[35]

It was only to be expected that the partisans of the Old and the New Left would ultimately consign Habermas to the dustbin of history along with other erstwhile heroes. While he did not belong to the Old Guard of the Frankfurt School, Habermas had been very much part of the school since the 1950s. When the fierce debate over the destiny and role of social theory and philosophy moved into full view at the Fifteenth German Sociological Congress held in Heidelberg in 1964 to commemorate the centenary of Max Weber's birth, he sided with Horkheimer, and more especially with Marcuse, on the question of value freedom and objectivity. Habermas suggested that the business of an ideologically critical examination of the methodology of sociology could not be relegated to the sociology of knowledge. More specifically, if Talcott Parsons, Reinhard Bendix, and Benjamin Nelson credited Max Weber with breaking the trilogy of historicism, utilitarianism, and Marxism, "I envy our American colleagues their political traditions which permit such a generous and (in the best sense of the word) liberal interpretation of Max Weber." Stressing that in Germany Max Weber's political sociology had had a different history, he went on to say: "If we are to judge Weber here and now, we cannot overlook the fact that Carl Schmitt was a legitimate pupil of Weber's. Viewed in the light of the history of influences, the decisionist element in Weber's sociology did not break the spell of ideology, but strengthened it."[36] Such considerations were closely in line with Marcuse's own undertaking on the same occasion to show up Max Weber's theory of the internal value freedom of science "for what it is in practice: the freeing of science for the acceptance of valuations imposed from outside."[37]

A few years later Habermas took pains to differentiate his position from "the fundamental attitudes that find expression in the features of a neo-anarchist worldview whether emotionally on the level of the Beatles and folksongs, politically on the level of Castroism and quotations from

Chairman Mao, or reflectively on the level of a theory that somewhat existentializes Marx and Freud, as in the works of Herbert Marcuse."[38] The key element in his own formulation of critical theory was the concept of "knowledge-constitutive human interests." In the political and philosophical controversies inside and outside the halls of academe, no other part of Habermas's *Wissenschaftstheorie* has gained the same currency. Small wonder, for what Habermas hoped to achieve by a critique that sought the destruction of "the illusion of scientific objectivism" was something that had proved increasingly elusive to the exponents of critical theory—greater acceptability both as philosophical and social theory and as the guide to revolutionary praxis.

What kind of theory leads to knowledge capable of truly orienting action? In response to this question, Habermas suggested as a starting point exactly the sort of theory that had defined the tradition of great philosophy since its beginnings. That tradition had insisted on the pursuit of knowledge freed from "mere" human interest, that is, knowledge that had taken a theoretical attitude. To illustrate, Habermas quoted from Schelling's *Lectures on the Method of Academic Study:* "The fear of speculation, the ostensible rush from the theoretical to the practical, brings about the same shallowness in action that it does in knowledge. It is by studying a strictly theoretical philosophy that we become most immediately acquainted with Ideas, and only Ideas provide action with energy and ethical significance."[39]

This concept of theory and life, theory in the traditional sense and in the sense of critique, had been the object of "one of Max Horkheimer's most important studies," said Habermas, referring to Horkheimer's early essay "Traditional and Critical Theory." Now, one generation later, Habermas considered it important to turn to a reexamination of this theme via a critical interpretation of Husserl's *The Crisis of the European Sciences.* Habermas, like Husserl, was concerned with crisis—not with crises *in* the sciences, but with their crisis *as* science. For "in our vital state of need this science has nothing to say to us," he quoted from Husserl. And, like Husserl, he took as the norm of his critique an idea of knowledge that preserved the Platonic connection of pure theory with the conduct of life. What ultimately produced a scientific culture, he explained, was not "the information content of theories but the formation among theorists themselves of a thoughtful and enlightened mode of life."[40]

In an elaborate argument, rich in subtleties and allusions, making his "way over abandoned stages of reflection" and in that way hoping to "recover the forgotten experience of reflection,"[41] Habermas unfolded his idea of "knowledge-constitutive human interest" as conjoining *theoria* and *kosmos, memesis* and *bios theoretikos,* knowledge and interests from the life world. And he offered five specific theses to explain the relation between knowledge and interest.[42] Fundamental methodological decisions, he said, such basic distinctions as those between analytic and synthetic statements or between descriptive and emotive meaning, were either appropriate or inappropriate; for their criterion was the metalogical necessity of interest that we can neither prescribe nor represent, but with which we must come to terms. Thesis number one therefore was: "The achievements of the transcendental subject have their basis in the natural history of the human species." Because the cognitive processes to which social life is linked function not only as means to the reproduction of life but also determine what a society defines as a good life, the second thesis held that "knowledge equally serves as an instrument and transcends mere self-preservation." As the interests constitutive of knowledge become part of the productive forces accumulated by a society, as they constitute the cultural tradition through which the society interprets itself and the legitimations it adopted, thesis number three maintained that "knowledge-constitutive interests take form in the medium of work, language, and power."

Habermas observed that the language of German idealism, according to which "reason" contained both will and consciousness as its elements, was not so obsolete after all. For reason also meant the will to reason, and in self-reflection knowledge attained "congruence with the interest in autonomy and responsibility." The fourth thesis thus told us that "in the power of self-reflection, knowledge and interest are one." It is true, the ontological illusion of pure theory behind which knowledge-constitutive interests become invisible promotes the fiction that Socratic dialogue is possible everywhere and at any time. When philosophy discovers in the dialectical course of history the traces of violence that deformed repeated attempts at dialogue, it must do something—it must "further the process whose suspension it otherwise legitimates: mankind's evolution toward autonomy and responsibility." Habermas's fifth and final thesis therefore found that "the unity of knowledge and interest proves itself in a dialectic that takes the historical traces of suppressed dialogue and reconstructs what has been suppressed." Of course, only in a fully emancipated society would communication develop into the nonauthoritarian and universally practiced dialogue from which "both our model of reciprocally constituted ego identity and our idea of true consensus are always implicitly derived."

So much, in rough outline, for Habermas's argument. If we now ask, How, precisely, could one identify the specific social interests that determine the direction from what is to what ought to be, the answer provided by Habermas contributes little, if anything, to resolve the dilemmas of the Frankfurt School. "These interests," he said, "define the social system so much as a whole that they coincide with the interest in maintaining the system."[43] Something strange has happened since the end of the nineteenth century, Habermas explained. Capitalist society has changed to a point where two key categories of Marxian theory, "namely class struggle and ideology, can no longer be employed as they stand."[44] Without doing violence to the subtleties of his own thought, he might even have said that they "cannot be employed at all." Why? Because the fusion into a system of large-scale industrial research, science, technology, and industrial utilization has made them obsolete. To wit:

> The system of advanced capitalism is so defined by a policy of securing the loyalty of the wage-earning masses through rewards, that is, by avoiding conflict, that the conflict still built into the structure of society in virtue of the private mode of capital utilization is the very area of conflict which has the greatest probability of remaining latent. It recedes behind others, which, while conditioned by the mode of production, can no longer assume the form of class conflicts. . . . Hegel's concept of the ethical totality of a living relationship which is sundered because one subject does not reciprocally satisfy the needs of the other is no longer an appropriate model for the mediatized class structure of organized, advanced capitalism. The suspended dialectic of the ethical generates the peculiar semblance of *post-histoire*. The reason is that relative growth of the productive forces no longer represents *eo ipso* a potential that points beyond the existing framework with emancipatory consequences, in view of which legitimations of an existing power structure become enfeebled. For the leading productive force—controlled scientific-technical progress itself—has now become the basis of legitimation. Yet this new form of legitimation has cast off the old shape of *ideology*.[45]

Of course there were conflict zones even in advanced industrial societies, Habermas was willing to admit. But they did not seem to matter much. As to what interested the student radicals most, Habermas just could not say who would form the revolutionary force to replace the revolutionary working class in which his elders of the Frankfurt School had lost confidence. His intellectual efforts thus appear to culminate in an updated version of Mannheim's sociology of knowledge on the one hand and a valiant espousal of the virtues of speculative philosophy on the other.

The Meaning of History

Among the things that aroused the special scorn of the apocalyptic visionaries and redemptionist millenarians of the Old and New Left was

Horkheimer's persistent concern with "meaning"—the meaning of life and history. They belittled his increasing interest in religion in general and Judaism in particular, and the ultimate triumph of Schopenhauer over Marx in his philosophy, as the deathbed confessions of an aging patrician. Nothing could be further from the truth. Horkheimer's novellas, written by the precocious adolescent and morally sensitive young adult, easily reveal the specifically religious and moral themes and motivations of his later thought.[46] At no time was there a fundamental departure or breach. The appeal of critical theory to "*ein ganz Anderes,* an entirely other than this world," Horkheimer reaffirmed time and again, had primarily a social-philosophical impetus. It led finally to "a more positive evaluation of certain metaphysical trends, because the empirical 'whole is the untrue' [Adorno]."[47]

Horkheimer's argument proceeded patiently, methodically, almost pedantically, in the critical manner of Kant. Sensuous data, in themselves wholly disconnected and disordered, were the given material of experience. These constituted the building blocks of our knowledge, as it were. The order and connection that were established among them, the spatial-temporal and other relations which they exhibited—in short, all the regularities and laws to be discerned in this manifold—had their exclusive source in the rational subject. Thus the world can be seen as falling into two hemispheres. On the one side we have phenomena, things as they are to us, the unity of our thinking minds with the material of sense; on the other side stand the things as they are in themselves or, if we please, the unknowable. These things-in-themselves, regarded as reality, are precisely what our minds can never know: there can be no knowledge of reality at all.

Horkheimer could never bring himself to accept Hegel's main argument that if the Kantian categories were to be forms of thought, and thought was the substance of the world, the categories must also be the forms of the world-in-itself and that, therefore, thought was constitutive of reality. With Kant he held that "the things we know about are appearances only; we can never know their essential nature, which belongs to another world which we cannot approach." That his *Sehnsucht nach dem ganz Anderen* (1970) was a nonscientific concern, he realized only too well; but it did express "the hope that earthly horror does not possess the last word." One can, indeed, as David Hume suggested, erect "religious faith on philosophical skepticism." In Horkheimer's case, it was his way of reaffirming that even as a philosopher he was still a Jew who was bound by the biblical injunction against making an image of God.

Horkheimer and Adorno, whatever their earlier views and visions, were never the leftist gurus their more impassioned disciples and detractors believed them to be. Horkheimer's veiled references to "the wholly other" and Adorno's mysterious allusions to a world "in the messianic light"[48] contained no blueprints and no marching orders for revolutionaries chafing to establish the red millenium. A profound pessimism had permeated the thinking of the two leading spirits of the Frankfurt School ever since their first joint venture, *Dialectic of Enlightenment* (1947, 1972). Hegel and Marx believed that the movement toward freedom was irreversible or that the progressive expansion of freedom was the general law of development. To their followers they held out the comforting thought both that salvation lies in your own hands and that history is on your side. Horkheimer and Adorno now turned Hegel and Marx on their heads by professing the opposite. Reason and history, they insisted, were moving not toward greater progress but toward greater regress, not in the direction of bliss and salvation but in the direction of hell and damnation.

It would be foolish to fault Horkheimer and Adorno for reminding us that knowledge can be used for evil purposes and that the situation is made more threatening when the increase of power over nature is accompanied by an increase of power over the minds of men. Since Auschwitz it has become only too obvious that the optimism of the early theories of progress, which assumed that intellectual, scientific, and technological development was the chief determinant of social progress, is dead and gone. Beyond the moods of optimism and pessimism, the real problem with Horkheimer and Adorno lies elsewhere—in their unwavering commitment to the same eschatological interpretation of history. The rhythm and plot of history which empirical inquirers cannot detect has always been clear to them.

Those of us who are less certain of the consummation of history, feel that it is futile to rail against science and technology, instruments which can be used both for oppression and destruction and for freedom and welfare. The *Wertfreiheit* of the sciences leaves the road open to both progress and degeneration. The choice is ours. While knowledge is not sufficient, it is a necessary condition of progress. It can make no promise of ultimate success, and it can offer no apocalyptic visions. By pointing up the possibilities open to men, however, it provides them with a choice and thus with a chance to make their own history before the end of days is reached.

Notes

1. C.V. Wedgwood, *William the Silent* (London: Jonathan Cape, 1967), p. 35.
2. Edward Shils, "Tradition, Ecology, and Institution in the History of Sociology," *Daedalus* (Fall 1970):773.

3. *The Autobiography of Bertrand Russell* (London: Allen & Unwin, 1967), p. 13.
4. Max Horkheimer, *Kritische Theorie* (Frankfurt: S. Fischer, 1968), 1:97.
5. "Soziologie und Philosophie," in *Sociologica II,* ed. Max Horkheimer and T.W. Adorno (Frankfurt: Europäische Verlagsanstalt, 1962), p. 5.
6. Horkheimer, *Kritische Theorie,* 1:263.
7. Ibid., 2:197.
8. Karl Marx, "Letter to Arnold Ruge" (1843), in *The Marx-Engels Reader,* ed. Robert C. Tucker (New York: W.W. Norton, 1972).
9. Ibid.
10. Alfred Schmidt, *Zur Idee der Kritischen Theorie* (Munich: Carl Hanser, 1974), p. 138.
11. Horkheimer, *Eclipse of Reason* (New York: Oxford University Press, 1947), p. 145.
12. John Dewey, *Freedom and Culture* (New York: G.P. Putnam's Sons, 1939), p. 6.
13. Theodor W. Adorno, *Stichworte: Kritische Modele 2* (Frankfurt: Suhrkamp, 1969), p. 110.
14. S.M. Lipset, *Group Life in America* (New York: American Jewish Committee, 1972), p. 12.
15. Herbert Marcuse, "Beiträge zu einer Phänomenologie des Historischen Materialismus," *Philosophische Hefte* (July 1928):52.
16. Ibid., p. 68.
17. Herbert Marcuse, *Negations: Essays in Critical Theory* (Boston: Beacon, 1970), p. 149.
18. Ibid., p. 156.
19. Ibid., p. 155.
20. Herbert Marcuse, *Reason and Revolution* (Boston: Beacon, 1968), p. xv.
21. Martin Jay, *The Dialectical Imagination* (Boston: Little, Brown, 1973), p. 80.
22. Marcuse, *Reason and Revolution,* p. x.
23. Ibid., p. xii.
24. Ibid., p. xiv.
25. "Marcuse Defines His New Left Line," *New York Times Magazine.*
26. Ibid.
27. Raymond Aron, *The Elusive Revolution* (New York: Praeger, 1969).
28. "Marcuse Defines His New Left Line."
29. *New York Times* (27 June 1973).
30. Horkheimer, *Kritische Theorie,* 1:xii.
31. Raymond Aron, *Marxism and the Existentialists* (New York: Harper & Row, 1969).
32. Jay, *Dialectical Imagination,* p. xvii.
33. Ibid., p. xi.
34. Aron, *Marxism and the Existentialists.*
35. Jürgen Habermas, "Die Scheinrevolution und ihre Kinder," in *Die Linke antwortet Jürgen Habermas* (Frankfurt: Europäische Verlagsanstalt, 1968).
36. Habermas, in *Max Weber and Sociology Today,* ed. Otto Stammer (New York: Harper & Row, 1972), p. 66.
37. Ibid., p. 133.
38. Jürgen Habermas, *Toward a Rational Society* (Boston: Beacon, 1970), p. 28.

39. Jürgen Habermas, *Knowledge and Human Interests* (Boston: Beacon, 1971), p. 301.
40. Ibid., p. 302.
41. Ibid., p. vii.
42. Ibid., pp. 312–15.
43. Habermas, *Toward a Rational Society,* p. 105.
44. Ibid., p. 107.
45. Ibid., p. 108; cf. Habermas's most recent book on the *Legitimation Crisis* (Boston: Beacon, 1975) of "late capitalism." While going beyond the Frankfurt School's almost exclusive preoccupation with "bourgeois ideology" to an economic, political, and cultural critique of modern society as an integrated whole, Habermas argues that the crisis tendencies in our economic and politco-administrative subsistence were not necessarily beyond our ability to cope with them. The trouble was, however, the independent evolution of the normative structures which destroy, without replacement, the historic motivations for economic performance and political compliance.
46. Max Horkheimer, *Aus der Pubertät: Novellen und Tagebuchblätter* (Munich: Kösel, 1974).
47. Jay, *Dialectical Imagination,* p. xii.
48. T.W. Adorno, *Minima Moralia* (Frankfurt: Suhrkamp, 1951), p. 481.

2

The Frankfurt School
in New York

Jürgen Habermas

For that special group of emigrants whom the public has come to associate with the name of Critical Theory, albeit from the late 1960s on, the *Zeitschrift für Sozialforschung* was a vital part of its life: It was both its organizational core and intellectual center. Editorial meetings more often than not turned into scholarly discussions; research assignments and publication plans coincided in most cases. The journal was more than just an outlet for a group of scholars; it played a constitutive role in establishing a school of thought. And the editor of the journal, Max Horkheimer, never let his readers doubt its importance. In the foreword to volume 6 he emphatically justified the journal's selection of lead articles by stating:

> We have decided to continue a philosophical tradition in that we were guided in the selection of articles not just by their scholarly quality but more importantly by their representative thinking and the direction of their research. The lead articles in various disciplines should develop and apply a common philosophical viewpoint. Since in all other areas of life indifference toward universal human concerns and the renunciation of rational decision are steadily gaining hold, and relativism is becoming the avowed intellectual attitude precisely among sincere men, scholarship should hold on to certain ideas even more resolutely.

These words were by no means signs of dogmatism; they merely indicated a decided preference for research interests by the choice of themes that the journal's very first volume had already indicated.

Theoretical Emphasis

Horkheimer had initiated the first issue of the journal with an essay on "Science and Crisis." The essay outlined the principal features of a critique of science (*Wissenschaftskritik*), bringing out a dual frontal attack that remained operative until the positivism dispute of the 1960s: the stand against scientism and metaphysics. These two variants of an understanding of a theory that had its roots in the same traditions formed the background against which Horkheimer—together with Herbert Marcuse—in the years that followed worked out an approach to a critical theory of society. Similar to Husserl's investigation of "The Crisis of European Sciences," Horkheimer's works intended to penetrate beyond the objectivistic self-understanding of the empirical sciences in order to expose the life-world context of research, that is, to lay bare the threads extending from social praxis to methodology. This very first issue, published while still in Frankfurt, distinctly contained the seeds of later theoretical developments. Fromm wrote, for example, on the task of an analytical psychology; Löwenthal and Adorno on the sociology of literature and music; Friedrich Pollock and Henryk Grossmann on capitalism, the economic crisis, and on the "prospects of a new social order with the help of a planned economy."

With a few bold, energetic strokes, Erich Fromm outlined the foundation for a fruitful Marxist adaptation of psychoanalysis. The revolution that had not come to pass, the success of fascist dictatorship in Germany, the bureaucratic distortion of socialism in Stalinist Russia—those were the contemporary historical events that made for sharpened sensibilities of the possibility of psychic mediation between changes in consciousness and socioeconomic changes. It was up to psychoanalysis to demonstrate how the pressure of economic conditions on the institutional structure was converted into behavioral modes and ideologies. An equally momentous integration of Freudian developmental psychology with social theory was accomplished again only by Talcott Parsons at a much later date. It was not long before the members of the Frankfurt Institute made good use of this tool developed by Fromm.

A similar situation applies to cultural theory, represented by the works of Adorno, Löwenthal, and Benjamin. In his first essay, Löwenthal complained not only about the "distorted relationship" of literary criticism to psychoanalysis, history, and sociology, but also about its inclination to put a metaphysical spell on its subject matter and to metaphysically mistify the subject of its investigation. On the other hand, the "connection between cultural and economic processes" should by no means be investigated empirically, as a subfield of sociology, so to speak. The approach of the Frankfurt group confined itself to the work at hand; but the investigation of aesthetic forms was radicalized to the extent that the social mechanism, the psychodynamics rooted in the economic structure, could be deciphered even out of the seemingly most remote, esoteric, and mysterious cyphers of the work of art. Löwenthal's approach, ideology critique, to literary works belonging to the narrative and dramatic genres that had been produced by the European bourgeoisie paved the way for a methodology that has since been practiced widely by generations of students of Germanic studies. Löwenthal was just as persistent in the investigation of the formal elements of literary works such as the narrative framework and dialogue development as well as the composition and selection of themes. This detective-like search for the social content of aesthetic forms was even more pronounced in Adorno's studies on Schönberg and Wagner and in Benjamin's essay about Baudelaire, all of which are a fascinating documentation indeed for an aesthetics amounting to a thoery of society that has its parallel only in the works of Georg Lukács.

The most conventional among the theoretically significant articles are the contributions on the fourth theme that were first most meaningfully addressed by the essays of Pollock and Grossmann. In any Marxist-oriented journal we would expect the political economy to dominate. It is true that reviews of the literature on planned economy (by Kurt Mandelbaum and Gerhard Meyer) are safely ensconced in the volumes of the journal; it is also true that the book-review section recounts the main issues of the workers' movement under the heading "Social Movements and Social Policy." However, economic theory is not elaborated upon; Pollock's extremely interesting theses on state capitalism (and Wittfogel's famous studies on oriental despotism) merely confirm the steady shift in the theoretical perspective that is symptomatic. Less attention is paid to the conflict-producing mechanisms of the economic system than to the postcrisis interceptive mechanisms of conflict management by the state and of cultural integration. The works of Franz Neumann and Otto Kirchheimer regarding political science and the theory of law all point in this direction; both of these legal scholars who first joined the institute after its emigration from Germany and whose social democratic orientation remained outside the close circle of original members made contributions to the development of a theory of democracy that is still relevant today.

All the elaborate essays reflect the incomparable productivity of a small group of scholars who banded together around the journal which became their focal point as emigration shrunk their sphere of activity. The journal provided a sort of focus; if there was ever a Frankfurt School that could be pinpointed, it existed between the years 1933 and 1941 and settled in a house provided by the generosity of Columbia University at 429 West 117th Street, on New York City's Upper West Side.

What Makes the Journal a Document

It is this previously discussed main part of the journal that has been badly plundered. In 1970, when the first reprint appeared, all the important essays by Marcuse, Adorno and Benjamin, Löwenthal and Fromm, and Neumann and Kirchheimer had already been published in separate editions. After years of hesitation, even Horkheimer had finally consented to a reprint of his essays from the journal. However, in his 1969 foreword to the two volumes, Horkheimer put some distance between himself and his early work. He no longer wanted to acknowledge the validity of the "economic and political ideas" that had comprised the horizon of his reflections in the 1930s. He warned students: "Careless and dogmatic application of critical theory to praxis in a charged historical reality can only hasten the process that it sought to denounce" (*Critical Theory*, p. v). We may then ask: If everything important—complete with this caveat— had already been published, why a reprint of the magazine with all the trimmings?

It was Horkheimer who by chance put me in the fortunate situation of being able to answer this question. During my assistantship at the Frankfurt Institute in the 1950s, Horkheimer discouraged us from reading the journal because of the above-mentioned reservations. A complete set of the *Zeitschrift* was kept in the institute's cellar, crated, nailed shut, and out of grasp. Consequently, I became acquainted at that time only with scattered issues and could not put my hands on the whole set of journals until after substantial parts had been published elsewhere. Thus I was surprised to discover the material lying around in those "compendious review sections" announced on the back of each individual issue: a journal, I learned, can be quite different from the key theoretical articles it contained.

Books have their destinies. They can be lost, forgotten, and then reappear. Even books that remain in circulation for a while have their own destinies. New editions are like shorelines, against which, with every change of situation and the appearance of every new generation of readers, a new stratum of unexpected reactions surfaces. The case is different with periodicals: they themselves prevent such a continuous reception. Journals limit their own timeliness by the rhythm of their appearance. Every new issue devalues the preceeding one, and with its last number a journal wanders into the archives. Periodicals are more intimately bound up with the date of their publication than monographs are with the year of their first printing. To be sure, periodicals can be effective in different ways: If they have absorbed enough of the spirit of the time, they can become a document. And sometimes even documents have their destinies. Perhaps that is the key for the analysis of the effects that the *Zeitschrift für Sozialforschung* produced.

Essays defining the Frankfurt School's theoretical positions take up less than half of each issue. The book review section occupies more than a third of the space. And since the editors insisted on short, extremely concentrated reviews, more than 350 publications were reviewed each year—a total of almost 3,500 titles over the years. Among the guidelines of the book-review policy that Horkheimer made clear in the previously-mentioned foreword is the elaboration of a theoretical standpoint:

> Because the existing intellectual confusion makes the undaunted pursuit of certain ideas in the various fields of social theory particularly necessary, it is in the best interest of each and every philosophical thinking to keep track of work done within individual disciplines. This orientation should be made easier for the reader of our journal mainly by the book reviews offered. We will try to at least mention every single publication of any importance for the theory of society, even if it is in remote fields. The main article-section is supplemented by such studies by specialists, which have some connection to questions of the social sciences. In this case, differences in theoretical attitude play a far lesser role than the clarification of particular contents. Our criticism of the positivistic school does not prevent us from recognizing and promoting its achievements in particular fields [vol. 6, no. 2].

Articles by Otto Neurath and Paul Lazarsfeld thus appear in the same volume with the works of Horkheimer, Marcuse, and Fromm; Neurath comes from the Vienna Circle, and Lazarsfeld specializes in social upheavals, in techniques of social research. The understated allusion to keeping track of work done within individual disciplines refers mainly to the book-review section, behind which is the well-concealed impressive achievement of Löwenthal who expertly pulled the editorial strings. Without him, that is, without the book-review section he ran, Horkheimer's idea of "social research" in the foreword to the first issue could not have been realized—a theory of society oriented to the present epoch and subject to the criterion of empirical research in all the social science disciplines.

Unity of the Social Sciences

The background philosophy of the German historical school provided two or three generations of the humanities (*Geisteswissenschaften*) with a unifying force, which then was conceptualized by Dilthey. Horkheimer achieved something similar with this journal for the social sciences, although it lasted only a decade. The literature discussed in the book-review section provided the raw material that fit quite naturally into the theoretical framework; it seemed to be the test for the organizational power of the central research interests. It was divided into philosophy, general sociology, psychology, history, social movements and social policy, specialized sociology, and economics. Subdivisions of special sociology were: political science, cultural anthropology, and theory of law. Never again have both disciplinary and national distances been bridged so strikingly in the social sciences; never again has the unity of the social sciences been so convincingly portrayed as here, and, to use the definition of Merleau-Ponty, from the perspective of an unorthodox, modified "Western Marxism," which fused the heritage of German philosophy from Kant to Hegel with the tradition of social theory from Marx to Durkheim and Max Weber.

Nevertheless, an internal (Marxist) discussion hardly plays any role here. To be sure, Lukács or Borkenau wrote about the old Marx-Engels Complete Edition (MEGA), Korsch did so about Lenin, Paul Mattick about the early Sidney Hook, and Marcuse about Cornue and on Marxology in France. Labriola was reviewed as was Natalie Moszkovska's famous article on crisis theory. All this, however, remained free from the otherwise usual bickering among factions. Korsch for example, was more interested in Donoso Cortes, in the build-up of state power in fascist Italy, in Michael Freund's studies on Sorel, in the instructive ambivalence in the book of a young conservative author such as Wilhelm Eschmann (on the "revolution" of 1933).

Horkheimer and Löwenthal could never have achieved the ambitious goals of their editorial policy without the collaboration of internationally renowned experts such as Alexander Koyré, Maurice Halbwachs, Raymond Aron and Georges Friedmann from Paris, Maurice Ginsberg and T.H. Marshall from England, and Charles A. Beard, Margaret Mead, Harold D. Laswell, and Otto Lipmann from the United States.

The journal had enviable financial resources; thus it was able to persuade many of the German émigrés to contribute their work. There are gaps that are characteristic of the setup: Ernst Bloch and Hannah Arendt are missing from the list of contributors, as is Hans Morgenthau. From the scholars associated with the New School for Social Research, only Adolf Lowe and Hans Speier contributed to the journal. Still, the impressive list of reviewers included: Ernst von Aster, Otto Fenichel, Paul Honigsheim, Karl Landauer, Karl Löwith (first from Rome, then from Japan), Ernst Manheim, Siegfried Marck, Paul Massing, Hans Mayer, F. Neumark (from Istanbul), Arthur Rosenberg, and Günther Stern. Individual articles were contributed to the journal by Ossip

Flechtheim, Hans Gerth, Bernhard Groythuysen, A.R. Gurland, Herta Herzog, Ernst Krenek, Frieda Reichmann, Ernst Schachtel, and Paul Tillich.

The editors were able to use this wealth of experts to carefully report on the most varied research orientations. The journal could familiarize its German public with the newer movements abroad such as the functionalist school of American cultural anthropology (Malinowski, Mead, Benedict), different sociological developments be it within the Durkheimian School or the Chicago School; further with A.C. Pigou and the beginnings of welfare economics, with the pragmatism of G.H. Mead and Dewey, and with the great historical works of Pirenne or Toynbee. And the journal was especially qualified to critically evaluate such theoretical innovations as Kurt Levin's field theory, the beginnings of analytical ego psychology, the revolutionary work of Keynes and the works of Joan Robinson, or the Unified Science movement that had its roots in logical empiricism. These are but a few examples of this unusual scholarly instrument's ability to be an integrating force, and to illustrate the wide range of intellectual stimuli for which the journal had an especially sensitive and selective antenna.

Had the only significant achievement of the journal been to contribute philosophical inspiration for uniting the social sciences at a specific historical moment, it would still have become an important document. But I have serious doubts that this achievement could have been accomplished without the impulses provided by contemporary historical events. Helmut Dubiel in his exemplary *Studies on Early Critical Theory* (Suhrkamp, 1978), traces how the historico-political experiences including the end of the revolutionary workers' movement, the Nazi regime, and Stalinism, deeply affected the development of Critical Theory itself, and how these developments gradually dashed the hopes that had existed at the beginning of the project and led to the negative dialectical theory of totalitarianism that Horkheimer and Adorno, having only the critique of instrumental reason left at their disposal, took back with them to Germany. The journal as a whole reflected this process.

Contemporary Historical Events as a Motive Force

Horkheimer's foreword for the first English-language issue in July 1940 betrays the journal's earlier motives:

> We have until now not published the journal in America mainly because in the last eight years most of our readers were Europeans. Since almost all of the articles appeared in German, they were able to fulfill their real

purpose: to keep alive, in the mother tongue, philosophical and scientific traditions that could no longer be followed in Germany. The language in which articles were written influences the ideas they contain. But now this consideration fades before our wish to place our work, even in its external forms, at the service of American social life. Philosophy, art and science have lost their homeland in almost all parts of Europe [vol. 8:321].

A look at the book-review section of the four English-language issues clearly shows why the journal had to fold: the umbilical cord to the scientific culture of the homeland was cut. Till then the émigrés had looked to Germany with love and dependency mixed with sadness, bitterness, and horror. These alarmed looks caught something that makes the reading of the reviews a depressing experience for everyone to whom the names meant anything; this part of the journal reflected the spiritual disintegration that was happening at German universities.

The first issue published in Frankfurt fully reflected the world of the 1920s. The abundance of short reviews surveyed a familiar terrain; there were famous social scientists such as Vierkandt, Tönnies, and Thurnwald, Karl Mannheim, Alfred Weber, Emil Lederer, Robert Michels, Theodor Geiger, or A. von Martin. Discussed side by side were C.G. Jung and Freud, Hans Freyer and Neurath, Ludwig von Mises and Lenin, Kurt Breysig and Franz Mehring. There were spans from Eugen Rosenstock to Nicolai Hartmann, from Lujo von Brentano to Kautsky, from Alfred Schütz and Eduard Heimann to Kuczynski, from Malinowski via Bergson to Croce. Only a few shrill tones could be heard in this peaceful, amicable circle, for example when Adorno spoke of Spengler's noisy, profuse pathos and the young Dolf Starnberger displayed an unerring political estimation for Othmar Spann's valency as time-symptomatic. Richard Löwenthal was equally critical: In a Marxist vein, he tore to pieces the theory of democracy inspired by Schumpeter and Weber, which he himself was to embrace later. But Karl Korsch still emphasized the strengths of Carl Schmitt's theory; and Hans Speier cautiously started to express his reservations about the reduction of politics to friend/foe relations.

Two issues later, the atmosphere had suddenly changed: when the same book, Carl Schmitt's Begriff des Politischen, appeared in its third edition, Marcuse restricted himself simply to enumerating the partly opportunistic, partly inflammatory textual changes that the author had tacitly considered necessary to undertake after January 30, 1933.

At the same time, however, Horkheimer still warned against blanket judgments, alluding to the then dominating "sociologically extremely complicated intellectual currents existing in Germany." Consequently, the reviews of German-language publications presented a complex picture. Of course, the journal followed the work of émigrés, including those with whom there seemed to be no personal contact, such as the work of Karl Mannheim, Ernst Heller, Helmuth Plessner, Leo Strauss, E. Voegelin, W. Hallgarten, or Gotthard Günther. But attention was paid mainly to authors who could continue the German intellectual tradition within Germany: Jaspers, Litt, Nicolai Hartmann or Franz Schnabel in philosophy, Friedrich Meinecke, Erich Kahler, and Hermann Oncken in history. Progress on editions of collected works (Hegel, Dilthey) was just as diligently recorded as the complicated political differentiations within well-known schools (such as the Heideggerian one in Freiburg or that of Felix Kruger in Leipzig). With Marcuse, Löwith, and Günther Stern (who become famous after World War II under the name of Günther Anders), the journal had three philosophers who matured intellectually in the Freiburg of a Husserl or a Heidegger. With a sigh of relief, Marcuse at the end of 1936 began a review stating that a few works from Heidegger's circle, though they ordinarily would not belong within the scope of a journal of social research, deserved reviewing because without accommodating the dominant ideology, "they are striving for an objective treatment of their subject matter." There appears to be a strenuous effort to bring the far away blurred contours into focus.

Typical of the situation is what Adorno wrote about Erich Rothacker's book *Die Schichten der Persönlichkeit* (The Strata of Personality), the same book by the way that we, as Rothacker students, were still using in our psychology courses after the war without recognizing the sharp distinction of a New York observer who in 1938 wrote:

> The book shows the scholarship of the Dilthey school and is well organized. Its political reserve is noticeable. The customary practical application of the organically stratified personality is omitted. The chapter on the psychology of nations can be considered a disguised polemic against the race doctrine because of its emphasis on historical factors over the invariables. Authors like Bergson, Koffka, W. Stern, Geiger, Kurt Goldstein are mentioned. Of course, Freud is not. We miss him all the more since the only idea that goes beyond the textbook framework, that of the "strata" of the person and his relations, is directly based on Freudian theory of the "systems": unconscious, preconscious and conscious, and on Freud's statements about their typological and dynamic interpretation" [vol. 7:423].

On another page, one reads Günther Stern's bitter remarks on C.G. Jung's American lectures, published in the same year, in which the psychologist expressed himself more cautiously than he did right "after the New Order" in Germany: "It would be unjust to hide Jung's sensitivity to geographic differentiations under the bushel." Elsewhere we find Erich Trier's report from Frankfurt on the newest developments in Protestant theology (Barth, Gogarten, Müller), or the reports of Hugo Marx and Hans Mayer from Zurich about the travesty that Carl Schmitt and his students as well as people like Ernst Anrich, E.R. Huber, Ernst Forsthoff, Otto Koellenreutter, Herbert Krüger, and Karl Larenz were staging at the time in German penal law.

Marcuse's article on "The Struggle against Liberalism in the Totalitarian Concept of the State," published as early as 1934, fits in this context. It marks Marcuse's first break with his teacher Heidegger, whose inaugural address and article in the Freiburg student newspaper of November 10, 1933, was immediately circulated among his exiled students. Marcuse breaks with Heidegger by an artifice. Carl Schmitt's decisionism was considered the solution to the riddle of an abstract existential ontology that turns its back on the context of social life: "Existentialism breaks down at the moment that its political theory is realized." And, ironically, in agreement with Carl Schmitt's statement that on the day of the seizure of power "Hegel had died," Marcuse wrote: "Existentialism had rejected the greatest spiritual heritage of German history. Not with Hegel's death but only now does the titanic fall of classical German philosophy take place" [vol. 3:194].

An End with Two Postscripts

This mood became more pronounced in the following years. It undermined the normative foundations of Critical Theory itself and consequently led to the end of the journal. Martin Jay, in his historical portrayal of the Frankfurt School (*The Dialectic of Imagination*, 1973, p. 168) refers to the financial difficulties that killed the institute's programs. But in reality, the journal folded because its inner clock had wound down.

The decision to direct the journal toward an American readership was on the surface the expression of a desire to engage the institute more intensely in empirical research and integrate it with the scientific mode of investigation existing there. The radio research group around Paul Lazarsfeld represented the point of contact; consequently, one of the issues of the journal was dedicated to problems of mass communication. Horkheimer's "Notes" in the same issue are even more revealing. They display not only a certain helplessness, but more importantly, a half-heartedness in the declared effort to insert the critical contents of theoretical concepts like hidden explosives in techniques of revolt. The attempted salvation came too late: Critical Theory had already lost too much ground and surrendered to a dialectics of enlightenment that eroded reason and faith in reason. Resignation had already set in by 1941.

In the penultimate issue, Horkheimer published his essay "The End of Reason" that already anticipated the *Critique of Instrumental Reason.* All confidence had been lost in the power of philosophical tradition, in the utopian content of bourgeois ideals, that is, in the rational potential of bourgeois culture that would, under the pressure of the already developed productive forces, be unleashed in social movements. The rationalistic core of Critical Theory that had at one time believed it could, by means of an immanent critique of the forms of objective spirit, distinguish "between what man and things can be, and what they in fact are" (vol. 5:27), had been undermined. Marcuse had rightly called this distinction the "central lever of theory." But now all reason seemed to have fled. The productive forces had turned into the destructive forces of the war machinery. And where was the social movement which, having remained a "subject," was to carry theory—"the consciousness of certain groups and individuals engaged in the struggle for a rational organization of society"? What is left, since 1941, is the diagnosis of a process of self-destruction of reason, anticipating all important motifs of the critique of progress that was revived in the 1970s—though of course without the cheekiness of those who today transform the dialectics of enlightment into a simple philosophy of postenlightenment.

Two lines lead from the point where the journal ceased to exist and the classical form of theory fell apart to the late 1960s. Adorno and Marcuse drew opposite conclusions from the "dialectics of enlightenment." While Marcuse relegated reason's historically darkened claim below the threshold of culture by a theory of instincts, Adorno set his by-now empty hope on the solitary exercise of a self-negating philosophy. Löwenthal, who was overshadowed by the two others, represented a third possibility: One can object to the accusatory thesis of the end of reason without having to choose between metaphysics, on the one hand, and one of the fashionable or scientifically promoted forms of the liquidation of reason, on the other. The philosophical exhaustion that cripples the intellectual scene today—and not only in West Germany—is arousing again curiosity about Critical Theory's attempts that was terminated in the early 1940s. Maybe the termination of the undertaking can partly be explained by the fact that even those who have given Marxism the pseudonym of "Critical Theory" still did not proceed in an unorthodox enough manner. Because they understood what Marx had called "productive forces" too traditionally, they soon had to discover that the growth of the forces of cognitive-instrumental rationality do not by themselves guarantee forms of life worthy of man. It might just be possible that the real productive forces, the rational potentials, are more a matter of communication than of relationships of production.

3
The Idea of Critical Theory

Alfred Schmidt

Let us examine some of the Horkheimerian statements of problems that seem to be especially helpful when dealing with contemporary issues of philosophy such as (1) the question with regard to the structure of history, (2) idealism versus materialism, and (3) traditional versus critical theory, the latter being clearly related to the first two.

While we may observe around us the increasingly formalistic and ahistorical nature of the social scientific and philosophical consciousness, it is apparent that Horkheimer's treatises (in the essay collection *Kritische Theorie*, published in 1968) adhere faithfully to the Marx and Engels insight stated in *German Ideology* that "there is only one science, the science of history."[1] Horkheimer then proceeds to develop an economic-materialistic concept of the science of history in opposition to contemporary forms of unhistorical philosophical thought that are not so much scientific as ontological. Heidegger amply demonstrates how this is true in *Being and Time*. While seemingly radicalizing historical consciousness, he subordinates world history to "authentic historicity" as a "state of being of 'process' of existence as such."[2] As a consequence, the integration of individual existence into the historical process is relegated to a position of indifference and externality. "An investigation of the actual historical events," states Horkheimer, "can help to find answers to the single enigma of being just as the analysis of single beings will lead to historical understanding."[3]

Dilthey has the definitive advantage over Heidegger in that he recognizes and examines historical processes together with their supraindividual structures. In spite of his criticism of Dilthey, Horkheimer time and again refers to Dilthey's historical methodological considerations. That Dilthey perceives an essential "spiritual unity"[4] in the structure of each and every epoch makes him an immediate precursor of philosophical anthropology. He is convinced that "in each great cultural period we see universal human essence developing and displaying all of the facets that are innate in each human being."[5] Dilthey holds that history should be investigated through intuitive (*verstehende*) psychology; it is first and foremost a history of the spirit (*Geistesgeschichte*). Horkheimer emphatically rejects this kind of "overtly harmonizing mode of approach."[6] The relatively similar character traits of leading personalities of an epoch who are considered ideal types by the method of the history of ideas should not cause us to ignore the fact that the societal existence of the economically dependent individuals must also be taken into consideration because they presuppose the psychic essence of the ruling ones. Furthermore, not merely the spiritual but the empirical totality of what Marx called the "relations of production" becomes brittle not just because of objective antagonisms but also because every new mode of production drags along surviving remnants of the preceding one. The notion of a uniform image of man that was stubbornly upheld by Scheler following the lead of Dilthey and is still alive today in some forms is an ahistorical concept albeit it attempts to incorporate the process of "becoming and change." Horkheimer states in no uncertain terms that such a positing of the question clearly presupposes a "solid conceptual hierarchy"; it "contradicts the dialectical character of the historical process (*Geschehen*) in which the basic structure of being of both groups and individuals is integrated."[7]

"Structure" and "type," the two Diltheyian categories, are cemented only in a theory of history that exposes those economic dynamics that constitute the basis for the succession of epochs. This is equally true of Dilthey's demand that the study of history should be supplemented with "analytic psychology." (Freud, it should be noted, has in fact developed this concept.) Although (Hegelian) historical materialism insists on the objectivity of the historical process and consequently rejects its reduction to individual psychological motives, it does not overlook the fact that the objectivity encountered by men is mediated through their own actions. It also keeps in mind that the objective economic determination of their actions becomes understandable only through the analysis of "men's own way of reacting to it."[8] While psychology had been the basic science of man in bourgeois theories since the Renaissance, it will now become the "indispensable auxiliary science of history."[9] If we agree that there is no "eternal human nature" as such that can serve as a universal basis for the whole historical process or at least for any of its individual periods, then it stands to reason that "the theory of being relating to man as well as to all the types of philosophical anthropology is bound to change from a (basically) static ontology to a psychology of man living in a specific historical period."[10] Horkheimer replaces any metaphysically oriented notions about man in general, which Marx and Engels had previously sharply criticized in connection with the writings of the leftist

Hegelians and those of Feuerbach in the pre-March (1848) period, with a notion of exact research into what makes up the human essence. Horkheimer writes: "For every and each period, differentiation has to be made between those spiritual motivating forces unfolding in man which underlie all of his achievements as well as of those spiritual factors that enrich societal and life processes, on the one hand, and between the relatively static psychic constitution of individuals, groups, classes, races and nations which are determined by social structures, on the other."[11] Consequently, Horkheimer understands a comprehensive "science of history" to be neither a history based on the critical use of sources and archival material, that is, a purely descriptive history in the conventional sense (although he is willing to take into consideration its methods and findings), nor a philosophy of history to be understood as a priori constructs—Hegel had already said that it was not to be understood as such. Rather, it is to be understood as critical historical scholarship and a "materialistic anthropology" and is thus diametrically opposed to the endeavors of a Dilthey, Scheler, and others. Since its point of departure is the unity of bourgeois society mediated through commodity production, it can successfully bring home the meaning of the past, relating it to the daily struggles of the present while maintaining detachment, and it can also comprehend the uniqueness of the past. History is perceived by Horkheimer as having a dual meaning: it represents both an ongoing confrontation with the past and the remembrance of injustices past that may never be remedied. Good examples of this Horkheimerian approach to history are the essays "Egoism and Freedom Movement" and "Montaigne and the Function of Skepsis." Contrary to the tendency often encountered in philosophical literature, Horkheimer's essays present an analysis of the total social-psychic makeup of individuals, groups, strata, and classes, as well as an analysis of their conscious and unconscious behavioral patterns against the background of their dependency on societal reality. The fact that the method applied here is more of the *erklärende* than the *verstehende* one does not so much result from the author's lack of insight into the qualitative character of social processes as apart from the natural processes but rather from his conviction that although until now history has been made by men, it "has not as yet been made with a collective will according to a collective plan,"[12] meaning that history assumed the character of a blind natural process that has become estranged from its maker.

The difference between idealism and materialism has seldom been adequately treated in academic philosophy; their specific meanings remain unclear. One of the aspects of the Horkheimerian essays which accounts for their actuality is the attempt to illuminate this divergence without ignoring the epistemological reservations of idealism with regard to materialism, and not accepting materialism as a *Weltanschauung*. Furthermore—and this is an important distinction—the essays discuss in general the extremely complex relationship between the historical concept of materialism and philosophical materialism.

By critically delineating his theory from the Diltheyian doctrines of *Weltanschauung* and from some representatives of ontology in which materialism is seen to offer a perennial possibility for the human mind (*Geist*) to interpret the whole world in a metaphysical manner, Horkheimer arrives at an approach that incorporates history into the essence of the theoretical construct. He demonstrates that as far as the range and content of its propositions and their focus is concerned, materialism is subject to change according to the state of human affairs and the ensuing conflicts. In the seventeenth and eighteenth centuries, for example, materialism reduced reality to mathematically defined matter and its mechanical movements to serve the interests of the ascending bourgeoisie; present-day materialism has "economic theory of society" as its main content. Materialism is much less characterized by those "formal traits which oppose it to idealistic metaphysics."[13] The mistaken belief that materialism was primarily an answer to metaphysical questions must be attributed to the philosophical representatives of materialism who started with metaphysical questions and then set up "their own thesis in opposition to idealist positions."[14] This practice prompted academic philosophers to dismiss materialism as epistemologically primitive and to reject as dogmatic materialism's thesis that matter and motion are the only realities. In addition, the thesis itself, which admittedly is inadequate, receives an ethical twist, that is, it is taken as "the basis for certain practical consequences, and, in fact, for a consistent way of life, just as the idealist metaphysics is taken as the intelligible basis for idealist ways of acting."[15] Horkheimer makes the valid points that such a unity of action cannot be proven by materialism. Whenever materialist philosophers make an attempt at a "system" they fail to realize that "the content of materialist theory itself makes any such unified structure impossible. . . . The principle that is defined as reality by the materialist doctrine is not fit to furnish a norm. . . . Matter in inself is meaningless; its qualities cannot provide maxims for the shaping of life."[16]

What Horkheimer wants to emphasize is that materialistic dialectic does not aim at ascertaining the ultimate substratum of reality. It transcends (*aufhebt*) the philosophical opposition between *Geist* and nature as well as between matter and consciousness into what is called sensual-objective (*sinnlich-gegenständlich*) praxis by the "new materialism" of the *Feuerbach-Theses* (of Marx). In Marx's opinion, the opposition to idealism is an opposition to philosophy per se in the sense that materialism so far has been of contemplative nature and considered "knowledge as the only objective means of proceeding [*Verhalten*]."[17] The question of materialistic dialectics are not unimportant against the belief of present-day logical empiricists; they only acquire a less emphatic meaning in the context of comprehended history. The "priority of nature"[18] to man and his consciousness has been understood by materialists of natural science orientation as having an absolute validity, but it reveals itself to be a moment of changing value in its relation to the state of the forces of production. "Nature too,"[19] stated Marx, "taken abstractly, for itself—nature fixed in isolation from man—is *nothing* for man." The achievements of the individual sciences which serve as a basis for the doctrines of physical and physiological materialism must not be evaluated in absolute terms. They must be seen against a sociohistorical background or they will turn into rigid and unreasonable dogmas. Once "it is recognized that the key to the understanding of the whole history of society lies in the history of the development of labor,"[20] as Engels suggested, then it will become impossible to proceed from the assumption that there is "a logically pre-ordained insight" to it.[21] What Horkheimer has in mind is nothing other than Hegel's mistaken attempt to describe historical dialectic as a kind of applied case for the logic of the absolute spirit. To be sure, Horkheimer's critique applies also to dogmas of present-day Soviet ideology, which has general dialectical laws that govern the development of the physical universe, meaning that there are immutable laws that are not integrated into the dialectical process. Nature, stripped to its bare bones and thus separated from any "negative" mediating activity of man, is then structured dialectically. It is solidified to a *Seinsgrund* of the historical movement of society that will thus become a secondary phenomenon only; we find a similar concept in Heidegger's work. Not quite unlike Hegelianism, the Russian (*sic*) ideology views "everything that surrounds us . . . as an example of the dialectical."[22] Codified to a doctrine of ontological categories, on the one hand, and to an empty methodology, on the other, dialectics comes to represent *par excellence* what the Eastern countries mean by the problematic label "Marxist philosophy." Horkheimer in his essays makes no concession to any such view. He is indirectly critical of any attempt to superimpose a normative structure on human-societal reality, for it may be an (allegedly) materialistic one. According to Marx, who was always more cautious in dealing with problems concerning nature than was the later Engels, who adhered more faithfully to the Hegelian view, no investigation should make matter and its motion its point of departure; what alone matters is what during the course of history man in the production process may accomplish with them. "The correct theory," states Horkheimer referring again to *German Ideology*, "can only be the result of observing men living under specific conditions and maintaining their existence with the help of specific instruments of production."[23] If we assume that man's history has neither a uniform goal nor a specific universal spiritual meaning, then dialectic is not to be reified materialistically; history is bound to man and disappears with him. Should dialectic be declared the supreme law governing the world, it will inevitably become a means to the end of a state religion. The interconnection between Marxism and metaphysical materialism is not to be found where the Soviet ideology would like it to be. Soviet ideology follows in the footsteps of that problematic materialism that tends to speak in universal terms and to transfix nature in its pantheistic glory. There is another aspect of materialism which Horkheimer likes to refer to because its presence is latent in the critique of political economy: It is the insistence on the sensual happiness of the individual and the moment of humility and sadness in face of the radical finitude of man and his efforts. This aspect is not emphasized so much by academic experts of ideology.

It was self-evident to Horkheimer from the very beginning that the Marxian doctrine just like any other theory is "subject to epistemological scrutiny."[24] Keeping this in mind, one finds his articles strikingly appropriate for contemporary discussions. Post-Stalinist writers from Poland, Czechoslovakia, or Yugoslavia have been developing lately some of the ideas that Horkheimer advanced as early as the 1930s. For example, some Horkheimer essays discuss the object-constituting role of human praxis that now concerns these late-comers. The essays also call attention to the importance of *Lebenswelt* in *The Crisis of European Sciences and Transcendental Phenomenology* (1936), a book by Husserl, whom Horkheimer calls "the last real epistemologist." Horkheimer also anticipated certain problems relating to the logic of science that were later raised by the Althusser School in Paris in its "structuralist" interpretation of Marx's *Kapital*. Clearly, Horkheimer's assessments are more acceptable than those of the French interpreters who give the historical character of Marx's work short shrift.

The question then arises: What precisely is the theoretical position of Critical Theory with regard to epistemology and science? Horkheimer's answers are to be found in a series of essays of which three should be singled out here: The essay on the "Problem of Truth" (1935); the programmatic article ("Traditional and Critical Theory" [Ed.]); and the one on logical empiricism, both from 1937. In comparing and contrasting Critical Theory with "Traditional Theory," Horkheimer's theoretical position can be traced back to Descartes's *Discours de la méthode*. The

Cartesian deductive method of the seventeenth century became absolutely binding for the modern notion of scientific exactitude. Descartes already had wanted to apply the deductive method of mathematics to the whole of science; he advocated a unity of science which, in due course, became the key idea of positivism: "The division of sciences is sublated (*aufgehoben*) by deriving the principles for special areas from the same basic premises."[25]

It matters little in consequence whether one interprets these premises—these universal propositions—as evidential insights, conventional stipulations, or as judgments based on experience. With regard to the genesis of the modern notion of perfected theory construction, Horkheimer points out that the philosophical difference between empiricism and rationalism turned out to be relatively unimportant. What is alone decisive is that the propositions related to a substantive field are "linked together in such a way that a few are basic and the rest are derivatives. The smaller the number of primary principles in comparison with the derivations, the more perfect the theory."[26] Therefore, "the basic requirement which any theoretical system must satisfy is that all the parts should be interlocked thoroughly and without friction." The usefulness of this conception of theory which is ultimately based on a "purely mathematical system of symbols" is solely operational.[27] Propositions are valid only to the extent that they present actual processes. If systematically interconnected, they merely contain "stored-up knowledge" in the form "of the closest possible description of facts."[28]

For the time being, this Horkheimerian conception permits a self-understanding of modern science as sketched above. It takes fully into consideration the extent to which it has contributed to the progress of technological domination of nature, thereby becoming itself, to use Marx's expression, an "immediate force of production."[29] At this point, Horkheimer criticizes a certain type of pragmatic rationality that empirical researchers feel at home with and which gets confused with the scientific process per se. What scientists pretend to be an immutable essence of theory in principle is in reality nothing but the expression of a work situation that is socially predetermined. Talking about theory, they remain unaware of the fact that what they describe is not an unchangeable idea at all but a product of abstraction that has its origins in "scientific activity" as "carried out within the division of labor at a particular stage in the latter's development."[30] Because the activity of the scholar takes place alongside the activities of numerous other groups of professionals, the societal interconnection of all the various sectors of production remains opaque. Thus the ideological illusion of the "self-sufficiency of work processes whose course is supposedly determined by the very nature of its object"[31] in reality is inevitably a historically mediated element of the reproduction of life. Scientific thought remains satisfied with classifying experience in the light of questions which arise out of everyday social life. What they may mean beyond their abstract immediacy for the societal whole cannot be discussed within the categories of traditional theory: "The social genesis of problems, the real situations in which science is put to use and the purposes which it is made to serve, are all regarded by science as external to itself."[32] We are thus faced with the paradoxical situation that the reason conventional science rejects a non–praxis-oriented thinking is more abstract and removed from reality that is mediated by the totality of the praxis of an epoch than is Critical Theory, which does not intend to imply that a pragmatic epistemology is correct from the societal relevance of science but rather prefers autonomous reflection that does not regard proof and the truth of an idea as identical.

Critical Theory goes beyond the subjectivism and relativism of positivism (in which the interpretation of science must not be thought to be identical with its content) to the extent that it has "for its object men as producers of their own historical way of life in its totality."[33] It aims to reveal the *cognitive* content of historical praxis, to perceive it as something that will in reality—and not merely theoretically—be able to transcend (*aufheben*) the positivistic "dualism of thought and being, understanding and perception."[34] In his detailed analyses, Horkheimer develops the idea that the concrete world, which in itself has to become the object of scholarly scrutiny and which is passively received by the precritical individual consciousness, is also "a product of the activity of society as a whole." Facts of sensual perception which positivists consider to be irreducibly given "are socially performed in two ways: through the historical character of the object perceived and through the historical character of the perceiving organ."[35]

Some important consequences result from this materialistically colored *Konstitutionslehre*: First, an undogmatic evaluation of the social role of the sciences, and second, a dialectical theory of the process of cognition. What so far has been considered to be an intrascientific process, namely, the relationship of matter (that is already structured) and theory (that unifies), the verification of propositions, the bringing of hypotheses to bear on facts, has now been defined as a sociohistorical process. To the extent that science has to orient itself to the peculiarity of its objects, its concepts are inevitably affected by subjective factors and interests; there are no "theory-free" facts. Subject and object cannot be separated from each other nor can there be a perfect congruence of knowledge and object (of knowledge). Both poles of cognition change continuously in relation to each other within the historical process: "The theoretical activity of men . . . is . . . a product of ever-changing reality. . . . The subject-object relation is not accurately pictured as two fixed realities that are conceptually fully transparent and move towards each other. Rather, in what we call objective, subjective factors are at work. . . . We must grasp the interplay of both aspects, the human and the extra-human, the individual and the classifiable, the methodological and the substantive, and not separate any of these, as realities, from the others."[36]

The above statements should have made clear that Critical Theory has nothing to do with the naive copy theory or reflection theory conception of cognition that has been put forth again and again ever since antiquity in the history of materialism. It even influenced the terminology of Marx and Engels and of their disciples; although their thought, which is grounded in German idealism, was aimed precisely at eliminating the rigid separation of subject and object, knowledge and being—a separation so characteristic of copy realism. Even though Horkheimer speaks of the "mirroring of the dynamic structure of history,"[37] of "reflection of the concrete whole in thought,"[38] we have to keep in mind that these metaphorically used terms which often lead to misunderstandings say nothing about the *art* (way) of the knowing subject to assimilate the world in a sensual, rational, and first of all, in a historical-practical sense. But the terms prevent Critical Theory from falling prey to the Hegelian illusion that reality is an absolute concept since it is conceptually mediated because the difference between the conceptual and the nonconceptual itself is part of the thought process. By contrast, scientific materialism has not abandoned the idea of mediation as was shown earlier; it made mediation finite thereby causing concept and object to remain in an "irreducible tension."[39]

More important for the characterization of the relationship between theory and reality are such terms used by Horkheimer as model (*Entwurf*) and construction, and especially, the term first used by Marx, "dialectical presentation" (*dialektische Darstellung*). These terms indicate that theory is neither simply a poor imitation of existing conditions (in which case it would be ideology) nor a passive description of facts (in which case it would be obtuse empiricism) on the one hand, and that it is an expression of the relationship between the analytical social sciences and dialectical theory of society on the other. The latter topic is hotly debated in present-day German sociology's "dispute of method." Be that as it may, dialectical concept has to deal with material already prepared by the empirical intellect which cannot be ignored and has to be incorporated into its (own) movement in spite of the material's initial opposition to it. Hegel himself distinguishes between the "process of the origination of science" and "its process 'in itself.'"[40] Following in his footsteps, Marx keeps apart "analysis" and "presentation," that although they must be kept separate, must also be related to each other: "But analysis is the necessary prerequisite of generical presentation, and of the understanding of the real, formative process in its different phases."[41]

Horkheimer's essays are credited with the fact that already in the 1930s they raised these issues, so important to the correct understanding of the critique of political economy. Regardless of how much Horkheimer appreciated the renunciaton of reification contained in the irrational *Lebensmetaphysik*, he does not overlook the regressive moments of those doctrines which deify isolated concepts such as "intuition," because in their understanding the limits of intellect (as demonstrated by Hegel) have been solidified into limits of articulated thought. "Unlike irrationalism, materialism attempts to transcend the one-sidedness of analytical thought without dismissing it completely."[42] Horkheimer's aim is to use it correctly, thus applying to analytical thought a more positive evaluation than Hegel's. One has to remember that it was Marx, the dialectician, who was strongly inclined "to calculate the principal laws of economic crises mathematically."[43] Yet he did not make mathematics an absolute. No matter how exact and indispensable the methods and results of the research processes of individual sciences, they constitute only the material not the content of theory.

As Horkheimer states: "The individual sciences provide only the elements for the theoretical construction of the historical process, and do not remain the same in the presentation as they were in the individual sciences. Rather, they attain new functions of meaning which they did not possess before."[44] Traditional theory is thus sublated in Critical Theory; dialectical logic has nothing to do any more with an atemporal realm of spiritual essences but becomes "scientific" in a sense that goes beyond Hegel. Horkheimer characterizes these essences as "the embodiment of all intellectual means by which it becomes possible to make fruitful those abstract moments which were separated from the intellect for the sake of depicting living objects."[45]

The concept of Critical Theory, however, would be insufficiently defined if we limited the discussion to its relationship to analytical research methods. Objective reality enters thought not only in this, through the individual sciences, filtered form. Theory, above all, represents the sum total of insights originating "in a certain praxis and in certain sets of objectives."[46] As far as materialism is concerned, there can be no unequivocally and irrevocably fixed character to the process of historical dialectic; its construction itself is a temporary phenomenon which has been "designed by men in the course of their confrontation with their societal and natural environment."[47] If anything, it is its unswerving reflection upon its own conditional state that characterizes Critical Theory. It does not pretend to be a perfect reflection of the *ordo sempiternus rerum* and readily admits that real human beings and their interest in more reasonable conditions determine its nature.

This interest is not added to the process of cognition as an external element but is effective already at its initial stages along with other moments. The dialectical theoretician considers even the most elementary facts of everyday perception not just as mere facts but rather as something that shall one day be controlled by men united by a common goal. As long as society remains bound to natural history only and fails to constitute itself as "the real subject [of history],"[48] men will not be free in spite of their triumphal domination of nature. Critical Theory does not despise progress (which would amount to bad romanticizing); however, it does not aim at the mere quantitative extension of the domination of nature but at taking hold of the reigns of that domination and thus contributing to the breakup of the primacy of the economy. It is not the creed of Critical Theory that societal being determines consciousness; it is the diagnosis of a condition to be transcended. The prehistory of mankind makes individuals into "personifications of economic catego- ries."[49] Only when individuals succeed in determining their life process in a common effort will blind fate turn into freedom and historical materialism cease to be the correct explanation of human affairs. This is the idea preserving the heritage of the great speculative philosophy of German idealism to which Horkheimer's essays are indebted. They intend to serve the overriding interests of a century that is about to abandon them.

Notes

1. In Marx-Engels, *Werke*, vol. 3 (Berlin: Dietz, 1962), p. 18.
2. Martin Heidegger, *Sein und Zeit* (Tübingen: M. Niemeyer, 1960), p. 20.
3. Max Horkheimer, "Geschichte und Psychologie," in *Kritische Theorie*, vol. 1 (Frankfurt: Fischer Verlag, 1972), p. 11.
4. Cf. Wilhelm Dilthey, *Gesammelte Schriften*, vol. 7 (Leipzig: B.G. Teubner, 1927), pp. 185ff.
5. Horkheimer, "Geschichte und Psychologie," p. 28.
6. Max Horkheimer, "Bemerkungen zur philosophischen Anthropologie," in *Kritische Theorie*, vol. 1, p. 200.
7. Ibid., p. 202.
8. Horkheimer, "Geschichte und Psychologie," p. 19.
9. Ibid., p. 18.
10. Ibid., p. 11.
11. Ibid., p. 18.

12. Engels to H. Starkenburg, letter of January 25, 1894, in Marx-Engels, *Aus-gewählte Briefe* (Berlin: Dietz, 1953), p. 561.
13. Max Horkheimer, "Materialismus und Metaphysik," in *Kritische Theorie*, vol. 1, p. 66.
14. Ibid., p. 34.
15. Ibid., p. 38.
16. Ibid., pp. 38, 40.
17. Marx, "Ökonomisch-philosophische Manuskripte," in Marx-Engels, *Werke*, suppl. vol., part 1 (Berlin: Dietz, 1968), p. 580.
18. Marx-Engels, "Die deutsche Ideologie," in ibid., p. 44.
19. Marx, "Ökonomisch-philosophische Manuskripte," p. 587. Translated passage cited in Karl Marx-Frederick Engels, *Collected Works*, vol. 3 (New York: International Publishers, 1975), p. 345.
20. "Ludwig Feuerbach und der Ausgang der klassischen deutschen Philosophie," in Marx-Engels, *Ausgewählte Schriften*, vol. 2 (Berlin: Dietz, 1966), p. 369.
21. Horkheimer, "Geschichte und Psychologie," p. 15.
22. G.W.F. Hegel, "System der Philosophie," part 1, section 81, appendix 1, in *Sämtliche Werke*, vol. 8 (Stuttgart: F. Frommann, 1927–40).
23. Horkheimer, "Geschichte und Psychologie," p. 15.
24. Ibid., p. 17.
25. Max Horkheimer, "Traditionelle und kritische Theorie," in *Kritische Theorie*, vol. 2, pp. 137ff.
26. Ibid.
27. Ibid., p. 139.
28. Ibid., p. 137.
29. Karl Marx, *Grundrisse der Kritik der politischen Ökonomie* (Berlin: Dietz, 1953), p. 594.
30. Horkheimer, "Traditionelle und kritische Theorie," p. 146.
31. Ibid.
32. Horkheimer, supplement to "Traditionelle und kritische Theorie," p. 192.
33. Ibid.
34. Horkheimer, "Traditionelle und kritische Theorie," p. 146.
35. Ibid., p. 149.
36. Horkheimer, "Materialismus und Metaphysik," pp. 49–50.
37. Horkheimer, "Geschichte und Psychologie," p. 15.
38. Max Horkheimer, "Zur Rationalismusstreit in der gegenwärtigen Philosophie," in *Kritische Theorie*, p. 140.
39. Horkheimer, "Materialismus und Metaphysik," p. 48.
40. G.W.F. Hegel, "Vorlesungen über die Geschichte der Philosophie," in *Sämtliche Werke*, vol. 19 (Stuttgart: F. Frommann, 1927–40), p. 284.
41. Karl Marx, *Theorien über Mehrwert*, part 3 (Berlin: Dietz, 1962), p. 497.
42. Horkheimer, "Zum Rationalismusstreit," p. 150.
43. Letter to Engels of May 3, 1873, in Marx-Engels, *Werke*, vol. 33 (Berlin: Dietz, 1966), p. 82.
44. Horkheimer, "Zum Rationalismusstreit," p. 141.
45. Ibid., p. 139.
46. Max Horkheimer, "Materialismus und Moral," in *Kritische Theorie*, p. 109.
47. Horkheimer, "Zum Rationalismusstreit," p. 146.
48. Horkheimer, "Materialismus und Moral," p. 78.
49. Karl Marx, *Das Kapital*, vol. 1 (Berlin: Dietz, 1955), p. 8.

4
The Dialectical Imagination
by Martin Jay

Heinz Lubasz

There is a fundamental ambivalence toward radicalism in the position of a certain type of middle-class left intellectual which at once reflects his social situation and points to a central problem in Marxism. He expresses a reasoned hostility to the "bourgeois society" within which he nevertheless actively enjoys a secure if moderate income, a civilized lifestyle, and a chance to be creative. He is in principle committed to the cause of a "proletariat" with which he nevertheless has no contact, about which he knows nothing at first hand, and which, as "the masses," he privately despises. Alert as he is to the unfreedom, injustice, and suffering in the world, he reconciles himself to his comfortable situation by setting his own existence in the context of a world-historical movement designed (so he imagines) to produce a world full of people like himself: cultured, sensitive, creative, and above all unvulgar (for he disdains the vulgar rich as much as he despises the vulgar poor). His own purely theoretical praxis he sees as somehow advancing that movement, but he scarcely concerns himself with the hard question—so central to Marxism— of the relation between theory and social and political practice. Criticism becomes an end in itself. The revolutionary transformation of society remains a distant prospect for him, in part because he fears the violence and oppression with which it may be attended. If, therefore, some of his disciples conclude that his radical critique of bourgeois society must be applied in radical practice, he is as likely as any solid citizen to respond to their practical initiative by calling the police.

It is this fundamental ambivalence which the Frankfurt School embodies and its so-called Critical Theory systematizes. The basic Marxian concepts which Critical Theory still vaguely echoes have all been neutralized, gaining in generality what they lose in radical bite. "Capitalist exploitation" turns into "domination by the system," be that system capitalist or socialist. The "exploited proletariat" becomes the "totally integrated underlying population." In place of analysis of capitalist production and distribution we are given references to "the totality of social praxis." And the idea of a classless society is replaced by the notion of a "rational" society (or, even more vaguely, of "an altogether different Something" ["ein ganz Anderes"], as Max Horkheimer, the "dean" of the school, calls it in his foreword to *The Dialectical Imagination*). It may well be the case—I cannot argue the point here—that it has become essential to go beyond Marx, to revise the fundamental concepts of Marxian theory, and to extend its critical range. Indeed, the strongest argument that can be made in favor of Critical Theory—and Martin Jay makes it—is that this is precisely what it has attempted to do. Yet I very much doubt whether anything so vacuous as the notion of a rational society—the meaning of "rational" remaining unspecified— can usefully serve as a critical tool or advance by a single step the quest for a better world. Indeed, since Horkheimer held (by 1945 if not earlier) that theory could *not* guide political practice, and T.W. Adorno, the school's "subdean" opted explicitly for a purely *theoretical* practice, it is fair to conclude that the notion of a rational society was not intended to serve any practical purpose but simply fulfilled the function of providing a conceptual focus for the intellectual systematization of an ambivalent stance. One is tempted to paraphrase Sorel and to speak of Critical Theory as the expression of a determination *not* to act. (One resists the temptation only in view of the attitude of Herbert Marcuse, the third coformulator of Critical Theory though never strictly a member of the Frankfurt School, whose position regarding the relation of theory to practice was, as we shall see below, substantially different from that of Horkheimer and Adorno.)

The systematic ambivalence of the Frankfurt School, indeed its virtual abandonment of the radical impulse, is one of several possible responses to what Jay calls "the dilemma of the left intellectual in our century." Jay errs gravely, I believe, in supposing that the Frankfurt School can be seen as presenting that dilemma "in quintessential form" (p. xv). He can see it that way because he conceives the dilemma precisely as Horkheimer and Adorno themselves conceived it: as the unpalatable choice between succumbing to the intolerable bourgeois system and embracing its equally intolerable "ostensible opponents." Had Jay been less swayed by Horkheimer's perspective, not only on this point but throughout his book, he would have recognized that the dilemma of the leftist intellectual in our century lies deeper and is more complex than that. Had Jay written the history of the Institute of Social Research, he would have seen that there were various ways of reacting to that dilemma, ways which were not only discernible in that history but actually shaped it. There *is* an interesting story to be told about the transformation of a Marxist institute concerned with empirical and theoretical research focused on the working class into a center focused on critical sociophilo-sophical theory. But Jay, for all the splendid work he has done, has not told it.

The history of the Frankfurt venture falls into three phases which differ decisively from one another regarding not only geographical setting but sociopolitical context and the thrust of the intellectual work under-taken. Every one of them, including the very initiation of the venture, was a complex of responses to felt crisis, to Jay's "dilemma." The first phase began in 1923 with the founding, in Frankfurt, of an Institute of Social Research, Marxist in outlook, oriented toward empirical and theoretical work bearing on the cause of the working class and of socialism, concerned with the reconstruction of a Marxism which had recently sustained defeat in Germany and appeared to many to be in process of being perverted in Russia. It ended amid the crisis years in which the Weimar Republic collapsed, the Nazis came to power, and all the forces of the Left—trade unions, political parties, individuals, and organizations like the institute—had a final reckoning to make. With a new director at the helm—Max Horkheimer succeeded Carl Grünberg in 1930—the institute's assets were transferred to Holland well before all seemed lost, in 1931. Subsequently the institute's members and members-to-be grad-ually scattered abroad. The second phase of its history began in 1934 with the reconstituting of the institute in New York and a substantial shift in its orientation, in response to what Horkheimer called "the defeat of the German working class." So long as it enjoyed institutional affiliation with Columbia University—which it did until 1941—the institute main-tained a considerable degree of organizational unity and continuity. But after 1941 this unity and continuity began to dissolve for a variety of reasons, and the institute came more and more to center in the person of Horkheimer himself, together with his friend and closest collaborator Adorno, who had joined the institute in 1938. By 1950, when this second, American phase came to a close, the institute had become a very loosely structured entity. It was at this stage that Horkheimer and Adorno, and they only, decided to return to Frankfurt and reestablish the institute once more, with new personnel, new concerns, and a substantially new program. Critical Theory, which had throughout the American phase taken second place to a variety of research projects, now became the dominant force in the institute's life. Critical Theory came into its own, so to speak, only in this third phase; it was now, in the fifties, that the Frankfurt School proper was born.

It is impossible to grasp the dimensions of this whole history if one does not see it in its successive settings. The original institute lived amid the turmoil of the Weimar Republic as one leftist organization among many. It could be perfectly open about its Marxism so long as anyone in Germany could. Its members could—and many of its current and future members did—take an active and committed part in the social and political struggles of the country. The bearing of theory on practice was therefore nothing if not a live issue. In its American exile the situation of the institute was strikingly different. Its members continued to focus their attention on a Germany which was not and could not be a field of action for them, and no longer had any ongoing leftist organizations or movements that might put theory into practice. About their new country they knew little and cared less—until the United States entered the war against Germany. (It is characteristic of their self-isolation that the institute's journal continued to be published in German, even in New York.) In the circumstances, the relation of theory to practice became a nonissue. What now mattered to Horkheimer and Marcuse was that theory should be preserved—presumably against the day when practice might again be possible. (In the event, Marcuse did return to the problem in due course; Horkheimer never did.) What mattered to the institute as a whole was to come to grips with the phenomenon of Nazism and with related manifestations: working-class attitudes to authority, fascism in general, the problem of authority in the family, the "authoritarian personality." It was the empirical work carried out by social scientists such as Franz Neumann, A.R.L. Gurland, Henryk Grossmann, and Otto Kirchheimer which alone found a public in the United States and created links between the institute and American social scientists. Critical Theory, published in German, remained a closed book.

The flourishing of Critical Theory in the third phase of the institute's history has to be understood in the light of the overwhelmingly con-servative mood of postwar West Germany. In that context even the faint echoes of Marx that could be discerned in Critical Theory were an exciting revelation to many a student: "Critical Theory" became a kind of code for "Marxist Theory," and the Frankfurt School—as it now came to be called—a haven for students who wanted something other than the established ideologies. That the Frankfurt School should have played an important role in the formation of the new, predominantly student Left in Germany is to be explained, however, in terms of the kind of historical error that can itself be productive: The unradical Horkheimer and Adorno were identified by many of their students with the rather more Marxist bent of the *original* Frankfurt Institute for Social Research, with their more radical former colleague Herbert Marcuse (then at Brandeis University), and even with their own seemingly more radical past. Whatever the political predilections of its staff, the new institute was seen as a direct link with the whole history of the Left in Germany, a bridge across the gap Nazism created. All this and more has to be grasped if one is to understand the symbolic significance of the "great confrontation" of 1968. Radical students, supposing that they were putting Critical Theory into practice, occupied the institute in support of their demand for radical reforms, only to be confronted with their mentor Adorno and the police whom Adorno promptly summoned—an incident which symbolizes the total divorce of theory from practice which Horkheimer and Adorno had in fact long since carried through in their writings. After that debacle the Frankfurt School ceased to form a focus for radical theorizing in Germany; and with the death, first of Adorno in August 1969 and then of Horkheimer in July 1973, it ceased to exist.

Martin Jay has performed a valuable service in making a substantial part of the Frankfurt story accessible for the first time. Out of interviews with surviving members of the institute (most of whom have since died), selections from their private correspondence, and a careful combing of their published and unpublished writings, he has skillfully constructed an eminently readable and intellectually sensitive collective portrait of the institute in the years of its American exile, 1934 to 1950. The claim that *The Dialectical Imagination* is a history of the Frankfurt School and of the Institute for Social Research from 1923 to 1950 is, however, ill-founded. The introductory chapter deals with the first phase of the institute's history so briefly and superficially as to amount to no more than a background sketch which sets the scene for the second phase. The history of the original institute remains to be written. So does the history of the Frankfurt School, which came into existence only after 1950. All we get here is its prehistory. Besides, the author quite unnecessarily confuses both himself and the reader by treating "Frankfurt School" and "institute" as coterminous, which they decidedly are not, even in the period with which the book deals.

What we do get is a description of the genesis of Critical Theory out of a variable mixture of Kant, Hegel, Marx, Schopenhauer, and Nietzsche, and an account of some of its main tenets. Then, in successive chapters, Jay portrays the institute's first efforts at making psychoanalysis fruitful for sociological inquiry (an enterprise in which Erich Fromm played an important part); its studies—largely theoretical—on authority and the family; its several analyses of Nazism, with particular attention to Franz Neumann's now classic *Behemoth*; its aesthetic theory and its critique of mass culture, where Walter Benjamin's influence made itself strongly felt, though he never actually joined the institute; and the studies of prejudice and of the so-called authoritarian personality conducted by members of the institute in conjunction with various outsiders in the 1940s. All this is interspersed with interesting information about the people involved, their fortunes, attitudes, and opinions. What is particularly helpful is that Jay frequently orients the reader by means of references to related intellectual currents. These chapters, which constitute the main body of the work, are framed by the opening chapter, which provides essential background information, and by a closing chapter on Adorno and Horkheimer's joint work, *Dialectic of the Enlightenment* (1947), which traces the transition from the second to the third phase in the institute's history and points the reader in the direction of the Frankfurt School without actually taking him there. Because so much of the book consists of careful and probing accounts of the institute's work, it will be particularly welcome to readers who are unacquainted with that work, to those who have so far known of Critical Theory only what they have gleaned from the writings of Marcuse, and to people who are already familiar with the work of, say, Benjamin, Neumann, or Fromm but know little or nothing about these writers' links with the institute. But the principal value of the work lies in the fact that it records a great deal of scattered and hitherto inaccessible information. As Horkheimer said in the letter to Jay which forms the foreword: "Much will be preserved which would be forgotten without your description." Truly it is very good description: clear, sane, conscientious, informed. It is in fact very good intellectual chronicle. What it is not is history.

The Dialectical Imagination falls short of being a work of history inasmuch as it fails to exhibit—and a fortiori to analyze—those connections among the phenomena it deals with which alone constitute the dynamics of the development it recounts. It exhibits neither the dynamics of the historical evolution of the world with which the institute was concerned nor the dynamics of the intellectual venture in which it was engaged. Nor, therefore, does it trace the links between the former and the latter, between the dramatically changing social and political conditions and the almost equally dramatic shifts in the thinking of the various members of the institute, and in the general orientation of the institute as a whole. Hence the reader cannot grasp the dynamics of the transformation from Marxist institute to non-Marxist school. Since he cannot grasp the dynamics of that transformation, he cannot either understand in what ways the story is supposed to present "in quintessential form the dilemma of the left intellectual in our century." As it is not a work of history, *The Dialectical Imagination*, for all its merits, sheds no historical light on that dilemma at all.

To grasp the dynamics of the institute's evolution between 1923 and 1950 and so to elucidate the dilemma of the left-wing intellectual it is essential to have a clear picture of the institute's situation in the Weimar period, especially during the critical years 1928 to 1933; to be able to trace the links between the various ways its members experienced the dilemma and the ways in which their thought and work developed; and, finally, to place the range of their responses within the overall structure of that dilemma. Jay's book is a grave disappointment in all three respects, though the information it presents is extremely useful to anyone who is already familiar with the period and with the work of the institute.

It seems extravagantly irresponsible of the would-be historian of the Frankfurt Institute for Social Research to condense into fewer than twenty pages (in a book of almost four hundred) his account of the very period in which, so far as the institute was concerned, that dilemma was most acute, the closing years of the Weimar Republic. A Germany torn by social conflict, experiencing the rise of Nazism and—indirectly—the emergence of Stalinism, with a working class cured of the hope of revolution and split among rival socialist, national socialist, and communist parties, driven by turns to despondency and violence by depression and mass unemployment—that, surely, is the very context in which we need to see the institute at work, wrestling with problems of theory, research, and practice in a situation in which the established conventions of Marxism are challenged and shaken to their foundations. *That* is the context within which we may hope to grasp how they experienced and how they variously responded to the great dilemma—*not* the United States of the 1930s, whose language they had not yet mastered, whose problems they neither understood nor cared about, from whose whole life they isolated themselves. (Horkheimer, who appears to have thought the German language the preeminent vehicle for the expression of truth, actually disapproved of those of his colleagues who were trying to master the English language, on the grounds that they were neglecting concern with truth in favor of improving their chances in the struggle for existence!) The history of the institute in the Weimar Republic is one crucial section of history we do not get; and for lack of it we cannot grasp the sense of the later evolution either.

Nor do we get even a glimpse of the variety of positions taken by members of the institute to the events of those years. All we get is a brief statement of how Horkheimer himself and an unspecified number of his closest friends saw the situation:

> After the failure of the German revolution [of 1918–19], [the institute's] members, at least those around Horkheimer, were alienated from all political factions. The SPD was treated with the scorn its craven capitulation before the status quo deserved—in fact, we might argue that the SPD's betrayal of the working class colored the Frankfurt School's subsequent distrust of all "moderate" solutions [p. 36].

Jay does not seem even to have asked himself whether the SPD was really guilty of "craven capitulation before the status quo" or whether all members of the institute treated it with "scorn." For, if he had, he must surely have wondered how to account for the fact that Franz Neumann, to take but one example, continued to be an active member of the SPD until the Nazis suppressed it, and worked until the very end as a lawyer for socialist trade unions. Had Jay pursued the matter he would have discovered that, long before the Nazis came to power, Horkheimer had repeatedly refused to lift a finger to help prevent an outcome which instead he calmly pronounced to be inevitable—itself an interesting comment on Horkheimer's conception of the relation of theory to practice. Had Jay then tried, as a historian is bound to try, to connect Horkheimer's and Neumann's practical dispositions and evaluations with their respective intellectual endeavors in the thirties and forties, he would have been able to shed some light not only on the difference between these two men (differences he faithfully records but does not elucidate) but on the distance, the coolness, even the intellectual hostility between what one might call the "tough-minded" and still committed empirical work of Neumann, Kirchheimer, Grossmann et al., and the "tender-minded" and very detached speculative writings of the critical theorists. Had Jay, in short, attended to the dynamics of the institute's development instead of simply chronicling it, the reader would have been able to appreciate the gulf that existed in the thirties and forties within an institute which produced both Neumann's rigorous social-scientific analysis of Nazi Germany, *Behemoth*, and Horkheimer's essay on "Reason and Self-Preservation," in which one reads that "the fascist order is the reason in which reason reveals itself as irrational" [p. 121].

Given Jay's intention of showing that the Frankfurt School "can be seen as presenting in quintessential form the dilemma of the left intellectual in our century," it is a great pity that he allows Horkheimer's view of the institute's history to dominate *The Dialectical Imagination*. Not that Horkheimer was not important. As the institute's director from 1930 onward and as the principal inspiration behind Critical Theory he certainly was. But his conception of the dilemma was not shared by most members of the institute, nor was his attitude toward it. Indeed, what makes the history of the institute so interesting as a case study in the history of twentieth-century Marxism is precisely the diversity of responses to be found among its members to a dilemma the roots of which lie embedded in the very origins of Marxism itself.

Understood in the light of its origins, Marxism is bourgeois theory about proletarian practice. In fact, it is bourgeois theory about proletarian practice conceived of as bringing about the actualization of the truths and values of bourgeois theory itself. It intends a twofold result: making the world into the kind of place German idealist philosophy says it can be, and raising the downtrodden masses to the level of full-fledged autonomous, freely active human beings. All this can be seen most clearly in Marx's early writings and in those later Marxian theories (Lukács, Korsch, Critical Theory) for which the Hegelian side of Marx is definitive: there the proletariat figures straightforwardly as the material instrument for the actualization of the ideals of philosophy. ("The emancipation of the German is the emancipation of man. The head of this emancipation is philosophy, its heart is the proletariat. Philosophy cannot actualize itself without the proletariat's being abolished, the proletariat cannot abolish itself [*qua* proletariat] without philosophy's being actualized." Marx, *Contribution to the Critique of Hegel's Philosophy of Right: Introduction* [1844].) It is worth noticing that Marx saw himself as a bourgeois theorist and realized that the conjoining of bourgeois theory with proletarian practice called for a word of explanation. In the *Communist Manifesto* (published in January 1848) he wrote:

> [As class struggle intensifies,] a small section of the ruling class cuts itself adrift and joins the revolutionary class, the class that holds the future in its hands. Just as, therefore, at an earlier period, a section of the nobility went over to the bourgeoisie, so now a portion of the bourgeoisie goes over to the proletariat, and in particular a portion of the bourgeois ideologists, who have raised themselves to the level of comprehending theoretically the historical movement as a whole.

The problematical nature of that alliance did not strike Marx until the events of the revolution of 1848 made it all too evident. (He revised his whole theory accordingly.) It was left to middle-class Marxist intellectuals of the twentieth century to experience its full force.

The essence of the problem becomes clear as soon as one explicates—however crudely—the nature of this conjunction of bourgeois theory and proletarian practice. A certain bourgeois theory—to wit, Marx's—identifies the one crucial flaw in society as it is and therewith the one essential desideratum of society as it should be, that is, it characterizes existing society as essentially class divided and future society as significantly classless (or, to use the terminology of Critical Theory, it characterizes existing society as essentially irrational and future society as significantly rational). As it is class riven (or irrational), society in its present form is not the locus of the self-determination of man in free activity. Since self-determination in free activity is man's very essence or nature, society must (and the force of this "must" is itself highly problematical) become classless (or rational). So at least says the theory. It also says that revolution is the process in which one type of society gives place to another, identifies the proletariat as "the great reserve army" of revolution, and so concludes that, by means of revolution, the proletariat is to bring into being the better society which bourgeois theory can envisage but which bourgeois critics are not powerful enough to create. The proletariat itself is not consulted; its wishes, its view of the world, the kind of better society *it* can envisage, even its willingness and ability to do battle for the cause—all these are declared (by Marx in 1846 as by Lukács in 1922) to be of no moment. After all, these are merely subjective matters; and what counts is objectivity, that which is scientifically (or, to use the vocabulary of Critical Theory once more, rationally) necessary. Bourgeois theory simply insists on the direction proletariat practice is to take.

Problems arise, of course, as soon as proletarian practice is seen to diverge from the path marked out for it by theory. As long as there is a working class with at least potential revolutionary thrust, the Marxist intellectual has something to theorize about, can hope that revolutionary theory and revolutionary practice will go hand in hand, and may plausibly feel that he is playing a constructive part in a powerful, world-historical movement. But once the proletariat can be clearly seen *not* to be revolutionary, theory is bereft of its bearing on practice. The Marxist intellectual can then take the view that the proletariat has been betrayed by its leaders, or that it has been so completely integrated into the established system as to be incapable of revolutionary action. In either case, he is left without an instrument for the realization of theory in practice. At that point theory can either cast around for an alternative "reserve army" of revolution, or it can give up the hope of revolution altogether and so cease being Marxist. If, on the other hand, socialist revolutions do succeed in peasant rather than bourgeois societies but establish regimes which do not obviously further the freely active self-determination of man, the Marxist intellectual who holds fast to the original vision is in difficulty of another kind. He then has the choice between, on the one hand, accepting the results of revolution on the grounds that tainted socialism is better than no socialism at all; and on the other hand, rejecting the results of revolution for the sake of holding fast to the commitment to human emancipation, on the grounds that no socialism at all is preferable to socialism that enslaves men anew.

What makes the dilemma of the left-wing intellectual in our century so complex is that it involves both of these sets of choices, and threatens at every turn to make him into a theorist with nothing practical to theorize about. The history of the Frankfurt Institute for Social Research and of the Frankfurt School affords an insight into the dimensions of this dilemma because it includes almost the whole range of responses to it. There is a broad acceptance of Soviet socialism (Grossmann) and, for a time at least, of the Communist Party (Wittfogel), as well as their systematic rejection (Pollock); there is the withdrawal into pure theory justified by the betrayal thesis (Horkheimer) and, for a time, by the total integration thesis (Marcuse), as well as the continued commitment to practical relevance at the cost of relinquishing the hope for socialist revolution (Neumann). There is also the eventual search for an alternative "reserve army" of revolution (Marcuse) and the final giving up of Marxism altogether. It is once again possible to do philosophy because the moment for its practical realization has passed (Adorno). (The only thing that does not seem to have occurred to these astute minds is that there is something radically amiss with the original conjunction of bourgeois theory and proletarian practice. But that is another story.)

Only the briefest possible indication can be given here of how the diversity of positions manifested itself in the history of the Frankfurt venture. Here are some examples. The economist Henryk Grossmann, an orthodox Marxist in the days of the original institute, took the pro-Soviet option, became increasingly alienated from the institute under Horkheimer and increasingly critical of what he took to be the shallowness of Critical Theory. His own analyses of the forces making for the collapse of capitalism and his study of Marx's relationship to the classical economists continued to reflect a Marxism for which economic factors were primary. Grossmann's political commitment somehow survived the shocks of the Moscow purge trials and of the Stalinization of Russia, and led him after the war to return to Germany—East, not West Germany—to take a chair of economics at the University of Leipzig. Karl August Wittfogel, the well-known sinologist, a Communist Party member in the days of the first Frankfurt Institute, took a different—and if anything even more familiar—route. At the end of the thirties he turned against the Soviet Union and against communism altogether. In due course he became a fanatical anti-Communist and assisted the red-hunting Congressional committees of the immediate postwar period. Friedrich Pollock, who from the first had belonged to the unorthodox circle within the institute and became an intimate of Horkheimer, worked out a critique of Soviet socialism which showed it to be a form of state capitalism. He then turned to a general analysis of state capitalism which suggested that, thanks to the new role of the state in the economy, capitalism might maintain itself indefinitely if state intervention could systematically counteract and neutralize the effects of those contradictions within capitalism which orthodox Marxists saw as the guarantee of its eventual collapse. Having through his work presumably convinced himself both of the unsocialist character of Soviet communism and of the durability of capitalism, Pollock withdrew to an early retirement in the Swiss mountains.

What is particularly striking in all three of these so very different intellectual careers is that the Soviet regime and the established Communist parties, however differently evaluated, have completely replaced the proletariat as embodiments of revolutionary practice, so that the force presumably making for the radical transformation of society has come to be seen as identical with the force making for a new establishment. This too belongs quite centrally to the history of twentieth-century Marxism, and represents a paradox which confronted leftist intellectuals with particular force in the forties and fifties. What it underlines, as I see it, is the extent to which the notion of the revolutionary proletariat functions in (bourgeois) Marxist theory as an abstraction standing for the power of practice, an abstraction whose theoretic function can be replaced by a functionally equivalent—if substantively very different— entity, such as "Soviet power," "the Third World," or "the revolutionary peasantry." Not until a New Left emerged in the late fifties and sixties in quest of a radical praxis that looked neither to established communism nor to the proletariat alone was an attempt made to overcome the paradox by going beyond it.

The emergence of the New Left brought the Frankfurt School to public prominence, revived interest in the earlier work of the institute, and gave Critical Theory a new lease on life. In this period Herbert Marcuse emerged as the most influential of the exponents of Critical Theory, for the simple reason that he was the only one to develop it in an expressly practical direction by applying it directly to social and political problems. Noteworthy in the present context about his writings in the sixties is his attempt to explore new possibilities of radical practice, and that the new directions were inspired less by new developments in theory itself than by fresh stirrings in the domain of practical life. The rise in the fifties and early sixties of a variety of non-Marxist, nonproletarian, and in some respects even nonpolitical movements, especially in the United States—Martin Luther King's campaign for Black civil rights, the anti-Vietnam War campaign, the emergence of the "drop-out" phenomenon (the "hippies," the "flower people," etc.)—these it was, and no theoretical discovery, which eventually suggested that there might be new roots, new impulses, and new forms of radical practice. Indeed, theory itself, in the form of Marcuse's *One Dimensional Man* (1964), had reached what looked like a complete dead end for practice with the thesis that advanced capitalist industrial society as a "totalitarian" system within which no kind of active initiative directed against the system can arise: The system tolerates only such human faculties as it can use, and thus completely integrates the population into the established order of things. By 1968, however, this total pessimism had given place to the qualified optimism of *Essay on Liberation*. Still convinced that the "system" itself is unitary and "totalitarian"—in contrast to the Marxian conception of a system drastically disunited by its internal contradictions—Marcuse now explored the idea that practical moves toward liberation might originate *outside* the system. He conjectured that there were five domains outside the established system which might hold the seeds of liberation, and these five he speculatively explored: the Third World which stands outside the Soviet-American orbit, the stance of "refusal" which simply rejects compliance with the system, voluntary "dropping out" of the system, the realm of art which stands outside and beyond it, and the unconscious, biological level of human experience which, so to speak, stands below it and can generate altogether new needs and faculties. This is not the place to examine Marcuse's arguments; it suffices for the present purpose to note that the significance of Marcuse's late work in the context of the history of the Frankfurt venture is that it attempts to restore, on fresh foundations, the unity of theory and practice, and so to escape from the paralyzing dilemma of the left intellectual in our century.

Horkheimer and Adorno, on the other hand—the Frankfurt School proper—bypassed the dilemma through withdrawal, through a return from practice-oriented theory to pure philosophy, to what Adorno called "theoretical practice." They had in any case always read Marx as a latter-day German idealist philosopher and retranslated the economic categories of Marxian theory into philosophical categories. In the end, Horkheimer valued Marxism only as "part of the individualist culture which is now perishing," as his literary executor, Professor Alfred Schmidt, told me last year. Adorno, for his part, told Martin Jay in 1969 that if Marx had had his way, the whole world would have been turned into a giant workhouse. None of this, of course, is to say that their intellectual work was of no value. There is much of great brilliance to be found in Adorno's writings, and there are suggestive ideas in some of Horkheimer's. It is only to say that their Marxism did not amount to much. What they cared about and were committed to was the heritage of German idealism: the freely active self-determination of the autonomous individual. Hence their concern with the defense of the individual against every conceivable form of domination, of non–self-determination: domination by society, domination by political power, domination by ideology, domination even by the sheer positivity of "fact" or the determinateness of the ego itself. To hold this sort of position and yet imagine oneself to be in some sense a Marxist—as they evidently did—is possible only if one takes the idealist moment in Marx for the whole of his theory. Certainly it is a grave misinterpretation of Marxian theory. But then Marx is often ill-served by his interpreters. It is not the least of the weaknesses of Jay's *Dialectical Imagination* that it conveys the impression that this sort of Marxism dominated the Frankfurt venture as a whole, and that "the dilemma of the left intellectual in our century" amounts to no more than the securing of theory against, and the defense of the individual from, "the absorbing power of both the dominant culture and its ostensible opponents."

Part Two
PHILOSOPHY

5

The Frankfurt School
and Critical Theory

Leszek Kolakowski

There is no summarized version of what is rightly regarded as the most complete and general exposition of Adorno's thought—*Negative Dialectics.*[1] It would probably be impossible to compile such a summary, and Adorno was probably well aware of this and deliberately made it so. The book may be called an embodied antinomy: a philosophical work that sets out to prove, by example or argument, that the writing of philosophical works is impossible. The difficulty of explaining its content is not only due to its extremely intricate syntax, evidently intentional, or the fact that the author uses Hegelian and neo-Hegelian jargon without any attempt to explain it, as though it were the clearest language in the world. The pretentious obscurity of style and the contempt it shows for the reader might be endurable if the book were not also totally devoid of literary form. It is in this respect a philosophical counterpart to the formlessness that manifested itself some time earlier in the plastic arts, and later in music and literature. It is no more possible to summarize Adorno's work than to describe the plot of an antinovel or the theme of an action painting. The abandonment of form in painting did not lead to the destruction of art, but actually liberated pure painting from "anecdotic" work; similarly, the novel and drama, although they consist of words, have survived the loss of form (which can never be complete) to the extent that we are able to read Joyce, Musil, and Gombrowicz with understanding. But in philosophical writing, the dissolution of form is destructive in the highest degree. It may be tolerable if it is due to the author's attempt to catch fleeting "experience" in words and to make his work directly "expressive," like Gabriel Marcel; but it is hard to endure a philosopher who continues to deal in abstractions while at the same time contending that they are a meaningless form of discourse.

With this reservation we may try to give an idea of Adorno's argument. The main theme that pervades his book and is expressed for example in his critique of Kant, Hegel, and the existentialists, appears to be as

95

follows. Philosophy has always been dominated by the search for an absolute starting point, both metaphysical and epistemological, and in consequence, despite the intentions of philosophers themselves, it has drifted into a search for "identity," i.e. some kind of primordial being to which all others were ultimately reducible. This was alike the trend of German idealism and positivism, of existentialists and transcendental phenomenologists. In considering the typical traditional pairs of opposites—object versus subject, the general versus the particular, empirical data versus ideas, continuity versus discontinuity, theory versus practice—philosophers have sought to interpret them in such a way as to give primacy to one concept or the other and so create a uniform language by means of which everything can be described: to identify aspects of the universe in respect of which all others are derivative. But this cannot be done. There is no absolute "primacy"; everything philosophy is concerned with presents itself as interdependent with the opposite. (This, of course, is Hegel's idea, but Adorno claims that Hegel was afterwards untrue to it.) A philosophy which continues in traditional fashion to strive to discover the "primal" thing or concept is on the wrong track, and moreover, in our civilization it tends to strengthen totalitarian and conformist tendencies by seeking order and invariability at any cost. Philosophy in fact is impossible; all that is possible is constant negation, purely destructive resistance to any attempt to confine the world within a single principle that purports to endow it with "identity."

Thus summarized, Adorno's thought may seem desperate or sterile, but it does not seem that we have done it an injustice. It is not a dialectic of negativity (which would be a metaphysical theory), but an express negation of metaphysics and epistemology. His intention is antitotalitarian: He is opposed to all ideas that serve to perpetuate a particular form of domination and reduce the human subject to reified forms. Such attempts, he argues, take on a paradoxical subjectivist form, especially in existentialist philosophy, where the petrification of the absolute individual subject as the irreducible reality involves indifference to all social relationships that increase the enslavement of man. One cannot proclaim the primacy of this monadic existence without tacitly accepting everything that lies outside it.

But Marxism too—especially in Lukács's interpretation, though he is not expressly mentioned in this context—serves the same totalitarian tendency under the guise of criticizing reification. "The remaining theoretical inadequacy in Hegel and Marx became part of historical practice and can thus be newly reflected upon in theory, instead of thought bowing irrationally to the primacy of practice. Practice itself was an eminently theoretical concept" (*Negative Dialectics*, p. 144). Adorno thus attacks the Marxist-Lukácsist "primacy of practice," in which theory is dissolved and loses its autonomy. Insofar as his opposition to the "philosophy of identity" is turned against the anti-intellectualism of Marxism and its all-absorbing "practice," he defends the right of philosophy to exist; he even begins his book with the statement that "philosophy, which once seemed obsolete, lives on because the moment to realize it was missed" (p. 3). At this point Adorno clearly departs from Marxism: There may, he argues, have been a time when Marx's hopes for the liberation of humanity by the proletariat and the abolition of philosophy by its identification with "life" were realistic, but that time has passed. Theory must abide in its autonomy, which of course does not mean that theory in its turn has any absolute primacy. Nothing whatever has primacy, everything depends on everything else and, by the same token, has its own measure of "substantiality." Practice cannot fulfill the tasks of theory, and if it claims to do so it is simply the enemy of thought.

If there is no absolute primacy it is also the case, in Adorno's opinion, that all attempts to embrace the "whole" by means of reason are rootless and serve the cause of mystification. This does not mean that theory must resolve itself wholly into particular sciences as the positivists would have it. Theory is indispensable, but for the present it cannot be anything but negation. Attempts to grasp the "whole" are based on the same faith in the ultimate identity of everything. Even when philosophy maintains that the whole is contradictory it retains its prejudices concerning identity, which are so strong that even contradiction can be made their instrument if it is proclaimed to be the ultimate foundation of the universe. Dialectic in the true sense is thus not merely the investigation of contradiction, but refusal to accept it as a schema that explains everything. Strictly speaking, dialectic is neither a method nor a description of the world, but an act of repeated opposition to all existing descriptive schemata and all methods pretending to universality. "Total contradiction is nothing but the manifested untruth of total identification" (p. 6).

In the same way there is no epistemological absolute, no single unchallengeable source of wisdom. The "pure immediacy" of the cognitive act, if it exists, cannot be expressed except in words, and words inevitably give it an abstract, rationalized form. But Husserl's transcendental ego is also a false construction, for there are no acts of intuition free from the social genesis of knowledge. All concepts are ultimately rooted in the nonconceptual, in human efforts to control nature. No concepts can express the whole content of the object or be identified with it; Hegel's pure "being" proves in the end to be nothingness.

The negative dialectic can, as Adorno says, be called an antisystem, and in that sense it appears to coincide with Nietzsche's position. However,

Adorno goes on to say that thought itself is negation, just as the processing of any substance is a negation of its form as presented to us. Even the statement that something is of a certain kind is negative inasmuch as it implies that that something is not of another kind. This, however, reduces negativity to a truism; it is not clear how there could be any philosophy that is not negative in this sense, or whom Adorno is arguing against. His main intention appears to be less truistic, namely to put forward no definite answers to the traditional problems of philosophy but to confine himself to exploding philosophy as it is today, since by its urge toward "positiveness" it inevitably degenerates into acceptance of the status quo, namely the domination of man by man. The bourgeois consciousness at the time of its emancipation combated "feudal" modes of thought but could not bring itself to break with "systems" of all kinds, since it felt that it did not represent "complete freedom." (From this observation of Adorno's we gather that he stands for "complete freedom" as against "systems.")

In his critique of "identity" and "positiveness" Adorno continues a traditional motif taken over by the Frankfurt School from Marx: the critique of society which, being subject to the domination of "exchange value," reduces individuals and things to a common level and a ho-mogeneous anonymity. This philosophy expresses and affirms that society cannot do justice to the variety of phenomena or the interdependence of different aspects of life; on the one hand it homogenizes society, on the other it reduces people and things to "atoms"—a process in which, Adorno observes, logic plays its part also. On this point he is faithful to the tradition of recent Marxist philosophy, which inveighs against logic while ignoring its modern developments.

Science, too, it appears, is a party to the general conspiracy of civilization against man, as it identifies rationality with measurability, reduces every-thing to quantities, and excludes qualitative differences from the scope of knowledge. Adorno does not suggest, however, that a new "qualitative" science is ready and waiting to take over.

The upshot of his critique is not to defend relativism, for that too is part of "bourgeois consciousness." It is anti-intellectual (*geistesfeindlich*), abstract, and wrong, because what it treats as relative is itself rooted in the conditions of capitalist society: "The alleged social relativity of views obeys the objective law of social production under private ownership of the means of production" (p. 37). Adorno does not say what "law" he refers to, and, true to his contempt for bourgeois logic, does not reflect on the logical validity of his criticism.

Philosophy in the sense of a system is impossible, he argues, because everything changes—a statement he enlarges on as follows. "The invariants, whose own invariance has been produced [*ein Produziertes ist*], cannot be peeled out of the variables as if all truth were then in our possession. Truth has coalesced with substance, which will change; immutability of truth is the delusion of *prima philosophia*" (p. 40).

On the one hand, concepts have a certain autonomy and do not emerge simply as copies of things; on the other, they do not enjoy "primacy" as compared with things—to agree that they do would mean accepting bureaucratic or capitalist government. "The principle of dominion, which antagonistically rends human society, is the same principle which, spiritualized, causes the difference between the concept and its subject matter [*dem ihm Unterworfenen*]" (p. 48). Hence nominalism is wrong ("the concept of a capitalist society is not a *flatus vocis*" [p. 50n.]), and so is conceptual realism: Concepts and their objects subsist in a constant dialectical association, in which primacy is obliterated. In the same way positivist attempts to reduce knowledge to that which is simply "given" are misguided, as they seek to "dehistoricize the contents of thought" (p. 53).

Antipositivist attempts to reconstruct an ontology are no less suspect; for ontology as such—not any particular ontological doctrine—is an apologia for the status quo, an instrument of "order." The need for an ontology is genuine enough, since the bourgeois consciousness has replaced "substantial" by "functional" concepts, treating society as a complex of functions in which everything is relative to something else and nothing has a consistency of its own. Nevertheless, ontology cannot be reconstructed.

At this point, as at many others, the reader may well wonder how Adorno intends his propositions to be applied. What are we to do if ontology and the lack of it are both bad and are both likely to involve us in the defense of exchange value? Perhaps we should not think of these questions at all, but declare ourselves neutral in philosophic matters? But Adorno will not have this either: It would be a surrender of another kind, an abandonment of reason. Science, just because it puts faith in itself and refuses to seek self-knowledge by any method other than its own, condemns itself to being an apologia for the existing world. "Its self-exegesis makes a *causa sui* of science. It accepts itself as given and thereby sanctions also its currently existing form, its division of labour, although in the long run the insufficiency of that form cannot be concealed" (p. 73). The humanistic sciences, dispersed in particular inquiries, lose interest in cognition and are stripped of their armour of concepts. Ontology, which comes to science "from outside," appears with the abruptness of a pistol shot (in Hegel's phrase) and does not help them to acquire self-knowledge. In the end we do not know how to escape from the vicious circle.

Heidegger's ontology not only does not cure this state of affairs, but proposes something even worse. Having eliminated from philosophy both empiricism and Husserl's concept of the *eidos,* he seeks to apprehend being—which, after this reduction, is pure nothingness. He also isolates phenomena and cannot conceive them as aspects (*Momente*) of the process of manifestation; in this way phenomena are reified. Heidegger, like Husserl, believes that it is possible to proceed from the individual to the universal without mediation, or to apprehend being in a form unaffected by the act of reflection. This, however, is impossible. Being, however conceived, is mediated by the subject. Heidegger's "being" is constituted, not simply given: "We cannot, by thinking, assume any position in which that separation of subject and object will directly vanish, for the separation is inherent in each thought; it is inherent in thinking itself" (p. 85). Freedom can be sought only by observing the tensions that arise between opposite poles of life, but Heidegger treats these poles as absolute realities and leaves them to their fate. On the one hand he accepts that social life must be reified," i.e. he sanctions the status quo, while on the other he ascribes freedom to man as something already gained, thus sanctioning slavery. He attempts to rescue metaphysics, but wrongly supposes that what he is trying to rescue is "immediately present." All in all, Heidegger's philosophy is an example of *Herrschaftswissen* in the service of a repressive society. It calls on us to abandon concepts for the sake of a promised communion with Being— but this Being has no content, precisely because it is supposed to be apprehended without the "mediation" of concepts; basically it is no more than a substantivization of the copula "is."

It would seem that, speaking in as general terms as possible, the main thrust of Adorno's attack on Heidegger's ontology lies in the Hegelian contention that the subject can never by wholly eliminated from the results of metaphysical inquiry, and that if we forget this and attempt to place subject and object "on opposite sides" we shall fail to comprehend either one or the other. Both are inseparable parts of reflection, and neither has epistemological priority; each is "mediated" by the other. Similarly, there is no way of apprehending by cognition that which is absolutely individual—what Heidegger calls *Dasein* or *Jemeinigkeit.* Without the mediation of general concepts, the pure "this thing here" becomes an abstraction; it cannot be "isolated" from reflection. "But truth, the constellation of subject and object in which both penetrate each other, can no more be reduced to subjectivity than to that Being whose dialectical relation to subjectivity Heidegger tends to blur" (p. 127).

The passage in which Adorno comes closest to explaining what he means by "negative dialectics" is as follows. "In a sense, dialectical logic is more positivistic than the positivism that outlaws it. As thinking, dialectical logic respects that which is to be thought—the object—even where the object does not heed the rules of thinking. The analysis of the object is tangential to the rules of thinking. Thought need not be content with its own legality; without abandoning it, we can think against our thought, and if it were possible to define dialectics, this would be a definition worth suggesting" (p. 141). It does not appear that we can infer more from this definition than that dialectic need not be cramped by rules of logic. In another passage we are indeed told that it is freer still: for "philosophy consists neither in *vérités de raison* nor in *vérités de fait*. Nothing it says will bow to tangible criteria of any 'being the case': its theses on conceptualities are no more subject to the criteria of a logical state of facts than its theses on factualities are to the criteria of empirical science" (p. 109). It would be hard indeed to imagine a more convenient position. The negative dialectician declares, firstly, that he cannot be criticized from either the logical or the factual point of view, as he had laid down that such criteria do not concern him; secondly, that his intellectual and moral superiority is based on his very disregard of these criteria; and thirdly, that that disregard is in fact the essence of the "negative dialectic." The "negative dialectic" is simply a blank check, signed and endorsed by history, being, subject, and object, in favor of Adorno and his followers. Any sum can be written in, anything will be valid, there is absolute liberation from the "positivist fetishes" of logic and empiricism. Thought has transformed itself dialectically into its opposite. Anyone who denies this is enslaved to the "identity principle," which implies acceptance of a society dominated by exchange value and therefore ignorant of "qualitative differences."

The reason why the "identity principle" is so dangerous, according to Adorno, is that it implies, firstly, that each separate thing is what it is empirically, and secondly, that an individual object can be identified by means of general concepts, i.e. analyzed into abstractions (an idea of Bergson's, whom Adorno, however, does not mention). The task of dialectic, on the other hand, is first to ascertain what a thing is in reality, not merely to what category it belongs (Adorno does not give examples of an analysis of this kind), and second to explain what it ought to be according to its own concept, although it is not yet (an idea of Bloch's, to whom Adorno does not refer either in this context). A man knows how to define himself, while society defines him differently in accordance

102 Foundations of the Frankfurt School of Social Research

with the function it assigns to him; between the two modes of definition there is an "objective contradiction" (again no examples given). The object of dialectic is to oppose the immobilization of things by concept. It takes the position that things are never identical with themselves. It seeks out negations, without assuming that the negation of a negation signifies a return to the positive. It recognizes individuality, but only as "mediated" by generality, and generality only as an aspect (*Moment*) of individuality. It sees the subject in the object and vice versa, practice in theory and theory in practice, the essence in the phenomenon and the phenomenon in the essence. It must apprehend differences but not "absolute" them, and it must not regard any particular thing as a starting point par excellence. There cannot be a point of view that presupposes nothing, such as Husserl's transcendental subject; the delusion that there can be such a subject is due to the fact that society precedes the individual. The idea that there can be a spirit which comprises everything and is identical with the whole is as nonsensical as that of the single party in a totalitarian regime. The dispute as to the primacy of mind or matter is meaningless in dialectical thinking, for these concepts are themselves abstracted from experience, and the "radical difference" between them is no more than a convention.

All these precepts concerning dialectic should, in Adorno's opinion, serve definite social or political ends. It even appears that criteria of practical action can be deduced from them. "For the right practice, and for the good itself, there really is no other authority than the most advanced state of theory. When an idea of goodness is supposed to guide the will without fully absorbing the concrete rational definitions, it will unwittingly take orders from the reified consciousness, from that which society has approved" (p. 242). We thus have a clear practical rule: First there must be an advanced (*fortgeschritten*) theory, and second, the will must be influenced by "concrete rational definitions." The object of practice, thus enlightened, is to do away with reification which is due to exchange value. For in bourgeois society, as Marx taught, the autonomy of the individual was only apparent, an expression of the contingency of life and the dependence of human beings on market forces. It is hard to gather from Adorno's writings, however, what nonreified freedom is to consist of. In describing this "complete freedom" we must not, in any case, use the concept of self-alienation, as it suggests that the state of freedom from alienation, or the perfect unity of man with himself, has already existed at some former time, so that freedom can be achieved by going back to the starting point—an idea which is reactionary by definition. Nor is it the case that we know of some historical design that guarantees us a joyful feature of freedom and the end of reification; up to now there has been no such thing as a single process of universal history: "History is the unity of continuity and discontinuity" (p. 320).

There can be few works of philosophy that gives such an overpowering impression of sterility as *Negative Dialectics*. This is not because it seeks to deprive human knowledge of an "ultimate basis," i.e. because it is a doctrine of scepticism. In the history of philosophy there have been admirable works of scepticism, full of penetration as well as destructive passion. But Adorno is not a sceptic. He does not say that there is no criterion of truth, that no theory is possible, or that reason is powerless. On the contrary, he says that theory is possible and indispensible and that we must be guided by reason. All his arguments go to show, however, that reason can never take the first step without falling into reification, and it is thus not clear how it can take the second or any further steps. There is simply no starting point, and the recognition of this fact is proclaimed as the supreme achievement of dialectic. But even this crucial statement is not clearly formulated by Adorno, nor does he support it by any analysis of his concepts and maxims. As with many other Marxists, his work contains no arguments but only *ex cathedra* statements using concepts that are nowhere explained. He condemns conceptual analysis as a manifestation of positivist prejudices to the effect that some ultimate data, empirical or logical, can provide philosophy with a starting point.

In the last resort Adorno's argument boils down to an assortment of ideas borrowed uncritically from Marx, Hegel, Nietzsche, Lukács, Bergson, and Bloch. From Marx he takes the statement that the whole mechanism of bourgeois society is based on the domination of exchange value, reducing all qualitative differences to the common denominator of money (this is Marx's form of romantic anticapitalism). From Marx also comes the attack on Hegelian philosophy for subjecting history to an extrahistorical *Weltgeist* and asserting the primacy of "that which is general" over human individuals, substituting abstractions for realities and thus perpetuating human enslavement. Again from Marx comes the attack on Hegel's theory of subject and object, in which the subject is defined as a manifestation of the object, and the object as a subjective construction, thus producing a vicious circle (but it is not clear how Adorno avoids this vicious circle, as he denies absolute priority to either subject or object). Adorno departs from Marx, on the other hand, in rejecting the theory of progress and historical necessity and the idea of the proletariat as the standard bearer of the Great Utopia. From Lukács comes the view that all that is evil in the world can be summed up in the term *reification* and that perfected human beings will cast off the ontological status of "things" (but Adorno does not say what the "dereified" state will be like, still less how it will be attained). Both the Promethean and the scientific motif of Marxism are discarded, and there remains only a vague romantic Utopia in which man is himself and does not depend on mechanical social forces. From Bloch, Adorno derives the view that we possess the idea of Utopia transcending the actual world, but that the especial virtue of this transcendence is that it cannot, in principle, have any definite content at the present time. From Nietzsche comes the general hostility to the "spirit of the system" and the convenient belief that a true sage is not afraid of contradictions but rather expresses his wisdom in them, so that he is forearmed against logical criticism. From Bergson comes the idea that abstract concepts petrify changeable things (or, as Adorno would say, "reify" them). Adorno himself, on the other hand, contributes the hope that we can create fluid concepts that do not petrify anything. From Hegel, Adorno takes the general idea that in the cognitive process there is a constant mediation between subject and object, concepts and perception, the particular and the general. To all these ingredients Adorno adds an almost unparalleled vagueness of exposition: He shows no desire whatever to elucidate his ideas, and clothes them in pretentious generalities. As a philosophical text, *Negative Dialectics* is a model of professorial bombast concealing a poverty of thought.

The view that there is no absolute basis for human reasoning can certainly be defended, as is shown by sceptics and relativists who have propounded it in various forms. But Adorno not only adds nothing to this traditional idea but obscures it by his own phraseology (neither subject nor object can be "absolutized"; perceptions cannot be abstracted from concepts; there is no absolute "primacy" of practice, etc.), while at the same time imagining that this negative dialectic can lead to some practical consequences for social behavior. If we do try to extract intellectual or practical rules from his philosophy, they reduce to the precepts: "We must think more intensively, but also remember that there is no starting point for thought"; and "we must oppose reification and exchange value." The fact that we can say nothing positive is not our fault and not Adorno's, but is due to the domination of exchange value. For the present, therefore, we can only negatively "transcend" existing civilization as a whole. In this way negative dialectic has provided a convenient ideological slogan for left-wing groups who sought a pretext for root-and-branch destruction as a political program, and who extolled intellectual primitivism as the supreme form of dialectical initiation. It would be unjust, however, to accuse Adorno of intending to encourage such attitudes. His philosophy is not an expression of universal revolt, but of helplessness and despair.

Critique of Existential "Authenticism"

Existentialism was clearly the main competitor of the Frankfurt School as regards the critique of reification, and was far more influential as a philosophy. German thinkers rarely used the term, but on the face of it the intention of their anthropological theories was the same: to express in philosophical language the contrast between the self-determining consciousness of the individual and the anonymous world of social ties conforming to rules of their own. Thus, in the same way as the attacks on Hegel by Marx, Kierkegaard, and Stirner contained a common element, namely their critique of the primacy of impersonal generality over real subjectivity, so the Marxists and existentialists were on common ground in criticizing the social system which confined human beings to socially determined roles and made them dependent on quasi-natural forces. The Marxists, following Lukács, called this state of things "reification" and ascribed it, as did Marx, to the all-powerful effect of money as a leveler in capitalist conditions. Existentialism did not concern itself with explanations such as the class struggle or property relationships, but it too was fundamentally a protest against the culture of developed industrial societies, reducing the human individual to the sum of his social functions. The category of "authenticity" or "authentic being" (*Eigentlichkeit*), which plays an essential part in Heidegger's early writings, was an attempt to vindicate the irreducible identity of the individual subject as against the anonymous social forces summed up in the term *the impersonal (das Man)*.

Adorno's attack on German existentialism was thus perfectly understandable: He wished to assert the claim of the Frankfurt School to be the sole fighter against reification, and to prove that existentialism, while appearing to criticize reification, in reality endorsed it. This is the purpose of *Jargon der Eigentlichkeit: zur deutschen Ideologie* (1964), in which he joins issue principally with Heidegger but also with Jaspers and occasionally Buber, Bollnow, and others. Adorno accepts the idea of reification and the Marxist view that it results from the subjection of human beings to exchange value, but he rejects the idea of the proletariat as the savior of humanity and does not believe that reification can be done away with simply by nationalizing means of production.

The main points of Adorno's attack on existentialism are as follows. First, the existentialists have created a deceptive language, the elements of which are intended, by some peculiar aura, to arouse a magic faith in the independent power of words. This is a rhetorical technique which precedes any content and is merely designed to make it appear profound. The magic of words is supposed to take the place of an analysis of the true sources of reification and to suggest that it can be cured simply by incantations. In reality, words cannot directly express irreducible subjectivity, nor can they generate "authentic being": It is quite possible to adopt the watchword of "authenticism" and believe that one has escaped from reification, while in fact remaining subject to it. Moreover—and this seems to be the essential point— "authenticism" is a purely formal catchword or incantation. The existentialists do not tell us in what way we are to be authentic. If it suffices simply to be what we are, then an oppressor and murderer is doing his duty by being just that. In short (though Adorno does not put the point in these words), "authenticism" does not imply any specific values and can be expressed an any behavior whatsoever. Another deceptive concept is that of "authentic communication" as opposed to the mechanical exchange of verbal stereotypes. By talking of authentic communication existentialists seek to persuade people that they can cure social oppression simply by expressing thoughts to one another, and conversation is thus turned into a substitute for what should come after it (Adorno does not explain what this is).

Secondly, "authenticism" cannot in any case be a cure for reification because it is not interested in its sources, namely the rule of commodity fetishism and exchange value. It suggests that anyone can make his own life authentic, while society as a whole continues to be under the spell of reification. This is a classic case of distracting people's attention from the real causes of their slavery, by conjuring up the illusion that freedom can be realized in the individual consciousness without any change in the conditions of communal life.

Third, the effect of existentialism is to petrify the whole area of "nonauthentic" life as a metaphysical entity which cannot be done away with but can only be resisted by an effort confined to one's own existence. Heidegger, for instance, speaks of empty, everyday chatter as a manifestation of the reified world, but he regards it as a permanent feature, not realizing that it would not exist in a rational economy that did not squander money on advertising.

Fourth, existentialism tends to perpetuate reification not only by distracting attention from social conditions but by the way in which it defines existence. According to Heidegger, individual human existence (*Dasein*) is a matter of self-possession and self-reference. All social content is excluded from the idea of authenticity, which consists of willing to possess oneself. In this way Heidegger actually reifies human subjectivity, reducing it to a tautological state of "being oneself," unrelated to the world outside.

Adorno also attacks Heidegger's attempt to investigate the roots of language, which he regards as part of a general tendency to glorify bygone times, Arcadian rusticity, etc., and consequently as related to the Nazi ideology of "blood and soil."

Adorno's criticism follows the main lines of conventional Marxist attacks on "bourgeois philosophy": Existentialism makes a pretense of fighting reification but in fact aggravates it by leaving social problems out of account and promising the individual that he can have "true life" by simply deciding to "be himself." In other words, the objection is that the "jargon of authenticity" contains no political program. This is true, but the same could be said of Adorno's own jargon of reification and negation. The proposition that we must constantly set our faces against a civilization subject to the leveling pressures of exchange value does not itself imply any specific rule of social behavior. The case is different with orthodox Marxists, who maintain that reification with all its baneful consequences will cease when all factories are taken over by the state; but Adorno specifically rejects this conclusion. He condemns society based on exchange value without giving any indication of what an alternative society would be like; and there is something hypocritical in his indignation at the existentialists' failure to provide a blueprint for the future.

Adorno is right in saying that "authenticism" is a purely formal value from which no conclusions or moral rules can be deduced. It is dangerous, moreover, to set it up as the supreme value, since it affords no moral protection against the idea that, for example, the commander of a concentration camp can, by behaving as such, achieve perfect fulfillment as a human being. In other words, Heidegger's anthropology is amoral inasmuch as it contains no definition of values. But is Critical Theory any better off? True, it includes "reason" in its higher dialectical form except that it is not bound by the trivialities of logic or the cult of empirical data, and as regards "freedom" we are chiefly told what it is not. It is neither bourgeois freedom, which enhances reification instead of curing it, nor is it freedom as promised and realized by Marxism-Leninism, for that is slavery. Clearly, it must be something better than these, but it is hard to say what. We cannot anticipate Utopia in positive terms; the most we can do is negatively to transcend the existing world. Thus the precepts of critical theory are no more than a call to unspecified action, and are just as formal as Heidegger's "authenticism."

Critique of "Enlightenment"

Although Horkheimer and Adorno's *Dialectic of Enlightenment*[2] consists of loose and uncoordinated reflections, it contains some basic ideas which can be reduced to a kind of system. Written toward the end of World War II, the book is dominated by the question of Nazism, which, in the authors' view, was not simply a monstrous freak but rather a drastic manifestation of the universal barbarism into which humanity was falling. They attributed this decline to the consistent operation of the very same values, ideals, and rules that had once lifted mankind out of barbarism, and that were summed up in the concept of enlightenment. By this they did not mean the specific eighteenth-century movement to which the term is usually applied, but the "most general sense of progressive thought . . . aimed at liberating men from fear and establishing their sovereignty" (*Dialectic of Enlightenment,* p. 3). The "dialectic" consisted in the fact that the movement which aimed to conquer nature and emancipate reason from the shackles of mythology had, by its own inner logic, turned into its opposite. It had created a positivist, pragmatist, utilitarian ideology and, by reducing the world to its purely quantitative aspects, had annihilated meaning, barbarized the arts and sciences, and increasingly subjected mankind to "commodity fetishism." The *Dialectic of Enlightenment* is not a historical treatise but a collection of haphazardly chosen and unexplained examples to illustrate various forms of the debasement of "enlightened" ideals; after some introductory remarks on the concept of enlightenment it includes the chapters on Odysseus, the marquis de Sade, the entertainment industry, and anti-Semitism.

Enlightenment, seeking to liberate men from the oppressive sense of mystery in the world, simply declared that what was mysterious did not exist. It aspired to a form of knowledge that would enable man to rule over nature, and it therefore deprived knowledge of significance, jettisoning such notions as substance, quality, and causality, and preserving only what might serve the purpose of manipulating things. It aimed to give unity to the whole of knowledge and culture and to reduce all qualities to a common measure; thus it was responsible for the imposition of mathematical standards on science and for creating an economy based on exchange value, i.e. transforming goods of every kind into so many units of abstract labor time. Increased dominion over nature meant alienation from nature, and likewise increased domination over human beings. The theory of knowledge produced by enlightenment implied that we know things insofar as we have power over them, and this was true in both the physical and social worlds. It also signified that reality had no meaning in itself but only took its meaning from the subject, while at the same time subject and object were completely separate from each other. Science ascribed reality only to what might occur more than once—as if in imitation of the "repetition principle" that governs mythological thinking. It sought to contain the world within a system of categories, turning individual things and human beings into abstractions and thus creating the ideological foundations of totalitarianism. The abstractness of thought went hand in hand with the domination of man by man: "The universality of ideas as developed by discursive logic, domination in the conceptual sphere, is raised up on the basis of actual domination" (p. 14). Enlightenment in its developed form regards every object as self-identical; the idea that a thing may be what it is not yet is rejected as a relic of mythology.

The urge to enclose the world in a single conceptual system, and the propensity to deductive thinking, are especially pernicious aspects of enlightenment and are a menace to freedom.

> For enlightenment is as totalitarian as any system. Its untruth does not consist in what its romantic enemies have always reproached it for: analytical method, return to elements, dissolution through reflective thought; but instead in the fact that for enlightenment the process is always decided from the start. When in mathematical procedure the unknown becomes the unknown quantity of an equation, this marks it as the well-known even before any value is inserted. Nature, before and after the quantum theory, is that which is to be comprehended mathematically. . . . In the anticipated identification of the wholly conceived and mathematized world with truth, enlightenment intends to secure itself against the return of the mythic. It confounds thought and mathematics. . . . Thinking objectifies itself to become an automatic, self-activating process. . . . Mathematical procedure becomes, so to speak, the ritual of thinking . . . it turns thought into a thing, an instrument (*Dialectic of Enlightenment,* pp. 24–25).

Enlightenment, in short, will not and cannot grasp what is new; it is only interested in what is recurrent, what is already known. But, contrary to the rules of enlightenment, thought is not a matter of perception, classification, and counting; it consists in "the determinate negation of each successive immediacy" (*bestimmende Negation des je Unmittelbaren*) (ibid., p. 27)—i.e., presumably, in advancing beyond what is to what may be. Enlightenment turns the world into a tautology, and thus reverts to the myth which it sought to destroy. By restricting thought to facts which must then be arranged in an abstract system, enlightenment sanctifies what is, that is to say social injustice; industrialism reifies human subjectivity, and commodity fetishism prevails in every sphere of life.

The rationalism of enlightenment, while enhancing man's power over nature, also increased the power of some human beings over others, and by this token has outlived its usefulness. The root of the evil was the division of labor and, along with it, the alienation of man from nature; domination became the one purpose of thought, and thought itself was thereby destroyed. Socialism adopted the bourgeois style of thinking, which regarded nature as completely alien and thus made it totalitarian. In this way enlightenment embarked on a suicidal course, and the only hope of salvation seems to consist in theory: "True revolutionary practice [*umwälzende Praxis*] depends on the intransigence of theory in the face of the insensibility [*Bewusstlosigkeit*] with which society allows thought to ossify" (p. 41).

According to the *Dialectic of Enlightenment* the legend of Odysseus is a prototype or symbol of the isolation of the individual precisely because he is fully socialized. The hero escapes from the Cyclops by calling himself "Noman": to preserve his existence, he destroys it. As the authors put it, "this linguistic adaptation to death contains the schema of modern mathematics" (p. 60). In general the legend shows that a civilization in which men seek to affirm themselves is only possible through self-denial and repression; thus, in enlightenment, the dialectic takes on a Freudian aspect.

The perfect epitome of eighteenth-century Enlightenment was the marquis de Sade, who carried the ideology of domination to its utmost logical consequence. Enlightenment treats human beings as repeatable and replaceable (hence reified) elements of an abstract system, and this too is the meaning of de Sade's way of life. The totalitarian idea latent in Enlightenment philosophy assimilates human characteristics to interchangeable commodities. Reason and feeling are reduced to an impersonal level; rationalist planning degenerates into totalitarian terror; morality is derided and despised as a maneuver by the weak to protect themselves against the strong (an anticipation of Nietzsche); and all traditional virtues are declared inimical to reason and illusory, a view already implicit in Descartes's division of man into an extended and thinking substance.

The destruction of reason, feeling, subjectivity, quality, and nature itself by the unholy combination of mathematics, logic, and exchange value is especially seen in the degradation of culture, a crying example of which is the modern entertainment industry. A single system dominated by commercial values has taken over every aspect of mass culture. Everything serves to perpetuate the power of capital—even the fact that the workers have attained a fairly high standard of living and that people can find clean homes to live in. Mass-produced culture kills creativity; it is not justified by the demand for it, since that demand is itself part of the system. In Germany at one time the state at least protected the higher forms of culture against the operation of the market, but this is now over and artists are the slaves of their customers. Novelty is anathema; both the output and the enjoyment of art are planned in advance, as they must be if art is to survive market competition. In this way art itself, contrary to its primal function, helps to destroy individuality and turn human beings into stereotypes. The authors lament that art has become so cheap and accessible, for this inevitably means its degradation.

Their concept of enlightenment is a fanciful, unhistorical hybrid composed of everything they dislike: positivism, logic, deductive and empirical science, capitalism, the money power, mass culture, liberalism, and fascism. Their critique of culture—apart from some true observations, which have since become commonplace, on the harmfulness of commercialized art—is imbued with nostalgia for the days when the enjoyment of culture was reserved to the elite: It is an attack on the "age of the common man" in a spirit of feudal contempt for the masses. Mass society was attacked from various quarters even in the last century, by Tocqueville, Renan, Burckhardt, and Nietzsche among others. What is new in Horkheimer and Adorno is that they combine this attack with an onslaught on positivism and science, and that, following Marx, they discern the root of the evil in the division of labor, reification, and the domination of exchange value. They go much further than Marx, however. The original sin of enlightenment, according to them, was to cut man off from nature and treat the latter as a mere object of exploitation, with the result that man was assimilated to the natural order and was exploited likewise. This process found its ideological reflection in science, which is not interested in qualities but only in what can be expressed quantitatively and made to serve technical purposes.

The attack is in line with the romantic tradition. But the authors do not offer any way out of the state of decadence. They do not say how man can become friends with nature again, or how to get rid of exchange value and live without money or calculation. The only remedy they have to offer is theoretical reasoning, and we may suspect that its chief merit in their eyes is to be free from the despotism of logic and mathematics (logic, they tell us, signifies contempt for the individual).

It is noteworthy that whereas socialists formerly denounced capitalism for producing poverty, the main grievance of the Frankfurt School is that it engenders abundance and satisfies a multiplicity of needs, and is thus injurious to the higher forms of culture.

The *Dialectic of Enlightenment* contains all the elements of Marcuse's later attack on modern philosophy, which allegedly favors totalitarianism by maintaining a positivist "neutralism" in regard to the world of values and by insisting that human knowledge should be controlled by facts. This strange paralogism, equating the observance of empirical and logical rules with fidelity to the status quo and rejection of all change, recurs again and again in the writings of the Frankfurt School. If the supposed link between positivism and social conservatism or totalitarianism (the authors treat these as one and the same!) is studied in the light of history, the evidence is all the other way: Positivists, from Hume onward, were wedded to the liberal tradition. Clearly, there is no logical connection either. If the fact that scientific observation is neutral toward its object and abstains from evaluation implies that it favors the status quo, we should have to maintain that physiopathological observation implies approval of disease and a belief that it should not be combated. Admittedly, there is an essential difference between medicine and social science (though the remarks of the Frankfurt philosophers in this context purport to apply to all human knowledge). In the social sciences, observation itself is part of the subject matter, if that is taken to include the entire social picture. But it does not follow that a scientist who abstains as far as he can from value judgements is an agent of social stability or conformism; he may or may not be, but nothing can be inferred in this respect from the fact that his observation is external and uncommitted. If, on the other hand, the observer is committed not only in the sense of having some practical interest in view but also in regarding his cognitive activity as part of a certain social practice, he is more or less obliged to regard as true whatever seems conducive to the particular interest with which he identifies, i.e. apply genetic, pragmatic criteria of truth. If this principle were adopted, science as we know it would disappear and be replaced by political propaganda. Undoubtedly, various political interests and preferences are reflected in various ways in social science. But a rule which sought to generalize such influences instead of minimizing them would turn science into a tool of politics, as has happened with social science in totalitarian states. Theoretical observation and discussion would completely forfeit their autonomy, which is the reverse of what the Frankfurt writers would wish, as they indicate elsewhere.

It is also true that scientific observation does not of itself produce aims; this is the case even if some value judgements are implicit in the rules prescribing the conditions under which certain statements or hypotheses become part of science. The canons of scientific procedures are not, of course, infringed by the fact that the investigator wants to discover something that will serve practical ends, or that his interest is inspired by some practical concern. But they are infringed if, on the pretext of overcoming the dichotomy of facts and values (and the Frankfurt writers, like many other Marxists, are constantly boasting of having done this), the truth of science is subordinated to the criteria of any interest whatsoever; this simply means that anything is right which suits the interests with which the scientist identifies himself.

The rules of empirical observation have evolved for centuries in the European mind, from the late Middle Ages onward. That their development was somehow connected with the spread of a market economy is possible, though certainly not proved. On this as on most other subjects, the proponents of Critical Theory offer only bare assertions, devoid of historical analysis. If there actually is a historical link, it still by no means follows that these rules are an instrument of "commodity fetishism" and a mainstay of capitalism; any such assumption is nonsense. The writers we are discussing seem to believe that there is, at any rate potentially, some alternative science which would satisfy the demands of human nature, but they cannot tell us anything about it. Their Critical Theory is not so much a theory as a general statement that theory is of great importance, which few would deny, and a plea for a critical attitude toward existing society, which we are invited to transcend in thought. This injunction makes no sense as long as they cannot tell us in what direction the existing order is to be transcended. From this point of view, orthodox Marxism is more specific, as it does at least claim that once the means of production are publicly owned and the Communist Party installed in power, only a few minor technical problems will stand in the way of universal freedom and happiness. These assurances are completely refuted by experience, but at least we know what they mean.

The *Dialectic of Enlightenment* and other works of the Frankfurt School contain many sound remarks on the commercialization of art in industrial society and the inferiority of cultural products dependent on the market. But the authors are on very doubtful ground when they say that this has led to the degradation of art as a whole and of the artistic enjoyment open to people in general. If this were so it would mean that, for instance, country folk in the eighteenth century enjoyed some higher forms of culture, but that capitalism gradually deprived them of these and substituted crude, mass-produced objects and entertainments. It is not obvious, however, that eighteenth-century rustics enjoyed higher artistic values, in the form of church ceremonies, popular sports and dances, than television offers present-day workers. So-called higher culture has not disappeared, but has become incomparably more accessible than ever before, and is undoubtedly enjoyed by more people. It is highly unconvincing to argue that its dramatic formal changes in the twentieth century are all explicable by the domination of exchange value.

Adorno, who refers to the degradation of art in many of his writings, seems to think that the present situation is hopeless, i.e. that there is no source of strength which would enable art to revive and perform its proper function. On the one hand, there is affirmative art, which accepts the present situation and pretends to find harmony where there is only chaos (for example Stravinsky); on the other, there are attempts at resistance, but, as they have no roots in the real world, even geniuses (for example Schönberg) are forced into escapism, shutting themselves up in self-sufficient realms of their own artistic material. The avant-garde movement is a negation, but for the present at least it can be nothing more; as far as it goes it is true for our time, unlike mass culture and bogus "affirmative" art, but it is feeble and depressing truth, expressive of cultural bankruptcy. The last word of Adorno's theory of culture is apparently that we must protest, but that protest will be unavailing. We cannot recapture the values of the past, those of the present are debased and barbarous, and the future offers none. All that is left to us is a gesture of negation, deprived of content by its very totality.

If the foregoing is a true account of Adorno's work, not only can we not regard it as a continuation of Marx's thought, but it is diametrically opposed to the latter by reason of its pessimism. Failing a positive Utopia, its final response to the human condition can only be an inarticulate cry.

Conclusion

When we consider the place of the Frankfurt School in the evolution of Marxism, we find that its strong point was philosophical antidogmatism and the defense of the autonomy of theoretical reasoning. It freed itself from the mythology of the infallible proletariat and the belief that Marx's categories were adequate to the situation and problems of the modern world. It also endeavored to reject all elements or varieties of Marxism that postulated an absolute, primary basis of knowledge and practice. It contributed to the analysis of mass culture as a phenomenon that cannot be interpreted in class categories as Marx understood them. It also contributed to the critique of scientistic philosophy, by drawing attention (though in fairly general and unmethodical terms) to the latent normative assumptions of scientistic programs.

The Frankfurt philosophers were on weak ground, on the other hand, in their constant proclamation of an ideal emancipation which was never properly explained. This created the illusion that while condemning reification, exchange value, commercialized culture, and scientism they were offering something else instead, whereas the most they were actually offering was nostalgia for the precapitalist culture of an elite. By harping on the vague prospect of a universal escape from present-day civilization, they unwittingly encouraged an attitude of mindless and destructive protest.

In short, the strength of the Frankfurt School consisted in pure negation, and its dangerous ambiguity lay in the fact that it would not openly admit this fact, but frequently suggested the opposite. It was not so much a continuation of Marxism in any direction, as an example of its dissolution and paralysis.

Notes

1. Adorno, Theodor W. *Negative Dialectics* (New York: Seabury Press, 1972).
2. Horkheimer, Max, and Theodor W. Adorno. *Dialectic of Enlightenment* (New York: Seabury Press, 1972).

6

Critique of Reason from
Max Weber to Jürgen Habermas

Michael Landmann

Max Weber

Two opposing camps met at a congress of national economists in 1909.[1] On the one side the socialist group around Schmoller, Wagner, and Knapp argued for the unity of theory and practice, science and politics. On the other, Weber, Sombart, and Eulenburg demanded the separation of these two areas, maintaining that value judgments can never be made with an objective claim to truth. As the example of the natural sciences showed, science must limit itself to factual judgments. Only as an *empirical* science could sociology become a science at all.

Along with the empirical postulate, Weber gave the famous descriptions of calculating, goal-oriented, rational behavior (as contrasted with traditional and emotional motivations), which led to both capitalist enterprise and bureaucratic officialdom, paralleling the rise of scientism. Reason seemed limited to finding increasingly more effective means for given objectives. The political function of modern sociology, so Weber said, could consist only in the selection and provision of means.

In Max Weber, the extrication of isolated means was connected with his studies of Calvinism. The Calvinist limited himself to methodical action, while leaving the end to the unfathomable decrees of an unapproachable God. It was no accident that positivism, with its asceticism concerning the question of the whole and of meaning, could take root best in the Calvinist soil of Anglo-Saxon countries. Conversely, the metaphysical question remained relatively open against the background of either Catholicism, with its natural theology, or Lutheranism with its tender emotional fervor toward God.

Max Weber, however, considered the relative emancipation of the means to be a great motive force even beyond this historical context. In his last major lecture "Science as a Vocation," he posed the exclusion of axiological questions as a precondition for science. "All natural sciences give us an answer to the question: What should we do, *if* we want to master life technically? *Whether,* however, we want to and should master it technically, and whether that really and truly makes sense, is never examined, or simply assumed." The scientist who does not restrict himself to determining facts, but also wishes to ask about value and right action should be told that "the prophet and the demagogue do not belong on the podium of a classroom."

"Purposive rationality" is a method-and-means rationality for achieving ends, but it is not responsible for the rationality of these ends themselves. Values are felt or posited, not known. Weber's position arose from both the fascination of his time with the precision and reliability of the natural sciences, and from his study of the history of religion. He knew the prophets and the false prophets. He knew that the questionableness of their convictions was matched only by the pathos with which they proclaimed them. He distrusted surreptitious value judgments and politics flowing from the "romanticism of revolutionary hope." He had seen Treitschke in his youth.

The negative side of this position is that it surrenders to subjectivity and power all the areas that cannot be mastered with the help of empirical science. Therefore, first von Krockow ranked Weber among the decisionists. At the Heidelberg Sociological Congress of 1965, a faction under the leadership of Herbert Marcuse (for whom the task of sociology consists in changing society) raised the objection against Weber that he, like all mere empiricists, strengthened the status quo as a sociologist—not as the politician that he also was.

Weber saw rationalization as the law of science and consequently he approved of it, while simultaneously remaining aware of its limitations and dangers. He followed the "shifting battle" between goal-oriented and charismatic action, between rigidity and originality in intellectual and political life. He often complained of the disenchantment resulting from rationalization. He also spoke of the drastic change whereby the economic and technical means, originally devised for the end of human emanci- pation, became ends in themselves and froze into a "steel-hard hull" of "submission." After the Russian Revolution of 1905 he himself hoped that this economic and technical prison might be smashed, and he asked "whether a mighty rebirth . . . or mechanized petrification" loomed in the future.

Georg Lukács

In his essay on reification (the objective basis for the subjectively-felt alienation), Lukács uses Marx as his point of departure. According to Lukács, the alienation described by Marx results from the variously applied but always identical principle of the artificial fragmentation of original wholes (a motif that can be traced back to Rousseau, Humboldt, and Schiller, who however hoped to regain the totality lost in reality only indirectly, through education and art). As economic rationalization, according to Marx, sees in things no longer their utility but only their value as commodities, it also reduces the worker simply to a function of his measurable labor power which is also bought and sold as a commodity. It ignores his individual qualitative characteristics unless they disturb the precalculated course of the work process. No longer the complete man living from his own center, he is now the bearer of the work process, fitted as a component into an alien system, which he finds preexisting and finished, without his participation, and demanding his submission to its mechanical laws. He produces only a part of the product and so does not objectify his personality in it. The end product does not belong to him for his use, nor does he receive compensation equivalent to his share of his input. Thus rationalization by no means frees man, but on the contrary reifies him. It also reifies the relations of men among themselves, as well as those of the individual to himself. This reification, however, is a necessary consequence of fragmentation, the separation of the parts from a living whole.

According to Lukács, while rationalization subjects every partial field of social life to necessity and order, chance prevails in the relation of the relatively independent partial systems among one another. Total calculation in matters of detail therefore coexists with the incoherence and irrationality of the total process, since rationalization, as we saw, divides the organically unified work process into artificially isolated partial functions, each carried out more effectively and with maximum timesaving by a specialist. Consequently, partial functions tend to become independent and further develop, each in its own way, unrelated to the others, following only the logic of their own specialty.

Here the objective whole of civilization no longer has any inner unity, which is absent as well on the cognitive level. Every science—the more highly developed, the more so—shuts itself off in its own field. It even loses sight of the whole of its field. It restricts itself to specialized sublaws of its field, but not to its concrete substratum of reality. Scientific understanding itself becomes reified. Thus, as Marx saw, use value lies beyond the field of observation of political economy.

By departing from the material substratum of the formation of their concepts, the individual sciences consciously reject the knowledge of the whole context of their field. Even philosophy does not see through the reification underlying the formalism of the individual sciences. Science gains precision and credibility precisely by leaving its substratum in unexplored irrationality. When philosophy is based on the conceptualizations of the individual sciences, the connecting whole of the fields remains unknown.

A multiplicity of individual sciences, separate from one another in object and method, move in rational partial systems. Within them reason can operate unimpeded, with unproblematic categories, but it thereby loses the "true category of reality," totality. It can thus neither conceptually reproduce society nor lead it. It could do both again only by consideration of the totality, unscientific as that may seem.[2]

Because the sciences give close, detailed views, a view of the whole gained at a greater distance is needed in addition to them, as Lukács's teacher Georg Simmel had already pointed out in his critique of positivism. Lukács's achievement consists in "deacademicizing" Simmel's theorem by demanding not only a metaphysics of all being, but a comprehension of the whole society, and concomitantly that real society again become truly whole. The impulse given by Lukács lives on in Sartre's "dialectical totalization" of the historical process (critique of dialectical reason), but even more so in the Frankfurt School. No element can "be understood even in its functioning without insight into the whole." "Every opinion about society as a whole necessarily transcends its scattered facts," resulting in a concept "in which the disparate data are organized" (Adorno). At the same time, the "totality" is not only a structural principle, but also the (axiomatic) principle of society. It contains a norm for the critique of existing reality and a goal for history. This two-pronged attack against empirical social research proceeds by showing the latter to be inadequate because it deals with incoherent details and is value-free.

Theodor W. Adorno

Following Lukács, Horkheimer and Adorno claim in their *Dialectic of Enlightenment* that we are witnesses to the Enlightenment's self-destruction. The Enlightenment has become retrogressive and must therefore reflect on its own regression. Abdicating reflection on the destructiveness of progress would seal its own fate.

This retrogression is based on two sources. Scientism, which limited science to determining facts and to mathematization replaces the concept by the formula, the cause by the rule and probability. It translates qualities into functions and the positivist censor rejects as fiction, illusion, or meaninglessness everything that goes beyond the ritual of these formalizations. The other cause is the uncritical instrumentalization of science, dependent in part on the aforementioned formalization. Science, as analytical method, can no longer reflect upon meaning and value, or upon anything incommensurable, because these things cannot be broken down into mathematical formulas. In part the instrumentalization is conditioned by the fact that in this context science is concerned only with power and so only a reified form of thought can result. The goal is not the truth of an appropriated content, but method, operation, the effective approach, technology, and organization. Enlightenment consequently degrades even awareness and revolution to mere means.

In its roots and idea, enlightenment, according to Horkheimer and Adorno, is antiauthoritarian: Reason is a means of criticizing all domination. It seeks not only to perceive, classify, and calculate what is, but also to negate by seeing through the surface of social constraint, and by measuring the present against an idea of better reality and fearless happiness. As bourgeois enlightenment however it loses itself to its positivist factor—not only in Comte, but as early as Turgot and d'Alembert—and thereby renounces its own fulfillment. The factual remains unchallenged, repeated by cognitive reason, merely perpetuated by pragmatic reason. In science, the Enlightenment's critique of the existent becomes indifferent toward the prevalent value system. Indeed science consents to it as a means for self-preservation and accommodation. Scientific enlightenment no longer serves freedom, but only the self-preservation of the apparatus, which by better providing for our maintenance, at the same time subordinates and equalizes us. "By putting everything individual under its discipline, it lets the uncomprehended wholes of freedom, of domination over things, strike back at man's existence and awareness." The whole itself becomes a positive fact, whose unchangeable givenness must be subdued and subordinated, together with the constraint it exercises upon things and men. "Under the title of the brute facts, the social injustice from which they stem is sanctified as eternally removed from any remedy."

So enlightenment reverts to mythology. The two hopelessly mirror only existing domination and elevate the existing reality to the level of an eternal norm. "The curse of incessant progress is incessant regression." Antirevolutionary rationalism establishes new domination. Reason, which freed man from nature's violence, now justifies man's violence. Society dominates by means of the same reason which broke nature's domination over man; one domination has merely been exchanged for another. Furthermore, man himself is counted as part of nature to be dominated. Reason does not grasp this, or at least draws no lesson from it. It continues to betray and subjugate us and to adapt us to a civilization which is inseparable from inhumanity and horrors. Reason, by shutting itself off from its own theoretical imaginativeness, surrenders the field to charlatanism, superstition, and political madness. The masses, educated only technically, are ready for despotism. That is not the work of the opponents of reason, but of the Enlightenment itself.

In late works such as *Negative Dialectics,* Adorno's negativism toward reason becomes even more acute. Emile Durkheim's sociologism already drew a parallel between the super- and subordination of concepts on the one side and the power of the tribe over the individual on the other; logical hierarchy reflects the social one. Classification is related to classes. The isolation of concepts from one another is an expression of the division of labor. In this sense, Adorno chooses a tertium between the sociological and logical realms, namely "domination," which embodies the essence of the enemy as such. Adorno seems to have adopted the Talmudic saying: "The difference between the present and the Messianic age is only that then the repression by the rulers will cease." For Adorno no such thing as legitimate or liberating domination exists. In a radio talk broadcast in 1965 Adorno opposed Arnold Gehlen's claim that the subject develops only in the framework and in the service of institutions. Adorno bemoaned the authoritarian and repressive essence of institutions, which violate and strangle the individual self. The relation between man's domination of nature and man's domination of man recurs, according to Adorno, structurally in the relation of the general concept to the nonconceptual particular being. When the general concept identifies particular being with its own conceptual content and so homogenizes it and disregards everything in the thing that could contradict this identity, it subjects the thing to itself. The particular is subsumed in the general and is completely determined by the general's tending to domination.

The parallelism between sociotechnical domination over nature and man and cognitive domination of the concept over the known is not merely formal. Rather, the cognitive domination also constitutes, for Adorno, the basic cause of the sociotechnical one. Thus, reason is by no means the humane authority to which we can appeal when faced with inhumane domination. Instead, reason itself is to blame for this inhumanity, because it too derives from the will to dominate. Indeed, for Adorno, this intimate affinity with domination characterizes not only instrumental, technological, scientific reason, but all reason, even when it apparently—and therefore never successfully—resists the former, as does intuitive or dialectical reason.

Like reason, our entire awareness and the structure of our self are stamped by domination. Human qualities and capacities no longer seem to belong to a living unity but rather appear split off as if one "owned" them. The instrumental attitude toward external nature avenges itself when it is redirected toward our own inner nature. The subjugation of the nonself implies that the self too be fashioned in the image of the "identical, purpose-oriented masculine character." The objectification of solid things in the world around him leads retroactively to "self-reifi-cation." Bergson's warning, echoed by Heidegger and Jaspers, is thus linked with the theme of reification.

The perversion of the self by models of domination and reality has, however, still not permeated the "mimetic" strata in us, which formerly were predominant and have survived to our day. This distortion did not begin at any particular point in history, but has grown increasingly serious. It is located in a natural propensity of our mind and this is, in part, even necessary. Consequently, it would be an illusion to believe that the self could, by its own enlightening power, abolish the alienating conditions to which it is subject.

While reason promises to free man as a subject from domination by nature, it really enslaves him as an object of its own domination. This reversal of the subject into an object, already described by Marx, cannot be grasped by reason precisely because it always operates from a subject and because external liberation appears to be successful. Thus reason lives habitually under the spell of a self-induced blindness.

Still Adorno does try to break free of the logic of domination by means of "unregulated experience," by grasping the individual from the core of its individuality, and not from a previously fixed conceptual schema. New Philosophy aims for the nonidentity of the liberated multiplicity. "The reconciled state does not annex other reality by philo-sophical imperialism, but would allow other reality to remain remote and different, though in permitted proximity." The other thing should, as John Duns Scotus said, never be a mere "example of" something; it should, as in Rickert, be respected in its ungeneralized historical unique-ness. This is not merely true of knowledge: even in action one should live and defend the particular against universalistic reason.[3]

In addition to an attitude in which man subjugates nature, Adorno recognizes another attitude which he calls "mimetic"; in it the magical early age in turn submits to nature to save itself from this superior power. Only civilization represses this mimetic basic attitude. However, for Adorno as for the romantics, prehistorical properties of man survive in art and reappear even today. In an instrumentalized, purposive, nature-exploiting world, art is the last asylum of mimesis. It indirectly represents this other world, in which the repressive identity constraint of the self would again be loosened. Art remembers and promises. It is memory as refuge in a world that keeps us from our destiny. It could disappear as soon as we are allowed to fulfill our destiny.

However, the logical relation is not a relation of domination, for the simple reason that it is not a relation in reality. While domination is exercised from the outside, the concept only selects isolated factors that already existed in the thing itself. The concept is not related to the thing as the stronger to the weaker, but as the general to the particular. It does not abuse it, does not despise it, does not subject it to serfdom, does not deprive it of its surplus value, but tries to understand it and to give it a place in the coordinate system of an intellectual order. If subsumption by itself were a crime of brutal, elitist occupiers, mankind would have to give up speech along with reason; for words too are subsumptions.

Conceptual knowledge tends to regard the subsumed concrete object as already totally known. Therefore the late eighteenth century rebelled against the autocracy of conceptual knowledge, as Meinecke showed in his book on historicism. Now one wants to observe things not only in their development but also in the unmistakable specificity of their being-more-than-a-specimen, which they share with no other being. Yet this represents no alternative to conceptual knowledge. The concept already grasps certain traits of the thing and so prepares the way for deeper penetration into its individuality, which then reveals the pallor of the concept and, in extreme cases, its inappropriateness. The opposition is old, but it was left to Adorno to use it to denounce generalizing reason in its entirety as a realm of Satan.

Simply because the classified can be better mastered, used, managed, exploited, and made profitable, Adorno ascribes to classification as such an *interest* in domination and use. As Bergson showed, mechanism stresses the quantitative aspect because it looks at nature from the standpoint of applicability. Only the decline of this perspective permits nonquantitative, nonapplicable aspects to come to the fore: predominance of classificatory subsumption can be explained by interest. However, while its predominance is thus explained, the ability to classify is not. This ability to classify and quantify are both genuine intellectual achievements. What they show us of the world may be one-sided but not false, since both apprehend realities. What Adorno could attack would thus be only that certain interests lead to a too exclusive use of subsumptive reasoning even where it should not be applied. Interest is on the part of those who use instrumental reason perhaps even falsely due precisely to interest. The problem does not lie in reason itself, which provides as such a neutral basis of its application (though genetically it perhaps originated for such application).

If reason, as such, exercises a domination, it is not so much over things or other men as over nonrational forces within consciousness, or given a narrow understanding of the concept of reason, over its rational competitors. There is also a sociology of the soul: in it victors and oppressed face each other. Romanticism in the psychological realm parallels revolution in the political. It rehabilitates previously repressed elements and their achievement. Yet, while the liberation of the down-trodden social strata seeks to have them disappear as such, on the contrary, the liberation of the repressed psychic strata reactivates them precisely in their separate existence.[4] The repression of a social class is accompanied by a parallel repression of a psychic and rational layer among the oppressed. The rulers want to lull revolutionary ideas among them, while at the same time power robs the rulers themselves of their alertness.

Max Horkheimer

In his *Critique of Instrumental Reason,* Max Horkheimer completes his friend's philosophy by arguing that reason evidently comes to its senses when it denies its own absoluteness. For antiquity and for Leibniz, reason was not only a faculty of a subject but was also an objective order of reality. Subjective reason grasped this order as the true nature of things. Thus, human goals were rational not only due to their utility, but also because they appeared in harmony with the comprehensive rationality of the world. The antireligious and antimetaphysical Enlightenment destroyed precisely this context in the name of reason. Formerly ethics commanded us to obey eternal ideas that contained intrinsic value, but in Hobbes only rules for a smooth functioning of society remain. This self-abolition and instrumentalization of reason apparently is, to a certain degree, a necessary part of its nature.

Thus a substantive and a functional rationality—the latter already stressed by Max Weber—stand in opposition: one perceiving ideas, the other merely finding means for purposes, which may themselves be extrarational. The latter is at the same time more subjective and formalized. The dangers of objective reason are romanticism and ideology, while the dangers of subjective reason are materialism and nihilism. The task of philosophy consists in uniting the two wings of reason intellectually to prepare their unification in reality. As Kant interweaves empiricism and rationalism into the transcendental method, Horkheimer attempts to link instrumental and substantive reason.

The formalization of reason has, in part, great merits, although pragmatism and positivism have followed too much in its wake. If concepts are only nominalistic abbreviations, work-saving devices in a thought process reduced to the level of an industrial process, then not only are such concepts as mind, consciousness, and self lost as themes of reflection, but so are others, such as justice and tolerance. They are still in the lawbooks, but they have been cut off from their intellectual source. Reason no longer sanctions them, for it is no longer capable of determining the goals of life. That justice and freedom are better than injustice and oppression cannot be verified positivistically. The neutralization of reason robs it of every relation to ideas and the power to judge and discover them. It registers facts, forgetting that they could be the product of alienation, and therefore stops prematurely without connecting them to the social process. Positivistic intelligence becomes the servant of the existing production apparatus. Thus, the greatest task of reason is to denounce what is now called "reason."

Reason, which performs a service in the given social whole, is confronted by Critical Theory. It is opposed to a reason which recommends subordination to strong force, if that is useful to the subject, a reason which, in a struggle for survival, will make an object of the other person and deny him his freedom. Critical Theory restores an idealistic concept of reason which is, as such, connected with "interest in the abolition of social injustice."

Herbert Marcuse

In *One-Dimensional Man,* Marcuse follows the last reformulaton of the idea of reason to the effect that instrumental, value-free, or technical reason, as he calls it—i.e., a partial rationality—is all that remains in advanced industrial society. Despite rising rational capacities in parts of the system, the political system as a whole is consequently irrational. The rational functioning of industrial civilization appears to conceal this deep irrationality, while it essentially reverses even its internal rationality in the partial areas into their opposite. For romanticism, progressive reason kills organic growth; for Marcuse, insufficiently perfected reason kills itself.

The irrationality of the rational leads to increased productivity accompanied by increased destructiveness. This irrationality appears in the welfare state's military adventures. Because the killing is calculated, the madness is accepted. Similarly manipulated needs are inculcated into men by the power of suggestion through the mass media to keep production stable or to increase it. Needs no longer arise in the individual but in the autonomous technical and economic process. The vicious circle of irrational needs and instrumental reason produces these needs and then in turn is supported by them because only it can satisfy them. Satisfaction of these apparent needs increases work but not happiness. Thus, Marcuse turns into an accusation what Galbraith and Brzezinski had observed to be a law: A system always programs men, it satisfies *their* needs as they adapt to *its* needs.

By stabilizing existing power relations, mere technological rationality becomes irrational. Apparently "only" technical, it also has political implications just as it historically sprang from a class interest. It raises and secures the standard of living and comfort of the individual, but not autonomy and freedom from coercion. Its rationality becomes suspect. The rational apparatus frustrates its original purpose of bringing about a humane existence in which all functions are freely developed. Its striving is now to perfect technological rationality only within the framework of existing institutions while maintaining the given conditions of domination. Its goal is only self-reproduction and not rational change, which is limited to a corrective within the given system. The enslavement of man is considered inevitable when unfreedom is rationalized.

A society so structured tends toward the totalitarian, toward the elimination of opposing individuals, even if it is (still) not politically terroristic. Instrumental reason increasingly dominates human life. The same scientific method that succeeded in subjugating nature now subjugates man, for it is as such neutral. While domination was criticized and abolished by Enlightenment reason, it is legitimated by technological reason. It produces "a rationally totalitarian society." Its triumph, however, is to so restructure the actual subjugation that it becomes unnoticeable. Heteronomy, whereby we must adapt and restrict ourselves, appears in the mask of autonomy. Technology becomes ideology, because coercion appears as submission to a reason that has arranged everything optimally. By fulfilling our material wishes better than ever, it lulls the desire for liberation so skillfully that men accept repression without protest, build it into their own self-consciousness. They find their soul in their commodities.

While formerly the dominated stood separate from their masters on the upper end of the hierarchy, today domination is no longer exercised by human subjects, but by the anonymous and almighty system itself. Of course, there are groups that have greater managerial power that profit more, and that therefore are all the more interested in preserving the system, but they too are only servants of the expanding apparatus. They become "more and more dependent on the machinery which they organize and operate." They cannot declare as false any of the needs whose satisfaction the machinery promotes and stop its satisfaction. The system is really dominated by the anonymous, inherent tendency to create ever new needs and produce ever new means to satisfy them.

The same quantifying reason which separates *what is* from *what should be* and therefore presents itself as value-free is also the one that does not understand contemporary reality. Operationalism in the natural sciences and behaviorism in the social sciences no longer transcend the status quo. Empirical sociology investigates, in false isolation, a single factory, but not the sociohistorical context in which it stands. Its measurements thereby obscure more than they clarify. Their exactness is a mystification, since the social context is what determines the fact. Without that context, which constitutes a higher order of reality, the fact cannot be understood. Of course, the social context cannot in turn be measured. Rather, a *theory* of society is needed. Modern society exercises domination but makes it invisible and intangible. Thus, it has created a corresponding sociology incapable of recognizing domination. Science no longer transcends the given form of society, but performs only a therapeutic function and thus helps conserve it: It promotes quietism.

Rationality is not an absolute, unchanging factor, but relative to the respective historical moment. Historical development and changing reality expose rationality to be still irrational: Reason becomes nonsense. Contemporary rationality is also disavowed by the fact that it wants to perpetuate the status quo. It calls theories that contradict the existing universe irrational, while they are the rational ones precisely because they refuse to cooperate with madness. It is always a function of philosophy to recognize the irrational in existing reality and to design the "concrete negation" to it. According to Marcuse, this function today is allotted to so-called posttechnical rationality. It can propose an alternative only if it does not shy back from passing a value judgment on the existing system and critically transcending it. Yet this has become a most difficult task since the system has so increased its efficiency, raised its standards of living, and is so skilled at obscuring its inner contradictions that the quest for an alternative soon comes to be seen as unreasonable.

Strengthening any of the partial rationalities of the present system can only contribute further to the irrationality of the whole. It would be an intensification of repression and destruction, which are the work of this false rationality. Therefore, mere reforms, improvements in detail, are of no help, but, on the contrary, serve the bad whole. What is necessary is a revolutionary change of the system itself, a "reversal of the trend." But that means a "break with the prevalent technological rationality."

The domination of nature and the production apparatus will remain in existence. Marcuse is not advocating a rejection of technology, but only a different one which would bring its now unguided, arbitrary, and unendingly expanding process under control. In the future, an authority would be needed to first decide on the worthiness of satisfying needs and to establish priorities among them. The domination of the means over the end must be reversed; the independence of technical forces by which they imposed themselves as a criterion for men must be ended. They must reappear as services for a meaning in life that they do not produce. The achievement principle, by which men are evaluated only by efficiency and utility, must be displaced by the pleasure principle.

A consciousness rejecting a work ethic that subjects things and itself to practical economic ends will develop a "new sensitivity: an emancipation of the senses." While the supposed autonomy of bourgeois knowledge still serves an interest, only a future society will give us the astonishing fascination of a utility-free perception. But can the social continuum be at all broken by rational critique? Does the truly rational, the idea of how life could be better, have a place today—so Marcuse deliberates in closing—only in fantasy and literature?

It has often been observed that two forms of criticism of the modern world run side by side in Marcuse: a conservative one and a Marxist one.[5] If he originally underemphasized the bourgeois values of "interiority" because in their apparent independence they left the status quo untouched, later, after technological rationality has become the main enemy, these same values become allies in the struggle against the "administrative pre-emption of culture by civilization." This formerly rejected aporia is now reaccepted (analogously to "community" and "society"). Likewise, Marcuse's "great refusal" does not want to be conservative, but it seems to be so, since it is not a "determinate negation" and thus represents an existentially anarchistic attitude rather than a political, society-changing force.[6]

Jürgen Habermas

According to Habermas, experimental science does not function in society as an enlightenment fostering emancipation, but merely broadens our power over objective processes. It perfects administration. All efforts to comprehend the living context as a whole, as well as all positions based on value (and thus also the sensitivity to repression and the feeling of attachment for individual freedom) seem dogmatic to it. These elements of enlightenment are dismissed by the binding interest of a disinfected reason. Its monopolization of the claim to shape human behavior rationally implies the rejection of all other possibilities. Thus Habermas too, like all the members of the Frankfurt School, contrasts two forms of reason: a higher one interested in essence, context, and value, and a lower, more superficial one.

On the other hand, the value orientation of our behavior remains unchanged as before, but since the priority of one value over the other cannot be established by empirical reason, the choice is left to unsupported subjective decision. The progress of mere technical rationalization is bought with a proportional increase of irrationality. Without becoming aware of its dependence, empirical theory depends on the interest of domination over natural and social reality and the interest in maintaining existing domination.

In contrast, Habermas considers our chances of clarifying value problems and attaining rational agreement on them limited, but greater than positivism believes. Contrary to a "false consciousness" that shuts off reflection at the limits of verifiable science and so gains a disguised normative function, he postulates a Critical Theory that keeps reason's interest in freedom, autonomy, and liberation from dogmatism intact.

According to Habermas (in "Technology and Science as Ideology" and elsewhere) it is necessary to make a distinction between work and "interaction" or "communicative behavior." The sphere of work is that of instrumental, goal-oriented reason, the type of reason that deals with the choice of strategies and the use of techniques under fixed goals and in given situations, but does not reflect on the context of interests within society as a whole. In the sphere of interaction, on the other hand, reason seeks an understanding of the suitability and desirability of the inter-subjective norms. In the former case, under "work," rationalization means increase of skills and productive forces, extension of technical disposable power. In the second case rationalization means the progress of emancipation, the liberation of humanity, individualization, domination-free communication, abolition of repressiveness and rigidity. Here the intention of rationalization is not a better functioning of the economic-industrial apparatus, but what Plato and Aristotle called the "good life" and with it a change of the institutional framework. Thus technical progress is a potential for liberation only when it is imbedded within such a change.

Today discussion centers on "what we want in order to live" and not on "how we would like to live." Technical questions are solved, while practical goals are assumed as given. Technology becomes a technocratic ideology. There is no authority to determine the goal of technical progress, rather progress takes its goal immanently from within itself and claims that it is therefore acquired rationally. Yielding to "technical requirements," the depoliticized society becomes, as it were, a self-regulating system. It does not act according to norms, since its behavior is conditioned and adaptive. This conceals the difference between goal-oriented rationality and "interaction," and represses the emancipatory interest. The system reproduces itself without reflecting on whether the results correspond to our ideas of ourselves. However, social science ought to recognize that scientific and technical progress by itself remains questionable as long as it is not mediated by an externally determined direction.

Weber criticized the prophets who wanted to introduce values into science. Critical Theory again takes up this discussion and seeks a middle ground retaining the validity of each pole: Valuations are necessary but science itself, a different science, will make them. Habermas sums up the nature of this science with Jaspers's term, the "communicative": Values are to be discovered and viewpoints brought closer in undistorted discussion. But this disregards two factors. First, viewpoints can, despite all discussion, remain unreconciled, when each claims to have reason on its side. The new science could turn out to be aporetic involving irresoluble contradictions. The discussion takes place not only between divergent views and interests but also between different forms of reason. That is one of its justifying motives, but it is also the source of its danger to fail. This already implies the second factor. The alternative between a form of reason that finds means to fulfill goals and a form of reason that finds the goals in communication is considered only from the viewpoint of science. However, goals are not found only—if at all— scientifically or philosophically, nor are they only postulated by "prophets." They are dictated by wielders of power (who then also appropriate science and change it into a pseudoscience).

Notes

1. Cf. Christian von Ferber, "Die Werturteilsstreit 1909–1959," in *Logik der Sozialwissenschaften,* ed. Ernst Topitsch, 3rd ed. (Cologne, 1966).
2. Cf. Lucien Goldmann, "Reification," in *Dialektische Untersuchungen* (Neuwied am Rhein: Luchterhand, 1966). Society is seen as a "structured totality" in which no single factor dominates. The economic sector predominates only because capitalism separates it off as an autonomous reality. Thus religion, morality, and art also become independent. Reification rules in all these arbitrarily isolated realities. The leap to freedom is the return to a totality in which the sectors are mutually interdependent.
3. Cf. Kurt H. Wolff, "Surrender and the Body," in *Cultural Hermeneutics,* vol. 2 (Dordrecht and Boston, 1974): We abandon "received notions" only in the experience of "surrender."
4. Landmann, *Die absolute Dichtung* (Stuttgart, 1963), pp. 32ff., 119ff., 189ff.
5. Cf. Jürgen Habermas, in *Antworten an Herbert Marcuse* (Frankfurt: Suhrkamp, 1968), pp. 12ff.; ibid., Hans Heinz Holz, "Utopie und Anarchismus," pp. 15, 55ff.
6. How widely Marcuse's allegations against modern science are accepted today can be seen in a book from a completely different movement (theological and Heideggerian), which deals with the same weakness. Cf. Georg Picht, *Der Gott der Philosophen und die Wissenschaft der Neuzeit* (1966); Karel Kosik's *Dialectic of the Concrete* (Boston: Reidel, 1976) might also be mentioned.

7
Irrationalism of the Left

Arnold Künzli

Originally, Adorno's dialectic was a more or less positive one. Three historical events transformed it into a negative dialectic in which Adorno distanced himself sharply from Hegel's historical metaphysics and somewhat less sharply from that of Marx. The events were: first, the revolution that never materialized in the West, and then, second, miscarried in the East. And finally, there was Auschwitz.

Marx maintained the hope that his theory would soon penetrate the consciousness of the real revolutionary subject, the proletariat, and would thereby be transformed into praxis. He based his expectations on the fact that the theory he put forth was mediated through societal and historical developments, revealing the immanent principles regulating them. This hope came to naught on two counts: In the West, what happened is best expressed by the theological term "delay in Parusie" (*Parusieverzögerung*), meaning that "the revolution suffered the same fate as the second coming" (ND, p. 205). Adorno adds: "The attempt to change the world miscarried" and "the moment to realize it [philosophy] was missed" (ND, p. 3). In the East, there was also disappointment. The expected revolution miscarried; the Messiah turned out to be a false one—to stay with theological metaphors. Marx and Engels "could not foresee what became apparent later in the revolution's failure and even where it succeeded," namely, that "domination may outlast the planned economy" (ND, p. 322).

Since praxis failed to materialize and even its timeliness had passed, a call for philosophy and for a theory of society was revived. For a theory that claims to have been derived from Hegel and Marx, the "delay in Parusie" implies that it be critical vis-à-vis itself. The fact that the fate of this self-critical Critical Theory ultimately turned into a radically negative theory can be explained not only by the failure of the revolution to materialize and by the rise of a false Messiah, but also by the third decisive historical event—Auschwitz. With Auschwitz, the unforeseen and even unimaginable happened: In the phenomenon of Hitler a personification of the anti-Messiah appears on the historical scene. Adorno

133

thus became convinced that "anybody who still desired to philosophize would only be able to do so if the Marxian thesis is negated that the reflection is outdated. That Marxian thesis was based on the belief that a radical change of the world order was an imminent possibility. Today, only the hopelessly obdurate could envision such a change occurring which Marx still could think possible" (E, p. 23).

The conduct of philosophy in the form of a critical Theory of Society which relates itself to society and tries to grasp its truth is, therefore, the new business of the day. This means, however, that one pursues "the melancholy science [of] the teaching of the good life" (MM, p. 15). It is indeed a melancholy science because "he who wishes to know the truth about life in its immediacy must scrutinize its estranged form" (MM, p. 15). Adorno's premises are therefore that truth and alienation interlock, giving his conception of truth a sociological character. "The idea of scientific truth cannot be split off from that of a true society" (PD, p. 36). It follows that truth means a value of life: The true life is the real and meaningful one, and the alienated one is false. Thus the criterion that distinguishes a true from a false life is not to be found within the realm of epistemology or of formal logic; they have, after all, nothing to say about values. The criterion has to be an existential one: the basic experiences of want, suffering, and guilt. This experience communicates itself to thought and philosophy as a need which aims at abolishing want, suffering, and guilt: "Thinking contains the need—the vital need—at the outset—in itself. The need is what we think from" (ND, p. 408), states Adorno. "The physical moment tells our knowledge that suffering ought not to be, that things should be different" (ND, p. 203). This means that the physical moment will be the judge of what is true and what is false. Need then acquires an epistemological dignity if truth in the Adornoean sense can be brought at all to relate to epistemology. Truth is to be found where the need for transcending want, suffering, and guilt is satisfied. Epistemologically speaking, the judgment on the basis of need turns out to be a prejudgment, meaning, that want, suffering, and guilt not only should not exist but cannot exist.

As far as guilt is concerned, connecting it up with the concept of truth appears to be especially problematic. Its knowledge cannot be deduced at all from a physical need; and the thesis can be proposed that "existence at large has become a universal guilt context" (ND, p. 372). This thesis, however, implies that once a life existed without this guilt context and it could happen again. This demonstrates clearly that Adorno's philosophy and Biblical theology are related. True and false are philosophical conceptions in Adorno's thought but they really represent theological notions (*Vorstellungen*) from the tension field of "primordial guilt and redemption." At a later point, we will encounter explicitly the concept of guilt in Adorno's reflections.

The method of a critical theory of society to be applied in order to discover the truth about society—true society, that is—cannot therefore be that of formal logic. The main concern of formal logic is with finding the right concept and not the true life. Consequently, it analyzes only thought structures and propositions. But "thought . . . need not be content with its own legality; without abandoning it, we can think against our thought, and if it were possible to define dialectics, this would be a definition worth suggesting" (ND, p. 141). This statement makes it clear that dialectics and not formal logic will be chosen as the right method. The highest principle of formal logic is, after all, the absence of contradiction. The aim of Critical Theory is, on the other hand, to grasp the meaning of socially conditioned contradictions. Thus the correct method has to fit the experience of contradiction. Consequently, Adorno's choice will have to be dialectics as method because dialectics that is in itself contradictory will have the capacity to think contradictorily against itself. Therefore, Adorno can state that dialectic "is a challenge from below" and "not a variant of *Weltanschauung* . . . not a philosophical position" (ND, p. 303); nor is it "the merely existing reality [*kein schlicht Reales*]," because "to proceed dialectically means to think in contradictions, for the sake of contradiction once experienced in the thing, and against that contradiction" (ND, pp. 144–45). Dialectics is forced upon us by our own way of experiencing life in its contradictoriness that is marked by need, suffering, and guilt. There is no choice, we are condemned to dialectic. "The guilt of life . . . is what compels us to philosophy" (ND, p. 364).

This dialectic is driven by the impulse to recognize the essence behind the appearing Being and the general in the immediately experienced particular. "Appearance is always also an appearance of essence and not mere illusion" (PD, p. 84), states Adorno. "Reflections about society take off at the point at which mere understanding ends" (G, p. 140). Any "dialectical theory of society has to deal with central structural laws that determine facts, are manifested in them and modified by them" (G, p. 151). However, to take cognizance of the general in the particular is possible only if a dialectician possesses an idea of the general, be it in a vague way. This "general" is called totality in the Hegelian-Marxian dialectic. Totality means the sum total (*Inbegriff*) of contradictions because "society is one" (PD, p. 76); society "has more in common with the system than with the organism" (PD, p. 81). Totality is an interconnection that goes beyond individual facts and mediates them. It is the force of the whole that makes its influence felt in the sphere of the particular.

The isolated particular as immediately experienced fact is mere appearance and one cannot infer anything from it; its essence can be recognized if it is mediated by the whole, that is, by our search for the general that is manifested in the particular. "Dialectics unfolds the difference between the particular and the universal, dictated by the universal" (ND, p. 6). No element can "be understood merely as it functions without insight into the whole which has its source [*Wesen*] in the notion of the individual himself" (PD, p. 107). It has to be stated that this insight into the whole—to the cognition of the universal—is the crux of dialectics, because it poses serious epistemological problems. Critical Theory, however, never addressed itself seriously to the question of how to prevent that totality be grasped and/or be reflected upon in a false manner that could result in dialectical mediation between the particular and the general and wind up in a dead end. The question has to be asked: Was the truth about the whole a priori as obvious to Critical Theory as it was to Hegel?

This gap in Critical Theory is the more baffling since the category of the universal is given apriority in Adorno's dialectic: "Society precedes the subject" (ND, p. 126). Thus, Adorno says "to grant precedence to the object" (ND, p. 184) in order to establish this dialectic as a materialistic one: "It is by passing to the object's preponderance that dialectics is rendered materialistic" (ND, p. 192). For this reason, "there is no sensation without a somatic moment" (ibid.). With regard to the societal, Adorno speaks of "the absolute predominance of the economy" (MM, p. 58) in an almost vulgar Marxist manner, further of the "primacy of economy over psychology" (G, p. 13); and he does not exclude from consideration the possibility that "even mass murder [Auschwitz] is . . . explicable by the falling rate of profit" (MM, p. 234). It is due to the apriority of the object that the eradication of Jews as a group is interpreted as a moment in the "prehistory" of mankind that is nothing other than "the faithful shadow of developing productive forces" (MM, p. 234). Aside from the problematic nature of the conception of "matter" (*Materie*) in the self-understanding of the Frankfurt "materialists," it becomes questionable whether such an absolute positing of the primacy of the object remains compatible with dialectics; it is to be pondered whether even a thinker such as Adorno did not become a *terrible simplificateur* by applying an economic interpretation to the incomprehensible event of Auschwitz. An enlightenment that degenerates into positivism can lead to the self-destruction of reason just as a materialistic dialectic that attempts to reduce everything to the economic moment. Adorno fails to prove in what way a genetic connection can be established between Auschwitz and the Marxian dialectic of forces of production and relations of production—a relation that has since been challenged by Habermas.

Adorno makes certain categories absolute to satisfy the demand of his dialectic, to relate everything particular to a totality that makes understanding possible; otherwise there would be no dialectic. Therefore, totality "from below" (*von unten her*) is to be held on to under all circumstances; to Adorno it becomes "the all-penetrating ether of society" that is, of course, "everything but ethereal" (G, p. 160).

However, Adorno perceives two different conceptions of totality but rejects one of them categorically: the Hegelian concept of the whole as *Heilsgeschichte*—a totality that coincides with the concept of identity. Adorno's negative dialectics rejects the latter. The missed and miscarried revolutions and the horror of Auschwitz are basic experiences for Adorno which would not permit a *heilsgeschichtliche* conception complete with a premature design of a historical totality that had found its peace in identity. Reality, with which philosophy once thought itself to be one, has established (*erwiesen*) the "untruth of identity" (ND, p. 5). Adorno thus reproaches Marx and Engels "whose idealism was hardly anywhere as pronounced as in relation to totality" and accuses the "atheistic Hegelians, Marx and Engels, of deifying history" (ND, p. 321). Dialectics, however, means the consequent consciousness of nonidentity. Therefore, "totality can no longer be expected by philosophy" (ND, p. 136)— although, as we will see, it still does. Furthermore, the knowledge of the whole is excluded from the principle of dialectic in Adorno's *Minima Moralia*. As we will see, Adorno nevertheless claims to possess the knowledge of the whole. Thus, negative dialectics is simply an "anti-system."

At a later point, Adorno rejects the idea of a historical totality "as a calculable economic necessity" (ND, p. 323), and states: "Marx's expectation was overoptimistic with the primacy of productive forces in history which would necessarily burst asunder relations of production" (G, p. 159). However, Adorno is not against the primacy of the economy per se but rather against the Marxian thesis that economic developments necessarily lead to the right society. If and when historical totality's "claim to be absolute is broken—only then will a critical social consciousness retain its freedom to think that things might be different some day" (ND, p. 323). Idealist philosophy, including dialectics, was so inspired by its drive for the identity of the particular and the general that it repressed—indeed, liquidated—the particular from above, by the general. In other words, the Hegelian and even the Marxian concept of dialectic is a positive one. It appears as mankind's long journey, a kind of Calvary with stations, through a deified history with a certain expected positive outcome. History is thus perceived as a *Heilsgeschichte*. "It was the prototype for the idea of progress from Hegel to Marx" (E, p. 32).

Auschwitz means the involution of the negative in the historical process to such an extent (to be sure, Marx and Engels were aware of the negative in history) that after Auschwitz it has become impossible to regard this negative as one of mankind's necessary Stations of the Cross. It just will not do to shrug one's shoulders like Hegel did and state that the individual may have been wronged but this has nothing to do with history itself. Adorno mockingly remarks: "The world spirit's Hegelian migration from one popular spirit to the next is the Migration of Nations blown up into metaphysics" (ND, p. 341).

Before discussing the implications of Adorno's reflection further, let us take a brief look at the second form of totality which Adorno himself approvingly applies. Essentially, it is the totality of the society we live in and it determines us as individuals dialectically but it will disappear along with society: "Formulated provocatively, totality is society as a thing-in-itself (PD, p. 12). Since dialectic intends to burst open the totality of existing, "totality is not an affirmative but rather a critical category. Dialectical critique seeks to salvage or help to establish what does not obey totality, what opposes it or what first forms itself" (PD, p. 12). Speaking of totality in this sense, Adorno means bourgeois society mainly.

Adorno did not make the distinction always clear between the two concepts of totality, that is, totality as *Heilsgeschichte* and as existing-but-transitory society; we are not always sure which concept he was using on a specific occasion. Misunderstandings occurred especially during the course of the so-called positivism dispute. For this reason, we need to take a second look at the *heilsgeschichtliche* concept of totality. Because Auschwitz happened, all that is negative in history—even in less brutal and radical forms—underwent a qualitative change. Auschwitz represents a culmination of this negative, not something basically different. Adorno thus speaks of an "eons-old repression" (G, p. 57) or of an "eons-old-block" (ND, p. 298). One could say that after Auschwitz everything negative carries the stigma of Auschwitz and can potentially be radicalized into Auschwitz. Therefore "the administered world" shall be discouraged from the "most extreme liquidation of its members" if only "out of self-interest" (J, p. 32). But "barbarism continues to exist as long as conditions which made that regression [Auschwitz] possible continue to exist. This is the whole horror of it" (EM, p. 92). Societal pressure "drives men to the unspeakable, the culmination of which at a world-historical magnitude was Auschwitz" (EM, p. 92). This means, however, that a conception of history as *Heilsgeschichte* is no longer possible after Auschwitz. Adorno emphasizes that "after Auschwitz, our feelings resist any claim of the positivity of existence as sanctimonious, as wronging the victims; they balk at squeezing any kind of sense, however, bleached, out of the victims' fate. And these feelings do have an objective side after events that make a mockery of the construction of immanence as endowed with a meaning radiated by an affirmatively posited transcendence." He adds: "Such a construction would affirm absolute negativity" (ND, p. 361). Adorno's statement reverses the central proposition of the dialectic of Hegel and Marx concerning the dialectical leap by which there arises a new positive out of the negation of negation. Negative dialectics destroys all claim for identity; it is the "negation of negation that will not become a positing" (ND, p. 106). There is a qualitative difference between the negative as understood by Hegel and Marx and as it appeared in Auschwitz: Auschwitz is the manifestation of the radically evil. This negative is evil in a radical way because it can neither be surmounted (*überhöht*) nor done away with (*aufgehoben*); it can only be recognized in its absolute negativity.

The question should be raised whether Adorno has anything concrete to say about the road that led to Auschwitz. It has previously been pointed out that Adorno tried to make the connection between Auschwitz and economic development. It is not by accident that he never elaborated on his oversimplified thesis. He would ultimately judge Auschwitz as the (provisional) culmination of a civilization characterized by its unlimited drive for domination over nature and man—a civilization that transformed the reason of the Enlightenment into a merely instrumental reason, a *zweckrational* reason. Before Auschwitz happened, Horkheimer and Adorno could still believe in the possibility of the emancipatory effect even of technology: "It is nothing less than the hypostasis of scarcity, which in its social form has now been made obviously obsolete by the very technological development. . . . The only adequate response to the present technical situation, which holds out the promise of wealth and abundance to man, is to organize it according to the needs of a humanity which no longer needs violence" (P, p. 93). Moreover, Adorno was still able to demand that we make "the possible real" (P, p. 94). Coming from the position of negative dialectics, such a statement sounds quite positivistic. Adorno granted technology that "the abolition of labor" (P, p. 113) lies in its "essential nature" and wished to "contemplate a praxis which would explode the infamous continuum" (P, p. 117). A complete reversal of positions came first with the *Dialectic of Enlightenment*. Technology and the "abolition of labor" are dropped from consideration; rather, technology is accused of referring to method, the exploitation of others' work, and capital" (DE, p. 4), concluding that "what men want to learn from nature is how to use it in order wholly to dominate it and other men. That is the only aim" (ibid.). Horkheimer and Adorno reverse their former statements completely when they write that "it is unleashed technology" that is jeopardizing "fulfillment" (DE, p. 41). Later, in *Minima*

Moralia, Adorno even speaks of "the downfall of technology itself" (MM, p. 108). There is a sentence in *Negative Dialectics* that could serve as a motto for today's ecology discussions: "There is a universal feeling, a universal fear, that our progress in controlling nature may increasingly help to weave the very calamity it is supposed to guard against, that it may be weaving the second nature into which society has rankly grown" (ND, p. 67). The reason for this situation has been narrowed down to *Zweckrationalität,* which serves the will for domination over nature and man that civilization and nature have been almost hopelessly separated. A reason, however, that is merely means can be used—and misused— for any purpose, even for a purpose that turned into Auschwitz. Dialectics should bring reason to its reason and should mediate between means and ends, civilization and nature, to effect their reconciliation one day.

Returning to Adorno's concept of totality, the basic question is: Is it true that what could be learned from Auschwitz, namely, that the historical concept of totality and the deification of history are neither absolute nor valid any longer, and the postulate derived from this experience should yield a critical relation to totality that has helped Adorno to develop a new dialectic that now "must . . . turn even against itself" (ND, p. 406)? Is Adorno's statement valid that "negative philosophy, dissolving every- thing, dissolves even the dissolvent" (MM, p. 245)? In other words, did Adorno truly put negation, which once had a positive *heilsgeschichtliche* function for Hegel and Marx and became thereby the handmaiden of the absolute, into the service of a critical—even skeptical—approach that will not allow any absolutism, not even of its own? Has the change from a positive to a negative dialectic affected dialectic as such to become a truly critical, self-critical method of permanent self-reflection?

At this point, we have to examine Adorno's relationship to nihilism and skepticism. While skepticism elevates doubt to principle in a more or less radical manner, nihilism chooses nothingness as its principle. It should come as no surprise that Adorno's concept of critique and that of negative dialectics has no relation whatsoever to the methodical doubt of skepticism. He regards skepticism as a bourgeois attitude and asserts: "Bourgeois skepticism . . . is obtuse" (ND, p. 37). It is equally difficult to envision the compatibility of skepticism and dialectic, especially if the latter upholds the concept of societal totality. The essence of this dialectic is a definite negation and not the doubt. On the other hand, we can perceive a certain inclination to nihilism in Adorno's melancholy science. He asks, for example, "whether a condition with nothing left to hold on to would not be the only condition worthy of man," or "whether it would be better for nothing at all to be than something" (ND, p. 380). These questions are asked from the perspective of the Auschwitz experience: "For a man in a concentration camp," states Adorno, "it would be better not to have been born" (ibid.). On further reflection, however, Adorno is unwilling to endorse the "idea of nothingness" (ibid.) and keeps on searching for that last "haven of hope, the no man's land between the border posts of being and nothingness" (ND, p. 381). This amounts to a coquetry with nihilism, and the answer to the question regards the essence of Adorno's nihilism found here. Nihilism is, after all, one kind of absolutism, the absolutization of nothingness—if such a thing is imaginable at all. But this coquetry of dialectics with nihilism does not make such a suspicion farfetched.

Adorno makes some essential claims on negative dialectics which it could not fulfill, such as the demand that it abstain from absolutization and that it practice permanent self-criticism and even self-dissolution. He projects the experience of Auschwitz from the sphere of societal totality into that of historical totality; consequently, the latter retains its absolute character albeit with a negative indication. After having criticized Marx for his deification of history, Adorno describes it as an infernal process; history as *Heilsgeschichte* is transformed into a history of damnation. He states that the whole of Hegel is "not the divine absolute but its opposite made unrecognizable by thought" (S, p. 35), that is, the "absolute turned into absolute horror" (S, p. 106). He speaks of the "condition of the world that is heading toward catastrophe" (E, p. 23) and relinquishes the idea to comprehend "why the world that could be a paradise on earth today, may become hell tomorrow" (E, p. 24). Theory has to reflect on "the whole in its untruth" (ibid.). History is made demonic: "Things and men have assumed" a "demonically distorted form" (DE, p. 28). What will survive is the "progress towards hell" (MM, p. 234). By claiming that "the true identity of the whole" is the "terror without end" (MM, p. 235), Adorno unexpectedly turns into a philosopher of identity. The question could be raised here: Where in this negative identity can nonidentity be found, that is, the dialectical contradiction? Only the dogmatic statement exists that the historical dialectics is a "permanent transition or unchanging change" (G, p. 81). Hegel's world spirit finds itself resurrected in negation: "The world spirit is; but it is not a spirit. It is the very negativeness, rather" (ND, p. 304); "the reason of the world spirit is unreason" (ND, p. 317). It is negative dialectics in a simplified equation: By giving Hegel a minus sign, the calculus of dialectics is restored. Mankind is perceived as dragging itself along like an endless chain gang as if under a ban that "has become as omnipresent as the deity whose place it is usurping" (ND, p. 345). The radically evil, *the* evil, is promoted here to the world spirit. Adorno's negative dialectics is a theodicy reversed under a negative sign, indeed, a satanology. Hegel's "pathos grants the world spirit the only reality, echoing a hellish laughter in heaven" (ND, p. 347). Thus, "absolute negativeness is in plain sight" (ND, p. 362).

Adorno does not make a clear distinction between a comprehensive historical totality and a limited societal totality. It remains somewhat unclear whether and to what extent his absolute negativity is applied to Occidental society or the history of mankind as such, e.g., when he writes: "The world is systematized horror" (MM, p. 113). Adorno's attitude toward universal history is ambivalent. He regards it as problematic; universal history "must be construed and denied" (ND, p. 320). He then turns around and states: "After the catastrophes that have happened, and in view of the catastrophes to come, it would be cynical to say that a plan for a better world is manifested in history and unites it. Nonetheless, the unity that cements the discontinuous, chaotically splintered moments and phase of history—the unity that controls nature and aims at controlling man and, finally, man's inner nature—cannot be denied. No universal history leads from savagery to humanism, but there is one leading from the slingshot to the megaton bomb" (ND, p. 320). It is this "horror" that "verified Hegel and stands him on his head" (ibid.). The world spirit "would have to be defined as permanent catastrophe" (ibid.). These sentences justify the conclusion that Adorno has adopted Hegel's concept of historical totality albeit changing the plus sign into a minus one. His concept is somewhat less of absolute nature than that of Hegel and Marx; after all, Adorno's thesis does not actually say that the decline (*Untergang*) is inevitable although at times it comes quite close to saying so.

But Adorno does not remain unequivocally committed to his negative dialectics either: The positive reappears without warning through the theological back door as a legitimate child of negation. Adorno cites Samuel Beckett approvingly: "To Beckett, as to the Gnostics, the created world is radically evil, and its negation is the chance of another world that is not yet" (ND, p. 381). Not only is the disappearance of Ernst Bloch's "not yet" concept instructive, but the characterization of Beckett as a Gnostic sheds light upon Adorno himself. The question arises: Has "satanology" been used as a cover for theodicy, and did the description of the evil serve as a justification for the yearning for an Other, for the "entirely Other"? The proximity of negative dialectics to a negative theology is striking: "Negatively, due to the sense of nonentity, theology turns out to be right against the believers in this life on earth" (ND, p. 378).

In the course of his discussion of Spengler's work, Adorno is capable of perceiving in the positivity of negativity the only hope against the decline of the West. Decadence becomes "the refuge of a potentially better life. . . . The powerless, who . . . are to be thrown aside and annihilated . . . are the negative embodiment within the negativity of this culture of everything which promises . . . to break the dictatorship of culture and put an end to the horror of pre-history" (P, p. 72). To be sure, this was written before Auschwitz. But in the conclusion of a 1958 essay on Hegel, Adorno ascribed to negative dialectics the function of being the last possible negation that can result in position: "Insofar as philosophy determines the negativity of the whole, it fulfills for the last time the postulate of definite negation which is position. The ray which illuminates the whole in its parts as untrue is nothing more than utopia, the utopia of the whole truth that is still to be realized" (H, p. 104). In addition, negative dialectics is filled with Bloch's eschatological "spirit of utopia" which mitigates any sharp contrast between negative and positive dialectics. The main difference remaining is the fact that Hegel and Marx speak of the necessity of a position born out of negation while Adorno escapes into *conditionalis* in order not to be nailed down to any firm statement.

As a consequence, negative dialectics that was originally conceived as history of damnation turns into a positive *Heilsgeschichte*. Adorno makes the emphatic reference to transcendence, that is, he speaks of "experience that if thought is not decapitated it will flow into transcendence, down to the idea of a world that would not only abolish extant suffering but revoke the suffering that is irrevocably past" (ND, p. 403). Even dialectical reason will yield to this transcendence, that is, to "fate which reason alone cannot avert" (DE, p. 225). If reason cannot avert fate, what else remains besides that which is beyond reason? Adorno strays into the mystical and Biblical sphere to call his utopia by its true name, a utopia that is in reality nothing other than an eschatological concept and not even an inner-worldly one. Adorno thus speaks of the "messianic light" (MM, p. 234), of the "light of redemption" (ibid.). "Knowlege has no light but that shed on the world by redemption" (ibid.); all else is mere technology. In the face of despair, philosophy is for Adorno the means of reckoning, "to contemplate all things as they would present themselves from the standpoint of redemption" (ibid.). In the midst of *Negative Dialectics* there has been the attribution to materialism, a longing for "the resurrection of the flesh" whereby it concurred with theology (ND, p. 207). Adorno once refers to Augustine to justify his hope for redemption: "Augustine has recognized that redemption and history exist neither without each other, nor within each other but in a tension in which the piled up energies will ultimately demand nothing less than the *Aufhebung* of the historical world itself" (S, p. 34). Having accused Marx of deifying history, Adorno now goes beyond Marx in that he designs a dialectics of redemption and history that has not only lost its negative character but also now aims at transcending history as such. Auschwitz thus becomes a negation so absolute that redemption can be imagined only as a total *Aufhebung* of a historical world in which it could first occur. In consequence, however, Auschwitz would appear as the last definite negation, the negation of which would lead to the last position, namely, to redemption. Auschwitz thus would take the same role in Adorno's dialectics as the proletariat does in Marx's scheme. Adorno's dialectics—a negation of negation that cannot lead to a position—would have to lead philosophically to nothingness; only a Kierkegaardian leap can promise salvation. Adorno at one point contemplates the possibility that "the spell explodes" (ND, p. 346). Adorno's last thoughts are hopeful: "In the end hope, wrested from reality by negating it, is the only form in which truth appears" (MM, p. 98). As was the case with Bloch, Adorno is unable to state either epistemologically or in a practical political sense how to manage a leap from untruth to truth, from the realm of evil (*Unheil*) into the realm of good, and from unreason to reason. For Adorno, the dialectical unity of theory and praxis is irrevocably lost, and yet he holds on to a dialectic in which societal totality has the character of the absolute determining the particulars. Thus, Adorno got into the same bind as Herbert Marcuse: If the spell is absolute—how can the particular attain a position outside the spell that totality has imposed on it? Adorno is aware of this dilemma: "So we come full circle. Men must act in order to change the present petrified conditions of existence, but the latter have left their mark so deeply on people . . . that they scarcely seem capable of the spontaneity necessary to do so" (G, p. 147). Adorno sees as the only possibility the fact that thought grasped its own impossibility for the sake of possibility. Concerning the principle of negation, we encounter here a kind of mental acrobatics that somersaults and lands in the net of absurdity. This philosophical *salto mortale* into paradoxical practice seems to emulate the example of Kierkegaard.

Only those who, like Adorno, have to resort to such philosophical trapeze artistry negate the possibility of even a partial autonomy because they describe the existing as an absolutely negative societal totality by means of a radical, undialectical, and irrational condemnation. "Nothing particular is true" (ND, p. 152), states Adorno. Consequently, individuality too has to be bad if anchored in the existing. "No single thing is at peace in the unpacified whole" (ND, p. 153); Adorno reveals the "secret": "No individual happiness is possible which does not virtually imply that of society as a whole" (P, p. 87). "The whole is the untrue" (MM, p.

50) because the "thesis of totality itself is the untruth and also the principle of *Herrschaft* that has ballooned into an absolute" (H, p. 104). A logical conclusion could be that in that case the statement itself, "the whole is the untrue," is untrue itself. "Essence to begin with is the fatal mischief," states Adorno (ND, p. 167). "Each statement, each piece of news, each thought has been performed by the centres of culture industry" (MM, p. 108). Adorno accuses whoever wants to discover something positive in the existing of having "homicidal" tendencies. The defamation of the positive and its branding as "homicidal" is suspect; it also conjures up an Orwellian world of 1984 in which war means peace and love is hatred. Again and again, Adorno becomes the victim of his own tendency to absolutize, leading astray many of his basically correct insights and playing into the hands of those who reject Critical Theory for the sake of the preservation of the status quo. *Dasein* has become here total ideology, "semblance has become total" (P, p. 27). Society as totality excludes completely individual spontaneity because the whole rendered it powerless. Adorno projects a transcendental a priori of society: "That men are dependent on space, time and forms of thought shows their dependence on the species. . . . Imprisonment has been internalized" (S, p. 159). Consequently, "the transcendental subject can be deciphered as a society unaware of itself" (ND, p. 177).

Adorno characterizes the totality of bourgeois society as the domination of the principle of exchange value with its deceitful and exploitive fetishism of commodities. The principle of exchange "is fundamentally akin to the principle of identification . . . ; it is through exchange that nonidentical individuals and performances become commensurable and identical. The spread of the principle imposes on the whole world an obligation to become identical, to become total" (ND, p. 146). And "the domination of men over men is realized through the reduction of men to agents and bearers of commodity exchange. The concrete form of the total system requires everyone to respect the law of exchange if he does not wish to be destroyed" (PD, p. 14). Exchange value is "the formula used to bewitch the world" and "the fatality of mankind unfolds itself according to the law of exchange" (PD, p. 80). The world of exchange is a "world in which everything only serves a purpose, does not exist for itself" (H, p. 40). The domination of the exchange principle makes it impossible a priori for the subject to be a subject only; and he owes to society "its existence in the most literal sense. All its content comes from society" (MM, p. 154). All the impulses of men are "commensurable variations of the exchange relationship a priori" (MM, p. 229).

Adorno constantly refers back to the whole as "the evil" that condemns man to "impotence and apathy" (ND, p. 190). "Human beings are absorbed by the totality" (MM, p. 220) and are "totally manipulated" (G, p. 157); they are "powerless against the system" (ND, p. 89) and "helplessly dependent on the whole" (ND, p. 178). Hegel's world spirit, as far as it manifests itself in the totality of society, is to be defined as the *Zwang,* the "absolute suffering" and "permanent catastrophe" (ND, p. 320). Moreover, "the mind has always been under a spell" (P, p. 32). Therefore, "what is called communication nowdays" is nothing "but the noise that drowns out the silence of the spellbound. Individual human spontaneities . . . are condemned to pseudo-activity and potential idiocy" (ND, p. 348). People are "without exception spellbound and none of them is capable of love" (ND, p. 363). Adorno terms all that talk about humanism loathsome (*abscheulich*). In this world "no individual is capable of morality" (ND, p. 299); therefore, one cannot philosophize "that it is man as such who is central" (PD, p. 72). Unlimited goodness "becomes affirmation of all the bad that exists" (MM, p. 77); work and pleasure are carried out "under the protection of [the] hangman" (DE, p. 217). Adorno reaches the conclusion that "liberalism was the ancestor of fascism" (J, p. 49). Almost like a maniac, Adorno repeatedly perverts relative truth into absurdity by his absolutization. His tendency to absolutize begins with language—as is true with Marcuse. To characterize the existing, Adorno uses concepts and terms such as nothing, all, no, absolute, total, without exception, powerless; his concept of societal totality turns out to be closely related to Hegel's historical totality but it is also influenced to a no lesser degree by the absolutizing thought process of post-Kantian German idealism.

The question should be raised whether one can still speak of dialectic at all in a case where the spell reigns absolute. Where is the dialectical mediation between the particular and the general to be found? Was not the particular eliminated here too as it was in Hegel's thought on totality? This is true although the liquidation was not carried out "from above," that is, from the spirit, but "from below," from society. Since negative dialectics was shown not to have been consistently presented by Adorno as exclusively negative we have to ask to what extent it can still be considered dialectic. In any case, mediation here is a one-way street and the concept "absolute negation" itself could hardly be identified as dialectical. Absoluteness excludes mediation while dialectic is but mediation.

Another curious aspect of Adorno's philosophy has to be discussed. He proposes the thesis that totality cannot be verified like individual facts can because "the isolated observation through which it [Critical Theory] is verified belongs in turn, to the context of delusion which it desires to penetrate" (PD, p. 69). Because of this functional structure the notion of society cannot be grasped immediately nor can it be subjected to drastic verification as the laws of the natural sciences can" (G, p. 138). Insofar as this is true, "genuine reflection on the nature of society would begin precisely where 'comprehension' ceased" (G, p. 140). Totality, "unlike the individual social phenomena . . . is not factual" (PD, p. 13). With this categorical denial of the possibility of verification— or rather, falsification, if one wanted to side with Popper—the concept of totality becomes immune to scientific discourse; it turns into metaphysics. To be sure, totality should not be compared to individual facts since it cannot be measured, weighed, quantified; but does that mean that it is automatically excluded from all and any scientific discourse or possible verification? If totality cannot be subjected to the method of *Verstehen* or to verification, how can Adorno continuously refer to it and make statements about it? Why is it that Critical Theory refers to itself as an "objective Theory of Society" (S, p. 182)? If, as Adorno states, societal totality manifests itself primarily as that of the law of exchange, then it is not made clear why we cannot test Adorno's statements about the total spell (*Bannwirkung*) cast by this law of exchange. For example, should we not try to discover whether the individual is totally under the spell of that law to see whether there exist possibilities for spontaneity be they only temporary or partial? One strongly suspects that this self-imposed abstinence from testing had the exclusive purpose to shield these dogmatically absolutized theses from the scrutiny of critical reason.

Another interesting aspect of the problem with regard to the immunization of the totality concept is that the central concept itself remains unexamined. There is no discussion of the probability of other essential manifestations of societal totality other than the law of exchange. Should we not consider as such totalities, for example, positive rights, bureaucracies, technology—today especially—or traditional values? Furthermore, is there not a hierarchy of "totalities" ranging from the family to nations? How are these different totalities related to each other? Could a conflict situation arise between them or could they cancel each other out (*aufgehoben*)? Should we not consider the dialectic of totalities which would engender the need for a concept of a comprehensive totality?

The decisive problem is whether the reality that can be experienced really corresponds to Adorno's concept of societal totality, that is, the concept that we are determined by the law of exchange to even the most hidden and intimate spheres of our existence to such an extent that real communication or love is impossible as long as we remain under the spell of that totality and, moreover, that we are unable to extricate ourselves epistemologically from that spell. "If there is no true life in

the false, then there can be no true consciousness either," states Adorno
(E, p. 169). We have to ask: How did Adorno manage to receive *his*
permit (*Freipass*) to cross the borders of that spell—be it only in terms
of consciousness? Were the thesis about the absoluteness of the spell of
totality valid, we could not have had the revolutions and evolutions
throughout history that occur even under the law of exchange.

Everything points to the fact that the concept of totality acquired a
mythical character with Adorno. His concept of totality is directly related
to primordial sin and is in essence a *heilsgeschichtliche* concept and not
a rational category. It cannot be denied—especially in our time—that
there are societal forces that can cast a spell on the individual. It is
important to investigate the range of the spell to see whether it could
be neutralized or made ineffectual (*aufgehoben*), and whether the individual
can extricate himself from that spell. What would be needed is something
akin to a sociology and psychology of the relationship between the
individual and totality. Paradoxically, we would need a dialectic of totality.
The inconsequence of Adorno's thought lies in the fact that he does not
want to confess to the theological origin of his concept of totality and
spell or to identify it openly with "original sin." Rather, he attempts to
pin it down as an empirical category and identifies it with the law of
exchange. Adorno does not broach such subjects as whether there was
a spell before the law of exchange and whether a prehistory without spell
is conceivable. Hence his negative dialectics seems more and more like
a critical irrationalism albeit quite often without the critical impulse
suppressed by his dogmatic absolutizing.

It should be further noted that Adorno does not perceive need, suffering,
and guilt which are, after all, basic to his philosophy, in a dialectical
way. He sees our existence and history as characterized by Auschwitz;
but in spite of Auschwitz and other horrors that go on, Auschwitz does
not dominate every day and everywhere. There are not only need, suffering,
and guilt, but there is also a certain freedom from them. One expects
a dialectician to maintain ideas about dialectic of suffering and happiness,
guilt and responsibility, spells and freedom, and finally, need and security.

Curiously enough, Adorno starts out from the basic experience that
history has up to now been determined by need, suffering, and guilt—
demonstrative that history until now has been an *Unwesen*. How is this
conclusion possible when he speaks of "the outside world's impenetrability
for conscious experience" (ND, p. 179)? How can one claim insight into
the "law" of fate if reality remains impenetrable for consciousness, on
the one hand, and the law of totality cannot be verified, on the other?
Furthermore, since verification or falsification of totality is impossible
for Adorno, it is difficult to see how the three historical events mentioned

earlier—nonoccurrence of revolution, its miscarriage, and Auschwitz—become his all-determining experiences since they are based upon the empirical falsification of that idealistic identitarian philosophy and its dialectics that found its way into Marx's theory. It is not to be denied that the Soviet regime represents that societal totality that determines the individual fundamentally in the Adornoean sense. If totality as such cannot be tested, in what way and by what criteria is the basic thesis for Adorno's philosophizing to be won, namely, that the October revolution turned out to be a failure? And if negative dialectics characterizes itself as "the epitome of negative knowledge" (ND, p. 405), what type of knowledge is it that refuses to be tested? Does not revelation mean "knowledge"?

The unexamined and dogmatic pronouncements about the absolute validity of the spell seem to suggest that they were written by a paranoid or a neurotic. There may be something else at work here which could only be illuminated by our more thorough knowledge of Adorno's conscious and subconscious relationship to Jewry. T.W. Adorno discarded the Jewish name of his father "Wiesengrund," reduced it to a nondescript "W" that could stand for "Walter," and took on the name of his non-Jewish mother. Is it conceivable that Auschwitz acquired its significance for Adorno's entire philosophy and world view because it triggered certain personal feelings of guilt for not having stood up to the Judaism of his father? Are there in *Negative Dialectics* also moments of a personal atonement by "one who by rights should have been killed" (ND, p. 363)? Is it possible that a personal guilt feeling turned into an ideological pronouncement about the absolute guilt of the world?

On the question of paranoia, Adorno suggests in *Eingriffe* that he may have considered this interpretation valid: "The objective world seems to approximate the picture projected of it by persecution mania" (E, p. 168). It is an astonishing sentence that may have been prompted by previous suggestions of paranoia. Adorno may have had such a diagnosis in mind when he gave the subtitle *Injured Life* to his book *Minima Moralia*. Be that as it may, the proponent of the undisputable primacy of the economy over psychology cannot possibly accept a psychological interpretation of his *Weltbild:* "Whomever tries to comprehend the pathogen character of reality within traditional categories of human cognition falls prey to the same irrationality from which he wishes to shield himself by not betraying common sense" (ibid.). This says that the picture Adorno projects of the world is, according to psychology and common sense, that of a paranoid. However, the objective world approximates this picture in an increasing degree, thus annulling the pathological character of Adorno's projection by revealing the pathology in reality itself. Folly (*Wahn*) turns out not to be such because it coincides with reality.

In the same vein, Adorno states in another passage: "The dialectic cannot stop short before the concepts of health and sickness. . . . Once it has recognized the ruling universal order . . . as sick—and marked in the most literal sense with paranoia, with 'pathic projection'—then it can see as healing cells only what appears, by the standards of that order, as itself sick, eccentric, paranoia—indeed 'mad'; and it is as true today as in the Middle Ages that only fools tell their masters the truth" (MM, p. 73). Kudos to the fool—but there are fundamental differences between philosophical fools such as the priest depicted by Kolakowski (see the chapter "The Priest and the Jester" in *Toward a Marxist Humanism,* 1969) and a paranoid. Adorno declares that the paranoid is the cell of healing, the only healthy person, because he alone recognized the essence of reality as *Unwesen*. It seems to us that we encounter here the self-justification of a paranoid at its highest philosophical level.

What has to be fully appreciated is the way human suffering in general and its provisional culmination in Auschwitz, complete with corresponding human guilt in particular have become an overwhelming experience for a philosopher; and it has been transformed into a problem that philosophy can no longer ignore. Nonetheless, one has the uncomfortable feeling that Auschwitz exerts a certain fascination on Adorno: "The observation of evil is a fascinating occupation" (DE, p. 230); thus, the paralyzing effect of that event makes legitimate a fear of and an escape from praxis that traditional concepts characterize as neurosis. He who reduces all history to Auschwitz and would not avert his gaze from this evil (*Unheil*) that is beyond imagination and description will remain paralyzed like a person about to be bitten by a snake. Adorno's occasional coquetry with neurosis begs the question whether this attitude stems from his wish to remain paralyzed. In a fictional conversation about praxis, for example, he characterizes one participant—who is "unwilling to give up his right to think rather than become directly involved in praxis" (DE, p. 239)— as "the neurotic partner B" who "needs superhuman power if he is not to become healthy too" (ibid., p. 240). What Adorno means is that since the world is by all traditional standards neurotic, one must be neurotic to understand it—or at least to interpret it.

The emphasis here is not just on not giving up thought vis-à-vis praxis, but on the fact that this thought of negative dialectics has from the beginning superposed a taboo on praxis: Praxis should not mystify "its own immediate impossibility," states Adorno (S, p. 188); it is presupposed that praxis today is impossible. Another of Adorno's unreflected, dogmatic, and absolutistic propositions! Indeed, the works of

Adorno have been written "without practical intentions" (S, p. 190). Taken literally, this would mean that Auschwitz has become an aesthetic phenomenon. Adorno calls constructive criticism a "groveling criticism" (ND, p. 336) and states: "Positivity runs counter to thought" (ND, p. 19)—thinking is always something negative for Adorno. However, one continuously finds statements that contradict traditional sense as rationalization of an unconscious paralysis: "Neuroses are pillars of society; they thwart the better potential of men, and thus the objectively better condition which men might bring about. There are instincts spurring men beyond the false condition; but the neuroses tend to dam up those instincts, to push them back toward narcissistic self-gratification of the false condition. A weakness that will mistake itself for strength, if possible, is a hinge in the machinery of evil. In the end, the intelligible character would be the paralyzed rational will" (ND, p. 298).

Here and there, Adorno strives to overcome his deep-seated aversion to positivity and praxis. He speaks of the "love of things" although immediately corrects himself: "The spell . . . does not permit us to love" (ND, p. 191). Whenever Adorno discusses praxis, he becomes disarmingly banal: "Due praxis would be alone the effort to extricate oneself from barbarism" (S, p. 179).

The impression that Adorno's philosophy is essentially determined by his adamant—perhaps individual, psychologically conditioned—shying away from praxis and, consequently, from responsibility, is strengthened by his definition of philosophy, referred to earlier. Philosophy "does not allow itself to be nailed down" (ND, p. 109), and "only thoughts which cannot understand themselves are true" (ND, p. 48). He adds: in philosophy, "nothing is meant in a completely literal manner" (PD, p. 34). Therefore, Adorno rejects categorically "the desideratum of clarity" which is "questionable in a double sense" (H, p. 116). Clarity is a "fetish" (H, p. 170); lack of clarity is obviously not. Philosophy is thus something "floating" (ND, p. 109). One is reminded of Mannheim's concept of free-floating intelligence, which, of course, is contrary to everything Adorno stands for. Philosophy seems to be able to extricate itself from the spell. In any case, "according to its ideal, philosophical language goes beyond what it says by means of what it says in the development of a train of thought" (J, pp. 11–12). The underlying critical tone is obvious in Jürgen Habermas's essay on Adorno, entitled "A Philosophizing Intellectual" (Ü, p. 35).

Lastly, mention should be made of the ban on images carried over from the theological to the societal sphere. Adorno never tires of demanding "extreme faithfulness" to the ban on images "going far beyond its original . . . meaning" (S, p. 28). This ban is linked up with Hegel's "determinate negativity" which is defined as "pursuit of its [image's] prohibition" (DE, p. 24). It is only "in the absence of images that the full object could be conceived. Such absence concurs with the theological ban on images. Materialism brought that ban into secular form by not permitting Utopia to be positively pictured" (ND, p. 207). Dialectically speaking, everything is a "thing that comes to be, not a thing that is" (ND, p. 298); thus, the right condition cannot be described "as in the Jewish *theologoumenon,* all things would differ only a little from the way they are; but not even the least can be conceived now as it would be then" (ND, p. 299).

Negative dialectics understands itself as the philosophical articulation of the Biblical ban on images whereby it tries to make itself a home in the Old Testament. It can be considered the dialectics of Israel as can the positive dialectics of Marx whose proletariat is so unmistakably related to the people of Israel. For—and I am grateful to Max Geiger for this suggestion—the ban on images has a significant meaning not only for the whole Jewish history and in the Old Testament but it also goes beyond it since it is responsible for the special position of Israel among nations, for the difference between Israel's belief in God and other religious forms of the antique world. It expresses the idea that the secret of God—of an entirely Other—cannot be comprehended as a secret of the world. It also represents a warning not to draw God into our world, to put him at man's disposal in order to acquire access to him through a realization in this world.

It is by way of reference to the ban on images which legitimized negative dialectics's refusal to become positive that negative dialectics derived its origin from the Bible, especially from the Old Testament, and revealed itself as philosophically related to dialectical theology. It could prove fascinating to confront Adorno with Karl Barth. Helmut Gumnior entitled his interview with Horkheimer "The Yearning for the Entire Other," and referred to Horkheimer's statement: "Marx's thought in my opinion, was determined by the Messianism of Judaism; as for me, the main idea is that one cannot depict God but that it is precisely this state of nonpredictability that is the object of our yearning" (SA, p. 77). But this yearning is akin to a messianic expectation which we can glimpse in Adorno's work; and thanks to it, negative dialectics does not end up in nihilism. Human reason can only recognize the absolute negativity of the existing and call it by name. Everything else is yearning, hope, and expectation. The object of this yearning remains inexpressible. Therefore, a move toward the right life and right society cannot be a matter of human action. The ban on images corresponds to a ban on praxis. Man is permitted only to fill out the waiting time for his expectations with theory, with Critical Theory, which prepares him for the great change; but he cannot induce the change. Hence Critical Theory abandons the two fundamental theses of its early period: the belief in the emancipatory power of the interest of reason mediated through praxis, and the possibility of supporting this emancipatory interest with the help of human will. Human reason appears mainly as a receptacle for the light of transcendence: "No light falls on men and things without reflecting transcendence" (ND, p. 404). Indeed, the ban on images is only sharpened in the following passage: "Once upon a time the image ban extended to pronouncing the name; now the ban itself has in that form come to evoke suspicion of superstition. The ban has been exacerbated: the mere thought of hope is a transgression against it, an act of working against it" (ND, p. 402). Taken literally, not even hope may be called by its name anymore. Hope must remain without image because it is directed toward the "entirely Other."

This ban on images raises still another question. It is amazing to note from the beginning how easily Horkheimer and Adorno transfer the ban on images from religion and theology to the realm of society and theory without even reflecting on the problem. Only those who let themselves be guided a priori by a religious and *heilsgeschichtliche* conception of society can extend a ban referring to God to society. Society is thus given a numinous character; it is mediated by transcendence and its totality receives its light from the absolute. Nothing else seems to indicate better the absolute character of the totality concept of Critical Theory as its evocation of the ban on images. This is a further demonstration of Critical Theory's departure from dialectics; it comes out again for the absolute; it is not for a better society to be created tomorrow but for the true and right society yearned for that has to come at the end of history. One can make images of a better society, but one cannot do so about the only true one. Bedevilment of the existing by negative dialectics is inspired by hope for redemption. It is absolute negativity out of yearning for the absolute positivity. But it is precisely this thinking in absolutes, so dear to German idealism, that has always had devastating consequences in politics, especially when coupled with irrationalism which conceives of philosophy essentially as an aesthetic phenomenon, as a sister of music.

The radical students misunderstood Adorno completely when they took his eschatology that expected salvation "from above" at the end of history to represent Utopia, which should be put into praxis here and now by their own heads and hands. This misunderstanding has its tragic moments. Perhaps the "injured life" of Adorno with the accompanying humiliating conditions broke him. Some think it broke Critical Theory too. This interpretation, however, would overlook the fact that this Critical

Theory of the Frankfurt School contains a wealth of insight still effective and still able to deal with basic unresolved philosophical and societal problems.

Abbreviations of References

DE   Max Horkheimer and Theodor W. Adorno, *Dialectic of Enlightenment* (New York: Herder & Herder, 1972).

E   Adorno, *Eingriffe* (Frankfurt: Suhrkamp, 1968).

EM   Adorno, *Erziehung zur Mündigkeit* (Frankfurt: Suhrkamp, 1970).

G   Adorno, *Aufsätze zur Gesellschaftstheorie und Methodologie* (Frankfurt: Suhrkamp, 1970).

H   Adorno, *Drei Studien zur Hegel* (Frankfurt: Suhrkamp, 1969).

J   Adorno, *Jargon der Eigentlichkeit* (Frankfurt: Suhrkamp, 1969).

MM   Adorno, *Minima Moralia* (London: New Left Books, 1974).

ND   Adorno, *Negative Dialectics* (New York: Seabury, 1973).

P   Adorno, *Prisms* (London: Neville Spearman, 1967).

PD   Adorno et al., *The Positivist Dispute in German Sociology* (London: Heinemann, 1976).

S   Adorno, *Stichworte* (Frankfurt: Suhrkamp, 1969).

SA   Horkheimer, *Die Sehnsucht nach dem ganz Anderen* (Hamburg: Furche, 1970).

Ü   *Über Theodor W. Adorno* (Frankfurt: Suhrkamp, 1968).

8

Reason or Revolution?

Karl R. Popper

The trouble with a total revolution . . .
Is that it brings the same class up on top:
Executives of skillful execution
Will therefore plan to go halfway and stop.
　　　　Robert Frost, "A Semi-Revolution," in *A Witness Tree.*

The following critical considerations are reactions to the book *Der Positivismusstreit in der deutschen Soziologie* (translated into English as *The Positivist Dispute in German Sociology*), which was published in 1969[1] and for which I unwittingly provided the original incentive. I will begin by telling some of the history of the book and of its misleading title. In 1960 I was invited to open a discussion on "The Logic of the Social Sciences" at a congress of German sociologists in Tübingen. I accepted; and I was told that my opening address would be followed by a reply from Professor Theodor W. Adorno of Frankfurt. It was suggested to me by the organizers that, in order to make a fruitful discussion possible, I should formulate my views in a number of definite theses. This I did: my opening address to that discussion, delivered in 1961, consisted of twenty-seven sharply formulated theses, plus a programmatic formulation of the task of the theoretical social sciences. Of course, I formulated these theses so as to make it difficult for any Hegelian or Marxist (such as Adorno) to accept them; and I supported them as well as I could by arguments. Owing to the limited time available, I confined myself to fundamentals, and I tried to avoid repeating what I had said elsewhere.

Adorno's reply was read with great force, but he hardly took up my challenge—that is, my twenty-seven theses. In the ensuing debate Professor Ralf Dahrendorf expressed his grave disappointment. He said that it had been the intention of the organizers to bring into the open some of the glaring differences—apparently he included political and ideological differences—between my approach to the social sciences and Adorno's. But the impression created by my address and Adorno's reply was, he said, one of sweet agreement; a fact which left him flabbergasted (*"als seien*

Herr Popper und Herr Adorno sich in verblüffender Weise einig"). I was and still am very sorry about this. But having been invited to speak about "The Logic of the Social Sciences" I did not go out of my way to attack Adorno and the "dialectical" school of Frankfurt (Adorno, Horkheimer, Habermas, et al.) which I never regarded as important, unless perhaps from a political point of view; and in 1960 I was not even aware of the political influence of this school. Although today I would not hesitate to describe this influence by such terms as "irrationalist" and "intelligence-destroying," I could never take their methodology (whatever that may mean) seriously from either an intellectual or a scholarly point of view. Knowing now a little more, I think Dahrendorf was right in being disappointed: I ought to have attacked them using arguments I had previously published in my *Open Society*,[2] *The Poverty of Historicism*,[3] and "What is Dialectic?"[4] even though I do not think these arguments fall under the heading of "The Logic of the Social Sciences"; for terms do not matter. My only comfort is that the responsibility for avoiding a fight rests squarely on the second speaker.

However this may be, Dahrendorf's criticism stimulated a paper (almost twice as long as my original address) by Professor Jürgen Habermas, another member of the Frankfurt School. It was in this paper, I think, that the term *positivism* first turned up in this particular discussion: I was criticized as a "positivist." This is an old misunderstanding created and perpetuated by people who know of my work only at second hand: Owing to the tolerant attitude adopted by some members of the Vienna Circle, my book *Logik der Forschung*,[5] in which I criticized this positivist circle from a realist and antipositivist point of view, was published in a series of books edited by Moritz Schlick and Philipp Frank, two leading members of the circle;[6] and those who judge books by their covers (or by their editors) created the myth that I had been a member of the Vienna Circle and a positivist. Nobody who has read that book (or any other book of mine) would agree—unless indeed he believed in the myth to start with, in which case he may of course find evidence to support his belief.

In my defense Professor Hans Albert (not a positivist either) wrote a spirited reply to Habermas's attack. The latter answered, and was rebutted a second time by Albert. This exchange was mainly concerned with the general character and tenability of my views. Thus there was little mention—and no serious criticism—of my opening address of 1961 and its twenty-seven theses.

It was, I think, in 1964 that a German publisher asked me whether I would agree to have my address published in book form together with Adorno's reply and the debate between Habermas and Albert. I agreed.

But, as now published (in 1969, in German), the book consists of two quite new introductions by Adorno (94 pages), followed by my address of 1961 (20 pages) with Adorno's original reply (18 pages), Dahrendorf's complaint (9 pages), the debate between Habermas and Albert (150 pages), a new contribution by Harold Pilot (28 pages), and a "Short Surprised Postcript to a Long Introduction" by Albert (5 pages). In this, Albert mentions briefly that the affair started with a discussion between Adorno and myself in 1961, and he says quite rightly that a reader of the book would hardly realize what it was all about. This is the only allusion in the book to the story behind it. There is no answer to the question of how the book got a title which quite wrongly indicates that the opinions of some "positivists" are discussed in the book. Even Albert's postscript does not answer this question.

What is the result? My twenty-seven theses, intended to start a discussion (and so they did, after all), are nowhere seriously taken up in this longish book—not a single one of them, although one or other passage from my address is mentioned here or there, usually out of context, to illustrate my "positivism." Moreover, my address is buried in the middle of the book, unconnected with the beginning and the end. No reader can see, and no reviewer can understand, why my address (which I cannot but regard as quite unsatisfactory in its present setting) is included in the book—or that it is the unadmitted theme of the whole book. Thus no reader would suspect, and no reviewer did suspect, what I suspect as being the truth of the matter. It is that my opponents literally did not know how to criticize rationally my twenty-seven theses. All they could do was label me "positivist" (thereby unwittingly giving a highly misleading name to a debate in which not a single positivist was involved). Having done so, they drowned my short paper and the original issue of the debate in an ocean of words—which I found only partially comprehensible.

As it now stands, the main issue of the book has become Adorno's and Habermas's accusation that a "positivist" like Popper is bound by his methodology to defend the political status quo. It is an accusation which I myself raised in my *Open Society* against Hegel, whose identity philosophy (what is real is reasonable) I described as a kind of "moral and legal positivism." In my address I had said nothing about this issue; and I had no opportunity to reply. But I have often combatted this form of positivism along with other forms. And it is a fact that my social theory (which favors gradual and piecemeal reform controlled by a critical comparison between expected and achieved results) contrasts strongly with my theory of method, which happens to be a theory of scientific and intellectual revolutions.

This fact and my attitude toward revolution can be easily explained. We may start from Darwinian evolution. Organisms evolve by trial and error, and their erroneous trials—their erroneous mutations—are eliminated, as a rule, by the elimination of the organism which is the "carrier" of the error. It is part of my epistemology that, in man, through the evolution of a descriptive and argumentative language, all this has changed radically. Man has achieved the possibility of being critical of his own tentative trials, of his own theories. These theories are no longer incorporated in his organism or his genetic system. They may be formulated in books or journals; and they can be critically discussed, and shown to be erroneous, without killing any authors or burning books—without destroying the "carriers."

In this way we arrive at a fundamental new possibility: Our trials, our tentative hypotheses, may be critically eliminated by rational discussion, without eliminating ourselves. This is the purpose of rational critical discussion.

The "carrier" of a hypothesis has an important function in these discussions: He has to defend the hypothesis against erroneous criticism, and he may perhaps try to modify it if in its original form it cannot be successfully defended. If the method of rational critical discussion should establish itself, this should make the use of violence obsolete: Critical reason is the only alternative to violence so far discovered. It is the obvious duty of all intellectuals to work for *this* revolution—for the replacement of the eliminative function of violence by the eliminative function of rational criticism. But to work for this end, one has to train oneself constantly to write and speak in clear and simple language. Every thought should be formulated as clearly and simply as possible. This can only be achieved by hard work.

I have been for many years a critic of the so-called sociology of knowledge. Not that I thought that everything Mannheim (and Scheler) said was mistaken. On the contrary, much of it was only too trivially true. What I combated was Mannheim's belief that there was an essential difference with respect to objectivity between the social and the natural scientist, or between the study of society and that of nature. The thesis I combated was that it was easy to be objective in the natural sciences, while objectivity in the social sciences could be achieved, if at all, only by very select intellects: by the "freely poised intelligence" which is only "loosely anchored in social traditions."[7]

As against this I stressed that the objectivity of natural and social science is not based on an impartial state of mind in the scientists, but merely on the fact of the public and competitive character of the scientific enterprise and thus on certain social aspects of it. This is why I wrote:

"What the "sociology of knowledge" overlooks is just the sociology of knowledge—the social or public character of science."[8] Objectivity is based, in brief, on mutual rational criticism, on the critical approach, the critical tradition.[9]

Thus natural scientists are not more objectively minded than social scientists. Nor are they more critical. If there is more objectivity in the natural sciences, this is because there is a better tradition and higher standards of clarity and rational criticism. In Germany many social scientists are brought up as Hegelians, and this is a tradition destructive of intelligence and critical thought. It is one of the points where I agree with Karl Marx who wrote: "In its mystifying form dialectic became the accepted German fashion."[10] It is the German fashion still.

The sociological explanation of this fact is simple. We all get our values, or most of them, from our social environment; often merely by imitation, simply by taking them over from others; sometimes by a revolutionary reaction to accepted values; and at other times—though this may be rare—by a critical examination of these values and of possible alternatives. However this may be, the social and intellectual climate, the tradition in which one is brought up, are often decisive for the moral and other standards and values one adopts. All this is rather obvious. A very special case, but all-important for our purpose, is that of intellectual values.

Many years ago I used to warn my students against the widespread idea that one goes to college to learn how to talk and write "impressively" and incomprehensibly. At the time many students came to college with this ridiculous aim in mind, especially in Germany. And most of those students who, during their university studies, enter into an intellectual climate which accepts this kind of valuation—coming, perhaps under the influence of teachers who in turn had been reared in a similar climate—are lost. They unconsciously learn and accept that highly obscure and difficult language is the intellectual value par excellence. There is little hope that they will ever understand that they are mistaken; or that they will ever realize that there are other standards and values: values such as truth, the search for truth, the approximation to truth through the critical elimination of error, and clarity. Nor will they find out that the standard of "impressive" obscurity clashes with the standards of truth and rational criticism. For these latter values depend on clarity. One cannot tell truth from falsity, an adequate answer to a problem from an irrelevant one, good ideas from trite ones, one cannot evaluate ideas critically, unless they are presented with sufficient clarity. But to those brought up in the implicit admiration of brilliance and "impressive" opaqueness, all this (and all I have said here) would be *at best,* "impressive" talk: They do not know any other values.

Thus arose the cult of incomprehensibility, of high-sounding language. This was intensified by the (for laymen) inpenetrable and impressive formalism of mathematics. I suggest that in some of the more ambitious social sciences and philosophies, especially in Germany, the traditional game, which has largely become the unconscious and unquestioned standard, is to state the utmost trivialities in high-sounding language.

If those brought up on this kind of nourishment are presented with a book written simply and containing something unexpected, controversial, or new, they usually find it difficult or impossible to understand. For it does not conform to their idea of "understanding," which for them entails agreement. That there may be important ideas worth understanding with which one cannot at once agree or disagree is to them unfathomable.

There is here, at first sight, a difference between the social and the natural sciences: In the so-called social sciences and in philosophy, the degeneration into impressive but more or less empty verbalism has gone further than in the natural sciences. Yet the danger is getting acute everywhere. Even among mathematicians a tendency to impress people may sometimes be discerned, although the incitement to do so is least here; for it is partly the wish to ape the mathematicians and mathematical physicists in technicality and difficulty that inspires the use of verbiage in other sciences.

Yet lack of critical creativeness—of inventiveness paired with critical acumen—can be found everywhere; and everywhere this leads to the phenomenon of young scientists eager to pick up the latest fashion and jargon. These "normal" scientists[11] want a framework, a routine, a common and exclusive language of their trade. But it is the nonnormal scientist, the daring, the critical scientist, who breaks through the barrier of normality, who opens the windows and lets in fresh air; who does not think about the impression he makes, but tries to be well understood. The growth of normal science, which is linked to the growth of Big Science, is likely to prevent or even destroy the growth of knowledge, the growth of great science.

The situation is tragic if not desperate; and the present trend in the so-called empirical investigations into the sociology of the natural sciences is likely to contribute to the decay of science. Superposed upon this danger is another danger, created by Big Science: its urgent need for scientific technicians. More and more Ph.D. candidates receive merely technical training in certain techniques of measurement; they are not initiated into the scientific tradition, the critical tradition of questioning, of being tempted and guided by great and apparently insoluble riddles rather than by the solubility of minor puzzles. True, these technicians, these specialists, are usually aware of their limitations. They call themselves specialists and reject any claim to authority outside their specialities. Yet they do so proudly, and proclaim that specialization is a necessity. But this means flying in the face of the facts which show that great advances still come from those with a wide range of interests. If the many, the specialists, gain the day, it will be the end of science as we know it—of great science. It will be a spiritual catastrophe comparable in its consequences to nuclear armament.

I now come to my main point. Some of the famous leaders of German sociology who do their intellectual best, and do it with the best conscience in the world, are nevertheless simply talking trivialities in high-sounding language, as they were taught. They teach this to their students, who are dissatisfied, yet do the same. The genuine and general feeling of dissatisfaction manifest in their hostility to the society in which they live is a reflection of their unconscious dissatisfaction with the sterility of their own activities.

I will give a brief example from the writings of Professor Adorno. The example is a select one—selected, indeed, by Professor Habermas, who begins his first contribution to *Der Positivismusstreit* by quoting it. On the left I give the original German text, in the center the text as translated in the present volume, and on the right a paraphrase into simple English of what seems to have been asserted (see page 162).

It is for reasons such as these that I find it so difficult to discuss any serious problem with Professor Habermas. I am sure he is perfectly sincere. But I think that he does not know how to put things simply, clearly, and modestly, rather than impressively. Most of what he says seems trivial; the rest seems mistaken.

So far as I can understand him, the following is his central complaint about my alleged views. My way of theorizing, Habermas suggests, violates the *principle of the identity of theory and practice;* perhaps because I say that theory should *help* action, that is, should help us to modify our actions. For I say that it is the task of the theoretical social sciences to try to anticipate the unintended consequences of our actions; thus I differentiate between this theoretical task and the action. But Professor Habermas seems to think that only one who is a practical critic of existing society can produce serious theoretical arguments about society, since social knowledge cannot be divorced from fundamental social attitudes. The indebtedness of this view to the sociology of knowledge is obvious and need not be labored.

My reply is very simple. We should welcome any suggestion as to how our problems might be solved, regardless of the attitude toward

Die gesellschaftliche Totalität führt kein Eigenleben oberhalb des von ihr Zusammengefassten, aus dem sie selbst besteht.	Societal totality does not lead a life of its own over and above that which it unites and of which it, in its turn, is composed.	Society consists of social relationships.
Sie produziert und reproduziert sich durch ihre einzelnen Momente hindurch.	It produces and reproduces itself through its individual moments.	The various social relationships somehow produce society.
So wenig aber jenes Ganze vom Leben, von der Kooperation und dem Antagonismus seiner Elemente abzusondern ist,	This totality can no more be detached from life, from the cooperation and the antagonism of its elements,	Among these relations are cooperation and antagonism; and since society consists of these relations, it is impossible to separate it from them.
so wenig kann irgendein Element auch bloss in seinem Funktionieren verstanden werben ohne Einsicht in des Ganze, das an der Bewegung des Eizelnen selbst sein Wesen hat.	than can an element be understood merely as it functions without insight into the whole which has its source (*Wesen*, essence) in the motion of the individual entity itself.	The opposite is also true: none of the relations can be understood without the totality of all the others.
System und Einzelheit sind reziprok und nur in ihre Reziprozität zu erkennen.	System and individual entity are reciprocal and can only be apprehended in their reciprocity.	(Repetition of the preceding thought).

Comment: The theory of social wholes developed here has been presented and developed, sometimes better and sometimes worse, by countless philosophers and sociologists. I do not assert that it is mistaken; only the complete triviality of its content. Of course Adorno's *presentation* is very far from trivial.

society of the man who puts them forward; provided that he has learned to express himself clearly and simply—in a way that can be understood and evaluated—and that he is aware of our fundamental ignorance and responsibilities toward others. I do not think that the debate about the reform of society should be reserved for those who first put in a claim for recognition as practical revolutionaries, and who see the sole function of the revolutionary intellectual in pointing out as much as possible that which is repulsive in our social life (excepting their own social roles). It may be that revolutionaries have a greater sensitivity to social ills than other people. But obviously, there can be better and worse revolutions (as we all know from history), and the problem is not to do too badly.

Most if not all revolutions have produced societies very different from those desired by the revolutionaries. *Here is a problem,* and it deserves thought from every serious critic of society. And this should include an effort to put one's ideas into simple, modest language, rather than high-sounding jargon. This is an effort which those fortunate ones who are able to devote themselves to study owe to society.

A last word about the term *positivism.* Words do not matter, and I do not really mind if even a thoroughly misleading and mistaken label is applied to me. But the fact is that throughout my life I have combated positivist epistemology under the name of "positivism." I do not deny, of course, the possibility of stretching the term *positivist* until it covers anybody who takes any interest in natural science, so that it can be applied even to opponents of positivism, such as myself. I only contend that such a procedure is neither honest nor apt to clarify matters. The fact that the label "positivism" was originally applied to me by sheer blunder can be checked by anybody who is prepared to read my early *Logik der Forschung.*

It is worth mentioning that one of the victims of the two misnomers "positivism" and *Der Positivismusstreit,* is Dr. Alfred Schmidt, who describes himself as a "collaborator of many years' standing" (*Langjähriger Mitarbeiter*) of professors Adorno and Horkheimer. In a letter to the newspaper *Die Zeit,*[12] written to defend Adorno against the suggestion that he misused the term *positivism* in *Der Positivismusstreit* or on similar occasions, Schmidt characterizes positivism as a tendency of thought in which "the method of the various single sciences is taken absolutely as the only valid method of knowledge' (*die einzelwissen-schaftlichen Verfahren als einzig gültige Erkenntnis verabsolutierende Denken*), and he identifies it, correctly, with an overemphasis on "sensually ascertainable facts." He is clearly unaware of the fact that my alleged positivism, used to give the book *Der Positivismusstreit* its name, consisted of a fight against all this which he describes (fairly correctly) as "positivism." I have always fought for the right to operate freely with speculative theories against all forms of sensualistic empiricism.

I have fought against the aping of the natural sciences by the social sciences,[13] and I have fought for the doctrine that positivistic epistemology is inadequate even in its analysis of the natural sciences which, in fact, are not "careful generalizations from observation," as it is usually believed, but are essentially speculative and daring. Moreover, I have taught, for more than thirty-eight years,[14] that all observations are theory-impregnated, and that their main function is to check and refute, rather than to prove our theories. Finally I have not only stressed the meaningfulness of metaphysical assertions and the fact that I am myself a metaphysical realist, but I have also analyzed the important historical role played by metaphysics in the formation of scientific theories. Nobody before Adorno and Habermas has described such views as positivistic, and I can only suppose that these two did not know, originally, that I held such views. (I suspect they were no more interested in my views than I am in theirs.)

The suggestion that anybody interested in natural science is to be condemned as a positivist would make positivists not only of Marx and Engels but also of Lenin—the man who introduced the equation of "positivism" and "reaction." Terminology does not matter, however. Only it should not be used as an *argument;* and the title of a book ought not to be dishonest; nor should it attempt to prejudge an issue. On the substantial issue between the Frankfurt School and myself—revolution versus piecemeal reform—I shall not comment here since I have treated it as well as I could in my *Open Society.* Hans Albert too has said many incisive things on this topic, both in his replies to Habermas in *Der Positivismusstreit* and in his important book *Traktat über kritische Vernunft.*[15]

Notes

1. This paper, which has been added to the English translation of *The Positivist Dispute in German Sociology,* T.W. Adorno et al. (London: Heinemann, 1976), was first published in *Archives Européennes de Sociologie* 11 (1970):252-62. It has been revised for the present publication.
2. Karl R. Popper, *The Open Society and Its Enemies* (London, 1945).
3. Karl R. Popper, *The Poverty of Historicism* (London, 1957).
4. Karl R. Popper, "What is Dialectic?" *Mind* (1940):403ff. Reprinted in *Conjectures and Refutations* (London, 1963).
5. Karl R. Popper, *Logik der Forschung* (Vienna: Julius Springer, 1934). English translation: *The Logic of Scientific Discovery* (London: Hutchison, 1959).
6. The Vienna Circle consisted of men of originality and of the highest intellectual and moral standards. Not all of them were positivists, if we mean by this term a condemnation of speculative thought, although most of them were. I have always been in favor of criticizable speculative thought and, of course, of its criticism.
7. The quotation is from Mannheim. It is discussed more fully in my *Open Society,* vol. 2, p. 225.
8. Popper, *The Poverty of Historicism,* p. 155.
9. Cf. Popper, *Conjectures and Refutations,* esp. ch. 4.
10. Karl Marx, *Das Kapital,* vol. 2 (1872), "Nachwort." (In some later editions this is described as "Preface to Second Edition." The usual translation is not "mystifying" but "mystified." To me this sounds like a Germanism.)
11. The phenomenon of normal science was discovered, but not criticized, by Thomas Kuhn in *The Structure of Scientific Revolutions* (Chicago: University of Chicago Press, 1962). Kuhn is mistaken in thinking that "normal" science is not only normal *today* but always was so. On the contrary, in the past—

until 1939—science was almost always critical, or "extraordinary"; there was no scientific *routine*.

12. 12 June 1970, p. 45.
13. I have done so, although briefly, in the lecture printed in *The Positivist Dispute* (see especially my seventh thesis).
14. See my book *The Logic of Scientific Discovery*, new appendix 1.
15. Hans Albert, *Traktat über kritische Vernunft* (Tübingen: Mohr, 1969).

9

The Frankfurt School:
An Autobiographical Note

Karl R. Popper

I first heard of the Frankfurt School in the 1930s but decided then, on the basis of some experimental reading, against conscientiously reading its output. In 1960, as I have recounted in my "Reason or Revolution?", I was asked to open a discussion at a conference in Tübingen, and I was told that Adorno would reply to my paper.[1] This led me to another attempt at reading the publications of the Frankfurt School and especially Adorno's books.

Most of Adorno's works may be divided into three groups. First, there are his essays on music, literature, or culture. These I found little to my taste. To me they read like imitations of Karl Kraus, the Viennese writer; bad imitations, because they lacked Kraus's sense of humor. I had known, and heartily disliked, this kind of writing in my days in Vienna. I used to think of it as cultural snobbery, practiced by a clique which regarded itself as a cultural elite. These essays, incidentally, are characterized by their social irrelevance. Then there was a second group of books, on epistemology or philosophy. And these seemed just the sort of thing one calls in English "mumbo jumbo" (or in German "Hokus Pokus").

Of course, Adorno was a Hegelian as well as a Marxist; and I am opposed to both; to Marxism and especially to Hegelianism. As to Marx, I have great respect for him as a thinker and as a fighter for a better world, though I disagree with him on many points of decisive importance. I have criticized his theories at considerable length. He is not always particularly easy to understand, but he always tries his best to be understandable. For he has something to say; and he wants people to understand him. But as to Adorno, I can neither agree nor disagree with most of his philosophy. In spite of all efforts to understand his philosophy, it seems to me that all of it, or almost all, is just words. He has nothing whatever to say; and he says it in Hegelian language.

But there is a third group of his writings. The essays which belong to this third group are mainly complaints about the times we live in. But some of them are interesting and even moving. They give direct expression to his fears: his anxiety, as he calls it himself, and his deep depression. Adorno was a pessimist. After Hitler came to power—an event which, he says, surprised him as a politician—he despaired of mankind, and he surrendered his belief in the Marxist gospel of salvation. It is a voice of utmost despair which sounds from these essays—a tragic and pitiful voice. However, so far as Adorno's pessimism is philosophical, its philosophical content is nil. Adorno is consciously opposed to clarity. Somewhere he even mentions with approval that the German philosopher Max Scheler asked for "more darkness" (*mehr Dunkel*), alluding to the last words of Goethe, who asked for "more light" (*mehr Licht*).

It is difficult to understand how a Marxist like Adorno could support a demand for more darkness. Marx, certainly, was for enlightenment. But Adorno has published, together with Horkheimer, a book under the title *Dialectic of Enlightenment*[2] in which they try to show that the very idea of enlightenment leads, by its inner contradictions, into darkness— the darkness which we are allegedly in now. This is, of course, a Hegelian idea. Nevertheless, it remains a puzzle how a socialist, or a Marxist, or a humanist, like Adorno, can revert to such romantic views and prefer the maxim "more darkness" to "more light." Adorno acted on his maxim by publishing intentionally obscure and even oracular writings. It can only be explained by the nineteenth-century tradition of German philosophy and by the "rise of oracular philosophy," as I call it in my *Open Society*—the rise of the school of the so-called German idealists. Marx himself was brought up in this tradition, but he reacted forcefully against it, and in *Capital* he made a remark about it, and about dialectic, which I always admired. Marx said in *Capital:* "In its mystifying form the Dialectic became the ruling fashion in Germany."[3] Dialectic is still the ruling fashion in Germany; and it is still "in its mystifying form."

I would also like to say a few words about Horkheimer. Compared with Adorno, his writings are lucidity itself. However, Horkheimer's so-called Critical Theory is empty, devoid of content. This is more or less admitted by the editor of Horkheimer's *Kritische Theorie,* when he says: "To cast Horkheimer's conception into the form of understandable (*eingängige*) propositions is . . . almost impossible."[4] There remains only a vague and unoriginal Marxian historicism; Horkheimer does not say anything tenable that has not been said better before. His views may be said to be objectively uninteresting, including those with which I can agree.

I *have* found in Horkheimer some propositions with which I can agree. I can even agree with Horkheimer's formulation of his ultimate aims. In the second volume of his book *Kritische Theorie* he says, after rejecting Utopianism: "Nevertheless, the idea of a future society as a community of free men . . . has a content to which we ought to remain loyal through all [historical] change."⁵ I certainly agree with this idea, the idea of a society of free men (and also with the idea of loyalty to it). It is an idea that inspired the American and French revolutions. Unfortunately, Horkheimer has nothing of the slightest interest to say about the problem of how to get nearer to this ideal aim.

Horkheimer rejects, without argument and in defiance of historical facts, the possibility of reforming our so-called social system. This amounts to saying: Let the present generation suffer and perish; for all we can do is expose the ugliness of the world we live in and heap insults on our oppressors, the "bourgeoisie." This is the total content of the so-called Critical Theory of the Frankfurt School.

Marx's condemnation of our society makes sense; for Marx's theory contains the promise of a better future. But the theory becomes vacuous and irresponsible if this promise is withdrawn, as it is by Adorno and Horkheimer. This is why Adorno found that life is not worth living. For life is really worth living only if we can work for a better world now and for the immediate future. It is a crime to exaggerate the ugliness and baseness of the world: it is ugly, but it is also very beautiful; inhuman, and also very human. And it is threatened by great dangers. The greatest is world war. Almost as great is the population explosion. But there is much that is good in this world; for there is much good will. There are millions of people alive today who would gladly risk their lives if they thought they could thereby bring about a better world.

We can do much *now* to relieve suffering, and most important, increase individual human freedom. We *must not* wait for a goddess of history or for a goddess of revolution to introduce better conditions into human affairs. History, and also a revolution, may easily fail us. It did fail the Frankfurt School, and it caused Adorno to despair. We must produce and critically try out ideas about what can and should be done now; and do it now. To sum up with a phrase of Raymond Aron, I regard the writings of the Frankfurt School as "opium of the intellectuals."⁶

Notes

In December 1973, I was asked by the BBC whether I would agree to be interviewed on the subject of the so-called Frankfurt School for use in a program on their work to be broadcast in January 1974. I prepared this brief paper (which was not, in fact, broadcast in this form because I was given only five minutes in which to speak).

1. See *Archives Européennes de Sociologie* 11 (1970):252–62; or the revised version of this paper in T.W. Adorno et al., *The Positivist Dispute in German Sociology* (London: Heinemann, 1976), pp. 288–300.

2. M. Horkheimer and Theodor W. Adorno, *Dialectic of Enlightenment* (New York: Herder & Herder, 1972).
3. Karl Marx, *Das Kapital,* vol. 2 (1872), "Nachwort."
4. Max Horkheimer, *Kritische Theorie,* ed. A. Schmidt, vol. 2 (Frankfurt: Fischer, 1968), p. 340f.
5. Ibid., p. 166.
6. Raymond Aron, *L'Opium des intellectuels* (Paris: Colmann-Lévy, 1955).

Part Three
AESTHETICS

10
On Walter Benjamin

Georg Lukács

Our purpose here is to demonstrate that the spirit of allegory manifests itself quite unambiguously both in the theory and in the practice of the modernist avant-garde. It is no accident that, for decades now, critics have drawn attention to the basic affinity between baroque and romanticism on the one hand and the foundations of modernist art and ideology on the other. The purpose of this tactic is to define—and legitimize— the latter as the heirs and successors of those great crises of the modern world and as the representatives of the profound crisis of our age. It was Walter Benjamin who furnished the most profound and original theorization of these views. In his study of baroque tragic drama (*Trauerspiel*), he constructs a bold theory to show that allegory is the style most genuinely suited to the sentiments, ideas, and experience of the modern world. Not that this program is explicitly proclaimed. On the contrary, his text confines itself strictly to his chosen historical theme. Its spirit, however, goes far beyond that narrow framework. Benjamin interprets baroque (and romanticism) from the perspective of the ideological and artistic needs of the present. His choice of this narrower theme for his purpose is peculiarly happy, because the elements of crisis in baroque emerge with unambiguous clarity in the specific context of German society of the period. This came about as a consequence of Germany's temporary lapse into being a mere object of world history. This led in turn to a despairing, inward-looking provincialism, as a result of which the realist countertendencies of the age were enfeebled—or became manifest only in exceptional cases like Grimmelshausen. It was a brilliant insight that led Benjamin to fix on this period in Germany, and on the drama in particular, as the subject of his research. It enables him to give a vivid portrayal of the theoretical problem without forcing or distorting the historical facts in the manner so often seen in contemporary general histories.

As a preliminary to a closer scrutiny of Benjamin's analysis of the baroque from the vantage point of the problematic character of contemporary art, it will be helpful to take a quick look at the distinction between symbolism and allegory established by romantic aesthetics. This will reveal that their position was here much less clearly defined than that of thinkers in the crises that preceded or followed them. The reasons for their intermediate position are manifold. Above all, there was the overwhelming impact of Goethe's personality, with his clear insight into this very problem—which he too regarded as crucial for the fate of art. This factor was intensified by the powerful drive toward realism in art active in Goethe, but by no means in him alone. Furthermore, romanticism thought of itself as a transitional phase between two crises. This led to specific, if questionable, insights into the historical nature of the problem, but also to a certain defusing of the inner dilemma implicit in any attempt to define allegory.

Schelling, in his aesthetics,[1] organizes the history of art according to the principle that classical art was an age of symbolism, while Christianity was dominated by allegory. The first claim is based on the tradition established by Winckelmann, Lessing, and Goethe; the second is intended to provide a historical underpinning for a specifically romantic art. It is not so much the absence of precise knowledge of the Christian era that makes this scheme so vague and ambiguous, as the fact that its perspective is all too monolithically romantic. It does away with that conflict already familiar to us between symbol and allegory in sculpture, and even interprets as allegorical authors and works where the primacy of realistic symbolism is indubitable. Solger takes over Schelling's distinction, but defines it more sharply at the level of general theory.[2]

The real theoreticians of the crisis tendencies of allegory in romanticism were Friedrich Schlegel and Novalis. Their sifting and propagation of the idea of crisis and of allegory as a means of expression appropriate to it has close affinities with the philosophies of history just outlined. But whereas, particularly for Schelling, the problem is rendered less acute by his incorporating it within an objective philosophy of history, Schlegel takes as his starting point the loss of a mythology that might serve as a foundation for culture, and above all for art. The loss is seen as the index of a crises, even though he still hopes and believes that the creation of a new mythology will make it possible to find a way out of the impasse of the profound crisis of his own day. Since for Schlegel every mythology is nothing other than "a hieroglyphic expression of Nature around us" transfigured by imagination and love, it comes as no surprise to see him conclude that "all beauty is allegory. Simply because it is ineffable, the highest truth can only be expressed in allegory." This leads to the universal hegemony of allegory in all forms of human activity; language itself, in its primordial manifestations, is "identical with allegory."[3]

Such an analysis tends to cut allegory free from its old links with the Christian religion—links which were precisely determined and even laid down by theology. Instead, it establishes its affinity with a specifically modern anarchy of the feelings and with a dissolution of form which leads in turn to the collapse of objective representation (*Gegenständlichkeit*). It is Novalis who finds an explicit formula for such trends. "Stories without [logical] links, only associations, like dreams. Poems that are merely melodious and full of beautiful words, but without any meaning or coherence—at best only a few stanzas which are comprehensible—like a mass of fragments composed of the most heterogeneous objects. At best true poetry can only have a general allegorical sense and an indirect effect, like music, etc."[4]

Compared to these uncertain, obscure, and self-contradictory statements by the romantics, the picture of German baroque tragedy etched by Benjamin is remarkable for its impressive internal consistency and coherence. This is not the place to enter into a discussion of his often brilliant polemics, such as the one against Goethe, or of his illuminating detailed analyses. We must start by emphasizing that his whole interpretation of baroque does not stop short with a contrast between baroque and classicism, or with the attempt (typical of some later eclectics) to establish mannerism and classicism as related, complementary tendencies. Instead, he makes a direct attack on his target: the unveiling of the principle of art itself. "In the field of allegorical intuition," he says, "the image is a fragment, a rune. Its beauty as a symbol evaporates when the light of divine learning falls upon it. The false appearance of totality is extinguished. For the *eidos* disappears, the simile ceases to exist, and the cosmos it contains shrivels up. . . . A deep-rooted intuition of the problematic character of art . . . emerges as a reaction to its self-confidence at the time of the Renaissance."[5] However, the logic of Benjamin's argument leads to the conclusion that the problematic character of art is that of the world itself, the world of mankind, of history, and society; it is the decay of all these that has been made visible in the imagery of allegory. In allegory, "the observer is confronted with the *facies hippocratica* of history as a petrified, primordial landscape." History no longer "assumes the form of the process of an eternal life, so much as that of irresistible decay." However, "allegory thereby declares itself to be beyond beauty. Allegories are, in the realm of thoughts, what ruins are in the realm of things."[6]

Thus Benjamin sees with absolute clarity that, though the opposition of symbol and allegory is crucial to the aesthetic definition of any work of art, it is not ultimately the spontaneous or conscious product of aesthetic considerations. It is fed by deeper sources: man's necessary response to the reality in which he lives and which assists or impedes his activities. No detailed examination is required to show that, with all this, what Benjamin is doing is to take up and extend in a more profound way the problem of modern art as defined two decades before him by Wilhelm Worringer in *Abstraction and Empathy*. Benjamin's analysis is deeper and more discriminating than that of his predecessor, and more specific and sensitive in its historical classification of aesthetic forms. The resulting dualism which was given its first, highly abstract definition by the romantics, now crystallizes into a firmly based historical description and interpretation of the modern crisis in art and ideology. Unlike Worringer and subsequent critics of modernist art, Benjamin feels no need to project its spiritual and intellectual foundations back into any primordial age in order to emphasize the gulf separating symbol and allegory. Nor is his achievement significantly impaired by the fact that sociohistorical undercurrents remain vague and unfocused.

Benjamin's study, therefore, starts from the idea that allegory and symbol express fundamentally divergent human responses to reality. His incisive criticism of the obscurities in the formulations of the romantics turned a spotlight on the fact that, in the last analysis, the allegorical mode is based on a disturbance that disrupts the anthropomorphizing response to the world which constitutes the foundation of aesthetic reflection. But since what we see in mimetic art is man's striving for self-awareness in his relations with his proper sphere of activity in nature and society, it is evident that a concern with allegory must undermine that universal humanity always present implicitly in aesthetic reflection. Without generalizing as broadly as we do here, Benjamin expresses himself very firmly on this point: "And even today it is by no means self-evident that the primacy of the thing over the personal, the fragment over the total, represents a confrontation between the allegory and the symbol, to which it is the polar opposite and, for that very reason, its equal in power. Allegorical personification has always concealed the fact that its function is not the personification of things, but rather to give the thing a more imposing form by getting it up as a person."[7]

This brings the key elements of the problem sharply into focus. However, Benjamin is concerned only to establish aesthetic (or trans-aesthetic) parity for allegory. For this reason he does not go beyond mere description, albeit a conceptually generalized one. He ignores the fact that to give things a more imposing form is to fetishize them, in contrast to an anthropomorphizing mimetic art, with its inherent tendency to defetishization and its true knowledge of things as mediators of human relations. Benjamin does not even touch on this issue. Subsequent theorists far less critical than Benjamin make frequent use of the word *fetish* in the later manifestos of avant-gardist art. But they use it to mean something primordial—as the expression of an authentically primitive, magic attitude toward things. Neither in their theory nor in their practice do they notice that an attempt to retrieve an archaic magic culture could take place only in the imagination, while in reality they uncritically accepted the capitalist fetishization of human relations into things. Nor is the situation altered in the slightest by the frequent substitution of "emblem" (in its more recently acquired meaning) for "fetish." For in allegorical contexts an emblem expresses nothing if not an uncritically affirmed fetishization.

In the baroque, Benjamin rightly discerns the indivisible union of religion and convention. The interaction of these two elements creates an atmosphere in which allegory undermines any real objective representation from two different angles. We have already considered the tendency toward fetishization. However, Benjamin has also perceived that this factor sets another, contrary one in motion. "Any person, any object, any relationship can mean absolutely anything else. With this possibility a destructive but just verdict is passed on the profane world: it is characterized as a world in which the detail is of no great importance."[8] This is the religious world of devalued particularity, a world in which the particular is preserved in its devalued state. An unfetishized thing is necessarily constructed from its qualities, its details; unfetishized thinghood is the way a determinate particular just happens to be. To go beyond this, the internal relationships between appearance and essence, detail and the objective whole must be intensified. An object can only be rationally organized, it can only be raised to the plane of the individual (*Besondere*), the typical, as a totality of rationally arranged details, if the details can acquire a symptomatic character which points beyond themselves to some essence.

When Benjamin rightly points out that allegory wholly abolishes detail, and with it all concrete objective representation, he seems to be diagnosing a much more radical annihilation of all particularity. But appearances are deceptive; such annihilation implies recurrence. Such acts of substitution only mean that interchangeable things and details are abolished in the concrete form in which they happen to exist. Hence the act of abolition affects only their given nature and replaces them with objects whose internal structure is wholly identical with theirs. Therefore, since what happens is that one particular is simply replaced by another, this abolition of particularity is nothing more than its constant reproduction. This process remains the same in every allegorical view of representation, and by no means implies a conflict with its general religious foundations.

In the baroque, however, and particularly in Benjamin's interpretation of it, a new motif becomes apparent. This is the fact that the transcendence which provides the context for the process we have just outlined no longer possesses any concrete religious content. It is entirely nihilistic—though without modifying the religious character of the process. Benjamin notes: "Allegory goes away empty-handed. Evil as such, which it cherished as enduring profundity, exists only in allegory, is nothing but allegory, and means something different from what it is. It means precisely the nonexistence of what it presents." And equally perceptive is Benjamin's insight that it is "the theological essence of the subject" that is here expressed.[9] And this subjectivity, whose creativity has exceeded all bounds and arrived at the point of self-destruction, has a mode of receptivity corresponding to it. Here too, Benjamin's unremitting rigor provides the essential commentary: "For the only diversion the melancholic permits himself, and it is a powerful one, is allegory."[10] Benjamin is much too precise a stylist for us to be able to ignore the pejorative undertones implicit in his use of the word *diversion*. Where the world of objects is no longer taken seriously, the seriousness of the world of the subject must vanish with it.

Notes

1. F.W.J. von Schelling, *Werke* (Stuttgart and Augsburg: Cotta, 1856–61), vol. 5, p. 452.
2. K.W.F. Solger, *Erwin* (Berlin: Wieqandt and Grieben, 1845), pp. 41–49.
3. Friedrich Schlegel, *Prosaische Jugendschriften* (Vienna: Conegen, 1908), vol. 2, pp. 361, 364, 382.
4. Novalis, *Werke* (Jena: Diederichs, 1923), vol. 2, p. 308.
5. Walter Benjamin, *The Origin of German Tragic Drama* (London: NLB, 1977), p. 176.
6. Ibid., pp. 166, 178.
7. Ibid., pp. 186–87.
8. Ibid., p. 175.
9. Ibid., p. 233.
10. Ibid., p. 185.

11
Lukács and Horkheimer: The Place of Aesthetics in Horkheimer's Thought

István Hermann

Of all the members of the Frankfurt School, Horkheimer had the least to say about problems relating to aesthetics. For the school as a whole, aesthetic problems presented a central concern, a fact that cannot be solely attributed to the one-time illustrious presence of Walter Benjamin, whose interests were not only aesthetically motivated but whose whole lifework was of an aesthetic nature. Nor can it be largely due to the well-known fact that Adorno was extremely interested in things musical and consequently was able to demonstrate the reality of a specific sense of life (*Lebensgefühl*) that had in due time become the basic philosophical principle of the Frankfurt School by laying bare the inner contradictions existing in music through his profound intellectual grasp of the Schönbergian concept of music.

I will return to the discussion of how a *Lebensgefühl* may evolve into a fundamental philosophical principle, and will also take a closer look at the various problems with regard to substance, paths, and the developmental process of that *Lebensgefühl*. What should be of vital interest to us now is the question of the motivating forces behind the evolving of a *Lebensgefühl* into a constitutive element of a *Weltanschauung,* that is, the evaluation of the expansion of a *Lebensgefühl* into a *Weltbild* that also encompasses other streams of thought. The indebtedness of Horkheimer and of the whole school to the basic ideas of German idealism is common knowledge. Classical German philosophy, the last of the bourgeois philosophical systems containing the belief in and the philosophical justification of the possibility of universal man, had been characterized throughout its development by a definitive aesthetic focus. This goes beyond the fact that whole life works such as Goethe's aesthetic theories and concept of man or the aesthetic of Schiller and the romantic school were, for better or for worse, organically embedded in the philosophical development of the same period. Even Kant's supreme epistemological treatise, *Critique of Pure Reason,* generally regarded as his major philosophical statement, can be assessed and understood best in light of his attempt to extend his ever-present anthropological interest that in itself is closely connected to the aesthetic of classical German philosophy, into a *Weltbild.* In addition, the epistemological work should also be seen in its interconnection to the study "Religion within the Limits of Reason Alone" and to the aesthetic treatise *Critique of Judgment.*

It is quite another matter that the epistemological line of inquiry beginning with Kant seemingly attained its independence through the work of Fichte in which the impression arose that philosophy had nothing to do anymore with aesthetic, or, more precisely, with the development of German poetry of that era. This impression will dissipate as soon as a closer look is taken at the extent to which Kantian ethic and epistemology influenced Kleist, or at the complementarity of Fichtean philosophy and the aesthetic in the philosophy of romanticism, and finally, at the phenomenon of the aesthetic becoming again a significant, albeit problematic, component of Schelling's philosophy and a constitutive element of Hegelian philosophy in a more fruitful way. (In his discussion of the Hegelian aesthetic, Lukács correctly points out the aesthetic origins of the idea of the identity of subject-object and reminds us in what way this aesthetically grounded idea was to provide the means for the elimination of the inner contradictions of the Hegelian philosophical system.)

A real need existed for this league between philosophy and aesthetic in a period that Heine called "the age of poetry," in which the aesthetic sphere alone could alleviate the dire state of the real world, a world at strife with itself, by advancing the idea of the possibility of universal man and the possibility of creating a harmonious existence through education that was akin to something referred to by the Flaubertian title "éducation sentimentale." It was due to the labors of a Goethe and a Schiller that this "éducation sentimentale" turned into an aesthetic education; that the concept of aesthetic education became commonplace has to be attributed to Schiller's giving the title "On the Aesthetic Education of Man" to his letters on the developmental path of man. The title was more than just that: It represented a program.

For thinkers who perceived the horrors of fascism and imperialism as clearly as did members of the Frankfurt School, twentieth-century German philosophy could have but one program only: It either had to ground its philosophy in the workers' movement that offered a more realistic perspective for human development than did aesthetic education, or it had to awaken to new life the concept of aesthetic education that had been lying dormant for over a century. There was a need to assess both the considerable differences and similarities between that fo. ....er period (of aesthetic education) and the present one. Horkheimer clearly saw the similarities in that he characterized the nineteenth century as a less wretched one than the preceding or following ones. The wretchedness of eighteenth-century reality comes alive in the vivid description of a minor character in Schiller's play *Kabale und Liebe* (Intrigue and Love. An old footman informs Lady Milford of what is really going on by telling her about how many young men of the dukedom are captured and then sold for a large amount of money to fight for the colonists in America.) This far surpasses the more "civilized" cruelties of the nineteenth century, but stands comparison with the sufferings inflicted on man in the twentieth century. In terms of suffering, we are back in the late eighteenth or early nineteenth century. Horkheimer assures us that "the apparatus of power has not really gotten less refined since Galileo's penance and recantation; if it took second place to other kinds of machinations in the nineteenth century, it has more than made up for its backwardness in the twentieth."[1]

After having commented on the similarities, Horkheimer turns his attention to the differences. His point of reference is Goethe's famous saying in the *Westöstliche Divan* that *"Höchstes Glück der Erdenkinder sei die Persönlichkeit"* ("Individuality is the greatest happiness that a human being can possess"), which he follows up with the reflection: "Should it be the case as Goethe said that individuality means happiness, we must call attention to what another poet just added, namely, that the possession of individuality is a social achievement and can be lost at any time. Pirandello who leaned toward fascism, knew his own times better than he himself realized." (To be fair, Pirandello did indeed write a letter to Mussolini in 1924 offering him his services. But as things developed, he chose to remain neutral. We cannot therefore speak of Pirandello's leaning toward fascism. We should also consider that Horkheimer wrote this essay in 1937.) Horkheimer wound up his reflections by stating: "Under the totalitarian rule of evil, men may retain not only their lives but their very selves only by accident, and recantations mean today even less than they did in the time of the Renaissance. A philosophy that thinks it can find peace within itself, in any kind of truth whatsoever, has therefore nothing to do with critical theory."[2]

By distancing himself from the Goethean position, Horkheimer clearly demonstrates the differences between the situation in which a thinker finds himself and the position taken by him. In Goethe's time, it seemed a proper response to employ aesthetic education in the quest for individuality. In Horkheimer's time, the attainment and continued possession of individuality could only be a matter of pure chance. I have to forego now any detailed analysis of the differences in concept. The main point is to see that as far as the Frankfurt thinkers are concerned, the concept of aesthetic education cannot be an appropriate response under the present circumstances. The potential usefulness of this concept is lost for several reasons, the first being that the very Utopian dream Goethe put forth in the final monologue of *Faust,* that a time will come when free men roam the free earth, had clearly remained just that: a dream. The second reason is that an art that consciously renounced its "aura," to use Walter Benjamin's words, could not be called upon to be the "teacher of mankind," to be the core of an aesthetic education. Thus, a great many of the studies produced by members of the Frankfurt School were to offer proof that the classical concept of aesthetic education is dead, never to be resurrected. Benjamin's hopeless search for a way to a functioning aesthetic education (including his episodic discovery of Brecht as a possibility), Adorno's use of the concept of *Lebensgefühl,* and finally, Horkheimer's reflections, all attest to this fact.

Just as the aesthetic sphere had a decisive significance for classical German philosophy in that it provided means for solution to problems, so is the relationship between the aesthetic sphere and Critical Theory a crucial issue albeit with a different outcome: Now the aesthetic sphere as last resort proved itself inadequate to the task. It would not do, however, to mistake this notion of futility with the concept of skepsis and thus make it absolute. The absolute has no place in Critical Theory. Horkheimer makes the difference between critical theory and skepsis very clear in his essay on "Montaigne and the Function of Skepsis": While skepsis renders absolute both the negative state of existing reality and the impossibility of the knowledge of the truth, critical theory points to a better future in spite of its pessimistic insights. This statement undoubtedly is related to Horkheimer's reflections on the possibility of attaining and continuing to possess individuality as a matter of chance.

It is the problematic nature of individuality that determines Horkheimer's attitude toward the aesthetic sphere. While returning time and again to the discussion of the loss and degradation of individuality, Horkheimer often refers back to art. Writing on the concept of man, Horkheimer employs the category of "mimesis" (assimilation and imitation) and finds it useful when elaborating on man as a biological being. "Among the capabilities," writes Horkheimer, "which every man possesses as a biological being is the ability to assimilate and imitate." Thus,

> psychic reactions are acquired, in the form if not content; moreover, if a rigid separation of form and content leads to error in the analysis of a work of art, how much greater the error in the interpretation of human

feelings. Sadness and happiness, attention sought and given, shyness and devotion come into existence with the repetition of behavior and gestures, for, as Goethe says, "the outward is the inward."[3]

It is not by accident that such an aesthetically colored comparative thought system dominates Horkheimer's reflections; after all, his work represents an ambitious attempt to revive classical German philosophy grounded in aesthetic, an altogether problematic enterprise. The idea of futility of an aesthetic education is an immanent part of the Horkheimerian system of thought. This is one of the decisive differences between the position taken by the Frankfurt School and Georg Lukács, a fact that remains unrecognized by many interpreters of the school who try to show that there is a basic agreement between Lukács and the Frankfurt School. Iring Fetscher, for example, expresses a supposed identity of positions as follows:

> Lukács, and later on Max Horkheimer, Walter Benjamin, Herbert Marcuse, and Theodor Adorno even thought that to stress the continuity of the bourgeois and the revolutionary movements was most important because of the fact that the German and Italian bourgeoisie in the age of fascism were about to betray their own past. They endeavored to show to the bourgeois intellectuals the gulf between the liberal principles and humanitarian aspirations of the early bourgeoisie and the meaning and scope of the modern barbarians which grew out, as they thought, of the antagonism of contemporary capitalist society and led to fascism.[4]

Such a point of view so clearly and openly voiced by Fetscher and often lurking in the background of other writings wants us to believe that in the fight against fascism, Lukács and the best of the Frankfurt School held identical positions. That point of view becomes untenable once we realize the differences with regard to the aesthetic sphere. For Lukács, the aesthetic sphere supplies the means to educate mankind toward historical consciousness, that is, an educational means for mankind to attain its historical consciousness. In Horkheimer's opinion, classical aesthetic forms do not serve a useful function in the manipulated world, not to speak of fascism; he cannot conceive of how the concept of man could be revived and upheld as a model to strive for—on the contrary. Speaking of such literary heroines as Julia, Gretchen, or Madame Bovary, Horkheimer remarks that "in view of the changes which have occurred in the family in the age of full employment [they] are now but curiosities."[5] (It is an entirely different question that Horkheimer may be right in charging that the older, more sentimental character of love underwent a vast change. Nonetheless, it is still incorrect to refer to the heroines as "curiosities," because all those Julias and Gretchens have a role in the modern concept of love even if in a sublated way.) In the final instance, Horkheimer simply does not believe in the usefulness of contrasting the aesthetic values of the bourgeois era with our modern world. He asserts that all the values connected with aesthetics or individuality have disappeared, become impossible to uphold, anachronistic, and perhaps even harmful. Horkheimer says just that in his discussion of everyday life and mimesis. The valuation of mimesis in relation to man's everyday life constitutes a significant aspect of the Lukácsian aesthetic too. The difference is in the way Horkheimer evaluates mimesis, or more precisely, its actuality:

> In the present crisis the problem of mimesis is particularly urgent. Civilization starts with, but must eventually transcend and transvaluate, man's native mimetic impulses. Cultural progress as a whole, as well as individual education, i.e., the phylogenetic and ontogenetic processes of civilization, consists largely in converting mimesis into rational attitudes. Just as primitives must learn that they can produce better crops by treating the soil properly than by practicing magic, so the modern child must learn to curb his mimetic impulses and to direct them toward a definitive goal. Conscious adaptation and eventually domination replace the various forms of mimesis. The progress of science is the theoretical manifestation of this change; the formula supplants the image, the calculating machine the ritual dances. To adapt oneself means to make oneself like the world of objects for the sake of self-preservation.[6]

The analysis is correct but the conclusion turns out to be not quite correct:

> If the final renunciation of the mimetic impulses does not promise to lead to the fulfillment of man's potentialities, this impulse will always lie in waiting, ready to break out as a destructive force. That is, if there is no other norm than the *status quo,* if all the hope of happiness that reason can offer is that it preserves the existing as it is and even increases its pressure, the mimetic impulse is never really overcome. Men revert to it in a regressive and distorted form. Like the prudish censors of pornography, they abandon themselves to tabooed urges with hatred and contempt. Dominated masses readily identify themselves with the repressive agency. Indeed, in its service alone are they given free rein to indulge.[7]

Mimesis comes to play precisely such a role in fascism and in more general terms in a totally administered world. In the case of Horkheimer, however, mimesis does not—and cannot—play the part that becomes a significantly contributing factor in the Lukácsian conception of the aesthetic. Rather, mimesis is degraded when it accepts the role allocated to it by the forces of manipulation. That this has to be so follows from Horkheimer's concept in which individuality either becomes irrevocably lost or its continued existence will be a matter of chance, and which can hold nothing but autonomous thought against the modern world. Thus, Horkheimer cannot go beyond autonomous thought in the search for a means of enabling man as an isolated individual to resist modern manipulative forces.

For Horkheimer, the aesthetic sphere reveals the same process of decomposition as does society in general; it is part of the modern process of decomposition as are other economic or intellectual phenomena of society. Consequently, this aesthetic sphere is unable to point toward an objective way of easing the tension. According to Horkheimer, only a few hundred years before, art was still intimately associated with other spheres of social life. His assertion is correct: Regarding the spheres of daily use, or at least, of consumption, art in the modern period has a different role to play from its role in the cultic period. To be sure, Horkheimer states that the arts have lost their former functions but gained new forms that are "suitable to any interior"; the aesthetic sphere became "pure." This says that during the same historical process man has become a private "atomic subject" who abstracts or at least tries to abstract from prevailing social trends and standards: "In his aesthetic behavior, man divested himself so to speak of his functions as a member of society and reacted as the isolated individual he had become."[8] What the German philosopher has to offer here is an excellent phenomenology of modern aesthetic attitude; it means that art has in its own way preserved in the private sphere the inalienable human kernel, that is, the integrity of the alienated and isolated atomized individual. Taking this position to its ultimate conclusion we arrive at an extreme formulation of the origins and social function of art. Man has to become alienated before he can transcend all that is mimetic in order to preserve his integrity vis-à-vis a badly flawed society. Alienation from society, that is, a dissociation from alienated society, is thus seen as the first step toward the preservation of man's integrity. Modern art therefore can by no means be mimetic since even the remotest connection with mimesis makes man succumb to an alienated social world; nothing but a categorical rejection of mimesis can ensure integrity. Ultimately it is true, Horkheimer argues (and his argumentation clearly reveals what, in an important sense, the Adornoean aesthetic is all about), that art has always been related to the private sphere, to the private realm. What is characteristic of modern society is that now "society tends to liquidate [the private realm]."[9]

There are two spheres of alienation facing each other. The first is the mimetic sphere which once existed at the primitive level and then made its reappearance at the modern industrialized stage; the other is the sphere of individual integrity in its splendid isolation from all social context. One has to make a choice. True art has chosen the latter sphere of alienation since it knows no other alternative. These two tendencies are the basic reference point for all that is characteristic of the aesthetic theories of the Frankfurt School. We find its clearest and most compelling formulation in Horkheimer's writings; further analysis of Adorno's and Marcuse's reflections reveals the same indebtedness to this duality of alienation. The positing of the alternatives enables aesthetic to become again a decisive factor as in the "age of poetry," with the difference that the advocacy of individuality and the emphasis on the autonomy of poetry were supposed to fulfill different functions in the "age of poetry." Then, it provided direction for one passable road leading to society, existing both in an abstract and concrete sense. Now, for the Frankfurt School it serves the cause of isolation from society in which there is nothing the undamaged and autonomous individuality could attach itself to.

Herbert Marcuse clearly refers to this and the above-mentioned alternatives in his statement:

> In contrast to the Marxian concept, which denotes man's relation to himself and to his work in capitalist society, the *artistic alienation* is the conscious transcendence of the alienated existence—a "higher level" or mediated alienation. The conflict with the world of progress, the negation of the order of business, the anti-bourgeois elements in bourgeois literature and art are neither due to the aesthetic lowliness of this order nor to romantic reaction—nostalgic consecration of the disappearing stage of civilization.[10]

Here Marcuse formulates in more concrete terms what was before a theoretical notion of Horkheimer, namely, that the function of art is to confront alienation in the customary sense with its own particular kind of alienation. Although at first glance it may appear so, this is not such an absurd notion. Horkheimer was the first, after all, who postulated theoretically the societal mission of art, i.e., provided the framework for the creation of a purely avant-garde art based on individual integrity which could effectively resist social integration.

Putting the question this way, the following conclusion presents itself: Since family life, the private realm is steadily menaced by a manipulative society, the individual may invest all his energies looking for a refuge be it in modern city housing projects or in the suburbs. Thus the situation arises in which man has lost his ability to even imagine a different world.

The other world that man was supposed to bring about was—in the concept of the cultic epoch—that of art. Horkheimer describes the fate of this other world:

> Today it survives only in those works which uncompromisingly express the gulf between the monadic individual and his barbarous surroundings— prose like Joyce's and paintings like Picasso's Guernica. The grief and horror such works convey are not identical with the feelings of those who, for rational reasons, are turning away from reality or rising against it. The consciousness behind them is rather one cut off from society as it is, and forced into queer, discordant forms. These inhospitable works of art, by remaining loyal to the individual as against the infamy of existence, thus retain the true content of previous great works of art and are more closely related to Raphael's madonnas and Mozart's operas than is anything that harps on the same harmonies today, at a time when the happy countenance has assumed the mask of frenzy and only the melancholy faces of the frenzied remain a sign of hope.[11]

Here Horkheimer expresses his conviction that only an alienated and solitary world can become the artistic sphere and fulfill the same functions as a Raphael or Mozart did. In our view, this modern reversal of the function of art is one of Horkheimer's great theoretical accomplishments which has a solid critical foundation but which in our opinion is one of his most debatable propositions. Horkheimer's critique of modern art produced for mass consumption is fully justified. The entertainment industry on the one side and pure art as a symbol of solitary and despairing life on the other are the two poles of modern artistic life for Horkheimer; there is nothing between them or beyond them. Horkheimer justly criticizes Mortimer Adler's definition of the external marks of the great work of art, as advanced in his book on Walt Disney,[12] that it has to have "gross popularity at any one time or over a period of time and the ability to satisfy the most varied levels of taste."[13]

Horkheimer is correct in his critique of Adler's view of art as being independent of time, and argues forcefully and well against Adler's unhistorical method; while isolated elements of art may appear as similar as rain drops, they are in reality vastly different. Thus, for example, when Disney makes use of Raphael's blue horizon for his landscape, it is supposed to serve quite a different function; the art of Raphael and the modern animated films are neither artistically equal nor grounded in the same artistic principle. Of course, such naive theses as Adler's are easy to refute. Horkheimer's perceptive analysis further shows how the Aristotelian doctrine of mimesis becomes a cliché in such a shallow aesthetic as Adler's and how a cliché can be easily adjusted to any conventional doctrine to suit the occasion. Even more important is

Horkheimer's evaluation of modern intellectuals, applicable to all and any moralizing, shallow philosophy, or aesthetic: "They still have in mind the individual's harmony and culture, at a time when the task is no longer to humanize the isolated individual, which is impossible, but to realize humanity as a whole."[14]

At this point, the validity of Horkheimer's critique seems apparent. His aesthetic position is correct insofar as it remains directed against naive attempts to deduce present conditions from those of the past, that is, to depict individuality as an "ought" that is a direct result of past conditions; in short, against that which lies at the center of such aesthetic attempts. It matters little whether the reference is to the Renaissance, the nineteenth century, or Greek antiquity. They all fail to recognize the changed function of aesthetic phenomena in the modern age and therein lies their grave mistake.

We have to ask here whether Horkheimer himself was aware of this. His concept of the integrity of the individual as well as his *Menschenbild* is not based on the concept of the integrity of the "harmonious personality" but on the defense—even apology—of the individual stripped of meaning. The existing reality from which the individual dissociates himself appears to each and all as repulsive. Hegel's dialectical remark has more validity— that all thinking men find the world null and sacred at the same time— and this can be applied to our modern world. There is no world of horror (*Schreckenswelt*) so imaginable as the horror that would not show up the antidote to the totally manipulated world. *Angst,* being extremely problematic as it is, can still possibly find—not from without but within the world—those explosive elements which lead to a blowup of this world. It is also true that *Angst* and the horror itself contain mimetic elements, and further, that these mimetic elements are present in all spheres of modern life. One could just as easily speak of the ambiguity and contradiction inherent in mimesis; of the possibility that the primitive, natural, and biological reflexes would produce—by means of *Aufhebung* (sublation)—a mimetic sphere which would *not* prove the futility of resistance in a totally manipulated world. In most of his later essays, Horkheimer himself comes to the same conclusion and still remains theoretically committed to his original position. The following two passages are a good example of this ambivalence:

> The story of the boy who looked up at the sky and asked, "Daddy, what is the moon supposed to advertise?" is an allegory of what has happened to the relation between man and nature in the era of formalized reason. On the one hand, man has been stripped of all intrinsic value or meaning. On the other, man has been stripped of all aims except self-preservation.

He tries to transform everything within reach into a means to that end. Every word or sentence that hints of relations other than pragmatic is suspect. When a men is asked to admire a thing, to respect a feeling or attitude, to love a person for his own sake, he smells sentimentality and suspects that someone is pulling his leg or trying to sell him something. Though people may not ask what the moon is supposed to advertise, they tend to think of it in terms of ballistics or aerial mileage.

The complete transformation of the world into a world of means rather than of ends is itself the consequence of the historical development of the methods of production. As material production and social organization grow more complicated and reified, recognition of means as such becomes increasingly difficult, since they assume the appearance of autonomous entities.[15]

Insightful and skillful as it is in drawing a picture of the manipulated world, Horkheimer's analysis shies away from any discussion of the resistant forces. On the one hand, he subjects the specific alienation of the artistic sphere to a sharp analysis but fails to apply the same treatment to the possibilities of resistance, on the other. To be sure, a glimmer of hope finds its way into Horkheimer's reflections:

Insight into the suffering involved in mankind's situation, the situation in which it finds itself today even at the points where it disposes of the greatest power, can finally help to bring reason into human affairs. For events do not seem to lend much credence to the view that men are concerned chiefly with power. In contrast to their dictators, the peoples of the world have in fact gone to war only with great reluctance; if they have not infrequently been keyed up for war, it is because they have overcome their repulsion through some form of rapture. Men are at bottom far less interested in being "authentic" and "real" than in being happy, even if they have forgotten what being happy means.[16]

Horkheimer touches upon a significant element here; he attests to the existence of a strong force of resistance, and this is bound to have philosophical and aesthetic consequences. Man's drive toward a more meaningful life free from total manipulation creates a range of ideas and, consequently, a kind of aesthetic sphere which differs greatly from the Joycean, the uncompromisingly alienated, purely aesthetic sphere. This aesthetic sphere will not succomb to the pseudoaesthetic of the culture industry either.

Thus we arrive at a little-known point wherein the basic differences between Lukács and Horkheimer lie. There is a basic agreement between Lukács and the Frankfurt School, that includes Horkheimer's philosophical position that the negative, the bad, is not perceived as a surface phenomenon of capitalism but as one inherent in capitalism. Both Horkheimer and Lukács regard fascism and other unspeakable horrors of modern times as the unfolding of the inner mechanisms of a totally manipulated world. It follows that they are not very sympathetic to leftist journalism, even though it is often represented by men of the greatest integrity. This integrity invited respect but also obscured the questionable value of the contribution. After all, the bourgeois-democratic Left did not pay the attention due the ascending fascist threat. It will suffice to mention the circle around *Weltbühne,* especially Ossietzky who later became the hero and martyr of the antifascist movement. But after the 1930 *Reichstag* elections, he still fought against the social democrats who, in his words, fight a "nobody like Goebbels who for all practical purposes does not exist instead of waging a campaign against Brüning, the real candidate of the dictatorship" (*Weltbühne,* 1930, September 6, p. 425).

Aside from these points of agreement, there is no complementarity between the positions of the Frankfurt theorists and the Marxist Lukács. This is clearly shown by the differences in their aesthetic: For Lukács, the point of departure is Thomas Mann and his type of art, realism, while for Horkheimer it is Joyce and his "queer, discordant forms." The Marxist analysis sees in Thomas Mann's Faustus concept the true continuance and the contemporary variance of the Goethean ideal, while for Horkheimer only a Guernica and an alienated artistic sphere come into consideration.

The question then arises: What is the social determination of the Horkheimerian aesthetic? We have seen that the recognition of the existence of man's native mimetic impulses necessarily led to an isolated existence and the grounding of the aesthetic sphere is alienation. Reference was already made to Horkheimer's concept of man and his *Kulturkritik;* thus it is logical that the private atomic subject, the isolated individual, the monadic individual who tries not to succumb to his barbarous surroundings has become the central category for Horkheimer and the basis for his concept of the isolated aesthetic sphere. In their aesthetic reflections, other members of the Frankfurt School picked up these elements and even elaborated on them; for example, for Adorno only the Schoenbergian music could become the central category of modern music. These elements make manifest that bourgeois ideology believes but in the negativity of aesthetic education as befitting the modern era; nothing less than the individual's cutting himself off from modern world can be the proper aim of the aesthetic sphere.

This brings us back to the point discussed earlier in a positive sense, to the attempts to revive the ideology of entrenchment of "the age of poetry." In Goethe's time, there existed indeed an entrenched camp. But as the novel *Wilhelm Meister* proves, the camp did not serve exclusively defensive purposes, it had also an offensive character. It intended to prepare for a new world and to cultivate all that was not part of official German politics but that was slowly growing in man himself. By means of erecting an entrenched camp, there would be a shelter against contemporary German conditions. The new attitude, however, is an entrenchment of the individual and even of the artistic praxis from reality itself. In Goethe's time, it was to serve as a fortification behind which the artist could unfold his talent. In Horkheimer's conception, the entrenchment overwhelms; while the individual is steadily engaged in building his fort, he loses sight of the horizon completely. The fortification takes precedence over all other activity; it will exist only autonomously in itself and for its own sake.

Whom then did Horkheimer intend to defend? Was it art itself? Primarily, yes, but in the process he severely limited the possibilities of art; the total entrenchment amounts to a wall of self-imposed boundaries which art does not need. It is true that modern art was now and then capable of blowing up those self-built walls as a Guernica illustrates. In the end, however, Horkheimer's aesthetic conception restricts not only art but individuality itself; in his self-entrenchment, the individual looks with the same critical attitude upon the manipulative and antimanipulative forces alike. Such an aesthetic understanding isolates the individual from a world of possibilities. As Göran Therborn puts it:

> The classical Frankfurt School preserved Marx's critique of the evils of capitalist society, but grew increasingly sceptical about the remedies he proposed for those evils; the proletarian revolution and the release of the productive forces it would bring about. But this scepticism did not lead them to a renunciation of Marxist theory or to a reconciliation with capitalism, but rather to a hyper-radicalization of their ideological and political stance and a retreat from any political practice into philosophy and aesthetics. The most striking example of this pessimism-cum-radicalism appears in Horkheimer's and Adorno's discussion of science and technology, which had generally been treated as progressive and revolutionary in the Marxist tradition, but which the Frankfurt School increasingly saw as the direct cause and justification for social oppression.[17]

Thus the Frankfurt theorists arrive at a radicalism which goes beyond the boundaries of the real world; its sole purpose is to help the bourgeois artist to hold on to his radical beliefs. Or more precisely, this radicalism enables the bourgeois artist to believe that *his cutting off from the social world* amounts to a radical progressive stance. In the final conclusion, this aesthetic serves only to reinforce the illusion of the avant-gardistic tendencies of bourgeois art.

Notes

1. Max Horkheimer, *Critical Theory: Selected Essays* (New York: Herder & Herder, 1972), p. 252.
2. Ibid.
3. Max Horkheimer, *Critique of Instrumental Reason* (New York: Seabury Press, 1974), pp. 8–9.
4. Iring Fetscher, "The Young and the Old Marx," in *Marx and the Modern World,* ed. Nikolaus Lobkowicz (Notre Dame, Ind.: University of Notre Dame Press, 1967).
5. Horkheimer, *Critique,* pp. 16–17.
6. Max Horkheimer, *Eclipse of Reason* (New York: Oxford University Press, 1947), p. 115.
7. Horkheimer, *Eclipse,* p. 116.
8. Horkheimer, *Critical Theory,* p. 273.
9. Horkheimer, *Critical Theory,* p. 275.
10. Herbert Marcuse, *One-Dimensional Man* (Boston: Beacon Press, 1964), p. 60.
11. Horkheimer, *Critical Theory,* p. 278.
12. Mortimer J. Adler, *Art and Prudence* (New York and Toronto: Longmans, Green, 1937).
13. Horkheimer, *Critical Theory,* p. 281.
14. Horkheimer, *Critical Theory,* p. 289.
15. Horkheimer, *Eclipse,* pp. 101–2.
16. Horkheimer, *Critique,* p. 33.
17. Göran Therborn, "Jürgen Habermas: A New Eclecticism," *New Left Review* (no. 67, May–June 1971):79.

12
Negative Philosophy of Music: Positive Results

Ferenc Fehér

An increasing body of established opinion has come to recognize Theodor Adorno as the apostle and apologist of avant-garde music, as the major opponent of the reflection theory, and consequently as the critic who has done most to loosen up the causal relationship between art and society. Or to view the matter on the simpler level of personalities, Adorno is seen as the antipode of Georg Lukács, the father of representative Marxist aesthetics. Certainly the often irritated, at times even bitter exchanges between the two thinkers would make such a distinction convincing.

Despite this seeming contrast, upon closer examination quite a different picture emerges, not only of this relationship, but also of Adorno's lifework in the theory of music. Imbedded in their differences are to be found *in the order and the temporal-topographical positioning of their chosen artistic values* common elements fundamental to both men's thought. In terms of human content and aesthetic perfection, the period from Shakespeare to Goethe, i.e., to the end of the artistic age, is for Lukács as a literary scholar very much what the span between Bach and Beethoven is for Adorno. Their theoretical imagination is moved to heights of critical passion *by the very same thing.* Just as in Lukács's oeuvre nothing surpasses his analysis of the fateful turning points in Goethe and Hegel, so in Adorno's lifework there is no equal to his anatomical outline of *Missa Solemnis.* These two men are also inspired by a *common source*: In their analyses, both are drawn to the great achievement of modern history, the birth of the autonomous freeborn subject, the free bourgeois individual. To be sure, at a later point they both "revoke" this achievement by exposing the subsequent reification and alienation of this free individual. Nevertheless, during this *intermundium* of a century or a century and a half the free individual was to attain unsurpassed heights of art. Thus both thinkers emphasize their unqualified admiration for the artistic microcosm of totality *created by the autonomous subject.* With the exception of antiquity, Lukács practically ignores preceding eras in his analyses. Similarly, Adorno's evaluations of earlier periods are little more than insinuating disparagement.

Despite their differing terminology, the golden age of art, the period of great realism, possesses identical characteristics for both theoreticians. It is the image of a socialized and liberated humanity which elevates the most banal literary or musical material to the level of world history. From every point of the horizon, music from a world not yet subject to developments in electricity radiates the motif "seid umschlungen Millionen" ("you millions, I embrace you"). The work of art is organized into a genuine totality. As such, it bears the stamp of the "realm of reason," the external reality which furnishes authenticity; and this is brought about by the self-realizing activity of the individual creating the artistic totality. This is the basis for both Lukács's theory of form derived from Goethe's novel and for Adorno's analysis of Beethoven's symphony. Both men assert rapturously that the work of art *does have its ontology* because its mere existence, the mode of its formation, *affirms* the given world, and this spontaneously profound affirmation is only rarely abused by ideology in the negative Marxist sense of the word. Both Lukács and Adorno are enemies of "Schillerizing" diction which for them reflects the totalitarian abuse of a flesh-and-blood individual at the hands of an idealized notion of the citizen. But just for this reason they admire the rare moments of fusion between high and low culture. Thus the Shakespearean stage with its crude, yet cunningly transfigured whirl of the marketplace almost imperceptibly comes to express the most abstruse moments of crisis in Renaissance philosophy; and the philosophical bestseller *Werther* evokes a nostalgia in Lukács similar to Adorno's response to the *Magic Flute*, that last perfect hybridization of the ditty and the highest order of classical music. Finally, philosophy and high art are regarded as twins in both theoretical systems. Both Lukács and Adorno oppose the slick cult of spontaneity and maintain that *The Phenomenology of Mind* together with Goethe's *Faust*—or for Adorno, all of Beethoven's symphonic compositions—sum up the same world: the world of the birth of dialectics. Only when understood in this way can the often hackneyed concept of dialectics have any meaning. Adorno uses *History and Class Consciousness*, which had been a formative experience of his youth, as a point of departure. For the music philosopher, dialectics is the expression of the subject-object relationship, the vehicle for the realization of the subject-object identity. For this reason, Adorno's analysis of Beethoven's developing variation and reprise becomes an important contribution to the yet unwritten history of dialectical reason.

If a topographical positioning of masterworks along with their axiological conception is shared by both men, a common measure for assessing the *decline* of these works must also exist. The term *decadence* may seem startling here, since Adorno himself rejected the expression and relegated it to the vocabulary of the petty bureaucrat or the football coach. But Adorno does indeed have a theory of decadence, a theory no less consistent than that of Lukács. His treatment of *Missa Solemnis* already reveals signs of the "rupturing of totality" in this work. According to his analysis, Beethoven is compelled to make the best of the "barbaric advantages," the problematic means of a willed and hard-won unity. For the same reasons a similar analysis can be found in Lukács's portrayal of the aged Goethe creating the second part of *Faust*. Of course the tragic figures of transition are not identical for both—or at least, not always—although students of Lukács's Raabe essay may well discover numerous features similar to Adorno's Brahms interpretation. The contrast between their selections is quite evident. Adorno finds in Wagner and Mahler the heroic and still representative rearguard of a great music, which had become increasingly problematic. In contrast, one can easily document Lukács's antipathy for Wagner; and he also denies all internal heroism to Mahler's Viennese literary counterparts. Yet who can help but notice the Wagner-Mahler issue in Lukács's comments on Baudelaire and in his recurrent analyses of Flaubert. Despite his ruthless analysis of value hierarchy, Lukács extends the *same* understanding to all who must battle with inner resolution but defeated hopes.

The two theoreticians' inventories of present-day art offer the next astonishing parellel. Here Adorno is just as inflexible and curt as the alleged "cultural conservative" Lukács with his lack of enthusiasm for the new. Of course, the great exception is the New Music of Vienna. But a survey of Lukács will reveal an equally great exception: the rebellion of humanism and the restoration of the great legacy of the past within socialist literature. In general, of course, Adorno shows little such consideration. He expresses, for example, pronounced contempt for Debussy's musical form because of its deeply atomistic-narcissistic character, linking it to Bergson's philosophy which he finds unacceptable. Similarly, the "vulgarizing" Lukács rejects the epic form of Proust, Debussy's literary counterpart. Even if his contempt remains concealed by a grand-seigneurial style, Adorno betrays his feelings when he draws a direct connection between the esoteric French composer and Duke Ellington. Another example is Adorno's list of Stravinsky's sins: first, his aimless repetitions which liquidate time are seen as the musical mirror images of Nietzsche's retrograde theory of *Wiederkehr des Gleichen* (the recurrence of the same); second, his static music is described as the art of a dead-end street where everyone is waiting for Godot. Just as the first reference deals a considerable blow to Nietzsche, whom Adorno otherwise respects, so the second is directed at the altogether too mature and revered Beckett. Thirdly and finally, the "asocial collectivism" of Stravinsky's music, which is nothing more than a paradoxical play on the notion of community, creates for Adorno a music of enslavement. Despite a lack of musical expertise, on the basis of deep subjective experiences I must concur with this opinion. Not even Schoenberg's radical experiments escape criticism. Here it is directed at Schoenberg's rejection of "animal warmth," which links him in part to the composer Leverkühn. More fundamentally, however, Adorno criticizes Schoenberg for having failed in his most profound aspiration. Schoenberg had not succeeded in eliminating the contradiction between substance and phenomenon, "latent organization and manifest music," because in his age the creation of a world by the musical subject, although *still* a logical necessity, was *already* an impossibility. Moreover, Adorno considers the extreme emphasis on technique in current music to be a reflection of the principle of "production for the sake of production," and this, in his terminology, is the gravest of insults.

In Adorno's phenomenology the *crisis of music* is exacerbated by *the degradation of reception and commission*. Both the sociology of art and his "pure" aesthetics are in essential harmony with Lukács. At this point we need not elaborate upon the phenomenology of cultural crisis as depicted in Adorno's uniquely rich arabesques. An outline of its basic stages should suffice. On the first level, we find a truly penetrating typology of the fetishized regressive listener, who wants to hear in everything the music of "fear because of freedom." Second, there is a biting critique of the carefully constructed apparatus employed in the factory production of music and of the increasing practice of the music makers to substitute the electronic brain for the human brain and systematic market research for inspiration. Third, we note Adorno's rejection of a pseudocollective musical community made to serve autosuggestive and deceptive goals. And finally, Adorno concludes that streamlined competition enables performing techniques to accomodate all of the above with a managerial flexibility. So monumental is this phenomenology that even its obvious biases are instructive. These biases, some of which will be touched upon later, reveal once again Adorno's relationship to his supposed antipode, Lukács. At this point we shall concentrate only upon the final result of Adorno's analysis. His historico-philosophical argument is the same one upon which Lukács bases his repeatedly attacked decadence theory, which holds that a society of generalized exchange value is inimical to intellectual production, especially to art. In short, we arrive at Marx's prognosis.

To prove the profound relationship of the two antagonists, let us briefly call to mind the decisive factors common to their systems of categories.

Human species character, the "concern of humanity," plays the same regulating and unifying role in Lukács's aesthetics as the call for a collectivized liberated humanity in Adorno's philosophy of music. It is their systems' conclusive point of reference and their ultimate paradigm. For both thinkers, however, this *universality* can be realized only in the perfectly developed *particular*. The destruction of the individual character and the didactic-rhetorical-ideological element are the adversaries of artistic consummation to both. Nevertheless, according to Lukács's aesthetics, only the artist who surpasses his own particular personality is capable of his consummation; and in Adorno's similarly conceived formula, only the artist who is not a private but a social individual is able to achieve it. Finally, Adorno's easily misconstrued thesis concerning the inevitable antisocial nature of art also has a Lukácsian equivalent in the constantly defetishizing function of art. This presentation of the essential parallel underlying the apparent contrast is not meant to serve philological ends. It attempts instead to reveal the historico-philosophical foundation of Adorno's monumental achievement, one which will undoubtedly guarantee his permanence in aesthetics. Only by drawing upon this historico-philosophical, anthropological conception was Adorno able to create *the first genuine and profound outline of the semantics of music* which has withstood all later corrections. For indeed, an extremely antinomic structure reigns within the traditional "semantics" of modern music. The musical creation is seen as a Platonic impression of an idea which draws its *raison d'être* from a chimeric Other, a totally mysterious "message" within the sphere of music. From this basis we must arrive at one of two theories of music. First, we can derive a naturalistic theory which attributes to the tones of music and their unity a "natural" force serving to evoke specific feelings, and to human nature an isomorphic, innate capacity for response. This theory is obviously nothing more than myth clothed in the robes of science. Or, we can derive the cruder, more transposed symbolic theory of "program music." This second possibility is equally fruitless. It is a negation of Schiller's "Wenn die Seele *spricht, spricht die Seele* nicht mehr" ("if the soul speaks, it is no longer the soul which speaks"). Thus the adversaries of program music consider every interpretation scandalous except the purely technological one. However, it is not enough to note the crude vulgarism on the one hand or the journalistic lyricism on the other; to comprehend the sterility of these antinomic poles one has to consider the sociology of music, which both theories neglect. If either theory were correct—How could we explain the impossibility of uniformization in the "translation" of musical reception and the infinite variability of interpretation, or further, the fact that subjective interpretations cannot be restricted to the limits of one sphere? And if the second interpretation were correct—How could we account for historical changes in the social attitudes toward music, changes that are somehow simultaneous with *the* historical changes themselves? Moreover, how could we account for the actuality and legitimacy of those attitudes which are an undeniable fact of music theory?

The *tertium datur* propounded by Adorno is based on a unique *conception of mimesis*. By mentioning mimesis we again bring Adorno close to Lukács. This is not the place to discuss the undeniably problematic nature of the reflection theory; we do want to make clear, however, that the mimesis principle of *The Aesthetics*, apart from the frequent use of the term *reflection*, implies or exposes an approach with which Adorno should not have fundamentally disagreed. The first step of Adorno's mimesis concept is a paradoxical one: it departs from a "reality" that orders, provokes, stimulates, conveys, and sustains the work and proclaims the musical piece to be a windowless monad. Certainly Adorno is correct in describing the musical composition as an entity existing for itself. The work "says nothing else" than what it "expresses" with the organized entirety of its tones and there is no transcendent Other (the famous "message") "for whose sake" it exists. On the other hand, the composition is the *organized* entirety of tones, themes, theme-developing methods, etc. Therefore it is necessary to ask: With *what kind of* organization are we concerned here? A question made relevant even by the most primitive material the sociology of music deals with. *In whose name* are the elements of a musical work organized? And finally, since every kind of "organization" is directed toward some order—*What kind of* order is established by the composition of the musical work? Undeniably, these are already questions of "content" and "society," and yet they are questions that, whether well articulated or not, are provoked by every kind of listening experience. The answer lies in the question itself. *The "content" of the musical work is not something that exists outside of itself but is contained in its own organization*, an order embodied in this organization (or perhaps its disintegration in all its variations). However, the concept of every kind of order, every kind of structure, and every kind of totality is still "external" to music, since it imposes itself upon the composer from the external world. Hence the work stands on its own as a windowless monad, a *being-for-itself*, yet at the same time it points beyond itself to the world where the idea of its organization originated—it is a *being-for-us*.

The composition of the work as a uniquely organized whole, a "world," is mimetic for Adorno to the extent that it takes "social interactions" (Marx) and their historical development as the external model of its own principles or organization. Naturally the composer rarely experiences the mimetic organization with full consciousness, and Adorno does not completely explain how the organization is achieved. But this question, fundamental to the psychology of art, has not yet been answered by anyone. And if we consider that only for little more than half a century psychology has known or suspected how a basic affective structure like that of sexuality corresponds to social interaction, we cannot be too demanding. We should rather be content with what we have already learned, what has been conquered by theory. The structure of social intercourse, as the "background structure," which consciously or unconsciously molds the immanent structure of music, must ultimately provide the key for musical semantics.

It is impossible for an essay such as this to shed light on all the richness of this "Copernican revolution." We can only point to its highlights. First of all, *for Adorno, musical organization is not simply an order but a totality*, at least in the case of matured and emancipated Western European music. For a detailed explanation of the differences between these two concepts, the reader is advised to consult Lukács's essays in *History and Class Consciousness* from which Adorno himself took the distinction. It is not to his credit that he carefully avoided mentioning the source of his youthful inspiration. Schematically, the essential difference is as follows: Order is the absolute interconnection of objects, and totality is their entirety consciously realized as being-for-us. This explains why, in Lukács's conception, bourgeois society, based on goal rationalism and an attempt to change futile heterogeneity into a rationalistic homogeneity, is the first historical formation of totality sui generis. In accordance with this conception, Adorno maintains that Renaissance and late Renaissance music is merely order formation (and thus judged inferior), whereas the music of the initial bourgeois period (whether called baroque or preclassical) is a *rationally organized totality*. His occasional reproaches of Bach's music as "mathematical over-organization" (kept to a whisper before the great authority of Bach) are made in the spirit of purposeful rationality which organizes orders into totality. Even in its suspicions and absurdities, Adorno's animosity is derived from the ideal of an unsurpassable world-historical epoch.

From the point of view of musical semantics *the relationship of subject and object and of individual and community* is another extremely important aspect. Of course the two pairs of categories are far from being philosophically identical. Only in the mentality of bourgeois society does everything which is different from or more than the individual left to himself become identical with the object. However, it is not Adorno personally but all post-Hegelian philosophy that is collectively responsible for this confusion of categories. Adorno always poses the same question (and the answer given determines Adorno's interpretation of the composer's world view): As a totality, is the work of art *of a totalitarian or of a free-collective character*? Consequently he inquires whether the musical subject, the musical individual (which, of course, for reasons of its own universality cannot be conclusively defined—being at times identical with the individual tone, at times with the "theme" or with the part for the concert instrument) is able to develop from within itself and to organize the totality of the musical work from the inner dynamics of the participating elements; or whether the order is organized for these elements, that is, forced upon them. Since this totality in the history of music from Bach to Beethoven was born out of the self-movements of the musical subjects, Adorno maintains that this was the golden period of a free and collectivist music, which may never recur. But he criticizes even his favorite composer Beethoven for forcing his concept of order on the musical individual. In other words, Adorno realizes that the "uncritical affirmation of existence," which is made possible by the unhampered emergence of totality organized out of the dynamics of individual movement, can no longer be maintained or developed. His best analytical achievements, the interpretations of *Missa Solemnis* and *Opus III* (magnanimously dedicated to Thomas Mann), grow out of this knowledge. As the tragic representative figure of transition, Gustav Mahler should already have acknowledged the divergent movement of the parts, the subjective elements, and should have adjusted his formless form to these divergences.

Perhaps the richest and most developed dimension of Adorno's semantics is his concept of the disintegration of the "thought content" of musical time. He states clearly that the "attitude" of music (music being a primarily temporal art) to the process of time is the most significant criterion in terms of its relationship to the concept of progress. As the coauthor of *Dialectic of Enlightenment* and an expert on Marx, Adorno is obviously not a simple evolutionist. However, he firmly believes that totality can only be dynamic and that musical subjects can find fulfillment and be organized into a communal order only in a progressive time. In other words, time progress is nothing but the dynamics of this self-organization and formation into order. To be sure, Beethoven's developing variations prove that the more problematic "progress" is, the more diversions, roundabouts, and returns are needed for the creation of the reprise as the self-affirmation and self-justification of the whole process. In the end the self-justification of dynamics is reached in Beethoven. However, the temporal essence of Mahler's music (here the composer represents a type) is the absence of the reprise, the deflection of time: The themes reach a different goal than intended, and musical dynamics become the mimetic copy of life's confused disorder. And if for a moment we look to Adorno's attacks on Stravinsky and see these as leveled against *a type*, then the main reason for his animosity becomes more understandable. According to Adorno, whoever is "antitemporal"—thereby creating static patterning in pseudodynamics—is "antiprogressive." It is this grandiose outline of musical semantics that is wholly in accordance with the mimesis concept of Lukács's aesthetics. The point where Adorno and Lukács diverge can be noted in Adorno's interpretation of the New Music of Vienna. In this regard it is not crucial that Lukács, in his few sporadic statements, always remained hostile to Schoenberg, while Adorno regarded the Schoenberg-Berg-Webern movement as the only creditable classical one in modern music. Nor should one locate their basic disagreement in Lukács's critique of the twelve-tone system as *technique*. Even if Lukács (mainly in the 1930s) made statements *a limine* connecting the utilization of certain techniques with the principle of disintegration, it follows from the whole of his aesthetics that techniques in themselves are artistically indifferent: They may do just as much service as disservice to the "concern of humanity."

In a peculiar way dodecaphony as a technique is not that indifferent to value for Adorno. In the twelve-tone system he sees the fulfillment and the perfection of Max Weber's well-known concept of rationalization. Adorno perceives the development of modern music as a process of rationalization becoming increasingly universalized and he regards *rationalization carried to the end as a value in itself.* The universal value of Weber's concept cannot be challenged, for it was his idea of rationality that aided the best Marxist analyses of capitalism. Nor can the value character of the rational organization of music be called into question. The latter is related to what we identified in Adorno's musical semantics as a totality, a consciously organized order. But even if Max Weber's idea of the gradually realized goal-rational organization of music is accepted as objectively correct, a few questions are in order. First, can we speak of a "teleological preformation"? Does it really follow from the premature gestures of the integrated composition that rationalization carried to completion must culminate in this form, in the twelve-tone technique? Adorno triumphantly points to Schütz as an example. This is not a rhetorical question, but a real issue to be resolved—by experts only. If expert opinion is unanimously affirmative on this issue, then the second question, which is actually an objection, can be raised: Is technological rationalization of music, ruthlessly pursued to its end, a summit and a consummation? Adorno himself indicated the numerous, deeply problematic elements of this process when it is realized by means of strict logic: the natural affinity to dispassion (in Schoenberg); the empty intimacy (in the later Webern); the impenetrable "expertise" characteristic for all of them (in Adorno's terminology a pejorative concept); and the decisive circumstance that in this superrationalized musical medium the subject of the new music undergoes primarily an irrational world experience—existential anguish. It was Adorno who showed all this, and yet he considered rationalization carried to completion a consummation. In terms of Max Weber's premises, this is logical and consistent, but it is much less so when viewed in connection with Adorno's veneration for Marx. After all, universal rationalization is the consummated world or the never attained utopia of bourgeois society, but under no circumstances is it Marx's projection of a free human society.

One need not refer specifically to Marx to realize that at this point a little romantic anticapitalism would do no harm. In a very personal sense, Adorno had a theoretical impulse at his disposal which might have assisted him in countering the one-sided program of musical rationalization—namely the impulse from Kierkegaard, who had been the subject of the brilliant dissertation of his youth. Yet he did not take advantage of this opportunity. According to Kierkegaard, music is the art of sensuous genius. Let us now approach the issue not from the point of view of the artist but from the point of view of the medium; that is, let us demand from music not genius but sensuous-melodic fullness. This sensuous-melodic fullness is simply a condition of emotional saturation, the banality of which should not be reason for embarrassment, since it is always to become manifest. Thus what Adorno regarded as consummation was instead ambiguity. For Adorno, technical perfection and the inexorable logical process of goal-rational construction (assuming this construction really was destined to emerge from the premises of Western European rational music) were accompanied by a degrading of the sensuous-melodic fullness of music, its banalization, and consequently, its expulsion from the realm of "elevated music."

Adorno is simply unwilling to acknowledge antinomy, and this compulsive disregard leads to those consequences of his negative dialectics which are most problematic with regard to music. What does the principle of negativity mean in Adorno's philosophy? It means the appropriation of Marx's concept of alienation as mediated by *History and Class Consciousness*. It also entails an analysis of bourgeois society and culture which traces the unfolding goal-rational praxis that gave birth to the free individual; or rather it shows how free individuals broke through medieval barriers to create the new goal-rational totality. The process, however, reverses at its peak. Totality, the result of the actions of free individuals, becomes an alien power dominating them. During this process the free individual loses his freedom and is degraded to the level of the "fortuitous individual." Focusing on the regressive character of this movement,

Adorno's dialectic is negative in a double sense: On the one hand, it negates what exists; on the other, it theoretically denies the *possibility* of collective counterforces opposing the existing order.

For music, this theoretical standpoint implies above all the rejection of the artistic validity and authenticity of all collective musical forms. Adorno brands one type of music as exotic-provincial, denying it any musical relevance for a member of a reified industrial society. The other he calls *völkisch*, describing it as a deceptively mythical music which promotes a false reproduction of the organic community and the myth of blood, race, and nation in a world of individualists torn from the community. The third type he indicts as pseudooppositional. Its nonconformism is in reality a conformism integrated into the system. It is very likely that in most instances Adorno's emphatic objections are correct. Nevertheless, two comments must be added to his analysis. In the first place, if his diagnosis is sound, Adorno cannot infer from his own premises any kind of consummation other than perhaps the joint decline of music and music interpretation. His critical improvisations which focus on the notion of musical consummation remind one at times of the comfortable and aesthetically deliberate posture of the man glancing into the depths from the glass veranda of the Grand Hotel Abyss. For in art, the severity of the Kant-Fichtean "what is necessary is possible" is not valid. What applies here is Wittgenstein's no less severe maxim: "Whereof one cannot speak, thereof one must be silent." Second, even without investing a lot of unnecessary optimism in the existence and possibilities of collective counterforces, one can defend the Wagnerian folksinger against Adorno's charge. When Hans Sachs looks to the people rather than to the realm of academic sterility, he is not a romantic demagogue. Of course, the question where there is really a people aware of this protest and capable of responding to it *with music*, or at least with the raw material of music, does not have to be answered by the composer. But to deny this possibility in principle is unjustifiable. That is why this writer, free from sophisticated musical knowledge, must necessarily view Adorno's analysis of jazz with profound suspicion.

In the outline of the typology of music listening, the negative dialectics is transformed into aristocratism. To Adorno every type of modern music listener is "regressive," that is, he experiences music as dissected into atoms, and thus he furthers and completes the already advanced state of disintegration of musical totality in the work itself. The only adequate music listener is the expert who immediately senses the whole structure and its possible deformations. True, Adorno is troubled occasionally by doubts. Did not Schoenberg's music, for example, which demands considerable technical knowledge for adequate understanding, change leisure time into working time for the receptor? But Adorno overcomes his doubts and remains loyal to the primogenitary right of the expert, the only unalienated listener. It is easy to see through the haughtily utopian character of this concept if we consider the numerous attacks upon the illusionism of the young Marx, who believed that the emancipation from the division of labor would make us all fishermen, hunters, and "critics of criticism," among other things. But if we imagine the musical life of a liberated future as one in which hundreds of millions will be entirely absorbed by the technical subtleties of an increasingly rationalized music— Will there be any time for hunting and fishing, let alone for the criticism of criticism? From another point of view, this concept is not merely utopian but aristocratic as well, for it simply does not acknowledge that within certain human communities—still small in number and predominantly intellectual—there is an increase in a particular kind of receptive attitude. With negligible expertise, but with much more active attention to music, these communities search for the "meaning" of music, very often feeling their way instinctively along the paths of Adorno's semantics of music. They view the work not as a pretext for an autosuggestive conjuring up of emotions, but as the objectified projection of an answer to their own human dilemmas. If there is to be a future of collective humanity free from alienation, then it is this attitude, rather than that of Adorno's idealized expert, which contains the greatest promise for universal acceptance.

From this perspective we can understand Adorno's great blunder in the Bartók question. His identification of all forms of the popular with *völkisch* and his unappeasable suspicion of pseudocollectivity behind every collective solution biased his view of Bartók's genius. He simply did not comprehend that it is possible to have a *single* synthesis of musical material and conception that is both provincially exotic and at the same time guided by world-historical considerations. For the sake of clarity let us take *Cantata Profana* as the model of synthesis. This synthesis "compresses" (Bartók's term) the patriarchal collectivity, from which it started, until the music raises the issue of all collectivity and of modern humanity's total alienation. But the adjective *single* before the word *synthesis* was emphasized for a reason. Critical opinions on this point are understandably voiced in diplomatic terms owing to the fact that this genius finally found a homeland and an audience after the unjust attacks leveled against him. Nevertheless this author shares the growing opinion that Bartók created a complete and *aere perennius* work, but that he did not open up a new path for musical development in general. And for good reason. As Adrian Leverkühn in a mood of "dies irae" said correctly, the composer must strive to give his work a respectable basis for life. But whether this "respectable basis for life and adaption" is actually realized is, in the final analysis, not up to the composer. A consistent error in Adorno's negative philosophy of music is his interpretation of Bartók as an eclectic composer. This error, however, is a natural consequence of Adorno's point of view. In much the same way Lukács—from whom this writer learned the language of philosophical thought—came to systematically misunderstand Kafka. Guided by a profound skepticism toward all collective action, Adorno could not understand Bartók's singular accomplishment. Similarly, as a result of his aversion to the miseries of torn and degraded individuality, Lukács remained unappreciative of Kafka's singular accomplishment. Perhaps it was no accident after all that it was precisely Adorno's late Bartók article that allowed Lukács to revise his consistent injustices toward Kafka by reviving the Swift-Kafka parallel. And even though one of them unjustly rejected masterpieces in the name of the omnipotence of real actions and the other in the name of the impotence of immediate action, their mistakes do not diminish the total value of their work, just as Lessing's well-known errors did not diminish his merits as the author of *Laokoon* and *Hamburg Dramaturgy*. Lukács and Adorno received their laurels at a conference on aesthetics in Royaumont in 1968 from an "angry young man" who wanted to tear some leaves from their wreaths: With a gesture of contempt for their "bourgeois concept" of the continuity of culture, he apostrophized Lukács, Lucien Goldmann, and Adorno as the "holy family."

13
Autonomy of Art: Looking Back at Adorno's *Ästhetische Theorie*

Peter Uwe Hohendahl

Theodor Adorno's major contribution to the philosophy of art, his *Ästhetische Theorie*, appeared in 1970.[1] The work was almost completed when the author died in 1969. Adorno meant to rewrite the introduction, but otherwise the text needed only formal revisions, which were carried out by Rolf Tiedemann, Adorno's faithful disciple and editor. Tiedemann rightly felt that *Ästhetische Theorie* deserved immediate publication since it was the legacy of Critical Theory. Yet it was precisely this aspect which marred the reception of the book. Except for a few voices in the liberal and conservative camp, the response was surprisingly negative. One might have expected that the East German critics would denounce Adorno's theory as a typical example of Western ideology—which they did; more alarming was the unfriendly or at least cool reception among the West German Left. If the members of the Frankfurt Institute considered *Ästhetische Theorie* Adorno's legacy, it turned out to be an *Erbe* which was clearly unwelcome. The charges varied, but there was almost a consensus among the critics of the left camp that Adorno's last book did not offer the materialist theory of art that everybody was looking for. It was particularly Adorno's insistence on the autonomy of the art work and his well-known indictment of *Tendenz* and political art which angered the Left. Adorno evidently had not changed his position. In his last work he reiterated his critique of unmediated *engagement* and once more presented modernism and the avant-garde as the only viable responses to the increasing brutality of advanced capitalism. His renewed claim that, in the final analysis, only the authentic work of art overcomes the stultifying atmosphere of the cultural industry met with disbelief and outspoken disapproval. The hostility was so strong that the German Left dismissed the book out of hand and left the appropriation to the conservatives who at this point were inclined to use some of Adorno's arguments for the defense of their aesthetic and moral beliefs.

What were the reasons for this bizarre development? After all, the leftist movement in Germany owed most of its theoretical insights to the Frankfurt School and especially to Theodor W. Adorno who taught the younger generation the critical approach to literature and music. When *Ästhetische Theorie* came out, the West German student movement had reached the climax of its public influence. At the same time, it faced its first major crisis. The remarkable public recognition did not translate into a lasting, serious impact on the social system which they critiqued and attacked. Unlike the American students, the West German students tried to solve this problem by forming more structured political organizations or moving closer to established political parties (DKP). In 1970 the student movement, entering its second phase, turned against its initial belief in spontaneous political expression and rallied around more orthodox leader figures like Lenin, Trotsky, or Mao Tse-tung. As much as these various groups fought among themselves and disagreed about strategy, they had one thing in common: their dislike of the Frankfurt School and its interpretation of Marxism.[2] They redefined their goals in terms of immediate political action and tried to establish a closer connection with the working class. Critical Theory became the victim of this reorientation. Since the New Left had been under the influence of the Frankfurt School at least until 1969, this critique was more than anything else a self-critique and therefore carried out with uncommon harshness. The members of the Frankfurt School were openly condemned as bourgeois and their theory denounced as liberal middle-class ideology. The liberal element in Adorno's writing—not only his concept of genuine culture, which clearly owed much to the eighteenth and nineteenth centuries and showed the *Bildungsbürger* in Adorno, but also his defense of individual freedom against the demands of the state and political parties—made him definitely unpopular with a movement that struggled to transform the social structure of West Germany. Using the yardstick of orthodox Marxism, Adorno's leftist critics found it easy to dismiss his late work, especially *Ästhetische Theorie*, as irrelevant for the Marxist project. It was either Lukács or Brecht and Benjamin who became the new cultural heroes, and their theoretical work was appropriated to develop an alternative position. Ever since the famous Benjamin issue of *alternative* in 1967 (no. 56-57), the extremely complicated personal relationship between Walter Benjamin and the younger Adorno, who became Benjamin's disciple, critic, and editor, was presented as a clear-cut opposition: on the one hand the smug Adorno who tried to suppress certain parts of Benjamin's oeuvre because they did not agree with his understanding of Benjamin's essential philosophy (which cannot be denied); on the other hand Walter Benjamin who moved closer to Brecht, transcended idealism and developed a truly materialist theory of art. We have to understand this emotionally charged debate as a political rather than philological discourse. The heart of the matter for the New Left was a defense of Benjamin's oeuvre against the authority of Adorno and its integration into the dogma of the Frankfurt School.[3]

The interest in Benjamin, particularly in his essays of the thirties, which support the Communist Party, reflects the yearning of the New Left to grasp and revive the element of political praxis in aesthetic theory. Since the Left placed the emphasis primarily on those elements in Benjamin's work which agreed with Brecht and overlooked other traditions, Adorno's critique of these essays, which he advanced already in letters during the thirties, could only fuel the aversion against the devious influence of Adorno's aesthetic elitism.

Altough this debate has not yet come to an end—the question of Benjamin's Marxism seems to be as undecided as ever—there is a growing consensus among the Left and its various factions that the initial approach and the way it shaped the discourse has lost its usefulness and its critical edge. While Benjamin scholars have realized that we have to get out of the old mold if we want to appropriate Benjamin's writings for the eighties, the discussion about Adorno's theory seems to linger without any direction.[4] It is time to take another look at *Ästhetische Theorie* and Adorno's essays on literature. This is not to make Adorno less controversial and thereby more acceptable to the established forces of the academy. The perspective which guided the interpretation and critique of Adorno in the early seventies was rooted, as I have tried to show, in a singular historical situation—the struggle between the student movement and the West German establishment. The historical distance from these events, which only the nostalgic observer can overlook, calls for a reappreciation. This rereading cannot simply dismiss the arguments of the early seventies and pretend to face the text for the first time, but it must be conscious of the limitations imposed on the interpretation at that time.

According to the Left, Adorno refused to apply his own theory to the political realm. He indulged in pessimism. Indeed the social theory of the Frankfurt School which started out in the thirties as a Marxist project became increasingly pessimistic with respect to Marx's prognosis that capitalism would ultimately self-destruct and give way to a socialist society. Faced with fascism in Germany and Italy on the one hand and monopoly capitalism in the United States on the other, Horkheimer and Adorno concluded in the forties that the Enlightenment, which was supposed to bring freedom and emancipation, had resulted in barbarism and slavery, not as an accidental relapse, as the liberal mind preferred to see this development, but rather as the logical outcome of the historical process. In their *Dialektik der Aufklärung* Horkheimer and Adorno argued that the political unfolding of *ratio* would lead to the increasing domination of nature by man who then would become the victim of his own structure of domination. Since Horkheimer and Adorno, unlike Lukács, had given up the belief that the proletariat would revolutionize the given social structure, their analysis of advanced capitalism did not include the revolutionary perspective of traditional Marxism. The Frankfurt School reached a position where man can analyze the logic of history but not organize political opposition. As late as 1969, shortly before his death, Adorno defended this stance against the demands of the students. The unity of theory and praxis, he argued, tends to privilege action.[5] And this emphasis becomes irrational when imposed on philosophy. Adorno denounced the call for praxis as dogmatic and insisted that the uncompromising rigor of theory which defends its realm against the onslaught of positivism offers the truly critical opposition. This last effort to preserve the priority of theory came close to the very position that the Frankfurt School castigated as traditional in the thirties. Adorno's use of the category of negation became abstract and thereby lost its critical edge.

Although Adorno refused to view his attitude as pessimistic, we cannot overlook that the gap between theory and praxis is widening in his later writings. His late work tends to dwell on the importance of art. It is not accidental that Adorno's last book deals with aesthetic rather than social problems. His concern with social questions leads to aesthetic rather than political theory. Adorno's philosophy of art is his final answer to the dilemma of social praxis. Adorno offers the authentic work of art as that emphatic opposition which can no longer materialize in political organizations. This perspective might look more attractive today than ten years ago when there appeared to be hope that the age of capitalism might come to an end. But is this kind of relevance a good reason for us to return to Adorno's criticism? Is Adorno perhaps becoming fashionable again because his aestheticism and pessimism appeal to the readers of the troubled eighties? By asking these questions I do not want to discredit the legitimacy of our present interests and simply restore the authority of Adorno and the Frankfurt School. Still, the question of what *Ästhetische Theorie* offers us today should be coupled with the complementary question of what do we offer to Adorno's theory and from where do we look at it.

Let me begin with a broad description of Adorno's philosophy. His oeuvre is clearly grounded in the tradition of German idealism, particularly in Hegel. The same can be said about Georg Lukács, but the results are strikingly different. When Lukács moved from an idealist to a Marxist position and attempted to work out a materialist basis for his criticism, he adopted Lenin's reflection theory which is supposed to support Lukács's concept of the organic work of art as the only authentic form of art. Adorno rejects this more traditional part of Hegel's aesthetics and insists that the rigorous historical approach should be extended to basic aesthetic norms and rules. Lukács also historicizes art and literature. However, coming from reflection theory and a general concept of realism he favors those forms of literature which express the interest and concerns of the proletariat—in other words social realism. Adorno, who admired the early Lukács, refused to accept this argument. In his essay "Erpresste Versöhnung"[6] he distanced himself from Lukács's theory of realism and at the same time harshly critiqued Lukács's concept of the organic work of art. Adorno denounces Lukács's struggle against modernism, i.e., writers like Kafka and Joyce, as the regressive part of Hegel's influence—a reduction of the work of art to considerations of content. Adorno on the other hand defends modernism precisely because he shares the historical approach with the Hegelian tradition. To put it more concretely, he rejects the attack on modernism because it is rooted in an ontological, ahistorical understanding of the organic work of art. Modern writers are not decadent and therefore unable to synthesize content and form; rather they try to work out the dialectic of social change and aesthetic innovation. What we call the history of literature, changes of style and genres, is not just a sequence of facts and events; it consists of a dialectical process in which the individual work is seen against the background of conventions and norms. Authenticity is reached only through the negation of the affirmative tradition. This stress on novelty should not be mistaken for an apology of the fashionable, it rather indicates that the aesthetic material itself is drawn into the historical process.

Adorno follows the idealist tradition of Kant, Schiller, and Hegel, and emphasizes the autonomy of the art work. Unlike the aesthetic theory of the later nineteenth century in Germany, which tends to view aesthetic principles as metahistorical, Adorno is much closer to Hegel's intention when he applies the historical critique also to the basic aesthetic categories—including the concept of autonomy. The legitimacy of this category is limited to the period between the eighteenth and twentieth centuries, although Adorno is never quite clear whether this period has come to an end. In his famous lecture on poetry and society of 1957[7] Adorno referred to the collective *Grundstrom* in the poems of Brecht and Lorca without indicating whether this grounding in a collective spirit marks the beginning of a new progressive era or the decline of poetry as a medium of philosophical truth. I shall come back to this ambiguity later.

First I would like to develop another important aspect of Adorno's theory: the correlation between the aesthetic and the social sphere.

When literary theory in the late eighteenth century developed the notion that art is autonomous, the intention was to free the art work from the demand of social praxis. The result is an abstract opposition between the social and aesthetic sphere. By historicizing the major categories of aesthetic theory Adorno brings these realms closer together again. Ultimately art and society belong to the same stream of history. This insight is certainly not new. The leftist Hegelians, beginning with Heine, used Hegel's model of history to understand the evolution of literature as representative for the development of social and political history. Adorno's approach stands in this tradition, but he is very much aware of its dangers. While he insists on the dialectic of art and society (the art work is also a social fact), he does not, unlike Lukács, conceive of it in terms of reflection. Adorno's *Ästhetische Theorie* is his final effort to grasp and theoretically refine the dialectic of the social and the aesthetic spheres.

Adorno's theory not only defends and legitimizes modernism and the avant-garde, it may well be called a theory of the avant-garde. Its author is clearly on the side of those historical forces which undermine the rule of European classicism. Adorno is a distant and skeptical observer of Winckelmann's ideas. Looking back at Greek classicism Adorno points out the material conditions of Greek history which were anything but ideal: brutal warfare, slavery, and oppression are the reality which have to be suppressed before we can enjoy the notion of perennial beauty and harmony in Greek art.

> Neoclassicism presented a unity of the general and the particular which already in the Attic period could not be attained, much less later. It is why the classic statues gaze at us with those empty eyes which, instead of radiating noble simplicity and silent greatness attributed to them by the neoromantic period, give us a[n archaic] scare. What is forced upon us as classicism has nothing to do with corresponding European classicism in the era of the French Revolution and of the Napoleons, not to speak of the time of Baudelaire [p. 241].

The object of this critique is the neohumanism of Weimar and its glorification of Greek art. This seemingly historical polemic has a methodological aspect which I want to bring to the foreground: Adorno, at least implicitly, speaks here against the model that was used by the early Lukács to situate the novel form. Adorno undercuts the fundamental assumption of Lukács's *Theorie des Romans* that early Greek literature was grounded in social conditions which were free of alienation.

This critique of classicism becomes important because it is at the same time a critique of a model which was further developed by Lucien Goldmann. For Goldmann the task of the critic and sociologist of literature is to establish a homology between the social and the literary structure.[8] Adorno's theory looks similar, yet this similarity is deceptive. While Adorno shares with Goldmann the interest in formal structure and rejects any kind of *Inhaltssoziologie* as vulgar materialism, he is careful not to press the correlation into the homology model. The difference becomes apparent when Adorno defines his approach as *immanent*. The critic is starting out from the text rather than beginning with an analysis of the social structure. It is the explication of the work of art which offers insight into the social conditions that defined the production of the work of art. In his essay "Rede über Lyrik und Gesellschaft" he unfolds the notion that the social meaning of the poem is expressed through its language. The poem relates to social history only indirectly. Adorno calls the poem a philosophical and historical sundial; by deciphering the structure of the poem the critic decodes the meaning of social history. Again, this sounds like Goldmann's theory, but we have to note the distinction: The interpretation of the poem refers to the *meaning* of history, not to the facts or objective structures. The two realms are mediated by philosophy—more specifically the philosophy of the early Marx. Unlike Goldmann, Adorno would never identify the work of art with an individual social group or class. This procedure which is typical of Goldmann's criticism, is unacceptable to Adorno on principle. The correspondence between art and society, the aesthetic and the social meaning, transcends the particular group or class. Authentic are only those works which are representative of the whole. The choice of the sundial as the key metaphor signals that for Adorno the important element in the text is its expressive force and much less the author and his/her intentions to build up a coherent vision of the world. The individual author enters the sphere of criticism only as the human voice, the historical subjectivity that objectifies the expression through the work. Thus the emphasis is placed on the objective side: The authentic work of art is given the status of a permanent testament of human history— it embodies the hopes and sufferings, the expectations and contradictions of the human race.

In *Ästhetische Theorie* Adorno tries to unfold this argument: "If [the authentic work of art] stands in opposition to empirical reality by means of its formal moment—and mediation between form and content cannot be comprehended without this differentiation—then a certain degree of mediation is to be found in the fact that aesthetic form is but a sediment of content" (p. 15).

Or another definition: "Only by separating itself from empirical reality—a separation possible, based on the need of art to manipulate the relationship between the whole and its parts—can a work of art become a being of second power" (p. 14). Here Adorno, following Walter Benjamin, introduces the concept of the monad. By comparing art works with monads Adorno tries to explore the dialectic of art and reality. Monads are closed, they have, so to speak, no windows and therefore offer no immediate access to reality. This, as it turns out, is quite necessary, since the outside world is already contained in a monad. Adorno then applies this idea to the understanding of aesthetic forms: "The unresolved antagonisms of reality recur in the works of art as immanent problems of its form. This and not the introduction of concrete moments define the relationship of art and society" (p. 16). These unanswered questions provide literary and art history with their dynamic force. The increasing contradictions of reality show up as dissonances of form, they propel the evolution of art to the point where the avant-garde artist negates the very principle of the art work itself. Thus only those works deserve to be called authentic which question their own formal structure.

By stressing the formal aspect of literary history Adorno arrives at a position close to that of Russian Formalism. He also argues that aesthetic criticism should be primarily concerned with questions of technique. The detailed analysis of seemingly technical points, in other words close readings, throws light on the social meaning. The comparison with Russian Formalism is fruitful with respect to considerations of form. There are also important differences. Adorno would have rejected the formalist notion that literary history can be fully understood in terms of its intrinsic evolution. As we shall see, Adorno insists on the totality of history no less than Hegel or Lukács. Therefore the approach of Tynyanov[9] that the critic has to look first at the literary sequence, then at the political or economic evolution, and finally try to relate these sequences would be shunned as undialectical and positivistic. While Adorno shares the concern of the Russian formalists with technique, his interpretation of history follows a model which is quite different.

In spite of his outspoken critique of the traditional dialectic which moves from thesis to antithesis and finally ends with a synthesis, Adorno's philosophy is still grounded in Hegel's philosophy of history. The concept of history which the formalists propose, although analytically sound, is unacceptable to Adorno, because it deprives the work of art of its emphatic truth value (*Wahrheitsgehalt*). Adorno's interest in literary evolution is not that of the historians who are satisfied when they have demonstrated how a genre changes or a motif is expressed in different ways. Adorno's theory puts a high premium on aesthetic innovation. Patterns, forms, genres are not fixed entities, but historical categories. However, the notion of change and innovation must not be fetishized. Its meaning can be understood only as a part of a larger historical context. Close reading is for Adorno, strange as this may sound, a contextual reading. When Adorno postulates that the sociologist of art must begin with the text, he presupposes a model of history in which the various spheres—social, political, philosophical, aesthetic—are part of a unified process. Thus Adorno's claim to *Immanenz* should not be interpreted as a German version of New Criticism, the equivalent of Emil Staiger for instance. Stressing the intrinsic approach means the opposite: It is the attempt to overcome the reification of traditional interpretation. Formalized professional scholarship insists on the rigorous definition of its object, the separation of the researcher and his/her material, without paying attention to their dialectical relationship in which the subject is very much part of the object and, on the other hand, the seemingly objective material the result of the subject's activities. When we talk about Adorno's approach we have to realize that he refuses to offer an objectified scientific method which can be abstracted from the individual act of understanding and then applied to various works.

Among the three approaches to the work of art, the interest in the origin and production of art, the interest in its structure, and the interest in its impact and reception, Adorno privileges, as we have seen, the structural procedure. He is less sympathetic to studies which try to understand art in terms of communication. Adorno argues:

> The objectivation of art [from a social standpoint, its fetishism] is in itself a social product of the division of labor. Thus, an examination of the relationship between art and society should not zero in on the sphere of reception as it precedes reception: it is to be found in the sphere of production. The interest in the social de-coding of art should turn to production and not be satisfied with analysis and classification; for societal reasons, they often are completely divergent from the works of art and their objective social content [p. 338].

This hostile remark against reception studies is primarily directed against positivism in musicology which tried to develop a quantitative method to demonstrate the success and significance of music.[10] Adorno himself was clearly interested in reception and wrote a number of important essays on the sociology of hearing.[11]

Adorno's emphasis on production as the key to understanding of the art work deserves closer scrutiny. What does he mean? Certainly not the kind of studies which were popular in the late nineteenth century, when the critic explained the work of art by documenting its sources and demonstrated the roots in the biography of the author. The individual author and his/her intentions receive rarely more than fleeting attention. Biography is in most cases treated on the anecdotal level. Adorno would agree with Lukács's argument that Balzac's intentions and the meaning of his novels were not identical. He carefully refrains from praising the genius, knowing well that this category is part of the liberal ideology: the self-promotion of the artist who has to deal with the market place. Adorno defines production of art in terms of the general economic and social conditions under which the artist has to work—feudal patronage, the competition of the capitalist market, or the situation of culture industry in advanced capitalist societies. Second, Adorno wants to emphasize artistic labor: the concrete struggle of artists with the techniques available at a certain time. By focusing attention on the process of production the critic at the same time reveals its meaning and truth value.

I want to give an example from *Ästhetische Theorie* to demonstrate what Adorno has in mind. There is no doubt that Adalbert Stifter was a conservative author. Both his critical prose and his works of fiction express a moderate and cautious stance. It is not accidental therefore that Stifter's reading public consisted to a large extent of educated conservative German *Bürger*, while the left camp remained indifferent or hostile. Typically enough, Lukács denied Stifter the status of a major German writer. Adorno agrees with neither side. His interpretation wants to rescue Stifter's work from his conservative admirers who find their own ideology confirmed in the message of the novels. Adorno is fully aware that this effort is problematical when he notes:

> The strata which granted him his somewhat esoteric popularity has since disappeared. This is not the last word about him, however. Especially in his late period, there is too much of reconciliation and reconcilability. Objectivity becomes a mere mask and the conjured life a ritual of resignation. But throughout his middle period, we perceive the suppressed and renounced suffering of the alienated subject and an unreconciled situation [p. 346].

This statement, however, is followed by another one which demonstrates Adorno's understanding of the authentic value within the conservative ideology: "The ideological overtension present lends [Stifter's] work its mediated nonideological truth content and guarantees its superiority over literature that can offer only solace and the overrated privacy of the countryside. It gives him the authentic quality Nietzsche so admired" (p. 346). Adorno clearly differentiates between the meaning that Stifter wanted to express in his writings and the *Gehalt* hidden in the structure

authenticity
hidden in
the structure of
the work

of the work. In the case of Stifter Adorno sets the utopian element apart
from the conservative ideology of the author. This is a significant move.
The sociologist who concentrates on the plot and the characters of, say,
Nachsommer, can read this novel as a typical example of the conservative
mood of the 1850s. The overriding themes offer plenty of evidence for
this thesis. Adorno, to be sure, does not deny the validity of this aspect,
yet ultimately the thematic conservatism of Stifter's novels is seen as
part of a larger context. Adorno's reading links the conservative component
to the industrial revolution of the fifties. The legitimacy of *Nachsommer*
is its negation of the new industrial society.

The category of negativity is crucial for Adorno's philosophy. Through
its negativity the work of art secures its authenticity and sets itself apart
from the convention of its time and genre. Indeed, Adorno deemphasizes
conventions because, as socially accepted models of artistic expression,
they indirectly also affirm the social status quo. This is the reason why
Adorno never feels quite comfortable with older literature or music. The
works of the sixteenth and seventeenth centuries rely heavily on conventional devices and moreover fulfill immediate social functions. They
are still embedded in social and cultural traditions of individual social
groups and classes. For Adorno they are less valuable because they belong
to a specific social setting and are not fully autonomous. Their truth
value appears to be more limited. This bias shows that Adorno's criticism
is not just another form of ideology critique. In this respect Goldmann's
theory is certainly closer to Marxist orthodoxy. Goldmann's procedure
focuses on a specific social and historical situation, for instance the
situation of the *noblesse de robe* in France, and then relates his findings
to the structure of individual works of literature, for example Racine's
tragedies. In the final analysis he maintains a base/superstructure model.
Adorno on the other hand, makes use of ideology critique to undermine
ossified structures and reified thought patterns. He firmly holds that those
works of art which deserve to be called *gelungen*. i.e., genuine and
excellent, cannot be reduced to the status of documents which reflect
the ideas of a particular class. Although the authentic work of art is
grounded in its historical moment, its truth value (*Wahrheitsgehalt*)
transcends the historical moment. This truth value, Adorno argues in a
key passage of *Ästhetische Theorie*, on which their rank ultimately rests
is historical through and through: "Truth value is not related to history
in a way that it, together with the status of works of art, changes with
the passing of the period. To be sure, some variations are possible; works
of art of high quality, for example, may unfold throughout history. This
does not mean, however, that truth value and quality devolve on historicism" (p. 285). Against any relativistic notion Adorno maintains that

there is an objectively correct historical consciousness: "Ever since the potential for freedom disappeared, correct consciousness . . . will be advanced consciousness about contradictions, with their possible reconciliation on the far horizon" (p. 285). The aesthetic analogy of this advanced consciousness are the forces of production within the art world, i.e., the craftsmanship of the artist, mastering the material, struggling against the general trend toward conformity. Artistic innovation, in other words, is the equivalence of the advanced historical consciousness.

It should be obvious by now that Adorno's theory summarizes the development of the last century. Its examples are the composition of Schönberg and his disciples and the evolution of modern poetry since Baudelaire. Whether this philosophy can be applied to medieval art seems doubtful, since the category of autonomy is central to the basic argument. This brings us back to my initial question. After outlining what Adorno "has to offer," we must ask ourselves where we stand and how we relate to this theory today. If we mean to take Adorno's philosophy of art seriously, we cannot evade this question, because theory itself is no less historical than literature and music. And Adorno was quite aware of this problem. In the introduction to *Ästhetische Theorie* he states: "Just as the concept of system or moral, the notion of a philosophical aesthetics today seems antiquated" (p. 493). Then the question arises: How can we develop a systematic aesthetic theory when most of the traditional categories on which this theory was built have become obsolete? The fact that recent history has liquidated basic concepts like the beautiful makes any attempt to systematize aesthetics highly problematical.

Baumeister and Kulenkampff have argued that Adorno could no longer follow Hegel's philosophy of art which places the emphasis on content rather than form because it privileges rational discourse and therefore imposes its concepts on art in such a way that art loses its status as an independent mode of expression.[12] Those elements of the work of art which cannot be grasped by theoretical concepts are indeed most meaningful ones for Adorno who is distrustful of rational discourse. By the same token Adorno cannot hark back to a more traditional genre theory which rests on metahistorical norms. Nor can he turn to Kant's aesthetic theory which is concerned with aesthetic experience. Still Adorno is convinced that modern art and literature are in need of aesthetic theory. Appreciation as a mode of criticism is not enough. Since philosophical criticism aims at the truth value of art, the critics must not confine themselves to subjective experience. The task is to decipher objective meaning and this can be accomplished only with the help of a theoretical framework. Especially the complexity of modern art calls for a theoretical approach. Adorno notes: "Precisely those moments of art which cannot be reduced to subjective experience and cannot be comprehended in their plain immediacy need consciousness, that is, philosophy. It is part of every aesthetic experience as long as it is not barbaric, alien to art. Art expects its own explication" (p. 524). So Adorno, in spite of his skepticism against rational discourse, clearly relates back to the tradition of philosophical aesthetics and turns explicitly against the concept of experience offered by positivism and pragmatism. He defines the goal of aesthetic theory as follows: "Aesthetics today should be above the controversy between Kant and Hegel without trying to form it into a synthesis" (p. 528). This reference to Kant and Hegel, Adorno's shorthand for two types of aesthetic theory, locates the realm in which Adorno tries to work out the tension between theory and history. He suggests that the categories of idealism still help us capture the emphatic meaning of modern art and literature, although modernism and the avant-garde are no longer grounded in idealism. Adorno is fully aware of the dilemma. The philosophical concepts of criticism are at the same time indispensable and inadequate. Because of this ambiguity the late work of Adorno tends to identify philosophy and art, since the process of deciphering and preserving, in other words criticism, is the only way in which truth in an emphatic sense can be revealed. Genuine art, for Adorno the last bastion that has not yet capitulated, is the sphere where the deception of instrumental reason is without consequence. This vision owes its force to Hegel, although it does not share Hegel's negative attitude toward postclassical art. For Adorno art and philosophy are inseparable but not identical. This position allows him to cling to the concepts of the work of art (*Kunstwerk*) and truth value (*Wahrheitsgehalt*) as his categories. When philosophy, as Adorno claims, in the phase of late capitalism, has lost most of its emancipatory functions, it becomes the task of the authentic art work to stand in and defend the tower of truth.

I started this essay with some remarks about the hostile reception of *Ästhetische Theorie* in the early seventies. This animosity was partly caused by the frustration of the student movement. The students were looking for a leader in their political struggle and had to realize that Adorno was unwilling and also unprepared to step into this role. This explanation, however, is insufficient. The lack of appreciation the younger generation showed in 1970 must be related to a broader phenomenon. Between 1967 and 1970 West Germany witnessed an almost unparalleled breakdown of the literary system. The radicals called for the end of literature and criticism, since the capitalist system had turned them into meaningless toys of the establishment. This crisis undermined the belief in the autonomy of art which Adorno defended against *Tendenz*. This debate is only the foreground for a deeper problem which had been lingering after World War II. I mean the fate of the avant-garde. Adorno's philosophy of art is closely related to the avant-garde of the early twentieth century. He takes most of his examples from works written or composed between 1890 and 1930. Seldom does he refer to later works. His literary criticism favors authors of the nineteenth and early twentieth centuries, such as Heine, Balzac, Eichendorff, George, Wedekind, Kraus, and Benjamin. The notable exception is his interpretation of Beckett's *Endgame* (1957)—a play which speaks very much to the mood of Adorno's late years.[13] Occasionally Adorno would play with the idea that the concept of autonomy of art might not be fully appropriate for the period that followed World War II. Here and there he cautiously alludes to the end of the avant-garde, yet he fails to pursue this perspective with any rigor.

Today it would be futile to suppress this question: Did the neo–avant-garde still have the same critical edge which Adorno saw in the works of the previous generation? The New Left answered this question in the negative. They appropriated the arguments of Horkheimer and Adorno's *Dialektik der Aufklärung* that there is no room for genuine culture in advanced industrial societies and therefore rejected the notion of aesthetic opposition. As I mentioned earlier, they discovered Benjamin's writings and followed his thesis that the autonomy of art, which was grounded in its ritual function, faded away with the advent of mechanical mass reproduction. Benjamin had argued: "But the instant the criterion of authenticity ceases to be applicable to artistic production, the total function of art is reversed. Instead of being based on ritual, it begins to be based on another practice—politics."[14] This thesis guided the theoretical efforts of the student movement. They wanted to tear down the walls of the aesthetic ghetto and apply the arts to the political realm. By 1975 it was clear that this movement had failed to reach its goal. The literary system slowly but surely returned to the status quo ante. I cannot go into the political and philosophical reasons for this failure.[15] My argument is exclusively concerned with the critique of Adorno's *Ästhetische Theorie* as it emerged from the crisis of the literary system.

As soon as we focus on this question we begin to realize what separates our situation from that of Adorno in the sixties. We notice that Adorno's philosophy of art has become historical. Adorno stresses the precarious state of modern art and emphasizes the negative impact of capitalism on culture, yet he maintains that the function of art has not changed since the advent of modernism. To put it differently: Adorno's theory takes the institution of art for granted. Peter Bürger advanced the argument in his *Theorie der Avantgarde* (1974) that Adorno failed to critique the concept of autonomy.[16] It was the aim of the avant-garde movement, according to Bürger, to overcome the gap between the aesthetic and practical spheres and regain political impact by eliminating the traditional aesthetic autonomy. Bürger convincingly demonstrates that Adorno, in spite of his hostility toward Lukács, shares basic philosophical assumptions with him. Their disagreement about realism and modernism is based on a common notion of the autonomous work of art. While Lukács tilted toward a model of organic works of art, Adorno placed the emphasis on the raison d'être of tensions and contradictions. In Bürger's analysis the sharp edge of the historical dialectic finally turns against Adorno himself. Following Benjamin, Bürger describes the avant-garde movement in terms of a self-critique which denounces the complacency of modern aestheticism. Compared with this radical stance where art moves toward its own destruction, Adorno's aesthetic theory reads like a somewhat belated summary of modernism—a recapitulation which is not quite ready to accept the extreme conclusions of twentieth-century avant-garde.

Not all critics and theorists have agreed with Bürger's thesis. W. Martin Lüdke for instance, in a response to Bürger, questioned whether *Theorie der Avantgarde* does justice to Adorno's category of modernism (*Moderne*).[17] He takes issue with Bürger's presentation of Adorno's theory of aesthetic innovation, and finally tries to show that Bürger's critique is not really intrinsic, but rather inspired by the social theory of Jürgen Habermas. Lüdke's rejoinder is persuasive as an interpretation of *Ästhetische Theorie*, but it is ultimately beside the point. Adopting a Habermasian position, i.e., looking at the Frankfurt School from a stance which has modified some of the basic tenets, enables Bürger to situate Adorno's aesthetic theory *historically*. Precisely because he stands outside of Adorno's theory he can point out that the logic of this theory is limited to a specific period of European art.

Although it may not be obvious at first sight, this argument has far-reaching consequences. It undercuts Adorno's key metaphor: The art work is no longer the sundial of history. The period after 1945, according to Bürger, is marked by a legitimate coexistence of different styles and tendencies. There is no stringent correlation between social and art history.

Bürger's critique and its strategy are sound and convincing. Yet I would like to go one step further. To some extent Bürger himself still operates within the confines of Adorno's model. His major thesis, i.e., that the production and reception of literature between 1780 and 1910 are determined by the concept of autonomous art, is obviously derived from Adorno. Looking back at this period today and viewing it within the broader context of preceding and following literary history, we realize that Adorno's idea of autonomy, which was then historicized by Bürger, never covered more than a part of the actual literary production of the nineteenth century. Much of the Restoration period (1815–48), with Heinrich Heine as the prime example, would not fit. Aesthetic autonomy as an episode of history: this perspective looks more familiar to us than to Adorno. He was not prepared to accept this interpretation, because it would have deprived him of any meaningful approach to history. In his essay "Das Altern der Neuen Musik" Adorno is ready to concede that modern music was more radical in its beginnings than in its later phases. Still he refuses to unfold the implications of this argument. He laments this development as a loss. His remark about Bartók's later work is typical of this attitude: "Partial responsibility for this is borne by the naiveté of the professional musician who goes about his business without partaking in the movement of the objective spirit."[18] This reference to the objective spirit indicates that Adorno, in the final analysis, relies on a Hegelian model of history in which all strands relate to one single center. The application of this model, however cautiously Adorno proceeded, seems to blind him with respect to the divergence of artistic trends and movements. While Adorno certainly rejected a reductive reading of history and was also skeptical of historical laws, his thinking is deeply rooted in the concept of a unified historical process. This idea then, since the project of the Enlightenment has failed, leads him to the notion that the evolution of modern music is regressive because there is less personal freedom and an increasing amount of alienating bureaucracy in our society.[19] In a way, this argument puts the blame on history for not following the course that the philosopher has mapped out for it.

What is problematical in Adorno's philosophy of art, in other words, comes from the historical determinism he inherited from the Hegelian and Marxian tradition. The link between this tradition and the Frankfurt School is the work of Georg Lukács, especially *History and Class Consciousness*. Those orthodox Marxists who denounced Adorno's theory as liberal ideology, failed to notice that they did not share his concept of the work of art and his approach to criticism, but based their aesthetic theories on the same understanding of history: history as a dialectical process in which the concrete is by definition part of the whole. For Adorno there is no philosophy without *Universalgeschichte*. As Russell Berman puts it in a recent article: "This historical scheme, an attempt to retain the universal history of Hegel and Marx, evidently precludes the possibility of perceiving the qualitatively new, for the new is only more of the old."[20] Although Berman underestimates the difference between Adorno and orthodox Marxism, he has a valid point.

What are we to learn from this critique? Does it mean that any project of defining aesthetic theory in historical-philosophical terms has become impossible, as Bubner[21] claims? Or are we to take the advice of H.R. Jauss and turn to a system of aesthetic experience? Both Bubner and Jauss[22] are prepared to eliminate history. This way they hope to regain a less problematical theory of art. I would not be willing to pay this price, for the loss of history would imply a fragmentation of experience which would decrease its meaning.

Notes

1. For a full account of the genesis of *Ästhetische Theorie* see Rolf Tiedemann's "Editorisches Nachwort," in Theodor W. Adorno, *Ästhetische Theorie: Gesammelte Schriften*, vol. 7 (Frankfurt: Suhrkamp, 1970), pp. 537–44. The following quotations from *Ästhetische Theorie* are from this edition.
2. For the development of the West German student movement and its impact on literature see *Literatur und Studentenbewegung*, ed. W. Martin Lüdke (Opladen, 1977); *Nach dem Protest: Literatur in Umbruch*, ed. W. Martin Lüdke (Frankfurt: Suhrkamp, 1979).
3. Cf. Jürgen Habermas, "Bewusstmachende oder rettende Kritik: Die Aktualität Walter Benjamins," in *Zur Aktualität Walter Benjamins* (Frankfurt: Suhrkamp, 1972), pp. 175–223; Philip Brewster and Carl Howard Buchner, "Language and Critique: Jürgen Habermas on Walter Benjamin," *New German Critique* 17 (1979):3–14.
4. Among the recent contributions to Adorno see Richard Wolin, "The De-Aesthetization of Art: On Adorno's *Ästhetische Theorie*," *Telos* 41 (Fall 1979):105–27. See also Anson Rabinbach, "Critique and Commentary/Alchemy and Chemistry: Some Remarks on Walter Benjamin and This Special Issue," *New German Critique* 17 (1979):3–14.
5. Theodor W. Adorno, "Resignation," in idem, *Kritik: Kleine Schriften zur Gesellschaft* (Frankfurt: Suhrkamp, 1971), pp. 145–50.
6. Idem, *Gesammelte Schriften*, vol. 11, pp. 251–80.
7. Idem, "Rede über Lyrik und Gesellschaft," in idem, *Gesammelte Schriften*, vol. 11, pp. 48–68.
8. Lucien Goldmann, *Pour une sociologie du roman* (Paris: Gallimard, 1964); idem, *Recherches dialectiques* (Paris: Gallimard, 1959).
9. Jurij Tynjanov, "Über die literarische Evolution," in *Texte der russischen Formalisten*, vol. 1, ed. Jurij Striedter (Munich: Fink, 1969), pp. 393–431.
10. Theodor W. Adorno, "Thesen zur Kunstsoziologie," in idem, *Ohne Leitbild* (Frankfurt: Suhrkamp, 1970), pp. 94–103.
11. Theodor W. Adorno, *Einleitung in die Musiksoziologie* (Frankfurt: Suhrkamp, 1962).
12. Thomas Baumeister and Jens Kulenkampff, "Geschichtsphilosophie und philosophische Ästhetik: Zu Adornos Ästhetischer Theorie," *Neue Hefte für Philosophie* 5 (1973):74–104.
13. Theodor W. Adorno, "Versuch das Endspiel zu verstehen," in *Gesammelte Schriften*, vol. 11, pp. 281–331.
14. Walter Benjamin, *Illuminations*. Ed. and with a forward by Hannah Arendt, trans. Harry Zohn (New York: Schocken, 1969), p. 224.

15. See my essay "Politisierung der Kunsttheorie: Zur ästhetischen Diskussion nach 1967," in *Literatur in der Bundesrepublik Deutschland seit 1965*, ed. Paul Michael Lützeler and Egon Schwarz (Königstein: Athenäum, 1980).

16. Peter Bürger, *Theorie der Avantgarde* (Frankfurt, 1974), pp. 117–27.

17. W. Martin Lüdke, "Die Aporien der materialistischen Ästhetik—kein Ausweg? Zur kategorialen Begründung von P. Bürgers *Theorie der Avantgarde.*" In *Antworten auf Peter Bürgers Bestimmung von Kunst und bürgerliche Gesellschaft*, ed. idem (Frankfurt: Suhrkamp, 1976), pp. 27–71.

18. Theodor W. Adorno, *Dissonanzen* (Göttingen: Vandenhoek, 1972), p. 140.

19. Ibid., p. 157.

20. Russell Berman, "Adorno, Marxism, and Art," *Telos* 34 (Winter 1977–78):165.

21. Rüdiger Bubner, "Über einige Bedingungen gegenwärtiger Ästhetik," *Neue Hefte für Philosophie* 5 (1973):38–73.

22. H.R. Jauss, *Kleine Apologie der ästhetischen Erfahrung* (Konstanz: Universitätsverlag, 1972).

Part Four
SOCIOLOGY AND
SOCIAL PSYCHOLOGY

14
Critical Theory
and Dialectics

Paul F. Lazarsfeld

Germany makes its contribution through what has come to be known as Critical Theory. This has created a schism among German sociologists and has had some repercussions abroad. One must distinguish a recent and a more remote history of this trend. In the mid-1920s the University of Frankfurt created an Institute of Social Research of which Max Horkheimer became director in 1931. Several years before Hitler came to power, the institute undertook a number of studies, the results of which suggested that the German working class probably would not resist the Hitler movement because the German family fostered submission to authority.[1] In 1932 the institute began to publish a journal which brought to public attention a number of younger men, all of whom were to make their mark: Theodor Adorno, Walter Benjamin, Erich Fromm, Herbert Marcuse. The introduction to the first issue emphasized that the journal would cover all social sciences because the group was striving for an understanding of the total course of history. The titles of the papers in this first issue were somewhat more specific. An economist discussed with approval the Marxian theory of prices, and two other papers dealt with the societal determinants of literature and music respectively.

The "Gesellschaftliche Lage der Musik" by Adorno is an article on music (forty-four pages long with a second installment of equal length in the next issue), which, in retrospect, set the direction for the program. A translation of the first three sentences will be helpful:

> Whenever music sounds today it reflects the contradiction and crevices which split contemporary society; at the same time the deepest gap separates music from just that society which creates it and its atomization, a society unable to absorb from its music more than its rubble and wreckage. The role of music in its societal setting is exclusively that of merchandise; its value is determined by the market. Music does not serve any more immediate needs and use but submits itself like any other merchandise to the constraints of the market.[2]

When Hitler came to power the institute left Germany for the United States. Because of this interruption it took several years before a programmatic statement was available. It appeared in 1937 in an article by Horkheimer entitled "Traditional and Critical Theory."[3] The paper has three themes. First, the structure of modern science is described as one element in the rise of the middle class out of the precapitalist world. This is a summary of the well-known Marxist position. The notion of a pure science following its own course had a liberating effect in the nineteenth century; today it implies the acceptance of monopoly capitalism.

The second theme concerns the nature of this new world. Here Marxist theory is treated more selectively. Poverty, unemployment, and even exploitation are barely mentioned. The emphasis is on alienation, fetishism, and false consciousness. People today still believe they act on the basis of individual decisions; actually, their behavior is molded by social mechanisms.[4] Their destiny is determined, not by the competition of independent individuals, but rather by national and international conflicts between ruling cliques in government and the economic system.[5] No one has ideas of his own any longer; so-called public opinion is a product of the ruling private and public bureaucracies.[6] Human solidarity is more likely to be found in criminal gangs than in established society.[7]

Sociological analysis practiced against this background of necessity becomes Critical Theory; this is the third and essential theme. As a matter of course, social analysis should point to the elements just mentioned. But it should not look at them as isolated shortcomings but as the consequences of the basic social structure, a system based on production for profit. The relation between research regarding what exists and social goals to be strived for is stated as follows:

> To see the course of history as a necessary product of an economic mechanism implies already the protest against the present order and the idea of an autonomy of the human race; this means an order in which social events are not any more the result of a mechanism but grow out of free collective decisions. The insight that what happened so far was necessary implies already the fight for a change from a blind to a meaningful necessity.[8]

On one point this neo-Marxism is quite different from the earlier variety. Marx was convinced that the proletariat was a social force which would provide the leverage for basic social change. Observations of Hitler's Germany, of American labor unions, and of the Russian bureaucracy have shaken this conviction. In subsequent publications this "Marxism without proletariat" became ever more pronounced. But it is already clearly implied in the programmatic article by Horkheimer. He assigns to the critical theorist the task of allying himself with "progressive" elements and individuals (presumably from all social classes) who are willing to "tell the truth." This alliance will lead to a dialectical process which will generate "liberating, propelling, disciplined and powerful forces."[9] This is a different position from that taken by former utopian socialists, because technological changes have made a new organization of society possible. "Critical Theory declares things do not have to be as they are now. Mankind can change its existence. The possibilities are now available."[10]

In this paper no concrete examples are given nor is the mode of analysis explicated. It was left to two of Horkheimer's associates to fill in the details. Herbert Marcuse provided the historical background in a brilliant review, "The Foundations of the Dialectical Theory of Society,"[11] and in a later edition of this work he added an instructive preface on dialectics and suggested as slogan: "the power of negative thinking."[12] For Marcuse dialectics and critical theory are the same. His 1960 preface succinctly summarized the 1937 Horkheimer article:

> Dialectic thought starts with the experience that the world is unfree; that is to say man and nature exist in conditions of alienation, exist as other than they are . . . to comprehend reality means to comprehend what things really are and this in turns means rejecting their mere actuality. Rejection is the process of thought as well as of action.[13]

Almost by definition an "outsider" cannot really tell what his critical theory is about, although Marcuse's historical review certainly helps one grasp the main intent.[14]

One must supplement these cues by turning to Adorno who became the contact man with the world of the professional sociologists. Adorno faced two fronts, with very different effects. On the one hand he discussed in principle the relation between theory and empirical research. On the other hand he commented extensively on concrete sociological topics. In this second endeavor, Adorno's analytical observations have generally been drawn from the sphere of culture, and especially from music on which he is an outstanding expert. His general approach here can be fairly easily located. In one sense it resembles Parsons's, who applies a number of his basic concepts to a variety of topics such as the medical system, child-rearing, relations among nations, etc. More specifically, Adorno emphasizes latent functions, that is, connections which are not easily recognized by the superficial observer. But he adds as a characteristic ingredient an emphasis on those latent functions which, in his opinion, serve to deceive modern man and to mask from him the nature of a basically bad society. Thus one finds in his writings many statements like the following: "Theory wants to point out what secretly keeps the whole machinery working"; "empirically observed facts do not reflect the underlying true social relations; they are the veil by which these relations are masked." Adorno keeps reverting to the idea that social reality must be observed and studied, but for purposes of demystification and unmasking.[15] As one illustration one can take his contention that music in our times has become a fetish. We live in a world of promotion, propaganda, and advertising which forces upon us the categories in which we perceive the world. We believe in star performances, although few of us could distinguish one good violinist from another. The same is true for fine instruments, and yet we flock to a concert where the performer is scheduled to use a genuine Stradivarius. Of a major symphony we can hear and remember only the main themes; in "music appreciation" courses we use devices which reinforce this reification;[16] serious, popular, and other types of music are forced upon us by radio schedules, etc. Only detailed study of this kind of analysis can convey its creative element; there is no doubt that it enriches sociological thinking.[17]

But on another front Adorno and his followers have done much harm. The matter is best explained by a brief retrospective account. When, after the war, the majority of the Frankfurt group returned to Germany, they at first tried to convey to their German colleagues the merits of empirical social research which they had observed in the United States. In 1951 they convened a general meeting on the role of empirical social research, chaired by the venerable Leopold von Wiese.[18] Adorno presented the main report. Obviously, the older generation of sociologists feared that these new methods would endanger the humanistic tradition of their work. Adorno provided many concrete examples to demonstrate how all aspects of sociology can be enriched by empirical studies.[19] Of course, quantitative findings have to be interpreted, but this is known by all intelligent research workers. He especially wanted to dispel the idea "widely held in Germany that empirical social research consists just in counting the opinions of individuals and overlooks the many problems due to the dynamics of group life. . . . In the majority of such studies one combines depth interviews with quantitative findings and compares the reaction of people in isolation and in group situations."[20] Together with some insightful criticisms, this paper could stand today as a most adequate discussion on the contribution of concrete empirical studies to general sociology.

Within a period of five years, however, the situation changed completely. Adorno embarked on an endless series of articles dealing with the theme of theory and empirical research. These became more and more shrill, and the invectives multiplied. Stupid, blind, insensitive, sterile, became homeric attributes whenever the empiricist was mentioned. According to Adorno the research worker was only interested in verbalized subjective opinions of individuals in which he had naive confidence. If one examines the paper most frequently quoted as the first major expression of this new line, one can hardly believe that it was written by the same author as that previously quoted.[21] Thereafter one paper followed another, each reiterating the new theme. All have two characteristics in common. First, the empiricist is a generalized other—no examples of concrete studies are given. (The 1952 paper contained several interesting examples.) Second, the futility of empirical research is not demonstrated by its products, but derived from the conviction that specific studies cannot make a contribution to the great aim of social theory to grasp society in its totality. Empirical research had become another fetish concealing the true nature of the contemporary social system.

Adorno's position gained increasing attention, and in 1961 the German Sociological Society found it necessary to call a special meeting to debate the issue. The main topic was Logic of the Social Sciences. The exponent of what one might call the official theory of science was the Austro-English philosopher Karl R. Popper, and the coreporter was T.W. Adorno.[22] Since this meeting the so-called positivist-dialectic discussion has become the central theme of German sociology.

Neither of the reports offered any surprises. Adorno stressed the continuity of his position: "Critical sociology, for its concepts to be true, is necessarily at the same time a critique of society, as Horkheimer in his paper on traditional theory has demonstrated." Dahrendorf, in summarizing the discussion, pointed out that both speakers were so polite that it was difficult to really perceive the basic differences. According to him, the only clear distinction was that, for Popper, theory is continually evolving by trial and error, while for Adorno, it is, at least at its core, an eternal verity. Dahrendorf underscored his disappointment in the meeting because there was so little reference to specific sociological problems and to the uses of sociology for concrete social decisions.

There is a striking contradiction between the continuing excitement over the debate and the paucity of lessons to be learned from it. One almost has the feeling that partisanship depends more on how one feels about the Vietnam War than how one wants to work as a sociologist. In a subsequent article on the Tübingen discussion Habermas gave expression to this difficulty. He is the first and, as far as I can tell, the only commentator who has tried to specify the differences between an "analytical theory of knowledge and dialectics." He discusses the disagreement under four points: (1) How the object of sociological analysis is constituted; (2) the relation between theory and factual evidence; (3) the relation between theory and history; (4) the relation between science and praxis.[23] Habermas's efforts to break down the issue into specific components are certainly helpful but again the sociologist attracted by the atmosphere of Critical Theory could not learn how to proceed if he wanted to study a specific topic in its spirit.

Each point is highlighted by a quotation from Adorno and additional comments are written in his style. The whole situation becomes aggravated by the position of the "positivists." One of the main German centers of empirical social research is undoubtedly the University of Cologne. Its senior sociologist, at the Stresa international conference, has given apt descriptions of Critical Theory backed by well-chosen references.[24] He comes to a pessimistic conclusion: One should make a sharp distinction between a "theory of society" and "sociological theory" and beware of the former. The critical theorist deals in speculation "where he uses material data in an uncritical and uncontrolled way and rushes in too hasty a way to its conclusion . . . ; research has no meaning in itself, e.g. in order to corroborate or reject hypotheses, but is just used for sustaining revolutionary action." By thus divorcing the two areas he in turn forecloses the possibility of using perceptive elements in Critical Theory for the enrichment of the total field. The consequence can be exemplified by the important German text on empirical social research which the Cologne group has published. The section on the philosophic foundations of social research makes no mention whatsoever of critical sociology. Neither does its author find a place for it in his reader *Foundations of the Social Sciences*.[25]

Notes

1. *Studien über Authorität und Familie*, Studien aus dem Institut für Sozialforschung (Paris: Librairie Félix Alcan, 1936).
2. Theodor W. Adorno, "Gesellschaftliche Lage der Musik," *Zeitschrift für Sozialforschung* 1 (1932). It is impossible to reproduce in another language the type of German in which this and all subsequent papers by Adorno are written. The length of the sentences, the rhythm of the words, and the piling up of nouns—often the same noun repeated with slightly different meanings—has an hypnotic effect on the reader which might well explain some of the attraction his publications have today for many young German students.
3. Max Horkheimer, "Traditional and Critical Theory," *Zeitschrift für Sozialforschung* 6 (1937):245–95.
4. Ibid., p. 253.
5. Ibid., p. 259.
6. Ibid., p. 287.
7. Ibid., p. 291.

8. Ibid., p. 280.

9. Ibid., p. 269.

10. Ibid., p. 279.

11. Herbert Marcuse, *Reason and Revolution* (Boston: Beacon), pp. 258–323.

12. For American readers this was an amusing allusion to a popular Protestant theologian who preached the "power of postive thinking."

13. Marcuse, preface.

14. In recent years Marcuse has ceased to be an historian of ideas and has become instead a political prophet who has influenced German students directly, and students in other countries indirectly. It is easily understandable that someone who is against injustice, poverty, and war would feel comforted and stimulated by the undertow of critical sociology. While Marcuse's recent pamphlet *One-Dimensional Man* has gone through many editions in many languages, it can hardly be included in a survey of sociological trends.

15. At one point he says that empirical social research accepts "was die Welt aus uns gemacht hat fälschlich für die Sache selbst." Such a sentence could not be understood without Marcuse's detailed discussion of what Hegel meant when he said that the dialectic method brings out the true nature of the objects it analyzes.

16. "This is the symphony which Master Schubert never finished."

17. I have tried to spell out this idea with more detail in an article on "Administrative and Critical Communications Research," *SPSS*.

18. *Empirische Sozialforschung 1952*, Institut zur Förderung öffentlicher Angelegenheiten, E.V. (Frankfurt am Main).

19. Adorno, pp. 30–33.

20. Ibid., p. 35.

21. Theodor W. Adorno, "Soziologie und empirische Forschung," *Logik der Sozialwissenschaften*, ed. Ernst Topitsch (Berlin: Kiepenheuer, 1965; originally published in 1957). It is difficult to interpret the changes in Adorno's position. If one were to apply his technique, one might say that in 1951 it was still profitable to take an "American position," while five years later the garb of the all-encompassing philosophy was more likely to lead to the elite position he now holds.

22. "Interne Arbeitstagung der Deutschen Gesellschaft für Soziologie, Tübingen," *Kölner Zeitschrift für Soziologie und Sozialpsychologie* 14 (2):1962.

23. Jürgen Habermas, "Analytische Wissenschaftstheorie und Dialektik," in Topitsch.

24. René König, "On Some Recent Developments in the Relation between Theory and Research," in *Transactions of the Fourth World Congress of Sociology*, vol. 2 (1959), pp. 275–90.

25. Hans Albert (ed.), *Theorie und Realität* (Tübingen: Mohr, 1964); and in *Handbuch der empirischen Sozialforschung* (Stuttgart: Enke, 1967), pp. 38–64.

15

The Struggle of
Reason against Total
Bureaucratization

Franco Ferrarotti

Max Horkheimer, who died in July 1973 in Montagnola, Switzerland, at the age of seventy-eight, was not the founder of the Institute of Social Research at the University of Frankfurt but he was its guiding spirit, the director who set its tone. The well-known Frankfurt School is not identical with the institute but is a derivative of it. Jürgen Habermas, who began his career as assistant to Adorno, would have us believe that the Frankfurt School did not exist until after the institute escaped from Germany and Nazism. In any case, more than Adorno or even Marcuse and Fromm, Horkheimer represents the basic point of reference for a very special intellectual climate that had a significant influence on both Marxist and non-Marxist thought in spite of its obvious limitations. Horkheimer, moreover, was a cautious man by nature, more rigorous a thinker than Adorno and more open to economic and everyday reality than Marcuse; he offers throughout the life of the Frankfurt School a more secure point of reference, especially after his return to Germany in 1950.

Horkheimer's "critical theory of society," however, has never ventured beyond its first basic explorations of the theme of authority and the family. All the key elements of Critical Theory—and all its ambiguities— were already present in Horkheimer's theoretical introduction to his essay *Autorität und Familie* (1936). These key elements are the centrality of the concept of authority: the family regarded as the privileged sphere for the social reproduction of the consensus; the acceptance of the most intolerable historical conditions as if they were natural forces and therefore unchangeable; necessarily taking a methodological position based on a global vision of the human situation instead of a compartmentalized one; the critique of the technical-formal rationality that supposedly ignores science as a human enterprise. These basic ideas were already thought out by 1936 and were refined, then perfected in the essay. The works that followed, such as *The Dialectic of Enlightenment* (coauthored with Adorno) and *The Eclipse of Reason* can be considered as thoughtful—if perhaps brilliant—extensions of the original essay and nothing more. For this reason alone, any attempts by the Right to claim the later Horkheimer as its own should be considered arbitrary when mistakenly based on his statements taken out of context, or sensationalized interviews with eye-catching headlines and freely interpreted formulations. Horkheimer himself was led astray by such practices in spite of his warning of the manipulatory tactics of contemporary journalism.[1]

Horkheimer's extraordinary intellectual and historical stature can easily be restored by returning to the texts themselves, texts that were inspired by his awareness of the links between the historical situation, the economic structures, and the conscious attitudes of human beings in society. It is a pity that such a global scheme was not complemented by an effective sociology that incorporated methodologically controlled and politically oriented field work. Horkheimer had neither the disposition nor the sociological tools to accomplish this; he was, after all, deeply attached to a typically nineteenth-century intellectual perspective.

Authority, the Family, and the Social Reproduction of Consensus

The key concepts in Horkheimer's *Autorität und Familie*, adopted by the Frankfurt School down to Habermas, are "culture," "authority," and "family." The novelty of this approach lies in that a strictly speculative and highly abstract investigation does not seek to justify its own propositions by purely theoretical arguments, but rather through historical reality. Here the concept of culture is clearly distinguished from its purely philosophical meaning as a complex of shared experiences and values. In this sense Horkheimer can affirm that "both the subjectivist-anthropological and objectivist modes of viewing cultural institutions have their justification." But he adds that "the preservation of outmoded structures too has its source in human nature."[2] He explains that he does not mean an "original essence" and still less one that is "eternal or uniform." Man has no nature, but a history. All theories that see in the movement of society a mere reflection of a "fundamental ahistorical unity" are therefore open to criticism.

For Horkheimer, practical human attitudes and behavior are historical realities: They follow no model of metahistorical human nature. The fixed character of habit is based, as Max Weber would say, on the "authority of the eternal yesterday," and though it appears as a complex of "natural" characteristics, it is nothing but the product of circumstantial historical conditions. The transformation of the given society into a more rational one, less conditioned by chance and accident, does not depend on the strength of individuals. Horkheimer is convinced that the problem of individuals is not a *particular* problem. To hope for historical change resulting from individual efforts means to fall into resignation, thus to accept a sterile moralistic hope. Horkheimer writes:

> The relatively stable system of long-practiced, effortless behavior which men of a particular period or class manifest, the manner in which they accept their situation with the help of conscious and unconscious psychic practices, the infinitely differentiated and continuously revised structure of preferences, acts of faith, evaluations, and fantasies. . . . This set of internal contrivances which, despite its complexity, is for the most part the daughter of necessity—all this is preserved in many instances simply because to leave the old way of life and adopt a new one, especially if the latter demands increased rational activity, requires strength and courage; in brief, it requires an immense psychic effort.[3]

Is it courage or immense psychic effort? Is all this truly sufficient? Is it really only a question of psychic energy and spiritual strength? On this point Horkheimer does not offer a conclusive answer to dispel the danger of a culturalistic interpretation of social development. He simply claims that authority—particularly faith in authority—is an instinctive historical force which is sometimes "productive" and sometimes "obstructive." Authority is a decisive but highly ambiguous category! "A general definition of authority would necessarily be almost empty of content, but this is true of all definitions which attempt to capture elements of social life in a way that would be valid for all of history."[4] The concept of authority acquires its full meaning when united with other interrelated concepts of a general theory of society not only on the analytical level but in the specific meaning of a specific theory, i.e., insofar as it refers to a particular historical phase and to specific forms of authority relations. This is what clarifies the contradictory character of authority, for

> authority as accepted dependence . . . can simply imply a relationship which fosters progress, is in the interests of all parties, and favors the development of human powers. But it can also sum up in one word all those social relationships and ideas which have long since lost their validity, are now artificially maintained, and are contrary to the true interests of the majority.[5]

But authority must not be confused with authoritarianism. To show why not, Horkheimer provides a broad historical summary of typical rank relationships from the age of absolutism to bourgeois thought. Beginning with the struggle against the authority of tradition in the name of individual reason as the legitimate source of law and truth, in his analysis of the social situation corresponding to late capitalism, he ends up showing that "in the present economic system society appears to be as blind as subrational nature. For men do not use communal reflection and decision to regulate the process by which they earn their living in association with others."[6] Horkheimer's conclusion contains the seeds of his later reflections in *The Dialectic of Enlightenment*: "The fullest possible adaptation of the subject to the reified authority of the economy is the form which reason really takes in bourgeois society."[7]

Horkheimer describes the process of the proletarianization of the peasants who were expelled from the fields in the sixteenth century when the landowners decided to raise cattle instead of crops. Those peasants were "liberated in a negative way," i.e., simply deprived of the elementary means of subsistence. The history of "free workers" is in reality an epic of misery. "The factories," Horkheimer writes, "were places of horror. Their usual connection with orphanages, asylums, and hospitals did not mean that the place of work was simultaneously a hospital but rather that the hospital became a workplace and that men died of toil rather than of illness."[8]

What Horkheimer finds extraordinary is that the majority of mankind considers the capitalist way of life—a product of the Industrial Revolution—to be "natural," whereas it is really a historical relation conditioned by particular circumstances and not a suprahistorical, unchangeable, and eternal relation. The authority implicit in the bourgeois system of labor, the power relation on which it is based, the state of subordination in which it places humans—all seem to be the necessary consequence of a natural state, or at least it masquerades as the result of historical rationality. Even the philosophical expressions of liberty, understood as the struggle and emancipation of the relation of authority, are deceptive, since the freedom of the individual emancipated from authority is no more than an appearance, severely conditioned by the objective character of social life.

This principle enunciated by Horkheimer is not new, and can be connected almost word by word with the Marxist formulations in *The German Ideology*. The intellectual who considers himself the unique and zealous repository of liberty and whom Mannheim supposes to be "free-floating" above the interests of the social classes locked in perpetual combat, the philosopher whom Husserl sees as guarding noble values, the true "defender of humanity"—all those who elaborated the universal, metahistorical worth of culture and its values relegated to the atmosphere of a presumably harmonious Olympus—get what is coming to them in Horkheimer's pages. He applies these notions to the intimate everyday affairs of social life, and cuts deeply into the binding, dogmatic thick skin of the social professions:

> A good instance of the liberal, as he still exists in a relatively strong bourgeois community, presents a picture of freedom, openness, and good will. He knows he is the very opposite of a slave. Yet his sense of justice and his clarity of purpose operate within definite limits set by the economic mechanism and do not find expression in an ordering of social reality as a whole. . . . He is less his own master than he first appears. His sense of personal independence and his corresponding respect for the freedom and dignity of his fellows are noble but abstract and naive as well.[9]

One is reminded here of Max Weber's "naiveté." On the very eve of his death, even when faced with the signs of Nazi regression toward barbarity already appearing in his own civilized Bavaria, Weber remained absolutely convinced that the values of the liberal tradition were an eternal achievement. The pseudoindividualism of the great bourgeois and its edifying mythology of success—"that good of the modern world"—and the self-deception of the enterpriser-demiurge, are unmasked with equal clarity.

The social institution that aids and sustains that relation founded "on an obtuse and only apparently rational authority" is, for Horkheimer, the family. It "sees to it that the kind of human character emerges which social life requires, and gives this human being in great measure the indispensable adaptability for a specific authority-oriented conduct on which the existence of the bourgeois order largely depends."[10] The numerous functions of the family have been variously studied and interpreted. For Horkheimer they are capsulized in the function of stabilizing authority by constantly asserting the apparent naturalness of paternal power: "The necessity of a division and hierarchy of mankind, resting on natural, accidental, and irrational principles, is so familar and obvious to the child that he can experience the earth and universe, too, and even the other world, only under this aspect; it is the pregiven mold into which every new impression is poured."[11]

He sees the ideas of triumph, money, power, happiness, as closely interrelated. In particular, "for the formation of the authority-oriented character it is especially decisive that the children should learn, under pressure from the father, not to trace every failure back to its social causes but to remain at the level of the individual and to hypostatize the failure in religious terms as sin or in naturalistic terms as deficient natural endowment."[12] This should not be taken as an explicit prescriptive pedagogical theory or a mere correction in educational methods and text books would suffice to substitute a liberating socialization in place of an authoritarian one which tends to reinforce internal and external behavior that is submissive to authority. Horkheimer's deeper analysis implies not only the provision of intentional educational measures but also the modulation of the power of suggestion exercised by the nuclear family.

This is the central issue in Franz Kafka's *Letter to My Father*. It is not simply a question of teaching fathers to be "reasonable," "democratic," and "open" toward the child. A course in progressive education, or even direct experience with Montessori methods, would be inadequte for these objectives. But a study of the family as the essential instrument for reproducing authoritarianism in these terms could reduce these problems and answer, or perhaps even abolish, the question. In the sphere of the bourgeois nuclear family, the formation of the authoritarian personality and the exaltation of the instinct of submission are not merely the result of a narrow preparation of the parents, but are constitutive functions which can disregard the nature of education and even the will of the parents.

> The child's character is formed far more by the very structure of the family than by the conscious intentions and methods of the father. . . . However rationally the father may be acting by his own lights, his social position in relation to the child means that every educational measure he takes, however reasonable, must carry overtones of reward and punishment.[13]

Horkheimer, and more broadly the Frankfurt School, is advancing here an analysis that goes beyond the sector-limited analysis of current sociology, which is technically quite elaborate but too narrowly circum-scribed and fragmentary. The study of the family is outlined in terms of the broadest framework of global society. This approach goes beyond merely descriptive sociology (which is by definition incapable of probing the deeper significance of the social phenomena it deals with) and specialized compartmentalization (which has no way of perceiving the dialectical link between important aspects of social life considered as a whole). The consequences are foreseeable. "As long as there is no decisive change in the basic structure of social life and in the modern culture which rests on that structure, the family will continue to exercise its indispensable function of producing specific, authority-oriented types of character." By means of the family, society will continue to produce the type of men that perpetuate it. To solve the problem this poses for the family, society itself must be revolutionized. This crisis of the family is not isolated; it cannot be dealt with in the abstract, apart from the whole, and it cannot be described, interpreted, and solved isolating it and "for good reasons" ignoring its social roots in a scientific manner. The family is subordinated to the service and needs of society. The family prepares the sort of people society needs for the current mode of production: It produces authoritarian characters, human beings prone to take upon themselves the responsibility that ought to be ascribed to causes of a structural and social nature.

But the family and society are always antagonists. The bourgeois nuclear family exalts and confirms the instinct of submission but it also values the element of love which is linked to the mother's ambiguous role: "To the extent that any principle besides that of subordination prevails in the modern family, the woman's maternal and sisterly love keeping alive a social principle dating from before historical antiquity."[14] The work of Le Play, and still more of Hegel, for whom the conflict between the family and public authority were typified by the figure of Antigone battling for her brother's corpse, and finally, the studies of Bachofen and Morgan on the death of matriarchy, all examine and enlighten this subject.

It is thanks to the woman and what she represents, i.e., the nonutilitarian factor that she embodies, that the present type of family still retains an antiauthoritarian dimension, unmediated by the market and separate from the logic of production. Yet for the very same reason, the development of woman is continuously blocked by artificial obstacles: social and public life is reserved for men, and within the family woman's role is one of pure dependency which has persisted through the centuries. The circle is completed. The family, which at the dawn of capitalism was always the "reproductive cell" in a rich dialectical relation with society, is now reduced to a pure instrument serving the needs of advanced industrial development, under the double profile of production and consumption. The father has become the employer.

Fromm writes about the task of exploring psychological aspects of the relation between authority and the family, including that of defining the components of the authoritarian-masochistic character. At least fifteen years before the sociopsychological concept of authoritarian character was systematically used in investigations of Adorno, Else Frenkel-Brunswik, D.J. Levinson, and R. Nevitt Sanford in *The Authoritarian Personality*, Fromm had already dealt with its basic constitutive elements and the typical dynamism of its development. Fromm's treatment seems particularly successful where, inspired by the work of Freud and Abraham on the "anal character," he reveals the perfect correspondence between the gratifying impulses of the authoritarian character and particular "social" virtues or values, i.e., the socially admissible and auspicious ones, such as avarice, order, scrupulousness, and obstinacy, on the one hand, and the pleasure that the authoritarian character derives from the obedience and submission of another person, on the other. "Though the pleasure of obedience and submission as such," Fromm writes, "remains subconscious and concealed by rationalizations such as legality, necessity, reasonableness, it remains decisive for the authoritarian character that the situations in which he can obey, give him satisfaction, and when he meets them in reality he finds no need to modify them, but instead confirms them."

Fromm does not limit himself to a description of the explicit behavior of the authoritarian character as shaped by objective circumstances. It is true that the first part of Fromm's article is dedicated to the many aspects of authority and to the various configurations of relations between superiors and subordinates. He examines numerous situations: from the relation of the son to the father in a particular type of family structure of small rural proprietorship, to that of a woman patient with her doctor, and the Catholic believer with his personal confessor. The conclusion is that the bond of authority is not a strictly coercive behavior, but is produced through a constriction. Using a formulation advanced by Simmel, Fromm stresses that the relation to authority is the emotional bond of a subordinate to a superior person or institution. The bond of authority, in other words, is complex. It always contains an element of fear together with an element of esteem, of admiration and love together with hatred. Fromm, following the Freudian model, understands this complexity in terms of two questions—that of mass society and that of the formation of the superego, initially designated by Freud as "the ideal self" and "the ideal of the self."

Fromm is not uncritical of Freud. While recognizing the great contributions of the master, he criticizes the high degree of formalism that allowed Freud to attribute to the superego all the functions that he did not intend to attribute to the ego and the id, without sufficiently distinguishing between the various types of identification that sharper analysis brings out. Fromm travels along the road to neo-Freudian revisionism freely applying Freud's extraordinary discoveries to particular problems. In analyzing the dynamics of authority in the family, Fromm masterfully captures the dialectical bond by which the family is linked with the formation of the superego of the child, on the one hand, and the legitimation of authority within global society on the other.

> The external power operating in society is encountered by the child who grows up in the sphere of the patriarchal family mainly in the person of

the father. By identification with the father and by internalization of his orders and prohibitions, the superego is vested with moral attributes and power. Once such an authority is established, if it corresponds with the process of identification, there is an inverse process. The superego is constantly reprojected onto the wielders of the dominant authority in society, or in other words the individual invests effective authority with the attributes of his own superego. By this act of projection of the superego onto authority, the latter is largely removed from critical reason. It is shaped in its morality, wisdom, capacity, to a great extent independently of real manifestations. In such a way authority in turn becomes continually internalized and representative of the superego.

This statement of the dialectical nature of authority together with the critique of Freud, including his observation that Freud paid greater attention to the social conditioning of the father's character than any previous writers, lays the foundation for Fromm's treatment of the social nature of personality, or social personality. This does not mean that all is done and that theory emerges fully armed from Zeus's head like Pallas Athena. But one cannot help foresee or at least notice the indispensable premises.

Fromm's approach is psychological. Starting with the Freudian definition of character not as a sum of particular traits but as a "determinate structure" for which the change of one aspect of character conditions all the others, Fromm elaborates the theory of the necessary relation between masochism and sadism, which implies that to distinguish between the two we need only say that in one case the sadistic tendency is dominant while in the other it is censured, repressed, and submerged:

> The masochistic tendency causes the individual to renounce the individuality of his own personality and his own happiness and to surrender to power, abolishing himself as it were in it, and to find pleasure and satisfaction in that dedication, which in pathological cases can reach the point of voluntary endurance of physical sufferings. The sadistic tendency has the opposite purpose of making the other person the pliant and defenseless instrument of one's own will, of dominating him absolutely and totally and in extreme cases of making him suffer and express such sufferings emotionally.

The point is that sadism and masochism are always mutually inclusive and correlated, so that in sado-masochism the censured, repressed, and displaced opposite does not disappear completely, but emerges at the most diverse points, however much it tries to conceal itself. Hence the extraordinary ambivalence of the sado-masochistic nature of authority which, while itself prostrated before greater strength, enjoys inflicting persecution and suffering upon the weaker. The phenomenology of the linkage and behavior of the sado-masochistic character studied by Fromm is rich and enlightening, but rarely transcends the limits of a strictly psychological approach.

One indication of the "cultural institutionality" which reinforces faith in the "omnipotence of authority," seen in the last part of Fromm's essay, deals with "sense of distance" as a means of presenting the bearers of authority as something special and increases the sense of unconditional inferiority in the subordinates. Authority, which by nature is powerful and generates fear, is thus transformed into a moral model that demands submission. Typically social and not just psychological factors have contributed to this model in which the family plays a critical role:

> The child is led to believe that its parents do not lie and that they are effectively adorned with all the moral qualities which they demand of the child. . . . This aspect is one of the family's most important functions: it educates the child to consider certain moral qualities to be connected with authority, thus contributing to the production of the authoritarian character. The child suffers one of the most serious traumas of his life when he begins to discover that his parents are in reality far from living up to their own prescriptions. But when this happens, he substitutes other authorities, such as the school, and later those presented by the press, etc., and authority remains impenetrable to him so that he retains the original illusions identifying authority and morality.

The negative side of the predominantly psychological approach of this analysis is felt mainly in the question of the rebellion against authority. Fromm recognizes that however solid authority may seem, the history of both individuals and society is "a series of rebellions." A correct evaluation of the various types of revolts requires the preliminary and accurate analysis of the historical, economic, and political conditions in which the event occurs. Fromm's evaluation, purely psychological and metahistorical, leaves much to be desired. The whole question of anarchy seems to be treated in a superficial and ambiguous manner.

> The anarchistic types are typical examples of that rebellious character and if they were transformed into adorers of power, little would be changed in them from a psychological viewpoint. From this type of rebel one arrives, via various intermediary stages, at the type that abandons the person who had until then been the object of authority, only to submit simultaneously to a new authority. The cause of this can be seen both as resentment for unjust treatment or denial of love on the part of the old authority.

Resentment, disillusionment, love, and so on—these are psychological concepts that must also be examined within an essentially economic and political framework. Fromm does not seem to be unaware of this complexity, but even when he ought to introduce a sociological mode of analysis, he reverts back to a perfect symmetry between psychology and political action, and he inevitably asserts the primacy of the psychic over the economic. Indeed, I fail to see how he can avoid the pitfall of moralistic reasoning. Fromm writes:

> This rebellion in which the object changes but the authoritarian structure remains intact and even is ultimately reinforced and whose ideal is the type of rebel who has acquired power, is sociologically of the greatest importance. Such rebellion can contain the seeds of "revolution." The new authority serves as a revolt against the former authority and increases the illusion that the struggle against the repressive authority is a struggle against repression in general. . . . It could be, but the basic psychic structure is not modified, the revolt turns out to be a passing explosion of resentment and rebellion and the new authority occupies the position that the old one was no longer able to maintain.

The old and the new authority are, however, substantially equal. They are the simple, almost mechanical response to unchangeable and inescapable "impulses." Their transformation should not be interpreted as the rational outcome of a political project or a historical-economic program. It is only the expression of a basic ambivalence whose causal matrix lies in the very psychic constitution. I spoke of the role of moralism and of the reversal that this implies for any project whose aim is the rational transformation of traditional society. Beyond moralism, which is a form of refined scepticism, an iconoclastic cynicism like Pareto's begins to flourish. The affirmation of the instinctive apparatus and of "impulses" from the unconscious is a step in that direction. From this perspective, history, i.e., the cumulative effect of human efforts within given economic and political circumstances, is reduced to a monotonous war between the weakened or declining power elites and the emerging elites, "new potential instances of authority," ready to scale the heights of power and, no less than the deposed ones, to use it for their own egoistic ends.

In his essay on authority in *Studies in Critical Philosophy*, Marcuse claims that Pareto "is the first writer in the monopoly phase of capitalism to deal with the psychological problem of class domination and even the first to put authority in a social context." Marcuse reconstructs in detail the relation between authority and the family found in the ideas of theorists from Luther and Calvin to Sorel and Pareto, by way of Kant, Hegel, and Marx. He succeeds in revealing the real bond and structures of domination, and at the end of his own investigation he points out that the "psychic constant" and its "rationalization" inscribed in a "theory of social domination" are decisive in Pareto. Indeed, "all domination is based on coercion and on the rationalization of coercion, but that is not enough to guarantee the stability and continuity of domination: the more or less spontaneous consent of the governed is necessary."

According to Marcuse, Pareto saw more clearly than Sorel the importance of the family for maintaining and perpetuating authority. Sorel sees the monogamous family as "the administrator of the moral code of mankind," but does not establish its connection with bourgeois society. Pareto's positivist analysis penetrates much more deeply into the dialectical substance of social reality. It is interesting to note how Marcuse's criticisms of the "psychological" and "irrational" elements of Pareto's system could apply against some proponents of the Frankfurt School, especially as regards their reliance on "determinate psychic mechanisms for the analysis and explanation of social phenomena." Despite the formal distinction between positivism and idealism, the two are closely related.

The authors of *Autorität und Familie* sought to connect their theoretical claims with empirical investigations meant to provide the material necessary for empirical verification. The second part of the work is dedicated entirely to this research. That the attempt is not completely successful is not due to theoretical errors in carrying out the study or to a lack of methodological skills, but mainly to the difficulty of the problems studied. The research could be superficially divided into three groups: (1) a survey of workers and employees; (2) a survey on sexual morals; (3) a survey among experts on authority and family.

The questionnaires used show a modicum of formalization; the foreseen responses are almost all open, i.e., qualitative and not precodified. No calculation of correlations is attempted, nor is it possible to establish any connection between the variables considered particularly significant, even given the need to stress the relation between psychic and economic structures characterizing the social context. This last objective remains more a programmatic expression than anything else. It should come as no surprise that the surveys do not produce substantial modifications and do not necessitate a reformulation of the basic proposition on sado-masochism and on the authoritarian character presented in the theoretical essays written by Horkheimer, Fromm, and Marcuse.

The survey focuses on two groups of problems: authority as it constitutes one of the most important factors of social dynamics, and the family as it constitutes the social basis of personality formation. Given the imprecise nature of the technical tools used, the survey can legitimately be considered a pretesting operation, essential for designing the questionnaire and weighting it according to the public and the interviewers. In the introductory note, Erich Fromm observes at length that with their emigration to the United States the collaborators of the institute will be presented with "the opportunity to familiarize themselves with the most advanced American methods of investigation."

It is difficult to say whether that opportunity is good or bad. The methods of social investigation in the United States seem traditionally to be tilted toward the psychological; in studying social phenomena, the tendency is to avoid both the economic and political dimensions—not to mention the historical dimension, which is simply ignored. Social problems thus lose their objective firmness and are transformed into problems of interpersonal adaptation. Instead of being an essential instrument for the preliminary clarification of questions and for the positive advancement to their solution by means of changes in the socioeconomic structure, sociological investigations in the United States are merely technical studies to obtain and confirm an acritical mass conformism.

The study of psychology must always be integrated with the analysis of the structural character and the economic and political dimensions of social phenomena, otherwise it falls into a psychological trap, which necessarily reduces the objective problems such as power relations to problems of a pure state of mind and interpersonal relations. In addition to this, there is the tendency, so strong and typical among the scholars of the Frankfurt School, to avoid particular historical and political situations and to attempt instead a speculative analysis of a wide category of "domination" as such, separated from empirical investigation and indifferent to the economic and juridical structure. The need for a global study of problems that has constantly been advocated by members of the Frankfurt School is certainly valid, but since they attach less importance to specific field studies and since their theory posits an opposition between positivism and critical reflection, the globality they speak of risks being reduced to an empty traditional universalism as the endpoint of a spurious totalization which has lost contact with the historically determined character of the structure.

"The Eclipse of Reason"

In this perspective, the problems posed to humanity become insoluble, the liberty of the Enlightenment is transformed into its opposite, and the dream of an emancipated humanity gives way to a new barbarism. The very radical quality of denunciated evil acquires the tone and dimension of a new metaphysics. Horkheimer discovered the definitive words to express this despairing impasse: "If one were to speak of a disease affecting reason, this disease should be understood not as having stricken reason at some historical moment but as being inseparable from the nature of reason in civilization as we have known it so far. The disease of reason is that reason was born from man's urge to dominate nature."[15] The philosophical confirmation of this cruel self-accusation that reason pronounces against itself is seen most clearly in Horkheimer's *The Eclipse of Reason.* Here three separate and previously antagonistic spheres are brought in contact: reason, the subject, and nature. The attempt to dominate nature, to understand its secret and "laws" in order to subjugate it, required the establishment of an impersonal bureaucratic, "scientific" organization which in the name of victory over nature ended in reducing the human object to a mere instrument. In this situation, the concept of formalized reason and the subject/object dialectic are necessary and inevitable results.

According to Horkheimer, the present crisis of reason "consists fundamentally in the fact that at a certain point thinking either became incapable of conceiving such objectivity at all or began to negate it as a delusion."[16] The critical element sustaining the basic achievement of modern philosophy is the prolongation of a methodical scepticism that eats at the roots of the concept of truth and robs it of all meaning, transforming it into a merely subjective convention, formalized according to arbitrary limits: "The process was gradually extended to include the objective content of every rational concept. In the end, no particular reality can seem reasonable per se; all the basic concepts, emptied of their content, have come to be only formal shells. As reason is subjectivized, it also becomes formalized."[17]

It is not a question of the relation between the natural and the social sciences, or of the cultural relation which was the crucial reference point of contemporary German thought that generated the famous *Methodenstreit* in which writers such as Rickert, Windelband, and Weber firmly opposed the possibility of a postivist analysis. Horkheimer's intention is different. "This book," he writes, "takes a different approach. Its aim is to inquire into the concept of rationality that underlies our contemporary industrial culture, in order to discover whether this concept does not contain defects that vitiate it essentially."[18] The essential defect of reason today in technically progressive industrial society must, according to Horkheimer, be regarded as an operational transformation in which reason is at once artifice and victim. This consists in substituting the means for the ends and winds up by instrumentalizing reason itself in the very name of reason, by reducing it to necessary, predictable, and programmed thought—an integral part of the process of production. This shows that the Enlightenment has been turned into its direct opposite.

The Enlightenment's individual liberty enters into crisis when change from an elitist to a mass culture occurs alongside the transition from liberal, competitive capitalism to a capitalism dominated by an ever smaller number of large oligopolistic and monopolistic concentrations. Horkheimer approaches the problem both philosophically and socially:

> Having given up autonomy, reason has become an instrument. In the formalistic aspect of subjective reason, stressed by positivism, its unrelatedness to objective content is emphasized; in its instrumental aspect, stressed by pragmatism, its surrender to heteronomous contents is emphasized. Reason has become completely harnessed to the social process. Its operational value, its role in the domination of men and nature, has been made the sole criterion.[19]

Domination is the truly universal and all-comprehensive category. But what kind of domination? It is no longer a personal domination—the lordly type of "employer." Nor is it a domination of the subjective ideas that have manipulated the world of objective relations toward their own ends and logic. It is rather an impersonal and anonymous domination, in pure flux, the consequence of decisions arising from the instinct of self-preservation but filtered through a rational calculation that undermines the self and negates existence as the instinctive, inventive reaction to objective conditions:

> As the end result of the process, we have on the one hand the self, the abstract ego emptied of all substance except its attempt to transform everything in heaven and on earth into means for its preservation, and on the other hand an empty nature degraded to mere material, mere stuff to be dominated, without any purpose other than that of this very domination.[20]

Thus objective spirit—unprejudiced liberty of individual criticism that once was the basis of the justification and progressiveness of the Enlightenment—now has the same "obscurantist," regressive function of the objective reason of authoritarian religions and metaphysical philosophy. Horkheimer's criticism of individual subjective reason does not mean a return to dogmatic reason. On the contrary, it is a revolt against the desiccation of instincts—those essential impulses that have been so impoverished in the rational process. Without any concession to irrational tendencies, Horkheimer traces the trajectory which led from authoritarian and dogmatic religion to a complex of arbitrary, subjectivist constructions, incorporated into the massification of society and new forms of domination. Horkheimer failed to provide us with its phenomenology, but he did produce a marvelous account of the stages in the proletarianization of the mind in the modern world.

Total Bureaucratization and the Fate of the Individual

Horkheimer's critical view covers the entire range of modern thought from neo-Thomism to neopositivism. For Horkheimer instrumentality is not alien to the philosophical enterprise as such:

> But the transition from objective to subjective reason was not an accident, and the process of development of ideas cannot arbitrarily be reversed at any given moment. If subjective reason in the form of enlightenment has dissolved the philosophical basis of beliefs that have been an essential part of Western culture, it has been able to do so because this basis proved to be too weak. Their revival, therefore, is completely artificial: it serves the purpose of filling a gap. The philosophies of the absolute are offered as an excellent instrument to save us from chaos. Sharing the fate of all doctrines, good or bad, that pass the test of present-day social mechanisms of selection, objectivistic philosophies become standardized for specific uses. Philosophical ideas serve the needs of religious or enlightened, progressive or conservative groups. The absolute becomes itself a means, objective reason a scheme for subjective purposes, general as they may be.[21]

This criticism covers all of modern philosophy. But how about art? Is it not possible through art to capture and express a meaning of reality not mediated by rational calculation and not preoccupied with relating ends and means, or that is a consequence of utilitarian objectives? Horkheimer's answer is negative:

> Once it was the endeavor of art, literature, and philosophy to express the meaning of things and of life, to be the voice of all that is dumb, to endow nature with an organ for making known her sufferings, or we might say, to call reality by its rightful name. Today nature's tongue is taken away. Once it was thought that each utterance, word, cry, or gesture had an intrinsic meaning; today it is merely an occurrence.[22]

On the other hand, we can expect nothing from traditional philosophical reflection: Neo-Thomism is futile; pragmatism can survive only to the extent that it proceeds to an ever greater and more coherent functionalizing of thought; neopositivism, finally, pronounces a death sentence on scientific thinking. But science, which rises victorious from beneath the ruins of traditional philosophy, has nothing to say about the fundamental demand for a meaning to life and the position of the individual in the world—questions that concern modern man. Proceeding from the formulation of the hypothesis to the act of verification, it shows its cool neutrality, behind which may of course be hidden a constellation of interests or a political stratagem—and even an aberration such as nazism. But the fact that while dealing with dynamic principles science must also take multiple phenomena into account does not escape Horkheimer. Yet, whatever the modes of thought and the specific conceptions of scientific thinking may be, it cannot be forgotten that they are auxiliary instruments of production. Beyond that, any scientific fact is an eminently social fact. From the wheel to antimatter, all scientific facts are not solely relevant for science and indicate no superiority of scientism as a model for culture and society: "Like any existing creed, science can be used to serve the most diabolical social forces, and scientism is no less narrow-minded than militant religion."[23] Horkheimer does not see clearly how, in the present process of production, science becomes a directly productive force instead of merely being applied via the mediation of technology. Thus, his position must not be confused with Marcuse's, nor with that of apocalyptic authors who, by denouncing science, really express the holy hope of a prompt return to the Middle Ages. For Horkheimer, science cannot save humanity. But in a free society, not fragmented and divided by objective contradictions of interests, science can attain an autonomous and coherent development: "Only under ideally harmonious conditions could progressive historical changes be brought about by the authority of science."[24] The present situation is far from being harmonious, however, and there is no ready consolation:

> If one were to speak of a disease affecting reason, this disease should be understood not as having stricken reason at some historical moment, but as being inseparable from the nature of reason in civilization. . . . Thus the derangement of reason goes far beyond the obvious malformation that characterizes it at the present time. Reason can realize itself only through reflecting on the disease of the world as produced and reproduced by man; in such self-critique, reason will at the same time remain faithful to itself, by preserving and applying for no ulterior motive the principle of truth that we owe to reason alone.[25]

One has to ask: Is it possible for reason to go outside reason? Is it possible for culture to transcend culture? Is an awareness of reason sufficient to heal the ailment and cure the essential vice of domination? Is it not perhaps necessary, in the desire to avoid falling into prohibitively dogmatic or metaphysical positions, to patiently explore that constellation of material interests and those objective contradictions of social life that Horkheimer considers the crucial distortions of human life? Mass culture, the industrial society of the masses, atomization of the individual and his subjection to the impersonal authorities of the administrative apparatus on a vast scale—all that does not stem from or affect just the intellectual plane, but it takes us to the objective conditions of the social process in its historical development.

These real contradictions were not sufficiently treated by Horkheimer or by members of the Frankfurt School. But if the questions raised by Horkheimer are squarely faced, it must be recognized that he has brought them to the programmatic stage. More clearly than others, he saw the necessity for culture to transcend culture if it is to change life. Horkheimer criticized abstractly philosophizing intellectuals. Yet, he himself remained a pure intellectual: one of Europe's last great "private intellectuals." Concepts and empirical facts were not connected and the totalization resulted in a vacuous synthesis. The venture failed, but it is hard not to admire the splendor of that failure.

Notes

1. Max Horkheimer, *The Eclipse of Reason* (New York: Oxford University Press, 1947).
2. Max Horkheimer, *Critical Theory* (New York: Seabury, 1972), pp. 66–67.
3. Ibid., p. 67.
4. Ibid., p. 69.
5. Ibid., pp. 70–71
6. Ibid., p. 222.
7. Ibid., p. 83.
8. Ibid.
9. Ibid., p. 92.
10. Ibid., p. 98.
11. Ibid., p. 106.
12. Ibid., p. 109.
13. Ibid., p. 114.
14. Ibid., p. 118.
15. Horkheimer, *Eclipse of Reason*, p. 176.
16. Ibid., p. 7.
17. Ibid.
18. Ibid., p. v.
19. Ibid., p. 21.
20. Ibid., p. 97.
21. Ibid., p. 62.
22. Ibid., p. 101.
23. Ibid., p. 71.
24. Ibid., p. 83.
25. Ibid., pp. 176–77.

16

The Positivist Dispute
in Retrospect

Reinhard Kreckel

It would seem that writing on the positivist dispute in West German sociology today is tantamount to writing a piece of history of sociology. Although the English translation was only published in 1976, the original dispute between Karl R. Popper and Hans Albert on one side, and Theodor W. Adorno and Jürgen Habermas on the other took place during 1961–65, with Adorno's open attack even dating as far back as 1957.[1] Since that time the *Positivismusstreit* has lost momentum, at least in its country of origin. New controversial issues, such as the revival of Marxist influences in sociology or the ethnomethodological challenge, have taken its place as focal points of theoretical self-clarification and self-presentation among West German sociologists. Furthermore, and more immediately related to the present subject, the positivist dispute is now antiquated for the very simple reason that its two most active participants, Habermas and Albert, both have reconsidered their positions since the end of the debate. Both published full-length versions of their epistemological conceptions in the late sixties.[2] In these writings "after the blows" it became clear that the two opponents had learnt a good deal from their involvement in the controversy. Although their basic disagreement was unaltered, their arguments were now much more carefully elaborated and had become more open for discussion as a consequence. This made their work less suitable for simplified polarizations and sweeping accusations.[3] On the other hand, the two senior contributors, Adorno and Popper, also published their concluding comments on the positivist dispute in 1969 and 1970.[4] But they mainly reiterated old polemics without changing their attitude of mutual incomprehension. This merely underlined that the original controversy had become somewhat stale by then.

It would seem that there are only two possible approaches left for the present paper: either to provide an analysis of a closed chapter of West German intellectual history or to try to reopen it again in this country, albeit with considerable delay.[5] I am not very tempted by either alternative. Instead, I wish to explore a third possibility: whether there are any

254 Foundations of the Frankfurt School of Social Research

epistemological and/or theoretical insights of enduring importance to be preserved from the historical *Positivismusstreit*. More precisely, I am going to discuss whether the challenge from the "unorthodox" side of the dispute, represented by members of the Frankfurt School, has uncovered any crucial problems in their "mainstream" opponents' position which would require some fundamental rethinking.

From the "Critique of Political Economy" to the "Critique of Positivism"

To set up my argument it may be useful to go even one step further back into German intellectual history. My thesis is that the critique of positivism became, and remained, the central pillar of Critical Theory ever since its founders detached themselves from Marxist orthodoxy in the 1930s. In the same measure as Max Horkheimer and his followers developed doubts as to the validity of the Marxian critique of political economy, it was replaced by the critique of positivism as basis of Critical Theory. This is not simply a contingent shift of emphasis. There is a compelling logic behind it which is due to certain shared characteristics in the perspective of Marx and Critical Theory.

The intentions of Marx and Critical Theory overlap insofar as their common theoretical efforts are not simply directed at interpreting, but at changing the world. The unification of theory and practice is their aim, the criticism of "false" realities their theoretical means. But to achieve this, purely moralizing and "idealist" forms of social criticism are ruled out. Both Marx and the Frankfurt theoreticians start from the basic assumption that all ideas about social reality, including scientific ones, are socially determined and in this sense historically and socially relative. Thus, superficially, there may be as many "true" but divergent interpretations of social reality as there are different social interests. But not all interests and ideas coexisting in a society are equivalent; certain ideas are "ruling ideas." To Marx it was clear that in capitalist society these ruling ideas, including "bourgeois" political economy, were an expression of the interests of the ruling capitalist class. This fact alone, however, does not make them any more (or less) valid than any other ideas which happen to exist in a capitalist society.

To avoid having to rely on "idealist" moral decisions or dogmatic fixations as safeguards against relativism, Marx had to devise a method of detecting the "true" standpoint among the empirically given plurality of socially based interests and ideas in society. This was the method of critique of ideology. Basically, it meant identifying the only standpoint within a society which was not just an expression of a particular interest, but coincided with the interests of the "historical subject," the moving force of history in that epoch. In capitalist society, this interest was the proletarian class interest, of course. To get to it, the barrier of the "ruling ideas" of the bourgeoisie had to be broken. Marx attempted this by means of an immanent critique of what he had identified as the most advanced expression of bourgeois ideology of his time, political economy. By uncovering the immanent blindness of classical political economy and demonstrating how this blindness was due to political economy being chained to capitalist interests, Marx arrived at his theory of alienation and surplus value, accumulation of capital, and the eventual crisis caused by the fall of the rate of profit. In Marx's view, this theoretical conception was welded together with political practice through the "historical subject," the proletariat. The proletariat was the only class both interested in the abolition of class exploitation and able to bring it about, once the material conditions for the final crisis of capitalism had been generated by capitalism itself. In Marx's view, the proletariat's partisan class interest of liberation from capitalist exploitation converged with the scientific insight in the "objective" course of history toward a classless world society. Consequently, a purely scientific and unbiased theory of societal transformation could only be formulated from the vantage point of proletarian class interest. This scientific theory was at the same time a critical theory with practical implications, as every contribution to "objective" scientific knowledge was an integral part of the class struggle against capitalism and bourgeois ideology. Needless to say, that consensus over the precise contents of the very cornerstone of Marxist theory of society—the "objective" class interest of the proletariat—has never been reached among Marxists. But as long as one is willing to neglect this as a "minor" difficulty, one will have to admit that the model is coherent indeed.

Yet it is clear that the whole argument is in danger once the role of the proletariat as "historical subject" is questioned and no substitute is available. This can best be demonstrated by means of Horkheimer's famous essay "Traditional and Critical Theory" (1937) which may be read as a document of transition from the critique of political economy to the critique of positivism.[6] At the time of writing, Horkheimer had to come to terms with the upsetting experiences of the fascist victories in Central and Southern Europe, the growing conformist tendencies of the working classes in the most advanced capitalist societies, and the emerging Stalinist variant of socialism in the Soviet Union. All this had cast increasing doubts on the revolutionary potential of the proletariat. But even as late as 1937, Horkheimer was not ready to abandon the idea of the historical role of the proletariat. He argued that Critical Theory was to act as a kind of custodian trying to keep the theoretical knowledge of the true interests of the proletariat alive, even against the prevailing political attitudes and ideologies in the working class itself. In thus maintaining the concept of proletarian class interest in its strategic place, Horkheimer was still able to keep his program of Critical Theory relatively close to the Marxian model. On the other hand, although Horkheimer followed Marx's method in unfolding his Critical Theory by means of a critique of ideology, the object of his critique was not any more political economy, but traditional theory. He focused on the social sciences and philosophy of his time whose ideal it was to "follow the lead of the natural sciences with their great success"[7] and to adopt their formalistic style of theorizing and research. They were now pinpointed as the most advanced expression of bourgeois ideology. In 1937, Horkheimer's picture of this new "scientific" ideology was still rather impressionistic. It comprised a wide variety of writers such as Poincaré, Husserl, Durkheim, Tönnies, Max and Alfred Weber, and the concept of positivism was still undeveloped. Furthermore, Horkheimer's critique of traditional theory had not yet led him to change his analysis of the underlying structure of capitalist society. It was still interpreted in Marxian terms.

In the long run, however, the growing disillusionment with the proletariat made more profound changes inevitable. Once the idea of the revolutionary proletariat as "historical subject" was abandoned without any substitute taking its place, the link between theory and practice was disrupted. This meant that Critical Theory was in danger of falling back into an "idealism" based on nothing but theoretically unfounded value judgments and wishful thinking. In the 1940s and 1950s Horkheimer and Adorno opted for "critical pessimism" instead. In *Dialectic of Enlightenment, Eclipse of Reason,* and *Minima Moralia* they set out to develop a Critical Theory without revolutionary subject, based on the method of critique of ideology alone: In search for the deep roots of exploitation and alienation in modern society, they tried to supersede and go beyond Marx's critique of the innermost logic of capitalism, which had culminated in his analysis of the fetishism of commodities. They uncovered "instrumental rationality" as the underlying principle both of technological progress and increasing wealth, and of the continuing inhumanity, repression, and false consciousness in late capitalist as well as state socialist societies. As they saw it, instrumental rationality had once been the essence of the Enlightenment and scientific progress, and it was at the basis of man's success in establishing his domination over nature. But it had been perverted into a pervasive ideology buttressing man's domination over man. All spheres of social and cultural life in advanced capitalist and socialistic societies had become increasingly affected by this "logic of instrumentalism," leaving little scope for hope. Swimming without illusions against this ideological mainstream of instrumentalism, commercialism, crude propaganda, militarism, consumerism, was the new "theoretical praxis" of Critical Theory.

Clearly, this type of social criticism may all too easily be taken for a mere expression of idiosyncratic resentments, if it is not backed up by a convincing theoretical foundation. This is why the critique of positivism is so crucial to Critical Theory. The target of this critique, positivism, is usually defined rather loosely. It refers to all science of man, society, and culture attempting to follow the example of natural science and trying to analyze human reality according to the same epistemological principles as the natural world. This type of positivist analysis is identified by Critical Theorists as the forerunner and purest expression of "instrumental rationality." It follows that only if a cogent critique of positivism is possible, Critical Theory is able to uphold its own claim to be more than a mere compilation of empirical generalizations and theoretically unwarranted moral judgments. This explains why any new variant of positivism becomes a provocation and intellectual test case for Critical Theory. Its theoretical integrity may only be upheld as long as a rational critique of positivism succeeds.

If one accepts this interpretation, it becomes evident that it would be totally incongenial to criticize Horkheimer, Adorno, and their followers for not adhering to the very criteria of positivist social science they are trying to refute. However, this is one of the most recurrent arguments leveled against Critical Theory from the beginning of the positivist dispute to this very day.[8] I do not intend to pursue this line of controversy any further. Instead, I shall concentrate on the question of whether the efforts of Jürgen Habermas, the outstanding representative of Critical Theory[9] during and after the dispute, were able to come to terms with what he saw as the most advanced form of positivism, the critical rationalism of Popper and Albert.

The Controversy between "Invariance-Seeking" and "Invariance-Breaking" Epistemologies

The meaning of the term *positivism* itself is highly controversial, and it is widely used as a derogatory label.[10] In any case, Popper and Albert, the two writers attacked as positivists during the positivist dispute, protested vigorously against being described as such; they saw themselves as antipositivists. I do not wish to get drawn too deeply into this terminological controversy, as it is mainly polemical and of no epistemological consequence.[11] What I am interested in here is the antagonism of Critical Theory against all concepts of social science trying to emulate natural science. But the epistemology of natural science itself is not uncontroversial. It follows that one may expect at least as many versions of positivist social science as there are models of natural science. In fact, there might be even more variants of positivism, as it is not at all inconceivable that a social scientist may hold an entirely mistaken idea of the methodology of natural science he is trying to follow. This seems to lead up to a somewhat unsatisfactory definition, namely, that any social scientist attempting to follow what he and/or his critics believe to be the model of natural science would have to be described as a positivist.

However, the object of Critical Theory's criticism during the positivist dispute was defined somewhat more precisely. Whereas Horkheimer's earlier notion of traditional theory still had indiscrimately included a wide range of positivist approaches to social science, now criticism focused on those conceptions of scientific method based on the explicit assumption that invariant laws determine social as well as natural reality and are susceptible to the same form of scientific investigation. Among these "invariance-seeking"[12] epistemologies, Jürgen Habermas singled out critical rationalism. It was particularly suitable for criticism, as it could be said not only to be one of the most highly sophisticated scientific expressions of the ideology of "instrumental rationality," but also to have found widespread recognition among social scientists.

The original version of critical rationalism was formulated by Karl R. Popper in numerous writings from the 1930s to the early 1960s. It is too well known to require a lengthy introduction.[13] But a few remarks on its structure are necessary. The following quotation from *Poverty of Historicism* may be read as a useful summary of the epistemological position which was to become the subject of criticism in the positivist dispute:

> It is an important postulate of scientific method that we should search for laws with an unlimited realm of validity. If we were to admit laws that are themselves subject to change, change could never be explained by laws. It would be the admission that change is simply miraculous. And it would be the end of scientific progress; for if unexpected observations were made, there would be no need to revise our theories; the *ad hoc* hypothesis that laws have changed would "explain" everything.

These arguments hold for the social sciences no less than for the natural sciences.[14] Three basic tenets of critical rationalism are directly referred to in the above quotation:

1. The logic and method of natural and social science are one, the natural sciences being the model; their common end is to develop and test explanatory theory (*principle of unity of method*).
2. Theories explain (or predict) empirical phenomena by relating them to invariant and universal laws; "historical" theories are impossible (*principle of nomological explanation*).
3. Scientific progress is based on the readiness to subject theories to empirical tests and to revise them, if previously unexpected facts come up; closer and closer approximation to the invariant laws governing reality is thereby achieved (*principle of trial and error*).

Two further important characteristics of critical rationalism may be inferred from the previous ones:

4. As scientific theories must be of universal (ahistorical) validity to be able to explain historical facts, the scientific concepts used to formulate such theories are ahistorical too. Debates about the real (or essential) meaning of concepts are futile; what counts is their suitability for theory building (*principle of antiessentialism*).
5. If one starts from the assumption that invariant characteristics of reality exist and that it is the task of science to approximate them as closely as possible, these invariant laws can be and ought to be investigated in a value-free manner; criticizing or moralizing about what is unalterably the case simply does not make any sense. It may only inhibit the rational progress of scientific discovery (*principle of value neutrality*).

Underlying these five principles is Popper's "falsificationist" conception of science according to which no absolutely certain knowledge of the invariant features of reality is ever possible. Scientific hypotheses and theories can only be approximations to the truth. To assess the degree of approximation to invariant laws, and thus the verisimilitude of theories, Popper developed the notion of "explanatory power" or "informative content."[15] It means that the higher the level of theoretical generalization *and* degree of empirical precision of a nomological proposition, the higher its content and explanatory power. This *criterion of explanatory power,* as I call it, may be used to compare competing theories to find out which one may be assumed to be the best approximation to the invariant structure of reality on account of its superior informative content.

My argument is that the criterion of explanatory power fulfills a pivotal function in critical rationalism analogous to that played by the notion of the "revolutionary subject" in Marxism. In both theories, serious epistemological difficulties are inevitable as soon as these core elements come under pressure. In the case of critical rationalism, this can best be demonstrated by looking at its reactions to criticism. Reference to "informative content" or "explanatory power" is the standard defense against all kinds of objections. Whether the unity of scientific method, the notion of universal law, the trial-and-error principle, the ahistorical use of concepts, or the claim of value neutrality are challenged, the strongest counterargument always is: As long as critical rationalism delivers informative nomological theories whose explanatory and/or predictive capacities can be demonstrated empirically, its validity as scientific method is established and its claim to provide theoretical approximations to invariant reality upheld.

However, the criterion of explanatory power is not only critical rationalism's strongest argument against criticism, it is its most vulnerable point too: As long as informative theories or hypotheses *exist* in a given field of knowledge, critical rationalists are in a much stronger position than say, Marxist social scientists, who can only point to an uncertain future to validate their revolutionary theory and critique of ideology. However, a closer look at the present state of the social sciences of nomological orientation reveals a situation not too dissimilar to that of Marxism: There is widespread hope for the development of nomological social theory in the future, but little evidence of it now. As Richard J. Bernstein neatly put it: "There is simply no . . . corpus in sociology and political science where one can point to powerful explanatory empirical theories. It seems that in the social sciences the stress on 'what theory is' is inversely proportional to the ability to come up with 'theory proper.'"[16]

It might be argued against this diagnosis that behaviorists or psychological reductionists, such as Homans, Festinger, Malewski, and Opp, have already developed a body of nomological theory. This may well be so,[17] but to my knowledge there is no social theory in sight which is both general in its range (i.e. unrestricted by time and space) and specific in its ability to explain the existence and change of concrete historical institutions, belief systems, relations of production, forms of government— the very bread-and-butter of sociology, especially macrosociology. In the classical fields of sociological investigation no theory of nomological character and high explanatory capacity is available. Consequently, the criterion of explanatory power is of no help when a sociologist of critical-rationalist persuasion is faced with the task of choosing his own theoretical framework for the analysis of concrete social phenomena. There seems to be no epistemologically satisfactory way for him to determine which "theory of the middle range" or set of hypotheses to adopt, as none fulfills the minimum requirements of genuine generality *and* precision.

Any consequent attempt at applying critical rationalism to sociology leads to the conclusion that, by its very own standards, its results are highly unsatisfactory. In his more recent writings, Karl Popper himself apparently has come to the same conclusion. He writes about the "sociological lunatic fringe," describes sociology as "riddled with fashions and with uncontrolled dogmas,"[18] and says that "social relations belong, in many ways, to what I have more recently called 'the third world' or better 'world 3', the world of theories, of books, of ideas, of problems; a world which, ever since Plato, . . . has been mainly studied by essentialists."[19]

However, I would be surprised if all critical-rationalist sociologists were altogether happy with this recent development of their master's views on the social sciences. I take the West German sociologist and philosopher Hans Albert, Habermas's main opponent in the positivist dispute, as an example. Albert maintains that the development of no-mological sociology on the basis of critical rationalism is possible. But the only existing nomological theories he points to are reductionist theories located on the borderline between sociology and psychology.[20] Thus, to defend the use of critical rationalism for the analysis of phenomena such as ideologies, institutions, power relations, mass communication, market structures, systems of social inequality, Albert is obliged to offer additional arguments, as the criterion of explanatory power does not (yet) apply in these cases. There are two, partly overlapping, lines of argument in support of the view that the results of critical-rationalist sociology are scientifically sound in spite of the conspicuous absence of nomological theory:

1. The first, weaker argument is this: Albert argues that the very method of intersubjective control and rational criticism itself, once successfully institutionalized in a community of social scientists devoted to the ideals of objectivity, value-freedom, and rational discussion, guarantees the scientific soundness of sociology.[21] Even as an auxiliary argument, this is not very convincing. The institutionalization of value neutrality and criticism may well be a necessary prerequisite of any scholarly endeavor which wishes to avoid simple partisanship, suppression of evidence, and similar crude forms of bias, known since the days of Karl Mannheim as "particular ideology." But Mannheim's more important problem of "total ideology," that is, of relativism with respect to the choice of scientific theories and concepts, remains unresolved.[22] Thus, as long as the criterion of explanatory power fails to have an impact on sociology, Popper's (self-) critical remark pertains that "the suggestion that we find anything here like 'objective, pure description' is clearly mistaken."[23] In other words, Albert's first argument is based on a simple *petitio principii*.

2. His second line of defense is to be taken more seriously. Albert concedes that sociology, being but a young science, so far has mainly produced so-called quasi theories and quasi hypotheses, i.e. theoretical propositions limited to historically and culturally restricted areas.[24] In his view it would amount to adopting a "standpoint of resignation"[25] to exclude the possibility that such quasi theories might one day be subsumed under genuinely nomological theories. This might be interpreted as a simple *petitio fidei*, an act of faith in the existence of universal laws in social reality. But it may also be argued that this act of faith is strongly supported by empirical evidence. Even its most outspoken critics, such as Jürgen Habermas, emphasize that critical rationalism is *successful*, its success being one of the reasons for being chosen as object of criticism.[26] Critical-rationalist sociology has proved itself successful in developing theories and hypotheses describing empirical uniformities which have been satisfactorily tested and applied for practical purposes such as planning and social engineering. Critical-rationalist sociology undoubtedly "works" and delivers tangible results. How is this possible? From the point of view of the "invariance seeker" whose epistemological background assumption is that invariances do exist, however difficult it may be to get hold of them, the practical success of critical rationalism can be taken as a first sign of theoretical success; he will be inclined to infer that sociological research, although not yet mature, is on the right track and had entered the process of approximating invariant structures of social reality. (This, incidentally, gives critical-rationalist sociology an important edge over Marxist sociology in Western societies: Both are obliged to justify themselves with reference to future achievements, either an anticipated nomological theory or an anticipated victory of the proletariat; but the former has something concrete to point to right now, whereas the latter has not, at least if one is not willing to count the reality of state socialist societies as harbinger of "concrete utopia.")

The burden of proof shifts as soon as the "invariance-seeking" background assumption of critical rationalism is abandoned. Then a new answer is required to the question of why "invariance-seeking" sociology is successful, although it has not found, and cannot find, any universal laws. The standard answer is that in all societies known so far, social life has been structured by more or less stable values, norms, institutions, relations of power which are man-made and hence changeable. The success of critical-rationalist sociology may be attributed to its simple inability to distinguish between man-made regularities and genuine invariances.

Albert is not deterred by this objection. He claims that "nowadays nobody will confound quasi-invariances with natural laws."[27] But on what grounds is this distinction to be made? According to Hans Albert, empirical generalizations limited in time or space are quasi hypotheses referring to quasi invariances only. Taken seriously this seems to imply that no sociological generalization explicitly or implicitly based on historical notions such as industrial society, capitalism, socialism, underdevelopment, could ever qualify as nomologically solid. This would exclude most sociology from the family of science, a consequence Hans Albert and other "invariance-seeking" sociologists prefer not to face. Their doubts are smothered by the combination of a *petitio principii* that invariances do exist, a *petitio fidei* that good nomological theory will be possible one day, and the *practical experience* that "invariance-seeking" sociology is "working" and successful.

This does not answer the question whether the widely recognized success of "invariance-seeking" sociology is genuine, or a mere pseudo-success due to the mistaken identification of historical regularities as invariant structures. This problem is the point of departure of the critique of positivism or critique of critical rationalism developed by the representatives of Critical Theory. Quite regularly their critique leads to a confrontation between two radically incompatible views, as the following quotation from Zygmunt Bauman shows: "One can take, as the founding principle of critical sociology, an a priori rejection of the possibility of invariant endowment—whether transcendental or natural—which characterizes the human species once and for all."[28]

Once this is taken as the only founding principle of critical social science, the complete breakdown of the dialogue with critical rationalism is inevitable. If to believe or not to believe in the existence of universal laws in social reality is the only inescapable alternative, the epistemological schism is complete and no compromise possible. There is a way to overcome this stalemate and prepare the ground for a partial joining of forces between critical rationalism and Critical Theory. I shall try to demonstrate this by making use of certain arguments from the work of Jürgen Habermas. A full discussion of his approach to Critical Theory is not intended.[29]

Critical rationalism's principle of unity of method is rejected by Habermas. He distinguishes between three "knowledge-constitutive interests" leading to an empirical-analytical, a hermeneutic, and an emancipative type of science.[30] I am not going to discuss the merits of Habermas's theory of knowledge.[31] I shall simply take up a few crucial points pertinent to the present argument:

1. One of the criticisms Jürgen Habermas levels at critical rationalism is that the methods of natural science it is using "are unable to

distinguish between Nature and History,"[32] that is, between genuine laws and mere historical regularities or quasi invariants. He sees the reason for this inability in critical rationalism's refusal to use the "operation called Verstehen,"[33] a refusal directly related to its commitment to the model of natural science. To Habermas, on the other hand, hermeneutic or interpretive methods inapplicable in the natural sciences are crucial for the historical and social sciences. From this basis it is possible to develop what I have called the "criterion of historical understandability," which may be characterized in the following way:[34] As long as we succeed in tracing back and understanding the historical genesis of even the most persistent and seemingly universal regularities of social reality, we can be certain that they are *not* invariant laws, but products (or objectifications) of meaningful human action. Whether produced intentionally or unintentionally, their origin is human and therefore accessible to criticism and to attempts at influencing and changing them, whereas genuine laws of nature are not.

2. The criterion of historical understandability is not only used for the purpose of unmasking quasi invariants. Habermas's thesis is that the historical and man-made character of crucial regularities of social life, for example the all-pervasive "logic of instrumental rationality," tends to be systematically forgotten, repressed, or ideologically misrepresented. Furthermore, these reified structures typically are closely associated with the ruling interests in a given society. They take on the solidarity of a second nature, no longer understood as possible objects of critical discussion and practical transformation. Critical rationalism is attacked for contributing to the social reification and mystification of second nature by its tendency to confound man-made regularities of social life with universal and therefore unalterable laws.

3. This leaves open the central issue whether universal laws are possible at all. Habermas's position in this matter is inconsistent. On the one hand, in *Zur Logik der Sozialwissenschaften* (1967), he clearly states that "there is no empirical regularity in the field of social action which, although unintended, is not understandable."[35] This would preclude any chance of agreement with "invariance-seeking" social scientists. On the other hand, in the published version of his inaugural address "*Erkenntnis und Interesse*" (1965), he writes:

> The systematic sciences of social action, that is economics, sociology, and political science, have the goal, as do the empirical-analytical sciences, of producing nomological knowledge. A critical social science, however, will not remain satisfied with this. It is concerned with going beyond this goal to determine when theoretical statements grasp invariant regularities of social action as such and when they express ideologically frozen relations of dependence that can in principle be transformed.[36]

I am not interested in the question as to whether the first or second of these two quotations represents the "genuine" Habermas. For the present discussion the second is more promising: There, the possibility of invariant regularities in the social world is taken for granted, and the criterion of historical understandability is called for to tell the difference between genuine laws and lawlike regularities. Consequently, Hans Albert's critical comment on Habermas's *Zur Logik der Sozialwissenschaften* does not apply here: "Why should there be no general laws concerning e.g. the learning, the change, and the stability of norms which could contribute to the explanation of social developments? Can Habermas have an a priori knowledge of this?"[37] Albert is right: Habermas cannot; but neither can he himself. At first glance this seems to leave us with a situation poised in complete symmetry: On one side, we are faced with the epistemological strategy of "invariance seeking," based on the criterion of explanatory power; on the other side, there is the epistemological strategy of "invariance breaking," founded on the criterion of historical understandability. Both appear to be equally justifiable. In the final section I shall try to draw a few conclusions from this.

Consequences

The symmetry between "invariance-seeking" and "invariance-breaking" approaches is not quite as complete as it might appear. The criterion of explanatory power so far has proved to be more or less inapplicable in sociology, especially macrosociology; on the other hand, the criterion of historical understandability is ready for use. This seems to give the "invariance-breaking" strategy a certain advantage.

A further important point emerging from the previous discussion is that the two epistemological strategies are neither self-sufficient nor as totally incompatible with one another as the original positivist dispute would have us believe. Or, to put my thesis more positively, *valid social theorizing is possible only if the mutual dependency of "invariance-seeking" and "invariance-breaking" strategies is recognized and taken into account:*

First, from the point of view of critical-rationalist social sciences, the dependency on the "invariance-breaking" tradition takes the following form: As we have seen, critical rationalism has no procedure of its own to distinguish between nature and history. But its overall inclination is to press for generalization, i.e. for theoretical propositions without explicit temporal and spatial limitations. To illustrate this, I shall quote at some length from Popper's early work, *The Poverty of Historicism:*

> Since the existence of . . . sociological laws or hypotheses (other than so-
> called "historical laws") has often been doubted, I will now give a number
> of examples: "You cannot introduce agricultural tariffs and at the same
> time reduce the cost of living."—"You cannot, in an industrial society,
> organize consumers' pressure groups as effectively as you can organize
> certain producers' pressure groups."— . . . "You cannot introduce political
> reform without causing some repercussions which are undesirable from the
> point of view of the ends aimed at."[38]

There is little doubt that hypotheses of this kind may be empirically
corroborated and successfully applied in "piecemeal social engineering."
But it is also quite clear that their validity depends on the existence of
definite historical conditions, some of which are spelled out, others are
not. Take Popper's first example to illustrate this: Agricultural tariffs are
an eminently historical phenomenon presupposing the existence of a
state, central legislation, borders, a system of customs and excise control,
etc. Even then, Popper's generalization only holds if further assumptions
are made which do not refer to any invariant conditions, but to still
more historical phenomena: It is presupposed that some kind of free
market system exists, that consumer prices are not subsidized, etc. However
realistic Popper's example may be when applied to modern market
societies, it may certainly not be considered as an approximation to
invariant characteristics of social reality. Even a minimum amount of
historical sensitivity reveals that it refers to man-made and historically
specific regularities only. In other words, as long as the "purifying" effects
of the criterion of explanatory power cannot be relied upon, social sciences
of exclusively nomological orientation risk to produce misleading results.
As an antidote to this, the criterion of historical understandability must
be explicitly introduced.

Second, from the point of view of Critical Theory, the necessity for
communication with critical rationalism is given by the fact that Critical
Theorists, like anybody else, can have no a priori knowledge that universal
laws do not exist. With respect to the identification of invariances, the
capacities of the criterion of historical understandability are restricted.
First, the question whether certain general regularities of social life can
be traced back to specific historical conditions often remains controversial.
The continuing debates on the universality of social stratification or
power may illustrate this. Second, even if it could be demonstrated that
all empirically known social regularities are historically conditioned, it
may still be argued that they are mere manifestations of nontrivial
universal laws, which are required for their explanation. The problem
is that the Critical Theorist, even if admitting this, still cannot get much
assistance from critical rationalism, as its criterion of explanatory power

remains largely inapplicable. The lesson he will have to learn nonetheless is that a basic scepticism with respect to the possible range of variability of social reality is necessary.

Third, from the diagnosis that, at present, the criterion of explanatory power operates much less efficiently than the criterion of historical understandability, one might conclude that the furtherance of "invariance-seeking" sociology is particularly urgent. However, I would not go along with this priority. First, it neglects the important empirical observation that the majority of Western sociologists (Gouldner's "mainstream sociologists") already are much closer to the "invariance-seeking" than to the "invariance-breaking" paradigm. Second, there is a more fundamental epistemological reason. It is neatly stated by Johan Galtung:

> A sentence, whether based on data sentences or theory sentences, *excludes* something. A value sentence, whether based on a goal or interest, *includes* something, that which is preferred. As long as what is preferred is also observed and/or foreseen by data or theory, there is no problem. However, the moment what is excluded by data and/or theory is preferred, there is a problem. To raise a confirmed theory sentence of that kind to the level of an invariance *is tantamount to saying that something preferred is unattainable.* This is vastly different from saying it was never attained in the past. The latter is only a statement about *empirical* reality, that which is or was; the former a statement about *potential* reality, that which might be—saying that it coincides with what was. In other words, it states . . . that only what already *is,* is possible, now and in the future.[39]

> . . . a science programmatically limited to *seek* invariances is at best only half a science, at worst a tool in the hands of status quo-oriented groups.[40]

Just as Galtung does, I think it is legitimate to believe that during its past history mankind has not yet tried out all possible variants of social organization it is able to create; some of the better ones may still be in store for the future. On the other hand, the existence and knowability of genuine social invariances cannot be denied a priori, and it would be detrimental to any responsible sociology to ignore this. I therefore advocate *delaying tactics* as the appropriate epistemological approach: While admitting the possibility of genuine invariances, even the most durable regularities of social life ought to be treated as historically conditioned and changeable, and to be investigated in view of their transformability until this assumption proves untenable. This minimizes the danger of any premature submission to quasi invariances mistaken for universal laws. A fight is put up as long as possible against the necessity of having to admit the existence of unalterable restrictions to human freedom which go beyond the well-known truisms about the physical limitations of the human condition. This epistemological strategy also obeys the rules of Popper's falsificationism. But its emphasis is not only on testing theoretical conjectures against empirical reality, but also on testing historical experience against alternative possibilities.

Fourth, I do not think that the debate on universal laws in social science can take us much further than this. But a point is now reached from which a new, perhaps even more intricate set of problems becomes visible: The range of freedom of how man could organize his social life is so wide that even genuine invariances, if there should be any, do not impose very drastic limitations. The restrictions typically to be faced are of an entirely different nature; they tend to be rooted in the institutional status quo of a given society and in the ensuing power structure and hegemony of a world view. That is, enough constraints on creative activity and utopian phantasy are exercised by *social* factors to give sociologists plenty to think about. This does not mean that an "invariance-breaking" (or rather: "regularity-breaking") sociology is propagated which envisages the practical alteration of every empirically observed social regularity. Quite a few of them may be found acceptable as they are; others may be less agreeable, but the costs of their overthrow might by heavy. In societies riddled with inequality and injustice, what is desirable to some people is often costly to others; and some regularities are costly to all, but it is feared that their abolition might be even more costly, etc. *No theory of society, however radical, can start from zero.* It will always have to take certain historically grown regularities as given. Some such regularities, e.g. modern technology, justice, literacy, etc., tend to be considered historical achievements, not to be abandoned under almost any circumstances. That is, any theory of society will have to operate with what I call "practical invariances," propositions about social regularities which are accepted as, and/or desired to be, unalterable for the time being, although their historical character is known.

Which regularities a theoretician accepts as practical invariances, to be taken for granted as stable frame of reference for social analysis, and which ones he treats as variable depends on considerations involving both value decisions and empirical arguments: Unless a sociologist's value commitments to a present or future form of society are not completely dogmatic, they tend to be affected by empirical considerations as to the practical possibility to preserve or create the desired state of affairs. These considerations themselves are not intensive to hypotheses concerning the likely costs of changing or preserving the status quo in a particular way, and to the relationship between the costs incurred and the end desired. It is vital to any sociological analysis to be aware of the practical invariances it is based on and to be explicit about the value premises and empirical assumptions underlying this choice. If this is neglected, reification and mystification threaten again.

It now appears that the debate over the possibility of "genuine" invariances in social reality, which once animated the positivist dispute, is no longer the central issue. Even a partial reconciliation between "invariance-seeking" and "invariance-breaking" epistemologies seems now possible, as I argued above. However, beneath the epistemological level of discourse the disagreement continues. It concerns the question of what to treat as practical invariances. In place of a conclusion, I simply illustrate this final point: As we have seen, orthodox Marxists still refuse to recognize the social integration of the proletariat in advanced capitalist societies as a practical invariance; representatives of Critical Theory increasingly do, however provisionally and grudgingly; "invariance-seeking" or "traditional" theorists are more likely to interpret working-class integration as an inevitable concomitant of the "logic of industrialism"; empiricists and many ordinary citizens just take it for granted; others do not. There is no way to avoid taking sides.

Notes

1. The various contributions are collected in T.W. Adorno et al., *Der Positivismusstreit in der deutschen Soziologie* (Neuwied-Berlin: Luchterhand, 1969). English ed.: *The Positivist Dispute in German Sociology,* trans. G. Adey and D. Frisby (London: Heinemann, 1976).
2. Jürgen Habermas, *Zur Logik der Sozialwissenschaften* (Tübingen: Mohr, 1967; idem, *Erkenntnis und Interesse* (Frankfurt: Suhrkamp, 1968). English ed.: *Knowledge and Human Interests* (London: Heinemann, 1971); Hans Albert, *Traktat über kritische Vernunft* (Tübingen: Mohr, 1968).
3. A systematic account of this second, more balanced phase of the Habermas/Albert controversy is given in Reinhard Kreckel, *Soziologisches Denken* (Opladen: Leske, 1975), ch. 3.
4. Adorno, "Einleitung," in *Positivismusstreit,* pp. 7–79; Karl R. Popper, "Reason or Revolution," *Archives Européennes de Sociologie* 11 (1970):252–62.
5. For the early history of Critical Theory see P. Connerton, *The Tragedy of Enlightenment* (Cambridge: Cambridge University Press, 1980); H. Dubiel, *Wissenschaftsorganisation und politische Erfahrung* (Frankfurt: Suhrkamp, 1980); Martin Jay, *The Dialectical Imagination* (London: Heinemann, 1973); Zoltán Tar, *The Frankfurt School* (New York: Wiley, 1977).
6. Max Horkheimer, *Traditionelle und kritische Theorie* (Frankfurt: Fischer, 1970), pp. 12–64.
7. Ibid., p. 14.
8. Cf. e.g. Albert's contributions to the original positivist dispute. For a recent example of this approach see Tar, p. 166ff.
9. Habermas never was Horkheimer's or Adorno's pupil in any strict sense. Habermas's doctoral thesis was supervised by the philosopher Eric Rothacker

in Bonn; his habilitation thesis did not find their support, and he had to seek the sponsorship of the political scientist Wolfgang Abendroth at the University of Marburg to get it accepted. Notwithstanding this, Habermas was appointed as Adorno's codirector of the Frankfurt Institut für Sozialforschung in 1964, and he certainly took Adorno's side during the positivist dispute.

10. The following remarks are indebted to N. Stockman, "Positivism and Antipositivism in Sociological Metatheory," Ph.D. thesis, University of Aberdeen, 1979.

11. In his later writings, Jürgen Habermas himself replaced the term *positivism* by the more neutral formula of "empirical-analytical science."

12. The terms *invariance-seeking* and *invariance-breaking* are borrowed from J. Galtung, *Methodology and Ideology* (Copenhagen: Eijlers, 1977), ch. 3.

13. I am referring to Karl R. Popper's major early writings: *Logik der Forschung* (1934–35); *The Poverty of Historicism* (1944–45); *The Open Society and Its Enemies* (1945); *Conjectures and Refutations* (1963). Since the introduction of the "principle of the three worlds" in his two essays of 1968, "On the Theory of the Objective Mind" and "Epistemology without a Knowing Subject" (reprinted in *Objective Knowledge* [New York: Oxford University Press, 1972]), Popper's views on the unity of scientific method have undergone a transformation. Cf. *Unended Quest* (Glasgow: Fontana, 1976), p. 20ff.

14. Karl R. Popper, *The Poverty of Historicism* (London, 1966), p. 103.

15. Cf. Popper, *Objective Knowledge,* p. 52ff.

16. R.J. Bernstein, *The Restructuring of Social and Political Theory* (Philadelphia: Pennsylvania University Press, 1976), p. 24ff.

17. The nomological character of these theories has been disputed too. Cf. Habermas, *Zur Logik,* ch. 4; or K. Holzkamp, *Kritische Psychologie* (Frankfurt: Fischer, 1972).

18. Cf. Karl R. Popper, "Normal Science and Its Dangers," in *Criticism and the Growth of Knowledge,* ed. I. Lakatos and A. Musgrave (Cambridge: Cambridge University Press, 1970), p. 57ff.

19. Idem, *Unended Quest,* p. 21. For Popper's earlier view cf. *Poverty of Historicism,* where he makes a strong case in favor of "sociological laws or hypotheses which are analogous to the laws or hypotheses of the natural sciences" (p. 62).

20. Cf. Hans Albert, "Probleme der Theoriebildung," in *Theorie und Realität,* ed. idem (Tübingen: Mohr, 1964), p. 41ff.; idem, *Traktat über kritische Vernunft,* p. 64.

21. Idem, *Traktat über kritische Vernunft,* p. 41ff.

22. Cf. Karl Mannheim, *Ideologie und Utopie* (Bonn: Cohen, 1930), p. 7ff.

23. Popper, "Normal Science and Its Dangers," p. 58.

24. Albert, "Probleme der Theoriebildung," p. 39ff.

25. Ibid., p. 42.

26. Cf. Jürgen Habermas, *Theory and Practice* (London: Heinemann, 1974), p. 263ff.

27. Albert, "Probleme der Theoriebildung," p. 40n.

28. Zygmunt Bauman, *Towards a Critical Sociology* (London: Routledge, 1976), p. 89.

29. A useful English introduction to the work of Habermas may be found in T. McCarthy, *The Critical Theory of Jürgen Habermas* (London: Hutchinson, 1978).
30. Cf. Habermas, *Knowledge and Human Interests.*
31. Cf. Reinhard Kreckel, *Soziologische Erkenntnis und Geschichte* (Opladen: Westdeutscher Verlag, 1972), p. 30ff., for a more extensive discussion.
32. Habermas, *Zur Logik der Sozialwissenschaften,* p. 26 (my translation).
33. Cf. T. Abel, "The Operation called Verstehen," *American Journal of Sociology* 54 (1948); Albert, *Traktat über kritische Vernunft,* p. 159ff.
34. For a more detailed presentation see Kreckel, *Soziologische Erkenntnis und Geschichte.*
35. Habermas, *Zur Logik der Sozialwissenschaften,* p. 81 (my translation).
36. Idem, *Knowledge and Human Interests,* p. 310.
37. Hans Albert, book review, *Kölner Zeitschrift für Soziologie und Sozialpsychologie* 20 (1968):344 (my translation).
38. Popper, *The Poverty of Historicism,* p. 62.
39. Galtung, *Methodology and Ideology,* p. 73ff.
40. Ibid., p. 91.

17

The Uses of Psychoanalysis in Critical Theory and Structuralism

Edith Kurzweil

Both Critical Theory and structuralism set out to provide unique and strong critiques of modern society; both addressed the crises of modernity and the increasing realization that reason and science have failed as paths to human redemption; both were committed to debunk all false notions and myths; both were hostile to any sort of closed philosophical structure and, instead, depended on dialectical methods to apprehend reality. They both acknowledged their strong debt to Hegel and Marx although structuralism, also, was to some extent Nietzschean; and both built on Freud's notions of the unconscious to understand the diverse meanings and interpretations of human actions in their social context. Both schools have also been termed existential, and subscribed to various aspects of idealism—notwithstanding the fact that for Critical Theorists scientific truth was not to be split off from that of a true society, that is from empirical inquiry, even as idealism was disclaimed (Hughes 1975:139; Lichtheim 1971: 19–21), and that the structuralists continuously emphasized the scientificity of their systems of thought (Lévi-Strauss 1955; Althusser 1972). Insofar as both schools looked to the institutions responsible for transmitting social customs and mores and their acceptance by new generations, they addressed the dualist tradition that, to a greater or lesser degree, pits human nature against the social order. Given the different periods and countries of origin, and political and economic contexts, we can easily understand the divergent premises of Critical Theory and structuralism and why in very special ways they both adopted many of Freud's ideas on culture, which promised scientific explanations and/or resolutions for human irrationality, thus enhancing the chances to "speed up" the final liberation of humanity Marx had promised.

This essay does not deal with the existential situation and milieux of these scholars, with successive and temporal intellectual influences on them, or with concerns of individuals' Jewishness or assimilationism as impinging on research choices. The latter topic, in particular, has been amply explored in connection with the Frankfurt group (Jay 1973; Tar 1977; Buck-Morss 1977; Hughes 1975; Friedman 1981) and was of lesser interest to the French, for whom Sartre's *Anti-Semite and Jew* (1965), until very recently, seemed to have settled this question. But the issues they all dealt with reflected the fact that the Institut für Sozialforschung was set up in Frankfurt in 1923; that it took a different direction after Horkheimer took over in 1931; that shortly thereafter its members dispersed; that it was centered around Horkheimer and Adorno in New York until 1950, when it was reestablished in Frankfurt; and that structuralism was conceived only in the late 1940s.

Structural linguistics had been of limited interest before Lévi-Strauss's *Structural Anthropology* was published in 1958, although Ferdinand de Saussure had taught his *Course in General Linguistics,* the basis of structuralism, in Geneva between 1906 and 1911, and some of his students had compiled his lectures by 1915; and there never existed an Institute for Structuralism (Poster 1975; Kurzweil 1980), although for a brief period, in 1966, there were the *Cahiers pour l'Analyse.* Still, ever since Lévi-Strauss indicated how structural linguistics could be adapted by anthropologists, sociologists, literary critics, philosophers, and others concerned with the ontological relation of nature to culture, and with uncovering their origins—structuralist, neostructuralist, poststructuralist, and deconstructionist theories have preoccupied French intellectuals. (They have become extremely fashionable in some English and American academic departments.) Thus structuralism is a recent system of thought which has steadily gained in importance, whereas Critical Theory is older, was of interest sporadically—in America during World War II and since then in Germany—as a means to uncover the roots of anti-Semitism, totalitarianism, and authoritarianism. Since 1968, especially in its Marcusean version, it served as a theory to energize the New Left, yet never inspired the general intellectual public as structuralism did in France. Moreover, Critical Theory did not reach Paris, whereas structuralism has been increasingly exported.

The timing of the advent of Critical Theory in Germany and America on the one hand, and of structuralism on the other, though part of intellectual history, was related to the development of both theories: Political events in the 1920s pushed the German critical contingent to pursue the dialogue of Marx and the young Hegelians from adversary perspectives, while their French counterparts, the "new Hegelians," joined the Communist Party or went underground—in either case they were silenced. Hence Martin Jay's observation that the Frankfurt School differed from the Hegelian insofar as it was separated from Kant and Hegel by

Schopenhauer, Nietzsche, Dilthey, Bergson, Weber, Husserl, and many others, and by the systemization of Marxism itself (Jay 1973:43), could also be made for the French Left—for the young intellectuals who, too, expected to help spread the promises of the Russian Revolution in the 1920s. Just like the Critical Theorists, they had begun by continuing Marxist explorations in relation to *Realpolitik,* and, in the process, had introduced the possibility of employing Freud's theories as a liberating force in a future socialist society. In the late 1920s, however, the Parisian new Hegelians had to disperse. Those who became associated with the surrealists (Paul Nizan) tended to focus their revolutionary activities on the arts; those who joined the Communist Party (Henri Lefebvre and Norbert Guterman) stressed Marxist materialism over Hegelianism in their writing; others (Pierre Mohange) stopped writing; Georges Friedmann became a sociologist; Paul Ricoeur, an "outsider" whose primary concern was with the links between individual and social morality and much later with Freud, as well as Jean-Paul Sartre, turned first to literature and later to existentialism and phenomenology; Jacques Lacan became a psychoanalyst. In any event, the theoretical search for a Freudian Marxism was postponed until after World War II. Georges Politzer alone had persisted in this task. Not unlike Fromm, he had argued that Freud's scientific endeavors were of potential use for Communists, even if ultimately the turning of the id into ego would subvert the true relationship between individual psychology and historical development (as envisaged by Marx) and would thus serve reactionary aims (Politzer 1928). That Politzer's works remained out of print for years and were reissued only recently was a byproduct of the long disrepute of psychoanalysis, as well as an indication of the recently renewed interest in a leftist Freudianism in France.

Intellectual interest in psychoanalysis had been stymied by the predominantly dialectical-materialist, that is the more Stalinist, tendencies of the Left. (The Frankfurt scholars' choice of immigrating to the West, in 1933, was itself an indication of their anti-Stalinism [Lichtheim 1971:129].) And because the French Left, in addition, had a strong trade union base which, in turn, was controlled or at least strongly influenced by the French Communist Party, discussions of psychoanalysis were ruled out as "bourgeois" and counterrevolutionary. Thus the more "revolutionary" climate in France—that is the possibility of drastic political change of some sort—militated against the spread of psychoanalysis, but later on, when it began to acquire radical overtones, became almost popular (Kurzweil 1980; Turkle 1978). Not that Lacan's structuralist psychoanalysis was really a revolutionary force. But his much touted opposition to classical Freudians, based on a new and radical reading of Freud's texts, reflected a cultural stance, just as Karen Horney's or Harry Stack Sullivan's appeal to interpersonal relations and Erich Fromm's appeal to idealism had reflected an American culturally accepted stance in the 1940s and 1950s. So after the late 1960s, the fact that Lacanianism was more rhetorical than revolutionary was overlooked, and Lacan inspired large audiences. This broad-based interest led in turn to fascinating inquiries into unconscious motivations within the society—inquiries that were more consequential to thought than to practice. In any event, French psychoanalytic controversies became quite intellectual and abstract, subsuming structural-linguistic theories (Saussure, Jakobson, or Barthes) and concepts of theoretical breaks (Bachelard, Althusser, or Foucault) while at the same time promising individual liberation. Althusser's call to Marxists that the Lacanian enterprise might finally unveil both individual and cultural unconscious mental structures and might thus help further revolutionary ends, endorsed Lacan's work even further.

The promises of Critical Theory, however, had never reached more than small and select groups of scholars, not even during their most fruitful years in America (1933–50). By 1969, shortly before he died, Adorno, who had given up on Marxist practice, had even been attacked as conservative by some of his German students—particularly for his "elitist" ideas of art and his negative views about the influence of mass culture. Nevertheless, since then, there has been a revival of the work of the Frankfurt scholars. Especially some of the dissident students of the late 1960s thought that the inquiries into the repressive features of modern society and the theoretical attempts to construct a Freudo-Marxism might be put to good use. Marcuse's treatise on one-dimensionality and "repressive desublimation" was probably the single most decisive influence for the Frankfurt resurgence.

Both critical theory and structuralism addressed some of the universal problems of human existence and consciousness central to Husserl and Heidegger, but more sociologically; they questioned the surrealists' nihilistic responses to political events, and Nietzsche's notion of the superman; and they went back to examine Freud's postulates of the pleasure principle and ego formation, of the self and narcissism, of the Oedipus complex and the authority of the father, in relation to the sociopsychological nexus they were observing.

Aware of all the philosophic discussions since Hegel, Adorno and Horkheimer asked at the beginning of *The Dialectic of Enlightenment* "why mankind instead of entering into a truly human condition, is sinking into a new kind of barbarism" (1972:xi). They had started, as Marx had, with critiques of bourgeois modes of thought and perception, although with more recognition that the accomplishments of reason and science could easily be turned to brutal ends. Thus their theoretical Marxism, all along, was being "cleansed," self-consciously, of vulgarizations, so that it might provide the theoretical means to apprehend the new social and political conditions created since Marx by the communist state in Russia, by the conflicts between socialist and communist parties in democratic systems, and by the rise of fascism. The Frankfurt School thinkers were intent on comprehending all the philosophical and practical repercussions of repressive regimes, on truly understanding sociological and psychological reasons for anti-Semitism. They wanted to know what circumstances would allow for the acceptance of totalitarian and authoritarian rule by free individuals. By learning about authoritarian personality structure, for instance, Fromm had expected to find out how to ensure the education for and dedication to democracy. The team of *The Authoritarian Personality* did the same thing, though more scientifically. These crucial issues which were of particular interest during World War II, led them to examine the importance of the domination of the media by political authority. Alerted by the events of the Weimar Republic, they wanted to get to the roots of mass psychology, to know how and why it was so easy to control individuals' ideas, if only to avoid future Weimars. Hitler's propaganda minister Goebbels had demonstrated how an entire nation could be manipulated, how easy it had been to make people believe, for instance, that Germany had a "right" to the Rheinland, that the Jews "controlled world finances," or that Austria and Czechoslovakia ought to be annexed. In the process, capitalist rhetoric, which creates artificial needs to consume and sells goods as well as ideas, became part of the investigations.

Eager to comprehend how social evils can be perpetrated by ostensibly ethical individuals, the school's theoretical inquiries relied increasingly on a vigorous dialogue with psychoanalysis, especially as the focus shifted from Marx's economics to notions of domination and alienation. This was partly due to the realization that, in Russia, the end of capitalism had not brought the concomitant emergence of a revolutionary consciousness; and that in Western countries neither the advance of science nor the accession to power by socialist parties had altered the psychic structures of the inhabitants. Because the Communist Revolution in Russia had not abolished alienation (a central focus of all Marxist investigations) and thus had proven the proletariat incapable of executing the task it had been assigned by Marx, the Critical Theorists moved increasingly to investigating the reasons for this "collective failure" in the psychological development of individuals. (In the West, of course, psychic transformation was deemed impossible because of the increasingly dehumanized and repressive culture industry.) Marx himself had not delved too deeply into human consciousness, which in any event he expected to be altered by history, or into psychopathology which was thought to have its roots, to a large extent, in economics (Friedmann 1981:87–88). Particularly Adorno, Horkheimer at various times, and Marcuse, kept addressing the theoretical possibilities of harnessing the emerging unconscious in individuals, and of applying psychoanalytic methods to social aggregates, to help induce radical social change by postulating interferences in psychodynamic processes. Thoroughly familiar with the sociologizing strands of Freudianism, as represented particularly by Sullivan, Horney, and Fromm (an original member of their Frankfurt circle, his gradual move toward clinical practice on the one hand and popularizing idealism on the other, had estranged him from the institute), they increasingly looked to Freud's cultural contributions such as *Totem and Taboo* or *Civilization and Its Discontents* and attacked all psychologizing which was thought to "dilute" Freud's basic concepts. Adorno was concerned not to "castrate psychoanalysis by replacing the fear of castration," with, for instance, fear of parental love (1962:99). In *Minima Moralia* he had stated that "in psychoanalysis nothing is true except the exaggerations" (1978:40–41). Instead of focusing on the manifestations of psychic content in individuals' interactions, even when these were used as means to uncover the formation of early pathology, Horkheimer as well refused to simplify Freud, and tended to rely on the notion of the pleasure principle as the governing element in human existence (1932:129). For Freud, this principle invariably regulated the course of events to lower psychic tension (1961a:21) "and to help the individual in dealing with the external world . . . with pain and unpleasure." (1961b:14). Referring to Freud's *Group Psychology and the Analysis of the Ego* (1922), Adorno linked the analysis of an individual's "willingness to yield unquestioningly to powerful outside, collective agencies" to these agencies' subversive influences on the modern psyche. So unlike Freud, who tended to locate individual traumatic conflict in nature, in the psychological competition for scarce resources, and in a person's maladjustment, the Frankfurt scholars postulated this conflict as historically caused. Later on, Marcuse argued that eliminating the inequities of the social order, it would no longer be necessary to suppress the pleasure principle, and thus psychic structure itself could be transformed (1955:120–21). Recapitulating Schiller's argument which was thought to resolve the antagonisms of civilization—the liberation of man from inhuman existential conditions—Marcuse went on to elaborate on Freud's notions of play, themselves connected to its uses in folk tales and tribal myths. He then focused on the play impulse as the vehicle of liberation. In play, Freud had argued, "children repeat everything that has made a

great impression on them in real life, and . . . make themselves masters
of the situation. . . . [Thus] the child passes over from the passivity of
the experience to the activity of the game" (1961:36–37). Marcuse focused
on the fact that play allows not just intellectual or transcendental inner
freedom, but freedom in reality. "Because it is the realization of freedom,
play is *more* than the constraining physical and moral reality" (1955:172).
The emphasis on play—linked as it is the imagination—by *all* who
wished to utilize psychoanalysis for cultural understanding was not
accidental: it allowed more freedom of expression, more leeway. By
stretching the flexibility of play, individuals' imaginations would be
enlarged so that play, for Marcuse, was to become a major tool for
liberation. Playful impulses were to be encouraged, in children and adults.
Lacan as well focused on this aspect of Freudian thought, and proceeded
to postulate it as one of the central organizing concepts of his psychoanalysis.

Lacan's notions of play and imagination, initially more based on
clinical evidence focusing on the emergence of unconscious material to
consciousness in the psychoanalytic session than on Freud's cultural
contributions, were primarily addressed to the practices of the classical
Freudians. The discourse itself derived from a very different reading of
Freud, so that Lacan's ideas have been disputed and enlarged upon by
some of his followers in an entirely novel framework—subsuming Hegelian
categories, the inevitability of misunderstanding, as well as much of
classical and French literature. Put simply, we are accustomed, on the
clinical level (whether with "deep" therapy, ego psychology, or any other
technique) to alleviate the consequences of childhood trauma with the
help of psychoanalytic insight. It has been argued that Freud's dictum
"where *id* was there *ego* shall be" has often been applied too literally
in clinical situations. Thus practicing psychoanalysts tended to neglect
the societal level except for rudimentary generalizations derived from
studies of socialization in primitive cultures such as those by Erik Erikson
of American Indians (1964), Abraham Kardiner of the Alorese or the
Comanche, and by Geza Roheim (1971) of Australian totemism. They
assumed too readily that the liberation of individuals would, ipso facto,
make for a better society. But whereas the Frankfurt scholars attacked
these approaches for their naiveté and disagreed amongst themselves
about the interpretation and adaptation of Freud's discoveries, they
remained within what Lacan dubbed "American psychoanalysis." They
all accepted, for instance, that in play and in dreams the unconscious
would emerge from what a patient said, felt, recollected, acted out,
associated to, and from what an analyst would perceive and hear with
his "third ear"; and they also talked of the "generalized individual."

Lacan argued that he did that too, but that language was the intervening structure in the psychoanalytic relationship, and that its neglect, especially by his American colleagues, falsified all of Freud. His statement that "the unconscious is structured like a language" was repeated and commented on by dissidents and Lacanians so often that it became a cliché. Still, when we recall that Lacan here assumed dialectical relationships between words and meaning, between specific discourse and personal relations, as well as between all the possible associations and reciprocal connections between them, we must admit that he was indeed challenging all previously used methods to uncover the unconscious. At the root of his approach was the denial of the validity of ego psychology, and of the emphasis by "American" psychoanalysts on too rigid an application of Freud's heuristic division of personality structure into id, ego, and superego.

Insisting that Freud's writings had been misinterpreted, Lacan proceeded to reread them with the help of Saussurean dialectical relationships—between *langue* and *parole* and between levels of speech and systems of signs, with their own dual aspects of concept and sound image. In this fashion, argued Lacan, we would eventually understand and overcome the repressive nature of society. Such legitimation of psychoanalysis in linguistics, in sharp contrast to conventional psychoanalysis which is tied to biology and to Freud's developmental model, and which was partly derived from the natural sciences and from neurophysiology, undercut the medicalization of American psychoanalysis. The endless polemics on this subject were internal to psychoanalysis, but they indicate the indivisibility of theory and practice—in their specific national contexts. Consequently, the Frankfurt theorists' discussions, though sharing structuralist aims, had remained completely within the American context which Lacan rejected out of hand. His central concept of the "mirror stage"—the child's first apprehension of itself as a total being and the psychological repercussions of the emotional, visual, tactile, and other sensate elements experienced at that particular moment— became central to all structuralists. Essentially, stated Lacan, a child's first glimpse and apprehension of itself in the mirror (at between six and eighteen months of age) is of fundamental psychological importance as the initial awareness of itself in the preverbal stage.

> The *mirror image* situates the agency of the ego, before its social determination, in a fictional direction, which will always remain irreducible for the individual alone, or rather, which will only rejoin the coming into being of the subject asymptotically, whatever the success of the dialectical syntheses by which he must resolve as *I* his discordance with his own reality [1977:2].

In this fixed and fleeting "drama," continued Lacan, the individual anticipates himself biologically, becomes cognizant of both the "mental permanence" and the alienation of the *I,* and establishes a relation between his *Innenwelt* and his *Umwelt.* Inevitably, the child's perception is distorted, thus creating a fragmented body image—an image Lacan allegedly recuperated through analysands' dreams, through aggressive disintegration of the individual, or in schizoid and spasmodic symptoms of hysteria.

The substantive aims of Lacan's theories could not be faulted and would not be challenged—either by conventional psychoanalysts or by the Frankfurt scholars. In very different ways, all of them underlined the importance of the family and the incorporation of paternal authority, although the Frankfurt theorists frequently couched the discussion in critiques of the "revisionists" who were excessively concerned with interaction. Adorno, for instance, attacked Karen Horney for sociologizing psychoanalysis by emphasizing the influence of milieu in character formation, for substituting character traits for drives and emotional impulses, needs or passions for libido, and for postulating an ideal totality of character that could exist only in a nontraumatic society (1962:94–112). This criticism was indicative of Adorno's Marxist premises, as was the accusation of the "reification of real experiences" (1962:98). Lacan, aware of these polemics and sympathetic to some components on both sides, attempted to remain on the "deeper" or unconscious level of influence of an individual's milieu, while expecting to avoid all the accusations of superficiality, simplification, and thoughtless acceptance of social reality the "revisionists" had suffered. He would agree with Adorno, who stated that "Freud's greatness, as that of all radical bourgeois thinkers, exists in that he leaves these contradictions unresolved, and that he refuses to pretend systematic harmony where there are rifts. He exposes the antagonistic character of social reality insofar as his theory and praxis reach within the available division of labor" (1962:111).

Lacan, however, found not only revisionist but all other American psychoanalysis Pollyannic and superficial, and argued that he alone was reading Freud properly, as well as counteracting the perpetuation of the bourgeois status quo. His references were to practicing analysts, and unlike the Frankfurt scholars, who primarily used Freudian insights to attack the mass culture of industrial society as fake enlightenment, and as the new ideology which captures the individual in its airtight organizational web, Lacan sounded more philosophical, when he promised to liberate the individual in his society by providing a new analytic framework that would undercut all conscious and unconscious hypocrisy and sham at the roots. Granting that the depths of the unconscious could never be fully exposed, Lacan predicted that his own method would bring more hidden meanings of human interactions and thoughts into the open than any other; that more of the id—or "it"—would be able to emerge. This "opposite" approach required not only different methodologies but different foci and assumptions. These will be illustrated by looking at how the Critical Theorists and the Lacanians understood Freud's notions of the family and of the Oedipal situation.

In the 1930s, the Frankfurt theorists argued, along with sociologists such as Ogburn, that the functions of the family in modern society had decreased; and with the psychoanalysts, that the family was the primary agency for identity formation. According to Horkheimer:

> The family has a very special place among the relationships which through conscious and unconscious mechanisms influence the psychic character of the vast majority of men. The processes that go on within the family shape the child from his tenderest years and play a decisive role in the development of his capabilities. The growing child experiences the influence of reality according as the latter is reflected in the mirror of the family circle [1972:98].

By now, nearly fifty years later, such a statement has almost become a cliché, as has the specific emphasis on the influence of larger social structures, particularly of the media and the organization of production. But at the time, a Freudo-Marxian critique of society was new, and the meshing of parental with state authority, that is the individual's capacity to "transfer" his/her mode of response, was still being explored.

> A son . . . may think what he will of his father, but if he is to avoid conflicts and costly refusals he must submit to his father and satisfy him. . . . The father represents power and success, and the only way the son can preserve in his own mind a harmony between effective action and the ideal, a harmony often shattered in the years before puberty's end, is to endow his father, the strong and powerful one, with all the other qualities the son considered estimable. . . . It is . . . impossible to separate rational and irrational elements in the respect given him by his children [Horkheimer 1972:107–8].

Whereas Horkheimer and Adorno tended to focus on those factors of identity formation which impinged especially on authority relations, that is on the development of the superego, they, as well as Marcuse, noted that the conditions of the Oedipal situation were changing, that the legitimacy of the father's authority was declining, and that identification with the father was lessening. As a result, the process of ego formation and differentiation Freud had described was said, increasingly, to be undermined, as individuals submitted to "totalitarian integration."

These observations based on empirical evidence, led them inevitably to grapple with the contradictions of the Oedipus complex. Questioning Freud's "fatalistic" acceptance of the suppression of the pleasure principle, without however relinquishing his theories of the unconscious of personality structure, and yet rejecting all the assumptions that look to the roots of neurosis and psychosis in the individual's maladjustment rather than in the social order, Marcuse's argument in *Eros and Civilization* was most complex. As he asked whether "the realization of happiness in a free civilization still necessitates suppression," he maintained that the Oedipus complex, insofar as it "passes," either under the rule of a repressive reality principle or for "lack of success," appears to be a "natural" event (1955:186). In its place, he postulated a "self-sublimating sexuality" which would no longer be subjected to the repressive organization of the Oedipus complex, and instead, would restore the primary structure of sexuality thus freeing the entire biological organism, and transforming sexuality into Eros—"a quantitative and qualitative aggrandizement of sexuality" (1955:187–88). This desublimation of libidinal relations rejected the centrality of the Oedipus complex—a rejection Lacan achieved by bypassing it at the "mirror stage."

Because an individual's first conscious encounter with a mirror occurs long before the beginning of the Oedipal drama, said Lacan, interference at that developmental stage promises the possibility of undercutting the perpetuation of patriarchal and bourgeois family relationships—with all their repression. The first glimpse of an infant's own body (as its own) was said to bear on its perception of self and on all its future relationships, including resolution of the Oedipus complex. But again, this perception, according to Lacan, was constructed with the help of language. In his 1949 version of the "mirror stage" he stated: "On the mental plane we find realized the structures of fortified works, the metaphor of which arises spontaneously, as if issuing from the symptoms themselves, to designate the mechanisms of obsessional neuroses—inversion, isolation, reduplication, cancellation and displacement" (1977:5). With this insertion of linguistics, Lacan "legitimately" allowed his imagination to take over. His discussions about the family and its name for instance, now centered—in florid prose—on the given name of the father, that is, on paternal authority, and on the accepted presumptions by others an individual's name entails. Engaging in long discussions of literary works, he entered realms the Frankfurt contingent never thought of. The complexities of his system multiplied further, as Lacan began to elaborate on the moment at which the "mirror stage" ends. That is when identification with "the *imago* of the counterpart and the drama of primordial jealousy" allegedly determined the formation of the "I" and resolution of the Oedipus complex. "Primary narcissism by which analytic doctrine designated the libidinal investment characteristics," awareness of separation from the Other (a situation Lacan always let his listeners define for themselves), and semantic latencies are allegedly invested in this moment—"with all the ambivalences and dynamic oppositions of the Oedipal complex." Here the "separate libidos" of language and sexuality were used once more to legitimize the centrality of language and speech in psychoanalysis itself, thus "delegitimizing" American Freudians. The latter, hard put to prove the existence of libido, had even more difficulty grappling with the notion of separate and interacting libidos. But Lacan tended to overwhelm the skeptic with repetitions of linguistic and Freudian truths, such as "the unconscious is not merely the seat of the instincts"; "the subject's speech makes its entrance into language and its structure at a certain point in his mental development and cultural experience"; "every spoken word is full of meaning . . . its utterance is rooted in a specific context." Although such statements were to reaffirm the Oedipal matrix and inexhaustibility of the unconscious, the Babel of internal ambivalences multiplied further through Lacan's "discourse with the Other"—discourse located in the speech of the patient, in the analyst's reply or his silence (he is the Other), and in the reality the patient would eventually ascribe to it. It was in this context that Lacan connected the individual to his group. Thus his critical use of Freud's thought differed from that of the Frankfurt School not only as a result of the linguistic overlay, but in the dialectical relationship he postulated between clinical psychoanalytic practice and theory, between general psychoanalytic theory and Freud's philosophy, and between his metapsychology and its specific applications.

Understandably the current revival of Critical Theory as well as the increasing interest in French structuralism reflect our concern with the issues and problems these schools addressed—the conflicts inherent in democratic society that have to do with the optimization of individual liberties, opportunities, and well-being of every member. Lacan was as preoccupied as the Critical Theorists in pointing to the negative adaptation of pluralist ideology which was said to blur the differences between superficial phenomena and essential concerns. That is why, for instance, Adorno kept attacking the postulate of character as a

> sedimented totality . . . which . . . is in truth the result of an objectification of real experiences. If one makes them absolute, they can readily become an ideological way out for the individual's status quo. . . . [Furthermore] not only the individual, but also the category of individualism is a product of the society [Adorno 1962:98–100].

Such relentless attempts to avoid objectification of subjectivity converge
with those of the structuralists and with the surrealists who preceded
them. In this respect they all returned to Freud, using "the very tools
with which Freud uncovered the explosive instinctual and social roots
of the personality" (Marcuse 1955:219).

Although the attempts to fuse Marx and Freud need to be put within
their social context, they tended to be reinterpretations and revisions of
psychoanalysis aimed to achieve "happy" lives and societies. Even such
non-Freudian and non-Marxist therapies as encounter, esalen, est, or
Gestalt psychology, which no longer contain the pretense of a critique
of society, aiming only to overcome individuals' inhibitions to achieve
"self-fulfillment," reflect some of the Freudian and Marxist promise. But
these newer claims for happiness and productive development—so much
more insistent and less informed than those of the revisionists—as Marcuse
argued, are in contradiction to the objective social dynamics of our
society, and thus become themselves repressive (1955:233). This is why
none of the sociologized psychoanalyses could conceivably accomplish a
radical critique of bourgeois society. The Frankfurt School as well as
structuralism needed an "uncontaminated" Freudianism, as sharp a
weapon to liberate the individual as Marxism had offered to liberate
society. (Although I have my doubts about the ultimate viability of
linguistic psychoanalysis, its insistence on getting to the roots of Freudian
thought presents a similar program.)

Susan Buck-Morss summarized the project for Adorno, who worked
out the implications of the mediated relationship between Freudian and
Marxist theory. He began with an immanent criticism of Freud, demonstrating, predictably, that the language Freud used to describe a
supposedly *biological* theory, in particular the "exchange schema" governing the "economy of instincts," unintentionally illuminated the *social*
origins of that theory and of the psychological structures which it described.
This meant from the materialist perspective, that what appeared as
shortcomings in Freud's theory when judged from the criteria of absolute
and universal truth, were seen as precisely the grounds for its validity.
But that validity was limited to a particular historical stage of bourgeois
society, which, so Adorno argued, no longer existed. The "subject" of
Freud's times had been replaced by a new anthropological type. Characteristic of its psychological formation was not repression, but the
immediate substitute gratification provided by mass culture, not anal
possessiveness, but the consumer readiness to treat all objects as fungible
and disposable (1977:179).

Marcuse took this argument further when, in *One-Dimensional Man,*
he demonstrated how advanced technology functions to repress all in-

dividual expression, and how it even confines the formation of concepts and restricts all meaning (1964:208). In this work, he referred, for instance, to critiques by Gaston Bachelard and Maurice Blanchot, not only picking up their call for "liberating the imagination," but for a "comprehended imagination that becomes, redirected, a therapeutic force . . . [which] may go much further than the cure of neuroses" (1964:249–50). Maintaining that individuals suffer from their own images which are mutilated by society (including their faculty of imagination) and thus would organize to destroy even more than they are now permitted to do, he appeared less optimistic in his critique of domination than they had been. But Marcuse's critique continued to subsume psychoanalysis as a tool, and to attack mass culture, very much in the spirit of Lacan—who was a colleague of Bachelard and Blanchot—though in less spirited fashion.

Lacan was always more playful and disrespectful than the critical theorists, who suffered from German seriousness and pomposity and from the heaviness of their language. Hoping to overcome the limitations of bourgeois language, Freud's tongue itself, Lacan claimed to rediscover its origins in his special reading. In this critical endeavor, the ideas and practices of the Frankfurt thinkers and of the structuralists converged: They all made use of language and literature to apprehend new subtleties and unconscious elements. And they all perceived a critical psychoanalysis as the only means to uncover the interstices of our social and psychological unconscious as the tool to arrive at true socialism.

They also shared the open-ended dialectic which goes back to Hegel and to the dialogue of the young Hegelians. So even if the studies of the Frankfurt School have become dated, due to the fact that we have fewer illusions about eradicating prejudice or totalitarianism, or that we now have more evidence about repression in both capitalist and so-called socialist societies, the critical method of the Frankfurt School appears to remain viable. Psychoanalytically informed criticism, whether in its Frankfurt or in its Parisian incarnation, continues to search for improvements in its method and for a new anthropology, recognizing that there are no easy solutions, that we have only better or worse ways of confronting inequality, domination, and all the other contradictions within individuals and societies.

References

1962   Adorno, Theodor W. "Die revidierte Psychoanalyse," 94–112; "Ideologie und Handeln," 38–47; "Soziologie und empirische Forschung," 205–22. In *Sociologica II*. Frankfurt: Europaeische Verlagsanstalt.

1978   _____. *Minima Moralia*. London: NLB.

1950 ——— , et al. *The Authoritarian Personality.* New York: Harper.
1972 Althusser, Louis. *For Marx.* New York: Pantheon.
1977 Buck-Morss, Susan. *The Origin of Negative Dialectics.* New York: Free Press.
1964 Erikson, Erik. *Childhood and Society.* New York: Norton.
1981 Friedmann, Georges. *The Political Philosophy of the Frankfurt School.* Ithaca: Cornell University Press.
1922 Freud, Sigmund. *Group Psychology and the Analysis of the Ego.* New York: Liveright.
1961a ——— . *Civilization and Its Discontents.* New York: Norton.
1961b ——— . *Beyond the Pleasure Principle.* New York: Bantam.
1963 ——— . *Character and Culture.* New York: Crowell Collier.
1965 ——— . *New Introductory Lectures on Psychoanalysis.* New York: Norton.
1932 Horkheimer, Max. "Geschichte und Psychologie." *Zeitschrift für Sozialforschung* 1 (no. 172).
1972 ——— . *Critical Theory.* New York: Seabury Press.
1973 ——— . "The Authoritarian State." *Telos* 15 (Spring):3–20.
1978 ——— . *Dawn and Decline.* New York: Seabury Press.
1972 Horkheimer, Max, and Theodor W. Adorno. *Dialectic of Enlightenment.* New York: Herder & Herder.
1975 Hughes, H. Stuart. *The Sea Change.* New York: Harper & Row.
1973 Jay, Martin. *The Dialectical Imagination.* Boston: Little, Brown.
1945 Kardiner, Abraham. *The Psychological Frontiers of Society.* New York: Columbia University Press.
1980 Kurzweil, Edith. *The Age of Structuralism.* New York: Columbia University Press.
1977 Lacan, Jacques. *Écrits: A Selection.* New York: Norton.
1977 Lemaire, Anika. *Jacques Lacan.* London: Routledge & Kegan Paul.
1955 Lévi-Strauss, Claude. *Tristes Tropiques.* Paris: Plon, and New York: Atheneum.
1963 ——— . *Structural Anthropology.* New York: Basic Books.
1971 Lichtheim, George. *From Marx to Hegel.* London: Herder & Herder.
1955 Marcuse, Herbert. *Eros and Civilization.* New York: Vintage.
1964 ——— . *One-Dimensional Man.* Boston: Beacon.
1975 Poster, Mark. *Existential Marxism in Postwar France.* Princeton: Princeton University Press.
1928 Politzer, Georges. *Les Fondements de la psychologie.*
1971 Roheim, Geza. *Australian Totemism.* Atlantic Highlands, N.J.: Humanities.
1965 Sartre, Jean-Paul. *Anti-Semite and Jew.* New York: Shocken.
1966 Saussure, Ferdinand de. *Course in General Linguistics.* New York: McGraw Hill.
1977 Tar, Zoltán. *The Frankfurt School.* New York: Wiley.
1978 Turkle, Sherry. *Psychoanalytic Politics.* New York: Basic Books.

18
Partisan Truth: Knowledge and Social Classes in Critical Theory

Michael Löwy

How did the Frankfurt School conceive of the relationship of Critical Theory to the viewpoint of certain social classes? In other words, what was, in the school's eyes, the ultimate foundation for the critical understanding of present society? This essay will deal only with two of the main thinkers of the Frankfurt School—Max Horkheimer and Herbert Marcuse—since it is mainly in their works that this question is discussed; it is also limited to the 1930s, the "classical" period of the Frankfurt School.

Among the greatest merits of Critical Theory are its uncompromising negation of the established order and its passionate antipositivism—both dimensions being intimately related and expressing the coherence of negative dialectics. It is particularly adamant in rejecting the positivist fallacy of a presuppositionless, ethically neutral, or value-free social science, which pretends to limit itself to collecting and classifying pure empirical facts—as if the selection of facts and their theoretical reconstruction did not necessarily imply certain presuppositions and a certain orientation. According to Horkheimer, the late apology of a value-free science is nothing but an attempt to reduce theoretical reflection to a humble maid at the service of the established goals of industrial society.[1]

Critical Theory, on the contrary, does not pretend to be axiologically neutral; it denies such a possibility for any social knowledge and it proclaims openly and proudly its commitment to certain values, its partisan character, its adherence to certain philosophical and ethical presuppositions. It believes in the objective validity of these presuppositions and values, avoiding therefore the dilemmas of relativism. Is this validity related to a social class position, a class viewpoint? For Horkheimer, Mannheim's sociology of knowledge, by linking every thought to a certain social group, to a social position (*Standort*), leads inevitably to a relativist position.[2]

Horkheimer has always been hostile to Mannheim's conceptions, but his first tentative answer to the challenge of sociology of knowledge is somehow awkward and inadequate. In 1930 he published a review of *Ideology and Utopia* which sweepingly rejected the whole book, insisting, among other things, that Mannheim's relativism "confused true and false with authentic and unauthentic."[3] Ten years later, in an essay written in 1940, he was willing to concede that Mannheim's analysis of ideology, stressing the links between each structure of thought (*Denkgebilde*), each philosophical or cultural production and specific social groups, is "without a doubt to a certain extent correct." But he once more accuses Mannheim of being prisoner of a purely relativist idea of truth: "The stereotyped application of the concept of ideology to each *Denkgebilde* is ultimately grounded on the conception that there exists no philosophical truth— and therefore no truth at all—for humanity, that all thinking is existentially determined (*seinsgebunden*). Which means that it belongs in the last analysis, by its methods and results, to a specific stratum and has validity only for this stratum."[4] This criticism is unable to touch the inner core of Mannheim's argument; Horkheimer seems strangely blinded to the fact that Mannheim *has* a solution for overcoming relativism: the synthesis of the various partial (and partially true) world views by the free-floating intelligentsia (*freischwebende Intelligenz*). It is impossible to develop a coherent Marxist criticism of *Ideology and Utopia* without tackling *this* solution; by avoiding it or ignoring it, Horkheimer's polemics appear surprisingly off the mark, even if they are able to reveal several contradictions in or limitations of Mannheim's position.

Marcuse's discussion of the sociology of knowledge is much more to the point; in an essay published in 1929, he recognizes as a *positive* element the fact that Mannheim—in opposition to the revisionist and neo-Kantian conceptions of Marxism as a value-free sociology—presents Marxist theory as "the concrete theory of the proletarian praxis" and as "the way through which the proletariat as a class, from its social situation, must live, seize and form reality." According to Marcuse, this sociological interpretation of Marxism is identical with the conception that Marx himself had of his scientific socialism. On the other hand what he does criticize is Mannheim's presupposition that "synthesis" is the road to objective truth: The "synthetic" character of a theory does not give it any advantage in relation to the viewpoints it is trying to mediate; it may even have less validity than they do.[5] But Marcuse fails to confront the idea of a free-floating intelligentsia, which according to Mannheim is the social basis (and guarantee) of an objective and all-embracing "dynamic synthesis."[6]

Critical Theory openly acknowledges its commitment to certain pre-suppositions, denying the comfortable myth of a value-free knowledge of society. But since it rejected (or ignored) Mannheim's solution of the "dynamic synthesis"—How could it avoid the pitfall of total relativism? How could it conciliate its avowedly partisan nature with the claim of objective truth?

The most coherent solution to this dilemma, in the framework of a dialectical Marxist conception, is probably Lukács's *History and Class Consciousness* (1923), a book which left a deep and lasting imprint on the whole Frankfurt School. For Lukács, Marxism is true not in spite of but *because* of its partisanship, because it is the class viewpoint of the revolutionary proletariat. Why is that so? Mainly for two reasons: (1) The proletariat is the universal class, which has no particular interests apart from those of humanity as a whole; (2) the bourgeoisie could achieve its historical aims without a clear understanding of the historical process—the cunning of reason (*List der Vernunft*) of the socioeconomic evolution led to its triumph. The proletariat, on the contrary, is confronted by history with the task of conscious transformation of society; the objective and true knowledge of its situation is a *vital need*. Truth is for the proletariat a weapon necessary for victory. At the same time Lukács was careful to distinguish between the empirical, given con-sciousness of the working class and its authentic class consciousness, its imputed consciousness as the rational understanding of the historical situation of the class. It is true that this conception raises as many problems as it solves: What does "the rational interests of the proletariat" mean? And what is the historical expression of the "imputed con-sciousness?" There is no simple answer to these questions, but they have the advantage of giving the debate a concrete context, in a specific, politically and socially defined sphere: the proletariat, its situation, its movement, its struggle, its historical aims. The trouble is that Lukács added to this bold dialectical solution of the complex problem of a "partisan truth" the much more controversial thesis that the Communist Party was the embodiment of the imputed consciousness.

Both Marcuse and Horkheimer rejected this thesis and kept a critical distance from the Communist movement. But they were very much attracted by the main argument of *History and Class Consciousness:* Unable either to reject or accept it entirely, they seemed to struggle internally with it during the 1930s. The whole problem of the relation between the proletariat and Critical Theory occupies an important place in their writings of those years; they experiment with one solution after the other, sometimes explicitly debating Lukács's views, sometimes im-plicitly relating to them. This struggle is probably not without a link to their peculiar political position as independent revolutionary intellectuals, who at the same time are deeply committed to the aims of the proletarian revolution and rather critical of the contemporary labor movement (particularly its Social-Democratic and Stalinist leaderships).

Marcuse's evolution during the late 1920s and 1930s seems to take him from a semi-Lukácsian position to an increasingly uprooted rationalist stand. In his well-known essay "Contributions to a Phenomenology of Historical Materialism" (1928), the name of Lukács does not appear, but the influence of his views is very much there. The concept of consciousness is defined, in Lukácsian terms, as part of the sociohistorical totality, as grounded on the concrete historical being. Moreover, according to Marcuse, the class becomes mature for its task as bearer of the historical action, through class consciousness. If a revolutionary situation is given, only the class which is conscious of its historical position can seize upon it— an affirmation which seems to be borrowed directly from *History and Class Consciousness.* Theory is linked to praxis and both are linked to the historical role of the "universal class," the concrete bearer of the radical action.[7]

One year later, in his review ("Zur Wahrheitsproblematik der soziologischen Methode," 1929) of Mannheim's essay, Marcuse is still—without mentioning Lukács—very near to his conceptions, both by his criticism of the neo-Kantian interpretations of Marx and by his definition of Marxism as the theory of proletarian revolution as a "historical function of the social being" (*Seinslage*) of the proletarian class, whose meaning can only be understood through this function. In this same article one can also see very clearly the transition to a different approach. Marcuse recognizes the existentially grounded nature of theory, but at the same time he insists that this does not mean that its validity is limited to its own social bearer; theory can have a general validity, i.e. truth. So far, there is no disagreement with the Lukácsian approach; but he tries to discover a criterion or case for judging the validity or truth of a theoretical proposition—and here is where the new perspective appears: For him, this criterion is the *value* of the social aim which is at the heart of a theory. For instance, in the case of Marxism, "the evident value superiority [*Höherwertigkeit*] of the socialist 'way of life' [*Lebensordnung*] in relation to the capitalist" is the ultimate guarantee for the truth of the theory! The key word here is "evident": For Marcuse certain ethical values are as self-evident as natural rights were for the philosophers of the Enlightenment. We shall return to this typically rationalist proposition. Marcuse tries, at the end of this article, to suggest an objective instance for these value judgments and produces the idea of some ahistorical or transhistorical basic structures (*Grundstrukturen*) of human social life, in which whether realized or not a value hierarchy of the different historical ways of life would be permitted to be established.[8] In other words, Marcuse does not base (as Lukács does) the truth of the proletarian viewpoint on the *objective situation* of the proletariat as a class but on the axiological superiority (in terms of transhistorical criteria) of the *aim* for which the class is struggling—socialist society. He moves therefore in the framework of the same essay from a quasi-Lukácsian analysis of the proletarian class character of theory to an ethical, nonhistorical foundation for it, not necessarily linked to any social class.

In 1930 Marcuse wrote an essay against the neo-Kantians (Max Adler) in which he particularly criticized their reduction of Marxism "from the theory of proletarian revolution to a scientific sociology." Here Lukács is for the first time explicitly mentioned and Marcuse seems to come very near to his conception of theory as the imputed consciousness of social classes. Philosophy, he writes, is "the scientific expression of a certain basic human attitude [*Grundhaltung*], . . . and a social-historical situation can often express itself clearer and deeper in such a basic attitude than in its reified practical life-sphere."[9] Strangely enough, in the same year and even in the same issue of the journal (*Die Gesellschaft* 7 [1930]) there appears another essay by Marcuse in which this perspective is openly questioned. The article, a review of Siegfried Marck's book on dialectical philosophy, once more mentions *History and Class Consciousness* in a very favorable light, as a work that had "an essential, and not to be underestimated, significance for the development of Marxism." But at the same time he considers that Marck's criticism touched a weak point in the Lukácsian dialectic—the concept of the "correct class consciousness": "This concept (as already the conception of class consciousness itself) breaks beyond the dimension of historicity, and is a fixation 'outside' the events, from where it can only be linked in an abstract-artificial way with history."[10] This criticism is quite surprising, not only in relation to the above-mentioned article on Max Adler, but also if one recalls that just one year before, in the already quoted review of Mannheim's book, Marcuse insisted that the ideological class character of theory was to be transcended toward a deeper dimension, in which "through a specific transcendence of events, some relations become visible, which put into question the historical level of being [*geschichtliche Seinsstufe*] as the ultimate given"—a reference to the basic structures which are the invariant foundations of history itself.[11] In other words, the concept of class consciousness is first (in 1929) criticized for lacking a transhistorical dimension, and then, in 1930, for being "beyond the dimension of historicity"! Clearly Marcuse is still finding his way and struggles with the Lukácsian views, without being yet able to crystallize his own perspective in relation to this issue.

It was as late as 1932 that Marcuse seemed to attain a coherent conception of the relation between historical materialism and the proletariat. In his essay on Marx's *Economic-Philosophic Manuscripts* (1844) he argued forcefully that only the understanding of the human essence could be the basis for the radical revolution: "The factual situation of capitalism is not a question of an economic or political crisis, but of a catastrophe of the human essence—this perception condemns from the beginning any purely economic or political *reform* to failure, and requires immediately the catastrophic abolition of this factual situation through the *total revolution.* Only out of this sure ground, with a solidarity that cannot be menaced by any economic or political argument, can the question of the *historical conditions and bearers* of the revolution arise: the theory of class struggle and of the dictatorship of the proletariat."[12] This powerful and impressive formulation is of course influenced by the historical conjuncture: the crisis of 1929–33 and the menacing rise of fascism in Germany. But it goes beyond the immediate moment and expresses some very basic and lasting convictions of Herbert Marcuse: (1) A radical and uncompromising negation of the established order and the aspiration for its total revolutionary transformation; (2) the concept of human essence as the ethical and philosophical foundation of revolutionary theory and praxis; (3) the historical role of the proletariat as bearer of the revolution, as a subordinate and derivative conclusion. In other words, the ontological or epistemological basis of Critical Theory is not the proletariat (as in Lukács) but human essence, negated and oppressed by capitalism.

Where does this concept of human essence come from? In the same essay Marcuse points to Hegel as the philosopher who discovered that human essence proves itself through labor—an idea which was then taken over by Marx in the *Manuscripts of 1844.* He considers this concept of human essence as a proof of the "inner relationship of the revolutionary theory with the philosophy of Hegel," a relationship which has been wrongly reduced only to the dialectical method.[13] Here begins an intellectual development which will take Marcuse further and further away from the proletarian class reference and toward the attempt to root Critical Theory in a rationally defined (Hegelian) essence. The link to the class struggle is not severed, but it becomes looser and less defined. For instance, in the essay "Philosophy and Critical Theory" (1937) he writes that "the materialist protest and the materialist critique originated in the struggle of oppressed groups for better living conditions and remained permanently associated with the actual process of this struggle"—

a reference which is sufficiently broad to include both the *Tiers État* of the eighteenth century and the modern proletariat.[14] In a similar vein he asserts in an article in 1936 that "materialist theory moves beyond historical relativism in linking itself with those social forces which the historical situation reveals to be progressive and truly 'universal'"—a formulation that seems to consider the possibility that different social forces (and not only the proletariat) may become the bearers of universal values.[15]

Before examining all the implications and developments of Marcuse's new perspective in 1936–37, let us briefly review Horkheimer's ideas on this question since 1930. Paradoxically, his intellectual evolution seems to run in the opposite direction from Marcuse's, toward a greater significance of the proletariat in relation to Critical Theory. This is enough to show the inadequacy of the immediate and "easy" explanation of the changes in the Frankfurt School's attitude toward the proletariat that resulted from the defeat of the German working class in 1933. The historical background was the same for Horkheimer and Marcuse, but they reacted differently to it.

In the above-mentioned critique of Mannheim of 1930, Horkheimer seems to reject the whole problem of the existential determination of thought. Marxism appeared as a nonideological theory able to judge and criticize ideologies; but there is not the slightest reference to its social conditioning or its relation to the standpoint of a social class.

A few years later in 1933, Horkheimer was already willing to acknowledge that Critical Theory (at that period still designated as "materialism") was conditioned by and linked to certain social forces: "The undialectical concept of the free subject is alien to Materialism. It is quite conscious of its own social dependence [*Bedingtheit*]. This is to be found . . . in the link with those forces which want to implement the above mentioned aims"—economic equality and the abolition of domination in society.[16] The concrete nature of these progressive forces is not clarified and the proletariat as such is not mentioned, but a methodological step toward a social foundation of Critical Theory has been made. This step is further developed and made more precise in an essay of 1935, "On the Problem of Truth," in which Horkheimer speaks already of social groups: Critical Theory (materialism) "does not pretend to be an exception to the social dependence of every thought and every spiritual content [*Geistesinhalt*], but the fact that it corresponds to a certain social position, that it is linked to the horizon and the interests of certain groups, does not mean that it is not valid for the others, which deny and oppress its truth."[17] Horkheimer has now grasped that the general social conditioning of thought does not lead inevitably to relativism and/or to a negation of the possibility to know objective truth. The question however remains unanswered: Which are the social groups whose interests and horizon influence materialist (Critical) theory and how does this conditioning accede to general valid truths?

The next step is made in the now famous essay "Traditional and Critical Theory" (1937), one of the most perceptive seminal works of the Frankfurt School and one of the most significant attempts to a Marxist definition of the relation between revolutionary intellectuals and the revolutionary labor movement. It is also, as we shall try to argue, the writing of Horkheimer that comes nearer to the Lukácsian position. First, Horkheimer insists that the subject of Critical Theory is not an isolated thinker but an individual defined by his real links with other individuals and groups and by his contradictory relation to a certain class. This class is now explicitly designated by its Marxist concept, the proletariat, whose interest, according to Marx and Engels, is to discover the immanent tendency toward a rational social organization, already present in human labor. If so—Why is the relation of the critical theorist to the proletariat "contradictory"? The reason, writes Horkheimer, is that unfortunately "the situation of the proletariat is in this society no guarantee for a correct knowledge"; the opposition between personal and class interest frequently prevents the emergence of the authentic class consciousness. Recent history has shown, beyond doubt, that "the consciousness of every layer may under the present circumstances be ideologically narrowed or corrupted, even if it has, by its social position, a vocation to truth." In other words, Horkheimer recognizes the vocation of the proletariat for the knowledge of truth, resulting from its objective situation (although he does not elaborate on the precise reasons for this vocation); but at the same time he insists that this tendency or possibility may be thwarted by historical conditions. It follows from this that Critical Theory cannot subordinate itself passively to the "psychological state of mind" of the workers; moreover, if one is not able to present to the proletariat its own interests (which are at the same time those of society) but follows the occasional thoughts and opinions of the masses, one falls under "servile dependency of the existent." The similarity with the Lukácsian distinction between empirical and imputed class consciousness is obvious and manifests itself even in terminology.[18]

What should be, in these circumstances, the task of the critical theoretician? He is defined by Horkheimer almost as a professional revolutionary (in the Bolshevik tradition). "His calling [*Beruf*] is the struggle to which his thinking belongs, not the thinking as something independent and separated from the struggle." As such, his duty is to criticize not only the apologies of the established order but also the wrong tendencies (conformist or utopian) in the ranks of the emancipatory forces. This may lead to a tension between the theoretician and the class to which he directs his thought. The only way to overcome this contradiction is, according to Horkheimer—and this is one of the most fruitful and interesting ideas of the essay—through the dialogue between "the most advanced section of the class" and "the individuals, which express the truth about it," and, in a second moment, between his advanced section together with his theoreticians and the rest of the class. Horkheimer stresses that his is not a one-sided relation but a process of reciprocity (*Wechselwirkung*), in which the aim is to *reduce the tension* between the views of the Critical Theoretician and those of the oppressed humanity for which he fights.[19] Once more, the parallel with *History and Class Consciousness* is striking (although it is not even mentioned in a footnote in the essay): For Lukács the task of the revolutionary vanguard is to *reduce the tension* (the same term) between his level of class consciousness and that attained by the proletarian masses.

It would seem that the main difference between Lukács (in 1923) and Horkheimer (in 1937) is that for the Hungarian Marxist the Communist Party is the concrete form of the authentic class consciousness, while for the Frankfurt scholar Critical Theory remains the concern of individuals. But even here the distance between them is not so great as it seems at first. Horkheimer refers not only to theoreticians but also, very explicitly, to *small political groups:* "Before the general historical turn the truth can be limited to numerically reduced units. History teaches us that such groups, ignored or made hostile even by the oppositional section of society, may, thanks to their deeper understanding, win the leadership at the decisive moment." Could this be a reference to past revolutionary organizations, like the Russian Bolsheviks in 1917? And to which *present* groups is he referring? One would be tempted to see here above all a definition of the Frankfurt School itself, as a group with revolutionary aims, but the prospect of becoming a leading social force seems disproportionate to the reality of a small collectivity of exiled scholars. In another passage of the essay Horkheimer writes that "under the conditions of late capitalism and the impotence of the workers against the oppressive apparatus of the authoritarian states, truth took refuge in admirable small groups, which, decimated by terror, have little spare time to sharpen theory"—a description which certainly does not fit the exiled Frankfurt Institute of Social Research![20] Could it be the German (or other) Communist Party? No, since these small groups where truth found shelter are ignored or made hostile even by the "oppositional section of society" and since Horkheimer criticizes, in another passage of the article, the combative movements where the original unity of discipline with spontaneity has disappeared and bureaucracy took control (a transparent reference to the German Communist Party). Was Horkheimer perhaps referring to Trotskyist or other leftist oppositional Marxist groups that were indeed being decimated by terror in several authoritarian states (above all in the Soviet Union itself) and neglected or persecuted even by the forces of opposition—groups with which Horkheimer shared a world-revolutionary perspective and a common dislike of both social democracy and Stalinism? This is a purely speculative hypothesis, and further research is necessary before we could establish with some degree of precision who these small groups were with which Critical Theory could identify in 1937.

The problem of the party—formulated in theoretical, abstract terms—was not necessarily the main disagreement between Horkheimer and *History and Class Consciousness.* The essential difference lay deeper and relates, in our view, to the following question: *In the name of which criteria* can one (the theoretician, the party, or the small group) criticize the limitations of empirical consciousness, the shortcomings of the psychological state of mind of the oppressed masses? Where are the grounds, the basis, the *foundation* for such a criticism?

Lukács's answer is clear: the imputed consciousness of the proletariat, its authentic class consciousness, as rational and adequate understanding of its historical interests and situation. For Horkheimer, the answer is—at least implicitly—reason. While for the first the foundation is, in the last analysis *social*—a class position—for the second it is *theoretical,* an intellectual standard. Of course the polarity between both is not absolute: The Lukácsian authentic class consciousness includes the rational dimension, and Horkheimer's reason contains a reference to the interests of the proletariat. But the difference between them remains.

According to Horkheimer—and this crucial theme returns several times in the essay—Critical Theory is grounded on "the idea of a rational organization of society, corresponding to universality"; more precisely, Critical Theory consciously follows "in the constitution of its categories and in all the phases of its development, the interest in a rational organization of human activity."[21] This interest, this idea, this rational perspective which leads to truth, may or may not be adopted by the proletariat; it is *not* for Horkheimer (as it was for Lukács) the organic expression of a class standpoint, the coherent manifestation of a class perspective, the imputed figure of class consciousness.

This is why Horkheimer can easily dilute the proletarian reference of Critical Theory in a much broader context: "The aim of a rational society, which of course seems today only conserved in fantasy, is really rooted in every human being."[22] From such a presupposition it is difficult to see why the proletariat has to be privileged as the subject of either Critical Theory or revolutionary praxis.

This abstract rationalist orientation, which is to a certain extent neutralized or counterbalanced in this essay by Horkheimer's insistence on the link between Critical Theory and the proletariat, is more explicit in Marcuse's writings from the same period (1936–37). As we saw already in 1932 Marcuse considered the concept of human essence—as formulated by Hegel and critically elaborated upon by Marx in 1844—as the ultimate foundation of (critical) materialism, before and above any reference to the proletariat. Here, by the way, lies a significant difference with Horkheimer, who in his essay "Remarks on Philosophical Anthropology" (1935) calls into question any anthropological conception of human essence. In the article "On the Concept of Essence" (1936), Marcuse relates the fulfillment of human essence to the same historical task which occupies the central place in Horkheimer's essays: the rational organization of society. In this writing Marcuse links Critical Theory to the whole rationalist tradition from Plato to Descartes and from the Enlightenment to Hegel. He complains that late bourgeois philosophy, by abandoning this tradition, by sacrificing the idea of critical reason and the doctrine of essence, "lost the Archimedean point where it had anchored the freedom of the knowing individual, and without it, it has no bases from which the weapon of critique can be employed." Marcuse tries to reestablish such an Archimedean point by returning to the rationalist concept of human essence from which he believes that certain "materially objective values" can be deduced. For him, materialist (critical) theory advances a claim to objective truth which is not founded on a pretension to be value free, but on a partisan commitment to an aim which is general and objective in itself: the rational planning of social life. Consequently, theory is not related to a specific social class but to all those who are committed to the same aims and values: "Theory has moved to another subject; its concepts are generated by the consciousness of specific groups and individuals who are part of the fight for a more rational organization of society." However, this abstract rationalist belief in objective ethical values is to a certain extent limited by Marcuse's revolutionary activism; in the following passage he seems to take some distance from the purely ethical-rational "Archimedean point": "Of course these insights cannot be arrived at through a contemplative attitude; in order to justify them, knowledge can have recourse neither to evidence afforded by mere perception nor to a universal system of values in which they are anchored. The truth of this model of essence is preserved better in human misery and suffering and the struggle to overcome them than in the forms and concepts of pure thought."[23]

This problem is examined once more in an article published one year later, "Philosophy and Critical Theory" (1937). This time Marcuse tries to define the difference between traditional (idealist) rationalism and critical (materialist) rationalism: while the first was satisfied with the realization of reason in pure thought, the second aimed at the rational organization of society. But the principles of reason seem to be the same in both, and once more he deduces from them a system of explicitly ahistorical "objective" values, which he now designates as "universal truths": "Of course to the identity of the basic social structure in previous history certainly corresponds an identity of certain universal truths, whose universal character is an essential component of their truth content . . . that man is a rational being, that this being requires freedom, and that happiness is the highest good as are all universal propositions whose progressive impetus derives precisely from their universality. . . . Critical Theory's interest in the liberation of mankind binds it to certain ancient truths." And although he relates the materialist critique with the struggle of oppressed groups, the link between them is not of an organic nature but an exterior one: By demonstrating the possibility of a rational organization of society, critical social theory "could provide theoretical leadership for those strata which by virtue of their historical situation, were to bring about the change."[24]

It seems that the ultimate foundation for the values and the ultimate guarantee for the truth of Critical Theory is reason, as understood by the Enlightenment and by German idealism. Marcuse insists that "reason is the fundamental category of philosophical thought, the only one by means of which it has bound itself to human destiny"; it is "the highest potentiality of man and of existence" and the "critical tribunal" of the given world.[25] His great work of 1941 on Hegel, significantly entitled *Reason and Revolution,* is an extensive development of these ideas. Horkheimer seems to be more reserved and some of his essays contain substantial criticism of classical rationalism; but even there he explicitly claims that the reason (*Vernunft*) of Critical Theory is the inheritor of this rationalist tradition.[26]

One of the salient characteristics of the Frankfurt School's work was its stress on reason, but Critical Theory never really made an attempt to define what was meant by reason. It is enough to examine the key concept for both Marcuse and Horkheimer's political philosophy: the *rational organization of society*—not only as the supreme goal, but also as a "self-evident," "objective," "material," and universal value, and as the ultimate basis for the claim of Critical Theory to objective truth—to see where the problem of this (abstract) rationalist approach lies: Every social class in society has its own idea of what a "rational organization of society" is. The trouble is that social values and ethical assertions that are evident for one class are far from being so to others, and/or that the same values (equality for instance) are interpreted by the different social classes in opposite ways and attributed widely diverse concrete meanings. One can accept that, as Critical Theory insists, some rational values are universal, all-human, and to a certain transhistorical: human life as such, freedom, happiness. The question remains however: What are the *concrete ways* for implementing those values, for realizing them in social life? And here each social class has its own answer, its own solution, its own propositions, which seem to it "self-evident." Critical Theory, and in particular Horkheimer and Marcuse, were not only committed to these universal but abstract values, but also to the *concrete solution* advanced by Marxism and the revolutionary proletarian movement: the socialization of productive forces, the democratic planning of economic life by the producers themselves as the necessary preconditions for the rational organization of society. This means that even if they are not always willing to admit it, their theoretical perspective *is* rooted in the proletarian class struggle for socialism. In other words, Critical Theory's social and political views were more concrete than its (idealist) epistemological and ethical conceptions.

The moral greatness, the impressive ethical radicalism, the humanist sensibility, and the revolutionary aspirations of Critical Theory (as represented by Marcuse and Horkheimer in the 1930s) are undeniable. But their rationalism remains—at least to a certain extent—abstract, ahistorical, socially unattached. It is true that Marx and Engels also claimed allegiance to reason and to their tradition of Western rationalism; it is enough to recall their well-known assertion that the proletariat is the inheritor of German philosophy. But this formulation already shows where the difference lies: For them reason cannot be abstracted from class struggle; in each historical period it takes the concrete figure of a concrete social class. In the modern capitalist society there are no self-evident rational values; socialist values are evident from the rational standpoint of the proletariat. For Marx, these values are not deduced from an ahistorical human essence or reason as such, but from the rational interests flowing from the objective historical situation of the proletariat in capitalist society. They are universal insofar as the proletariat is the universal class, the class without particular interests aiming at the abolition of classes in general. In this sense Lukács's theory of the proletarian-imputed class consciousness is closer to the Marxian conceptions than the Frankfurt School's universal ethical truths. Both Lukács and the critical theorists share a common belief: only through a partisan and politically committed attitude can theory attain objective truth—a dialectical proposition which transcends the analytical platitudes of value-free positivism. But while for the author of *History and Class Consciousness* the guarantee for the objectivity of this partisan truth lies in its class position and is related to the specific nature of the proletariat as a universal revolutionary class, for Marcuse and Horkheimer it is located in the objective nature of its value presuppositions, their universal or self-evident character. By recognizing the link between Critical Theory and the proletariat and at the same time trying to ground it on a purely rationalist ethical perspective, Horkheimer and Marcuse were grappling with a real problem: It is true that neither theory (as the scientific search for objective truth) nor ethical values can be reduced to a class standpoint; they have their own spheres of existence, their relative autonomy in relation to social determinants, their specific mode of development.

While in 1937 Horkheimer still insisted on the essential link between Critical Theory and the proletariat, in *Dialectic of Enlightenment* (1944) the working class practically disappears from his theoretical horizon (and a similar evolution can probably also be traced in Marcuse); it appears only as part of the undifferentiated consuming mass in the chapter on cultural industry, or in allegoric form, as the deaf and obedient Greek rowers in the beautiful analysis of Odysseus's legend.[27] It is very plausible that historical events which deeply touched Horkheimer, like the defeat of the Spanish revolution and the German-Soviet pact of 1939, played an important role in this evolution. This "dissolution" of the proletariat in the Critical Theory of the 1940s would not have been possible if the class had not been, already in the 1930s, a contingent and derivative element, and not the essential foundation corner of their *Weltanschauung*. This distance in relation to the working class is probably one of the reasons for the relatively abstract character of Critical Theory and its difficulty in taking part in the concrete political debates of the labor movement: How to fight fascism? How to unite the working class? How to struggle against bureaucracy in the labor unions and workers' parties?

Although Critical Theory was able to illuminate the contradictions and weaknesses of Mannheim's sociology of knowledge, it could not produce a coherent alternative proposition in relation to the social roots of objective knowledge. Referring to Adorno—but the same could be said of Marcuse and Horkheimer—Critical Theory "failed to come to grips with the central challenge of the sociology of knowledge . . . what is the Archimedean point in which a true consciousness can be said to be grounded? Having long since abandoned Lukács's faith in the proletariat, having nothing but scorn for Mannheim's intellectual class with its implied role of advising the politically powerful. It offered no real alternative which transcended idealism."[28] Jay suggests that "there is an

Archimedean point in the Frankfurt School's thinking that is employed as a standard against which false consciousness can be measured" and this is "the reconciled totality that will accompany the end of the story," a final historical hope that functions "as the ultimate ground of cognition."[29] This is a debatable interpretation, among other reasons because it neglects the deep historical pessimism of Critical Theory—in particular Marcuse—for which there is no assured and guaranteed harmonious future. The "ultimate ground" for Critical Theory is not in the past, the present, or the future, but *above and beyond history.*

Marcuse himself clearly stated, in the already mentioned passage from his article on the concept of essence (1936), where Critical Theory's "Archimedean point" lies. Criticizing modern bourgeois philosophy, he considers that, by abandoning the idea of *critical* reason and of *essence* it "lost the Archimedean point where it had anchored the freedom of the knowing individual" and therefore "the basis from which the weapon of critique can be employed."[30] In other words, *critical reason itself* (and the concept of human essence derived from it) is the "Archimedean point." The problem is, as Archimedes himself knew, that in order to raise the world, one needs more than a spiritual reference; a concrete, material support is needed for the level to be applied. Lacking this support, Critical Theory was condemned to become more and more suspended in the air, socially rootless, and abstract.

Notes

1. See Max Horkheimer, "Der neueste Angriff auf die Metaphysik," in idem, *Kritische Theorie,* vol. 2 (Frankfurt: Fischer, 1968), pp. 82–136.
2. See Max Horkheimer, "Zum Problem der Wahrheit," in *Kritische Theorie,* vol. 1, pp. 229, 241.
3. Max Horkheimer, "Ein neuer Ideologiebegriff?" in *Ideologie,* ed. K. Lenk (Neuwied and Berlin: Luchterhand, 1967), pp. 294–95.
4. Max Horkheimer, "Die gesellschaftliche Funktion der Philosophie," in *Kritische Theorie,* vol. 2, p. 302.
5. Herbert Marcuse, "Zur Wahrheitsproblematik der soziologischen Methode," in *Ideologienlehre und Wissensoziologie,* ed. Hans Joachim Lieber (Darmstadt: Wissenschaftliche Buchgesellschaft, 1974), p. 381.
6. It was only later, in 1937, that the Frankfurt School would to a certain extent come to grips with Mannheim on this crucial question when Horkheimer proposed to the "free-floating intelligentsia" the alternative of the Critical Theoretician linked to the struggle of the oppressed masses. Max Horkheimer, "Traditionelle und kritische Theorie," in *Kritische Theorie,* vol. 2, pp. 137–91.
7. Herbert Marcuse, "Beiträge zu einer Phänomenologie des historischen Materialismus," in idem, *Schriften,* vol. 1 (Frankfurt: Suhrkamp, 1978), pp. 356–57.
8. Marcuse, pp. 383, 393–94.

9. Herbert Marcuse, "Transcendentaler Marxismus," in *Schriften,* vol. 1, p. 445.
10. Herbert Marcuse, "Zum Problem der Dialektik," in *Schriften,* vol. 1, p. 421.
11. Herbert Marcuse, "Zur Wahrheitsproblematik der soziologischen Methode," in Lieber, *Ideologienlehre,* p. 393.
12. Herbert Marcuse, "Neue Quellen zur Grundlegung des historischen Materialismus," in *Schriften,* vol. 1, p. 536.
13. Ibid., p. 555.
14. Herbert Marcuse, "Philosophy and Critical Theory," in idem, *Negations,* (London: Allan Lane, Penguin Press, 1968), p. 141.
15. Herbert Marcuse, "The Concept of Essence," in *Negations,* p. 78.
16. Max Horkheimer, "Materialismus und Moral," in *Kritische Theorie,* vol. 1, pp. 108, 102.
17. Max Horkheimer, "Zum Problem der Wahrheit," in *Kritische Theorie,* vol. 1, p. 249.
18. Max Horkheimer, "Traditionelle und kritische Theorie," in *Kritische Theorie,* vol. 2, p. 199.
19. Ibid., p. 164.
20. Ibid., p. 186.
21. Ibid., p. 189.
22. Ibid., p. 199.
23. Herbert Marcuse, "The Concept of Essence," in *Negations,* p. 73.
24. Ibid., p. 78.
25. Herbert Marcuse, "Philosophy and Critical Theory," in *Negations,* pp. 135–36.
26. Max Horkheimer, "Zum Rationalismusstreit in der gegenwärtigen Philosophie," in *Kritische Theorie,* vol. 1, p. 174.
27. Max Horkheimer and Theodor W. Adorno, *Dialektik der Aufklärung* (Amsterdam: Querido, 1947), pp. 38–43.
28. Martin Jay, "The Frankfurt School's Critique of Mannheim," *Telos* (no. 20, 1974):83.
29. Ibid., pp. 88–89. As an illustration for his interpretation, Jay mentions Walter Benjamin's "angel of history" in the *Theses on the Philosophy of History.* Far from representing a "reconciled totality," Benjamin's angel of history is the victim of the malefic "storm of progress" and reveals himself unable to "make whole what has been smashed."
30. Herbert Marcuse, "The Concept of Essence," in *Negations,* p. 62.

Part Five
POLITICAL SCIENCE AND POLITICAL ECONOMY

19
The Political Contradictions in Adorno's Critical Theory

Hans-Jürgen Krahl

Adorno's intellectual biography is marked throughout and right into its aesthetic abstractions by the experience of fascism. The mode of reflection of this experience, which reads in the creations of art the indissoluble unity of critique and suffering, constitutes the relentlessness of the claim to negate and at the same time confines this claim within its limits. Reflecting on the fascist violence brought forth by the uncontrollable economic disasters of capitalist production, the "impaired life" knows that it cannot extricate itself from entanglement in the contradictions of bourgeois individuality whose irrevocable decomposition it has recognized. The fascist terror does not only reveal the airtight coerciveness of highly industrialized class societies, it also injures the subjectivity of the theoretician and reinforces the class barriers to his ability of theoretical perception. Adorno articulates the consciousness of this problem in the introduction to *Minima Moralia*: "The violence which drove me away, at the same time denied to me the full insight into its nature. I did not yet admit to myself the complicity into whose orbit anybody comes who—facing the unspeakable that happened collectively—would still mention the individual."

It appears as if Adorno, going through the incisive critique of the ideological character of the bourgeois individual, was spellbound by its ruins. In this case Adorno could never really have left the isolation of emigration. The monadological fate of the individual separated from others by the economic laws of abstract labor is mirrored in its intellectual subjectivity. Because of this, Adorno was incapable of transforming his private compassion toward the "damned of the earth" into an organized partisanship of theory engaged in the liberation of the oppressed.

Adorno's sociological insight, according to which "the after life of fascism inside democracy" has to be deemed as potentially more dangerous than "the after life of fascist tendencies against democracy," turned his progressive fear of a fascist stabilization of restored monopoly capitalism into regressive anxiety regarding the forms of practical resistance against this tendency.

He shared the ambivalence of the political consciousness of many critical intellectuals in Germany who imagined that socialist action from the Left was arousing the potential fascist terror from the Right against which it was fighting. According to this reasoning any praxis will a priori be denounced as blind activism, and the possibility of political critique is boycotted, namely the distinction between prerevolutionary praxis which is on principle correct and the infantile disorders from which it may suffer in emerging revolutionary movements.

Unlike the French proletariat and its political intellectuals, Germany lacks an unbroken tradition of violent resistance and hence the historical preconditions for a rational discussion of the historical legitimacy of violence. The ruling class which, according to Adorno's own analysis, was after Auschwitz still pressing toward fascism would not have been a power at all but for the need to complement the Marxist "weapons of critique" with the "critique of weapons." Only then can critique be the theoretical life of the revolution.

This objective contradiction in Adorno's theory broke into open conflict and made the socialist students into political adversaries of their philosophical teacher. As much as Adorno saw through the bourgeois ideology of the disinterested search for truth as a fetish of commodity exchange, he equally distrusted the traces of political struggle in scientific dialogue.

But his critical option that any philosophy if it is to be true must be immanently oriented toward the practical transformation of social reality, loses its binding force if it is not also capable of defining itself in organizational categories. Adorno's dialectical concept of negation moved increasingly away from the historical necessity of the partisanship of theory, which had once been part of Horkheimer's specific differentiation between critical and traditional theory, when he postulated the "dynamic unity" between the theoretician and the oppressed class.

Detachment from these criteria finally drove Adorno, in conflict with the student movement, into a complicity with the ruling powers which he himself hardly saw through. The controversy was by no means only related to the issue of private abstention from political practice; the inability of Adorno's theory to deal with the question of organization pointed at objective shortcomings of this theory regarding the epistemologically and sociologically central category of social praxis.

In spite of this, Adorno's philosophy introduced to the politically conscious students concepts which demystified the ruling system and defined the need for emancipation; concepts which implicitly suited the changed conditions of revolutionary situations in the metropolis and which could no longer be derived from the experience of crude impoverishment.

Adorno's micrological power of description excavated from the dialectic of commodity production and exchange relations that buried the emancipatory dimension of Marx's critique of political economy—a dimension which turns the critique of political economy into revolutionary theory, that is, a theory analyzing society with a view to its radical transformation. This dimension had been forgotten by most contemporary Marxist economists. Adorno's reflections on the categories of reification and fetishization, on mystification and second nature, transmitted to a younger generation the emancipated consciousness of Western Marxism in the 1920s and 1930s, of Korsch, Lukács, Horkheimer, and Marcuse, as it articulated itself in opposition to official Soviet Marxism.

In his critique of ontology and of the positivistic ideology of factuality, Adorno decoded the concepts of genesis and identity. He saw these categories of domination emanating from the sphere of commodity circulation whose liberal dialectic—which once legitimized bourgeois morality, namely the pretence of the fair exchange between equal owners of commodities—has long evaporated.

But the same theoretical instruments which allowed Adorno to realize these sociological connections blocked his view of the historical possibilities of liberating praxis. A trace of justified mourning vibrates in his critique pronouncing the death of the bourgeois individual. But Adorno was never able to transcend immanently in the Hegelian sense this last radical bourgeois position of his thought. He remained fixed to it, gazing fearfully at the terrible past with the always belated consciousness of the one who only begins to understand at dusk.

Adorno's negation of late capitalist society has remained abstract and has closed itself to the requirement of the definiteness of the "definite negation," a category to which he knew he was committed by Hegelian and Marxist tradition. In his last work, *Negative Dialectic,* he no longer pursues the concept of praxis in historical materialism in the context of the historical process which defines its forms, and no longer relates it to bourgeois social relations and forms of proletarian organization. In his Critical Theory the paralysis of class struggles reflects itself as the atrophy of a materialist understanding of history.

Horkheimer's program had once defined theory as an integral part of liberating praxis, but even in those days the bourgeois organization of Critical Theory made it impossible to make this program a reality. The destruction of the workers' movement by fascism and its seemingly irreversible integration into the reconstruction of postwar German capitalism necessarily changed the meaning of the categories of Critical

Theory. Inevitably it had to lose some of its definiteness, but the process of abstraction went on blindly.

The concrete and material history which Adorno critically posed against Heidegger's "ahistorical concept of history" departed increasingly from his concept of social praxis and finally, in his last work, *Negative Dialectic,* it had evaporated to such an extent that it appeared to be assimilated to the transcendental poverty of Heidegger's category.

In the paper he delivered at the congress of German sociologists Adorno rightly insisted on the validity of Marxist orthodoxy: that the industrial forces of production were still organized within capitalist relations of production and that political rule was still based on the economic exploitation of wage workers. Although at that conference such orthodoxy brought him into conflict with established sociology, it nevertheless remained ineffective as long as such categories had no connection to material history.

As it moved more and more away from historical praxis, Adorno's critical theory fell back into traditional forms of contemplation which could hardly be justified. The process of traditionalization in his thinking shows up his theory as a historical form of reason which outlived itself. The materialistic dialectic of the fettered forces of production reflects itself on the level of his thinking in the image of theory that fetters itself, inescapably entangled in the immanence of its categories.

"The age of interpretation of the world has passed and when the task is finally to change it, philosophy is bidding farewell . . . the time has come not for the first philosophy but the last." The last philosophy of Adorno has been unable or unwilling to depart from this farewell.

20

The Anti-Semitism Studies of the Frankfurt School: The Failure of Critical Theory

Ehrhard Bahr

Since Hitler's rise to power in 1933, the members of the Institute of Social Research had been preoccupied with the idea of the defeat of German fascism and the reconstruction of a post-Nazi society. Yet strangely enough, a study of anti-Semitism and its relationship to Nazi ideology and the Nazi regime was strikingly absent from the institute's projects in the 1930s, after the institute had gone into exile. Though one of the arguments of the founders in the 1920s to persuade Hermann Weil to endow the institute had been the need to study anti-Semitism in Germany, it was not until 1943 that the institute launched such a study which, oddly enough, was concerned with anti-Semitism in the United States rather than in Germany.[1]

The reasons given for the peculiar absence of any study of anti-Semitism in Germany during the 1930s were tactical rather than analytical and, viewed in retrospect, appear strangely evasive and misplaced. As one of the founding members remarked: "One did not want to advertise that [relationship between anti-Semitism and Nazi ideology]," and one was unwilling "to draw unnecessary attention to the overwhelming Jewish origins" of the institute's members.[2]

Though the main goal of the Frankfurt School from 1933 to 1945 was to explain German fascism to hasten its defeat, during the 1930s anti-Semitism was not considered a topic of the same importance and urgency as the studies on authority and family (*Studien über Autorität und Familie*) planned by the institute and published in Paris in 1936. To be sure, this work contained the model of the later studies on authoritarianism, but it did not identify the problem of anti-Semitism.

The first three phases of anti-Jewish legislation and activity in Nazi Germany—the boycott of Jewish businesses and professions and the legislation against Jewish professionals of April 1933, the Nuremberg laws of 1935, and the Kristallnacht pogrom of 1938[3]—had to occur before the institute officially recognized Nazi anti-Semitism as a major threat to the peace of Europe. Even the representatives of the thirty-two nations, so fruitlessly assembled at the Evian conference of July 1938, identified the problem more promptly, despite their failure to provide a solution. The year 1938 was of crucial importance since it marked the beginning of threats of deportation and mass arrests of Jewish minorities in Germany and Austria.[4] Yet it took the institute until 1939 to clarify its stand on anti-Semitism, when Max Horkheimer at last published his essay "The Jews and Europe."

This article, published in the *Zeitschrift für Sozialforschung,* was the first document to reveal the failure of Critical Theory in the most glaring fashion. Starting most promisingly with the statement that the scholar "who wishes to explain anti-Semitism must have Nazism in mind," the article, without warning, arrives at the non sequitur conclusion: "He who does not want to speak about capitalism should also remain silent about fascism."[5] Following doctrinaire Marxist theory, Horkheimer explained fascism/Nazism as the inevitable result of a capitalist society: "The liberal economic process [reproduces] the relations of domination by means of free contracts which are enforced by the inequality of property. The mediation has now been removed. Fascism is the truth of modern society."[6] After expounding this theory over almost fifteen pages, he finally returned to his topic on the last eight pages, when he criticized the Jews who had praised the liberalism of the recent past: "That they were better off with liberalism does not warrant its justice. . . . The order which, in 1789, set out on its way in a progressive fashion, contained from its start the tendency to Nazism."[7] Intensifying his attacks, Horkheimer declared: "If the Jews in their understandable nostalgia glorify the . . . Weimar Republic, then . . . the fascists are right," since they helped monopoly capitalism to enter its next logical stage of development, namely, the totalitarian state.[8] Only the English and French abstracts of this article contain the positive statement that "the elimination of anti-Semitism is identical with the struggle against the authoritarian state."[9] However, Horkheimer did not have much faith in the Western powers to conduct this struggle, because he considered them to be in their pretotalitarian phase.

It is difficult to avoid the conclusion that the Critical Theory of the Frankfurt School failed to anticipate or to account for the rise as well as the systematic policy of anti-Semitism in Nazi Germany. When the facts of the historical development finally caught up with members of the Frankfurt School, some of them adopted a doctrinaire Marxist stance, while others continued to glorify the conditions of the Weimar Republic.

The ambivalence of institute members became obvious in the anti-Semitism studies of the Frankfurt School in the 1940s and 1950s, namely, the study of anti-Semitism within American labor and the study of the authoritarian personality, studies that were sponsored by the Jewish Labor Committee and the American Jewish Committee, respectively. Incongruities in these activities become obvious when one considers the following points:

1. The institute had to come to the United States and study American anti-Semitism within the American labor movement and among the American middle class before its members were ready to approach the problem of Nazi anti-Semitism.
2. Institute members proved to be more sensitive to the Jewish question and potential fascism in the United States than to the reality of concentration camps in Germany.
3. The institute had to abandon Critical Theory and employ the methods of psychology and empirical sociology before Theodor W. Adorno and Max Horkheimer were ready to deal with the problem in *Dialectic of Enlightenment (Dialektik der Aufklärung)*, published in 1947.[10] And even then, the final chapter of this book, "Elements of Anti-Semitism," was based partially on the data and results of studies on anti-Semitism within American labor and on *The Authoritarian Personality,* published in 1950.

For the history of the two American studies, it is interesting to note that the American labor study was never published; its results were considered too damaging to American labor. The institute, "with its characteristic caution, was hesitant about broadcasting its finding," as one member observed. Furthermore, its methodology and conclusions were considered oversimplifications.[11] In *The Authoritarian Personality,* the contributors saw their main task not in analyzing anti-Semitism as such, but rather in examining the relationship of prejudice to authoritarian ideology in general. Thus anti-Semitism gradually all but disappeared from the study of the authoritarian personality and became just one of the many topics under investigation. The aim of the study, as Max Horkheimer stated in the introduction, was to explain prejudice "in order to help its eradication." Nazi Germany only served as a "vivid example" of the past.[12]

The chapter "Elements of Anti-Semitism" in *Dialectic of Enlightenment* by Adorno and Horkheimer, is a philosophical attempt to account for the occurrence of anti-Semitism, with Nazi Germany only as one example among others. The authors claim to offer "the main lines of a philosophical prehistory of anti-Semitism."[13]

In briefly reviewing the seven theses on anti-Semitism which constitute the second document to reveal the failure of Critical Theory, it should be noted that the chapter is divided into seven separate sections, each of which deals with a particular aspect of the phenomenon. In the first section the authors briefly investigate fascist and liberal points of view. For the fascists, according to Horkheimer and Adorno, the Jews are "an opposing race, the embodiment of the negative principle." This view inevitably leads to the necessity of exterminating the Jews to secure a fascist world order and world domination. While this doctrine about German fascism was true to the extent that in Germany fascism had made it factually true and, therefore, it did not require extensive explanations, the case was different in the theory of the liberal point of view which denied the existence of Jewish national identity. As the authors stated, the liberal theory considers the Jews to have "no national or racial characteristics" but to "simply form a group through their religious opinions and tradition" (p. 168). Adorno and Horkheimer were among the first to recognize that assimilation was the heavy price paid by Jews for the realization of this theory. Yet its practice did not save the assimilated Jews from persecution. The harmony of society, in which the assimilated Jews believed, "turned against them in the form of the harmony of the *Volksgemeinschaft* [national community]," from which by definition they were excluded (pp. 169-70).

The second section treats the question of anti-Semitism as a populist movement. Here the authors considered the various elements which in their opinion contributed to the aspect of anti-Semitism as a mass movement, and they dismissed political, economic, and social reasons for its development. Anti-Semitism as a populist movement, they concluded, is based on an "urge for negative equality [*Gleichmacherei*]" on the part of the masses (p. 170), i.e., the pleasure of watching those more privileged being robbed of all their possessions and seeing them lowered below the level of the underprivileged masses. Economically anti-Semitism is considered useless for the people at large: "[anti-Semitism] is a luxury for the masses" (p. 170). Adorno and Horkheimer pointed to the "Aryanization" of Jewish property in Nazi Germany and to the pogroms in Czarist Russia which hardly ever brought any economic benefit to the masses, but were of obvious advantage to members of the privileged classes. Only as an outlet of blind anger of the masses does anti-Semitism appear to serve the social function of a ritual of civilization. Men who are robbed of their individuality in modern mass society are set loose as individuals to find collective approval of their anger. But since the victims are interchangeable according to circumstances—with gypsies, Jews, Protestants, Catholics, serving equally well as scapegoats—there is no genuine anti-Semitism as a populist movement, according to Adorno and Horkheimer. Everything alien that appears privileged becomes the target of the destructive impulse of the masses who are unable to fully participate in the process of civilization.

Part three deals with the question of bourgeois anti-Semitism which is regarded as having specific economic reasons: "the concealment of domination in production" (p. 173). The Jews are made the scapegoat for the economic injustice of the capitalist system whose development is attributed to them. Anti-Semitism, according to Adorno and Hork-heimer, is in one sense the self-hatred of the bourgeois projected onto the Jews, who in fact were relatively unimportant economically, since they were mostly confined to the sphere of distribution without having access to the means of production. But within the distribution sector they became the visible representatives of the whole system, drawing the hatred of others upon themselves. The masses, disappointed in the economic progress which had been promised them, turned their fury on the Jews in the mistaken belief that what was denied them was withheld and controlled by Jewish entrepreneurs. For the captains of industry the Jews constituted the trauma of their own existence: "The clap-trap of anti-Semitism announced a fact" characteristic of their situation "and for which they secretly despised themselves." Their anti-Semitism, Adorno and Horkheimer concluded in an explanation that combines Marxist and Freudian arguments, "is self-hatred, the bad conscience of the parasite" (p. 176).

In the fourth section, the question of religious anti-Semitism is considered and dismissed as nonexistent within fascism: "The nationalist brand of anti-Semitism ignores religious considerations in asserting that the purity of the race and the nation is at stake. The nationalists realize that men have long ceased to bother about their eternal salvation. . . . It is impossible to arouse the feelings of the masses today by suggesting that the Jews are obstinate unbelievers." However, Adorno and Horkheimer realized that secularized forms of religion were retained by fascism and proved beneficial to the Nazis: "Religion as an institution is partly embodied in the system and partly converted into mass culture" (p. 176).

While the authors clearly noted that Christianity had largely become neutralized, they nevertheless concluded that Christian rationalizations of anti-Semitism were still of considerable influence. As the religion of the "Son," as they put it, Christianity contains an implicit antagonism against Judaism, the religion of the "Father," and against its surviving witnesses, the Jews. This antagonism is further supported by the fact that the Jews, by clinging to their own religious culture, reject the religion of the "Son," and by the circumstance that the New Testament blames them for the death of Christ. Combining elements of Kierkegaardian and Barthian theology, Adorno and Horkheimer argued that the "weak" Christians resent the openly negative attitude of the Jews toward their religion, since they feel within themselves traces of a negative attitude based on the paradoxical, irrational nature of their creed—an attitude which they do not dare admit to and which they therefore punish in others. Anti-Semitism becomes a means of confirming their own insecure faith (pp. 177-79).[14]

In the fifth part of their excursus Adorno and Horkheimer introduced the concepts of idiosyncracy and mimesis. Anti-Semites are wont to use idiosyncracy as an explanation of their behavior. Adorno and Horkheimer argue that the emancipation of society from anti-Semitism depends on whether this particular idiosyncracy is elevated to a rational concept, i.e., whether its meaninglessness is recognized. In order to explain idiosyncracy, the authors had to turn to some far-fetched theories pertaining to biological prehistory. According to their definition, idiosyncracy, which consists of the escape of single human organs from the control of the individual, is based on mimesis, i.e., adaptation to nature in a danger situation. Uncontrolled mimesis is condemned in modern civilization. Modern man experiences his mimetic heritage only in certain gestures and behavior patterns which he encounters in others and which strike him as embarrassing rudimentary elements that survive in his rationalized environment: What appears as repellently alien is in fact all too familiar. For example, the allegedly typical Jewish gestures of touch, soothing, snuggling up, or coaxing are enumerated by Adorno and Horkheimer as examples of mimetic behavior to survive old forms of domination. Such behavior arouses anger because it reminds modern man of his old fears which must be suppressed to survive in modern society. The anti-Semite cannot stand the Jew because he reminds him of his old anxieties which he does not dare to admit. He punishes his own fears in the Jew, who, as victim, becomes the false counterpart of the dread mimesis.

Part six continues the discussion of mimesis, contrasting mimesis, i.e., adaptation to the environment, with false projection, i.e., adaptation of the environment according to the individual perception. Anti-Semitism, the authors concluded, is false projection or repressed mimesis, not true mimesis: "For mimesis the outside world is a model to which the inner world must try to conform—the alien must become familiar." False projection, on the other hand, confuses the inner and outer world, defining as hostile the most intimate individual experience: "Impulses which the subject will not admit as his own, even though they are most assuredly so, are attributed to the object—the prospective victim." This process, in psychological terms, is known as transference. According to Adorno and Horkheimer, in fascism this behavior pattern is politicized (p. 187).

To make projection understandable as well as the manner in which it is deformed into false projection—a process regarded as part of the essence of anti-Semitism—the authors employed a rather naively realistic physiological theory of perception. This theory explains the perceptual world as the mirror reflection—controlled by the intellect—of data which the brain receives from actual objects. Adorno and Horkheimer maintained that "anti-Semitism is not projective behavior as such but the absence of controlling intelligence from it" (p. 189). The individual loses the ability to differentiate, he becomes paranoid and with this false projection he invests the outer world with the contents of his mind and thus perceives the world as being populated by people who, in his opinion, are bent on destroying him. The Jews appear as ready-made objects for such projection (p. 199). With a reference to history the authors declared that the persons chosen as enemies had already been perceived as such (p. 187).

Quite astoundingly, in the concluding section, the authors proclaimed with great confidence, yet without any sort of objective proof, that "there are no more anti-Semites," and, going even beyond this bewildering statement, they perversely maintained that the German fascists were not anti-Semites but "liberals who wanted to assert their anti-liberal opinions" (p. 200). Such an aphoristic statement, which contains only a kernel of truth inasmuch as it points to the decay of liberalism, can hardly be accepted as a historical analysis of German anti-Semitism in view of the evidence brought to light by the liberation of the concentration camps in Europe. It is revealing that the term *concentration camp* is absent from this chapter of more than forty pages.

Adorno and Horkheimer became the victims of their own theory of fascism as the perverted truth of liberalism.[15] Instead of pointing to the extermination policies practiced in the concentration camps, the problems of denazification, and the dangers of survival of latent anti-Semitism in postwar Germany, they concentrated their efforts in the last section on detecting potential fascism in the United States. This last thesis was added to the chapter "Elements of Anti-Semitism" in 1947.[16] The failure of Critical Theory becomes especially apparent at this point: Adorno and Horkheimer accused the United States of anti-Semitism in America, but to place it on the same level as the Nazi strategy of planned scientific extermination and to consider it even more dangerous for the future, reveals an alarming lack of differentiation. In developing their unique theory, the authors argued that anti-Semitism had always been based on stereotyped thinking. After the defeat of fascism in Europe, stereotyped thinking was all that remained of the anti-Semitism of the period before

1945. Adorno and Horkheimer regarded this type of thinking as especially prevalent in the American political party system. They saw anti-Semitism surviving in the United States, albeit in a different form. It had assumed a new shape in the "ticket mentality," a political behavior characterized by voting the straight ticket of "aggressive big business." The Allied defeat of Hitler's regime might have eliminated the most obvious forms of anti-Semitism, but the victors had done little to eradicate the causes at home. Equating capitalism and fascism in an unhistorical fashion,[17] Adorno and Horkheimer argued that anyone who "subscribes to the destruction of the trade unions and the crusade against Bolshevism . . . automatically subscribes also to the destruction of the Jews" (p. 201). As distasteful as reactionary politics may be, such a conclusion is necessarily neither historically nor logically true, in spite of the evidence of anti-Semitic remarks on the Watergate tapes. For Adorno and Horkheimer, anti-Semitism becomes an implied plank in the platform of not only reactionary but also of progressive parties, because the progressive parties in America also rely on "ticket mentality." Without any dialectical mediation the authors maintained that "the ticket mentality as such is as anti-Semitic as the anti-Semitic ticket" (p. 207). Therefore, Adorno and Horkheimer placed their hopes for the eradication of anti-Semitism not on the progressive parties, but on the absolute meaninglessness of the fascist program which could be permanently concealed from the undiscerning "only if they are wholly deprived of the faculty of thought" (p. 208). Thus only in the negation of the negative do the authors see a chance to break the vicious circle of anti-Semitism.

These obvious misjudgements can be attributed to certain inherent features of Critical Theory. Most evident is the absence of concrete historical data. Since Critical Theory does not seek merely to analyze a concrete historical situation but primarily to stimulate a change for the better, i.e., to transform the existing society into a more humane structure, the work tends to be subjective and speculative, in which facts are employed in an eclectic, not to say eccentric fashion. Historical data are drawn upon only to a limited degree and only if they are suitable for the authors' thesis.

Another obvious trait of Critical Theory is its Marxist commitment which becomes most evident in the third thesis on bourgeois anti-Semitism and in Horkheimer's article "The Jews and Europe" of 1939. Critical Theory associates itself with one of Marxism's historical failures, namely the inability to develop a positive answer to the phenomenon of nationalism, especially with regard to anti-Semitism. Marxists have always been divided on the issue of nationalism, the division being particularly sharp over the position of Jews in society. While Marx's essay "On the

Jewish Question" is a brilliant exposé of the difference between political and human emancipation, it is at the same time a scandalous diatribe against Judaism in modern society. Adorno and Horkheimer stayed within the confines of Marxist tradition and its historical failure with regard to anti-Semitism, going beyond Marx only insofar as they abandoned the Marxist commitment by admitting other than economic reasons as causes for anti-Semitism.

A further characteristic of Critical Theory is its integration of psychology into a Marxist philosophy of history and society, a historic achievement by itself. In the discussion of anti-Semitism as paranoia, however, historical and sociological analyses are reduced to the level of individual psychology. There is no doubt that Nazi anti-Semitism can be explained in psychological terms, but this paranoia is part of a mass hysteria and a historical phenomenon, namely, the paranoia of the nineteenth-century middle class which used Jews as a scapegoat for everything that went wrong in their society. Anti-Semitism provided an ideology to fit the needs and aspirations of the frustrated middle class, uprooted by industrialism.[18] Its behavior can be explained only in terms of mass psychology, not in terms of individual psychology.

The failure of Critical Theory becomes especially obvious when Adorno and Horkheimer had to resort to far-fetched psychological theories to account for sociopolitical phenomena. They advanced these theories amidst an array of material drawn from specialized scientific research and so created causal relationships that fitted their theory but which did not necessarily fit the facts.

Finally, the German origins of Critical Theory have to be considered. Since the members of the Institute of Social Research had disregarded the anti-Semitism of the Weimar Republic insisting that the integration of the Jews there had gone so far that discrimination had largely disappeared, they were forced to continue minimizing the independent importance of anti-Semitism and racism during the 1930s and 1940s. Even during the war, one member of the institute went so far as to call the German people "the least anti-Semitic of all."[19] His opinion was not regarded as extremist, but was shared by other members of the institute. Many regarded Germans as less anti-Semitic than Americans whom they had come to know after emigrating to the United States. It was only after their return to postwar Germany in 1949 that Adorno and Horkheimer arrived at a more realistic assessment of German anti-Semitism.

In the "Notes and Drafts" of *Dialectic of Enlightenment* two aphorisms are included which apply to the authors' theses on anti-Semitism: (1) "There is a historical tendency for cleverness to prove stupid"; and (2) "one of the lessons which Hitler taught us is that it is better not to be too clever."[20] Adorno and Horkheimer cited the example of the Jew who advanced all kinds of well-founded arguments to show that Hitler could not possibly come to power when his rise had become obvious to most people. The same could be said about the anti-Semitism studies of the Frankfurt School. They minimized the importance of German anti-Semitism, even at a time when its tragic results had become common knowledge. Most of the seven theses are too clever and therefore unconvincing in their lack of common sense, and have proved useless in political practice.

The chapter "Elements of Anti-Semitism" did not remain the last word on this problem. This is demonstrated by Horkheimer's later 1961 essay "The German Jews," in which he admitted that Theodor Herzl's forebodings had been justified,[21] and by Adorno's famous statement that one cannot write poetry after Auschwitz. As early as 1944 in passages of *Minima Moralia* Adorno had indicated that he was well aware of the existence of concentration camps which, however, he and Horkheimer had failed to mention in *Dialectic of Enlightenment*.

Notes

1. See Theodor W. Adorno et al., *The Authoritarian Personality* (New York: Harper & Row, 1950).
2. Quoted in Martin Jay, *The Dialectical Imagination* (Boston: Little, Brown, 1973), pp. 136–37.
3. See Karl A. Schleunes, *The Twisted Road to Auschwitz: Nazi Policy toward German Jews, 1933–1939* (Urbana: University of Illinois Press, 1970), pp. 62–110.
4. Nora Levin calls the events of 1938 "the great divide between emigration and annihilation of European Jewry." *The Holocaust: The Destruction of European Jewry, 1933–1945* (New York: Schocken, 1973), p. 74.
5. Max Horkheimer, "Die Juden und Europa," *Zeitschrift für Sozialforschung* 8 (1939):115.
6. Ibid., p. 116.
7. Ibid., p. 129.
8. Ibid., p. 135.
9. Ibid., pp. 136–137.
10. Max Horkheimer and Theodor W. Adorno, *Dialektik der Aufklärung* (Amsterdam: Querido, 1947).
11. Jay, pp. 225–26.
12. Quoted in Adorno et al., p. vii.
13. Max Horkheimer and Theodor W. Adorno, *Dialectic of Enlightenment* (New York: Herder & Herder, 1972), p. xvii.
14. Adorno et al., pp. 727–30.
15. See Göran Therborn, "The Frankfurt School," *New Left Review* (no. 63, 1970):79–82.
16. Horkheimer and Adorno, p. xii.

17. Göran Therborn has pointed out that the Frankfurt School "in effect took up the position adopted by the Comintern in the so-called Third Period, after the Sixth Conference of 1928: fascism was seen as an inevitable and culminating phase of capitalism." *New Left Review* (no. 63, 1970):84.

18. See Reinhard Rürup, *Emanzipation und Antisemitismus: Studien zur "Judenfrage" der bürgerlichen Gesellschaft,* Kritische Studien zur Geschichtswissenschaft, vol. 15 (Göttingen: Vandenhoeck & Ruprecht, 1975).

19. Franz Neumann, *Behemoth: The Structure and Practice of National Socialism, 1933–1944* (New York & Evanston: Harper & Row, 1966), p. 121.

20. Horkheimer and Adorno, p. 209.

21. Max Horkheimer, "The German Jews," in *Critique of Instrumental Reason: Lectures and Essays since the End of World War II* (New York: Seabury, 1974), pp. 101–18.

21

Political Economy and Critical Theory

Giacomo Marramao

Theoretical impotence is not the only reason that today men are unable
to rationally regulate economic relations, that is, their mutual relations to
the production and reproduction of social life, in a way corresponding to
the degree of understanding in other fields. Rather, the existence of economics
as an increasingly independent special discipline that allows less and less
determination by the general social problematic is but the expression of a
more profound state of affairs in which the existing power relations, nowadays,
sharply oppose any regulatory attempt to benefit the majority of men. This
is a problem of praxis, and its solution will constitute the content of history
lying immediately before us. The fortunes of coming generations depend
on the outcome.

So wrote Max Horkheimer in 1934 in an introduction to a study entitled
"Zur Theorie der Planwirtschaft" (On the Theory of Planned Economy)
by Kurt Mandelbaum and Gerhard Meyer.[1] The intervention of the main
exponent of Critical Theory in a seemingly exclusively economic debate
is itself symptomatic of the complex nature of those theoretical and
political questions that lie at the root of the problems regarding economic
planning in the 1930s. The Soviet experience and the monopolistic-
totalitarian tendencies of the German economy of the time prompted
the economic debate that had already begun with the first volume of the
Zeitschrift für Sozialforschung. The discussion was initiated by Friedrich
Pollock's essay "Die gegenwärtige Lage des Kapitalismus und die Aus-
sichten einer planwirtschaftlichen Neuordnung" (The Present Situation
of Capitalism and the Outlook for an Economically Planned New Order).[2]

All the discussants had in common the fact that they presented the
different ideal types[3] of a planned economy, both those that were hypothetical and possible; and in so doing, they consciously abstracted
from the empirical forms of historically determined economic processes.
Despite references to the necessity of praxis of which Horkheimer's
statement is a good example, the tendency to depict different models of
economic planning in historical terms only meant on the part of the
discussants a definitive retreat of theoretical analysis which was clearly
due to the failure of the revolution in Germany. This shows how far

removed they now were from the controversy over accumulation and collapse that Rosa Luxemburg's book provoked and from the heated debates about the future of capitalism, both of which presupposed a still open dialectic and different ways of conceiving and practicing revolutionary tactics. The freezing of the historical movement, a result of the ascending Nazi totalitarianism, manifested itself in the heightened interest in economic planning efforts then undertaken by the Soviet Union.[4]

The studies of Meyer and Mandelbaum, and, above all, of Pollock, contained important new elements, not to be underestimated in view of their influence on key theoreticians of the Frankfurt School: Horkheimer, Adorno, and Marcuse. Fundamentally new were the choice of the central aspects of an economic analysis: First, the *dynamic* aspect, i.e., the tendency of capitalism to overcome the crisis by means of an economically planned new order; second, the *static* aspect, i.e., the model of the planned economy; and finally, *state capitalism,* understood as an abstract form of economic organization, an "ideal type."

The presupposition that capitalism can definitely leave behind its competitive phase and move toward a planned economy is basic to this analysis. It also marks the main difference between Pollock's theory and that of Henryk Grossmann, who undoubtedly was the most important economist of the *Zeitschrift* but whose contribution will not be discussed in detail now. Although Grossmann's work represents the best attempt at a critical reappropriation of Marxian orthodoxy on the level of economic ("abstract") analysis, it marks the closing of an epoch, an historical cycle, which encompasses the development of capitalism as well as its theory. His theoretical efforts predate the profound structural transformations undertaken by capitalism after the 1929 crisis, meaning they came *before* the monopolistic and state capitalist form revealed itself more clearly in the course of the 1940s. Hence Grossmann's work, *Das Akkumulations- und Zusammenbruchsgesetz des kapitalistischen Systems,* published in 1929[5] and hailed by many as a historical event, closed with the radical claim that it is impossible to regulate production on the basis of the existing economic order. It also separates us from his work. Pollock's analysis, on the other hand, carried out in the broad and contradictory empirical context of the crisis, proceeds from the inverse presupposition that the crisis that had broken out on Wall Street on "Black Thursday" and spread quickly to all capitalist countries was not the beginning of the end but the end of the competitive phase of capitalism. Pollock stated: "It is not capitalism that is coming to an end, only its liberal phase."[6] In his opinion a closer examination of the dynamic of the crisis revealed the prospects for an "economically planned new order." To be sure, these prospects indicate only a tendential direction which in itself is not necessary; the art and nature of the "planned reordering" cannot be concretely determined beforehand but only outlined in abstract terms. Economic theoreticians can only outline different models of planning and so contribute to the construction of a "closed theory . . . which could serve a future economic policy as a means of orientation."[7] Pollock arranged these models in a scheme whose criteria are characterized by two main types of planned economy: the capitalist type that rests on the preservation of private ownership of the means of production and on the "general cartel" of Hilferding, and the socialist type that rests on the collective ownership of the means of production. Both models have in common the replacement of the old automatism based on self-regulation according to plan. Pollock's abstract description was by no means the result of a technocratic deformation; rather, it was grounded in the historical circumstance of the simultaneity of the crisis as well as in a theoretical phenomenon closely bound up with this circumstance: the profound process of revision to which the most important representatives of liberalism subjected their theories.

"It can be established without a doubt that the crisis can be overcome with *capitalistic means* and that 'monopolistic' capitalism be able to continue existing at least for the forseeable future." Pollock did not want to maintain, however, that the system was able to realize the perfect steering of the cyclic movement and a total transcendence of all contradictions. "To be sure," he stated, "there exists considerable evidence that in this administered capitalism the depressions will be longer, the boom phases stronger but shorter, and the crises more destructive than in the times of 'free competition'; nevertheless, the 'automatic' collapse of capitalism is not to be expected. There is simply no *purely economic* compulsion to replace it with another economic system."[8]

The statement of the problem on this point is much more complicated than it appears at first sight. Pollock does not deny the catastrophic character of the crisis—on the contrary. He rejects in no uncertain terms any harmonizing representation of prewar capitalism in which the huge destructions brought forth by the automatism of the market are defined as mere "frictions."[9] Pollock did not view the crisis as the *memento mori* of the system like Grossmann did; Pollock felt that the crisis could be overcome by *capitalistic means.* The market mechanism is no longer able to realize the "optimal adjustment" of productive forces to demand; thus the need arises for an economically planned new order: "The main reasons why today economic planning is being discussed everywhere are the manifest difficulties of the capitalist system on the one hand, and the existence of the Russian planning efforts whose collapse was wrongly prophesized by nearly all experts, on the other."[10] The abstract statement of the problem thus flows into the laborious economic and social transition process in the course of which both the Western capitalist states (above all the United States) and the Soviet Union began to discover new forms which could again set in motion the process of accumulation; but it is the Soviet experience that constitutes the continuing reference point for the "new course" of the capitalist economy. According to Pollock:

> It is part of the fundamental understanding of Marxian economic theory that a new economic system can come into being only when its economic and social presuppositions, at least in their rudiments, are prefigured at least *in nuce* in the older system and when the relations of production have become fetters on the productive forces. Just as in France toward the end of the eighteenth century, where the abandonment of the old bonds resulted in rapid economic development because under the rubble of the residual feudal economy the technical, economic and social presuppositions for the *laissez-faire* system were already at hand, the unleashing of the existing forces of production by an economically planned new order is only to be anticipated when its presuppositions are already given. The economic preconditions—disregarding for now the political ones—can be formulated in general terms as follows: the major weight of industrial production must be shifted to large-scale mass production enterprise and the process of centralization has to reach a certain level. Further: the technical and organizational means for mastering the tasks of a centralized economic administration must be known and a considerable reserve of productivity must be available for utilization by means of applying the method of economic planning. It can easily be seen that all of those economic preconditions are at hand to a considerable degree in the great industrial nations as well as in the world economy.[11]

This same development that had proven fatal for the "normal" operation of automatic market mechanisms also created the preconditions for the planned steering of the economic process. Both the character and the timing of this steering could take many different forms; they are a function of complex political conditions and of the initiative of the "economic subjects." The possibilities for a "socialist orientation" of economic planning are "slight so long as the influence of those strata which are interested in the change because of their class position remains insufficient for a transformation."[12]

Although Pollock's analysis was carried out with exemplary clarity and precision, it exposed the underlying problems but did not resolve them. His analysis took its departure from Marxian principles as it was based on the conflict between the forces and relations of production. However, the new qualities of contemporary processes necessitated if not a revision, at least a contemporary supplement to the old theoretical premises. The historical rupture of 1917 resulted in a decisive change within the world economy by introducing a new element in the overall dynamic of the process, the *political* element. This required a *political* reaction from the capitalist system. Otherwise the end of capitalism would have coincided with the end of the laissez-faire system. It would have been fruitless to have retreated to orthodoxy where very little attention would have been paid to the decisive role of the political factor. It would not have provided an answer to the *new* problems and would not have grasped the *morphological novelty* of the international situation. Horkheimer correctly noted in the first issue of the *Zeitschrift* that the objective weight of the general crisis was represented subjectively in an "inner crisis of science."[13] One must realize that it was a matter of critical circumstances in conjunction with the special historical situation (Russian revolution, defeat of the revolutions in the West, tendency toward monopoly capitalism) without which the genesis of Critical Theory and its *political conditioning* cannot be understood. Horkheimer called attention to the fact that as far as we can speak of a "crisis of science," it should be discussed together with the "general crisis":

> Historical development brought with it a fettering of science as a production force which in turn affects all of its parts: the content and the form, and the material as well as the method. Furthermore, science as a means of production is not correspondingly utilized. The understanding of the crisis of science depends on the correct theory of the contemporary social situation, for, nowadays, science as a social function mirrors the contradictions of society.[14]

Pollock's essay "Bemerkungen zur Wirtschaftskrise" (Remarks on the Economic Crisis) is symptomatic of the difficulty in adapting science to the new reality. Here Pollock found himself confronted with an adamantly resistant object of investigation which was also inadequately treated by Marx. Although the defender of an endogenous crisis theory, Pollock did not overlook—in agreement with Marx—the exogenous factors which could explain the particularities of the crisis; he rightly viewed it as a complex phenomenon brought forth by a variety of causes,[15] which may explain in part the lack of an adequate level of abstraction. Unlike Grossmann, however, Pollock lacked a consideration of the law of accumulation and any reference to the law of the tendential fall in the rate of profit (although, as we will see, the consequences of this approach seem to suggest an *implicit* revision of this law). Consequently, it is difficult to locate Pollock within the old and new discussions of crisis theory.

Marx had demonstrated the "general, abstract possibility of crisis"[16] in the separation of supply and demand. But the most general form of the crisis is not its cause. There is a distinction between simple commodity production and capitalist production which helps explain the phenomenon of the crisis. That distinction represents not only a qualitative difference but also a break between Marxian theory and those of classical economics. The *real* cause of the crisis lies in the *fall* of the profit rate; this determines the tendency of capitalists to retain capital in monetary form. (Keynes characterized this tendency as "liquidity preference.") Nevertheless, the determinant of the fall of the rate of profit is still hotly debated. In the famous third section of the third volume of *Das Kapital,* Marx associates it with the inadequacy of the rate of surplus value in relation to the organic composition of capital. In this case the value system would remain unchanged. The other cause for the sinking profit rate could be that a product cannot be sold according to its value, that is, it would be a matter of the lack of "real demand," or as Marx puts it, of the lack of "effective consumption." Both possibilities correspond to two different interpretations of crisis which we can schematize as follows: First, there is that interpretation which depends on the tendential fall in the rate of profit, and second, the theory of the "realization crisis" which can again be differentiated into two types—the "disproportionality theory" and an "underconsumption theory."

In the following, an attempt will be made to summarize the theses contained in the above interpretations and describe them in a very simplified manner. The cause of the crisis is not found in the disproportionality between production and consumption, but can be located within production itself, that is, in the basic contradiction between the forces and relations of production. The crisis then represents a forcible countermeasure of the system against the decline of the rate of profit— as the means to which capital reverts in order to repair the damages of "prosperity." The transition of the crisis into depression, the subsequent reformation of the reserve army, and the devaluation of capital are the connecting links in the cyclical chain through which the profitability of production and the bases for the resumption of accumulation are reconstituted. Preiser, Grossmann, Mattick, and, with considerable difference, Dobb are among the most important representatives of this theory.[17]

The fall in the profit rate is not to be explained by accumulation and the increase in the organic composition of capital, but by the impossibility of *realizing* surplus value because the capitalists do not succeed in selling commodities at their value. (One must be aware, however, that there are internal divisions within this interpretation because it is precisely in the realm of the "realization crisis" that the different currents of right- and left-wing revisionism as well as more up-to-date economic analyses operate.)

The crisis is the result of disproportionate production, that is, it is caused by an uneven division of social labor among particular spheres of production. The increase or decrease of market value on the basis of this disproportionality results in the wandering of capital from one branch of production to another. Marx himself did not discount the possibility that this disproportionality was traceable to *the lack of a plan* inasmuch as the entrepreneur in competitive capitalism can determine the level of real market demand only a posteriori. And if it affects an especially important sector of production, this leads to disequilibrium in the spheres essential to life and would in the end bring forth the crisis. Tugan-Baranowsky accepted the hypothesis of disproportionality as the sole explanation for crisis and thus contested the theory that depended on the tendential fall in the profit rate as well as the theory of underconsumption. After he came to deny the pathological character of the diseases of the system, he even tried, on the basis of the reproduction schemes in the second volume of *Das Kapital,* to prove the possibility of unlimited stabilization, so far as the proportionalities could be maintained. Such a maintenance would be guaranteed ever more strongly by the development of monopolistic concentration, by the trust and growing state controls which in turn would continuously reduce anarchy at the societal level. As Hilferding's discussion and Lenin's polemic against "economic romanticism" show, the theory of the "disproportionality crisis" had played an important role in the Second International.[18]

The crisis arises from the inability of capitalism to create an adequate market for the requirements of its own production. Sweezy, one of the best-known current representatives of this interpretation, formulated his thesis as follows:

> The real task of an underconsumption theory is to demonstrate that capitalism has an inherent *tendency* to expand the capacity to produce consumption goods more rapidly than the demand for consumption goods. To put it another way, it must be shown that there is a *tendency* to utilize resources in such a way as to distort the relation between potential supply of and the potential demand for consumption goods.[19]

The principle of this interpretation suggests that the logic of capitalism is one of *production for consumption,* and not, as Marx had emphasized, of *production for production.*

It is difficult to place Pollock's interpretation in this scheme. From a historical viewpoint, using the "crisis of science" as outlined by Horkheimer and demonstrated by the difficulties of economic theory after World War I as well as by the October Revolution, the interpretation of Pollock's thesis does not pose great difficulties. From a *theoretical* viewpoint, however, numerous problems arise. Pollock starts out from the classical scheme that rests on the contradiction between the forces and relations of production. Nevertheless, he is inclined to unite this scheme with the hypothesis which is typical of the "disproportionality crisis." According to this hypothesis, only a *plan* or some kind of self-regulation can stop the destructive process caused by the continuous wandering of capital from one sector of production to another and eliminate the disproportionalities which constitute the greatest obstacle to overcoming the crisis. Pollock's analysis represents an original combination of the classical Marxist interpretation and the "disproportionality crisis." Such a combination allows Pollock to establish a connection between controllability and the mutual correction between the two theories and to avoid one-sidedness while introducing the concept of plan. Pollock revises the dialectic between the forces and relations of production. Then "adjustment" of the conflict recognizes the menacing authoritarian consequences of the planned control of all economic processes as they appeared to be assumed by the state to an increasing degree. But let us take a closer look at the decisive points of Pollock's analysis.

In the essay on the crisis, Pollock claims that capitalist planning tends to intervene actively in the dynamic of the conflict between the forces and relations of production—a conflict that "has become more intense than it has ever been before"—introducing a kind of "adjustment process." This process operated in a twofold manner: through the forcible destruction of excess productive forces, described by Pollock as the "Procrustean method," and through the "relaxation of fetters" with which capital binds production relations. Both these methods "leave the *foundations* of the capitalist system untouched"; they can afford to be "differentiated sharply only in thought," since they are united in the practice of capitalist management.[20] The method of "relaxing the fetters" appears to Pollock stronger in the long run: In practice the individual owner's control over his own capital becomes increasingly limited. This control is increasingly transferred over to "large-scale units" or even the state. Pollock's train of thought gets complicated at this point because he is not quite successful in determining the limits of the process of concentration. When a central state authority steers the economic process, we reach an extreme point where the relations of production cannot be further modified without eliminating the foundations of the capitalist system.[21] Pollock's ambiguity mirrors a real process: Through his investigations of developments in the German and American economies he had come to realize that capitalist steering was on the verge of giving its "mocking" answer to the crisis. In an "inverted" way, capitalism was carrying out that model of planned economy which the theoreticians of the *Zeitschrift* had perceived as the only possible way out of the catastrophic crisis. Rather than placing such processes under the control of "associated individuals" and use them for the welfare and happiness of the "majority of men," the "rational" administration of economic processes resulted in further control by the strongest "monopolistic groups" in German national socialism and, with different methods, in the United States in the New Deal. It was up to these monopolistic groups to arbitrarily decide on "weal and woe of all remaining economic subjects, owners of capital and workers."[22] Thus the process that Pollock and Mandelbaum expounded in "Autarkie und Planwirtschaft" (Autarky and Economic Planning)[23] began to emerge. It proved to be the determining element of the present form of the capitalist social order: state intervention in the economy. Insofar as national socialism corresponded to this process (although it only expressed the first and most primitive phase), it was by no means the sign of a "backward step" or mere barbarism, but rather the logical result of the concentration process:

> Parliamentarianism was poorly suited to this end; it corresponded to a less advanced conglomeration of economic power. As a consequence of the release from the constraints of parliamentarianism and having at their disposal the entire apparatus of the psychic domination of the masses, during this period governments appear to be independent from classes and to stand above society without partisanship.[24]

Despite these important observations, the descriptive aspects of Pollock's analysis dominated the critical, as is particularly apparent in his essay "State Capitalism."[25] Here the pure description empties the object of all its contradictory components, lending it the character of the "bad" abstraction of the Weberian "ideal type." Obviously, Pollock has driven to an extreme point his own tendency already evident in his first works,[26] to rehabilitate "masks," that is, the different fetishized forms of capitalist economic processes: money, state, technology.

The historical force with which the tendency toward state capitalism had manifested itself, thus giving rise to the monstrous possibilities of despotic controls through the institutionalized forms of power, had prevented the economist from critically receiving the new developments and locating the dialectical elements within this new totality. Thus Pollock mistook as the essence the illusory character of the "alien power" of the fetishized forms of the economic process, while accepting as reality the uncontradictory and unidimensional facade of socialized despotism:

Governmental control of production and distribution provides the means with which the economic causes of depressions, cumulative processes of destruction, and unemployment due to lack of capital can be eliminated. We can even say that economics as a social science has lost its object under state capitalism.[27]

The connections between Pollock's conclusions and those of the most important philosophical representatives of the *Zeitschrift* are evident, both in the conclusions and in the complex development of the *Zeitschrift*. This observation not only provides a useful contribution to the analysis of the important current of thought imprecisely referred to as the "Frankfurt School,"[28] but it also shows the historical phases of the development of Critical Theory in relation to these economic-theoretical contributions which have, up to now, been unjustifiably passed over. After that one can move on to investigate in the most advanced phase— that of the 1930s—the causes of the inadequate elaboration of the relationship between theory and praxis.

Socialization of Work and Critical Theory: The Critique of Political Economy as a Condition of the Ability to Make History

In the essay "The Struggle against Liberalism in the Totalitarian View of the State" (1934), Herbert Marcuse described—with explicit reference to Pollock's analysis—the nature of the substantial continuity between the liberal and the totalitarian conceptions:

This rough sketch of liberalist social theory has shown how many elements of the totalitarian view of the state are already present in it. Taking the economic structure as a point of reference, we see an almost unbroken continuity in the development of the social theory. We shall here assume some prior knowledge of the economic foundations of this development from liberalist to totalitarian theory [reference to Pollock's analysis]: they are all essentially part of the transformation of capitalist society from mercantile and industrial capitalism, based on the free competition of independent individual entrepreneurs, to monopoly capitalism, in which the changed relations of production (and especially the large "units" such as cartels and trusts) require a strong state mobilizing all means of power. . . . The turn from the liberalist to the total-authoritarian state occurs within the framework of a single social order. With regard to the unity of this economic base, we can say it is liberalism that "produces" the total-authoritarian state out of itself, as its own consummation at a more advanced stage of development. The total-authoritarian state brings with it the organization and theory of society that correspond to the monopolistic stage of capitalism.[29]

The reciprocal relation between the investigations of Marcuse and Pollock appear also to extend beyond the 1930s when Pollock states in his work *Automation:*

> Among the most serious social consequences of automation [is] the danger that it strengthens the already existing trend toward a totalitarian society. But such a totalitarian development represents only *one* of the possibilities for society as a whole opened up by the new mode of production. It also shows, indeed for the first time in human history, a way toward the abolition of poverty and the oppressive labor that stunts men and this, not simply for the most developed countries, but in a not so distant future, for the entire earth. These are perspectives which appear utopian in the face of the tensions and struggles springing from the most bitter want of the greatest part of people living today, and yet would be realizable if a more rational use were made of the possibilities given today.[30]

The gap between theoretical formulation and practical critique has become very great here. The refusal of the system is similar to the peculiar ethical reasoning in Marcuse's *One-Dimensional Man;* it arises from the position outside "existing" reality and from which no *immanent* critique is possible.

More interesting and also more difficult is the relationship between Pollock and Adorno. Adorno always regarded Grossmann as the more profound and versatile of the economic theorists who worked on the basis of Marxian categories. However, he took over Pollock's character-ization of authoritarian socialization as it was being brought about by the oligo- and monopolistic developments of contemporary capitalism. Theoretically, the fundamental principle used to explain capitalist society is the dialectic between the forces and relations of production. However, as Pollock had shown in his essay on the economic crisis of 1933, this dialectic appears to be suspended because it admits a kind of "adjustment process" which, if it does not disprove the Marxian law of the tendential fall in the rate of profit, at least removes the concrete timeliness upon whose foundations this law's validity must rest. In his introduction to *The Positivist Dispute in German Sociology,* Adorno makes it clear that the theory of collapse still represents one of the most important questions of the social sciences today.[31] He makes similar remarks concerning value theory.[32] The Marxian laws, however, seem to have lost their object along with the medium of their practical verification. With the freezing of the real dialectic, critical thought appears to be in contemplative exile for an unforeseeable future. Even as Adorno's theory holds to Marxian orthodoxy, it still cannot allow it to become effective in the new form of the capitalist organization of domination. It becomes the negative totality, the reflex of the "absence of historical movement" (*Stillstand der historischen Bewegung*) of that objective process which Grossmann had outlined in his rigorous interpretation and which appears to be blocked by a series of countertendencies:

> Through the absolute rule of negation and in accordance with the pattern of immanent antithesis, the movement of thought, as of history, becomes unambiguously, exclusively, implacably positive. Everything is subsumed under the main economic phases and their development.[33]

The "mocking" realization of mankind as species-being in the planned economy has removed the practical-critical instance from revolutionary humanism's own object: "Self-preservation in the shape of class has kept everyone at the stage of a mere species being."[34] One can find a similar description of this phenomenon in Pollock's book on automation where he speaks of the paramilitary organization of modern manufacturing and describes this as the cellular form of the "despotism" of society as a whole. The process of the socialization of labor when completed becomes distorted; this is expressed in the respective absolutization of both moments of the process, that is, in an abstract rationalization in which variable capital is treated as constant capital and the worker as a machine, on one hand, and in an increase in the historical power of despotism in the factory, on the other.[35]

To draw parallels between an economist such as Pollock and a philosopher like Adorno would not surprise those who are familiar with the real issue—or even with the texts—of critical Marxism which tried, from the very beginning, to interpret the dynamic of the modern production process by recourse to the Marxian analysis of commodities:

> We are concerned above all with the *principle* at work here: the principle of rationalization based on what is and *can be calculated*. . . . Rationalization in the sense of being able to predict with ever greater precision all the results to be achieved is only to be acquired by the exact breakdown of every complex into its elements and by the study of the special laws governing production. . . . This destroys the organic necessity with which inter-related special operations are unified in the end-product. The unity of a product as a *commodity* no longer coincides with its unity as a use-value; as society becomes more radically capitalistic the increasing technical autonomy of the special operations involved in production is expressed also, as an economic autonomy, as the growing relativization of the commodity character of a product at the various stages of production.[36]

The mechanical fragmentation of the production process also shatters those ties that bound the individual subjects of work into a community of "organic" production. Mechanized production transforms these subjects into abstract, isolated atoms whose association is increasingly mediated by the abstract laws of the mechanism of society as a whole. In the system of social labor, time loses its qualitative character, its mutability, in congealing as a quantitatively measurable continuum which is correspondingly filled with measurable "things," i.e., the alienated operations of workers. The quantifying abstraction of work, the subsumption of the production process under the concept of calculability, is in the society of planned capitalism the *concretion* of the abstract presupposition that is implicit in exchange relations:

> Bourgeois society is universally subject to the law of exchange, to the "like for like" computations which leave no remainder. Exchange is in its very essence something timeless, as *ratio* itself—as the operations of mathematics exclude the moment of time by virtue of their pure form. In the same way concrete time ... disappears from industrial production. This ... scarcely requires accumulated experience any more.[37]

Such an abstraction of the production process and of the internal organization of the industrial enterprise would be impossible "were it not for the fact that it contained in concentrated form the whole structure of capitalist society."[38] The sphere within which "rational calculation" is effective is not only subjected to strict laws but also presupposes the absolute lawfulness of all events, meaning that the satisfaction of social needs is entirely realized in the form of commodity exchange. The atomization of individuals is therefore only the mirroring of the fact that the "natural laws" of capitalist production have seized all the life forms of the society on the level of consciousness. For the first time in history, all of society has been subjected to a unitary and uniform economic process which controls and decides on the activities and fate of all of its members. The commodity structure of "things" and the lawfulness of their relations lend to social relations the character of an innate naturalness which appears to the individual consciousness as an insurmountable fact. "The thesis that society is subject to natural laws is ideology if it is hypostatized as immutably given by nature. But these natural laws are real as the laws of motion of the unconscious society."[39]

This natural lawfulness has a specific repercussion in the theoretical dimension. What philosophers once termed "Life," which, by the way, is the leitmotif of Adorno's *Minima Moralia,* has been reduced to the sphere of the private, of mere *consumption,* which at the same time is the appendage and estranged form of the material production processes:

> The change in the relations of production themselves depends largely on what takes place in the "sphere of consumption," the mere reflection of

production and the caricature of true life; in the consciousness and un-
consciousness of individuals. Only by virtue of opposition to production,
as still not wholly encompassed by this order, can men bring about another
more worthy of human beings.[40]

Nevertheless, Adorno appears here to have forgotten the point of departure
as he directs his attention to the *socialized* form of reification and of
exchange, to the disadvantage of what is in reality the focal point of
this socializing process of labor: the modern factory. In clearly distancing
himself from Lukács, his original starting point, Adorno tends to reduce
the analysis of the modern capitalist enterprise based on the processes
of automation and parcelization of production activity to a purely
microsociological problem, and does not regard the enterprise as the
cellular form of the whole capitalist relation. Thus Adorno is able to ask
the "grimly comic" question: Where is the proletariat? This reduction
cannot be explained simply by resource to historical causes, important
as they may be. The failure of revolution, the crisis of 1929, fascism
and developments in the Soviet Union are perhaps responsible for some
of the characteristic features of Adorno's thought: the tacit adherence to
the fundamental categories of Marxian analysis (which were suspended
by the checkmating of the objective historical movement, that is, the
tendency toward crisis and to the collapse of the system), the abstracting
of concepts, and the evaporation of history in *Negative Dialectics,* where
the conception of history moves closer to the empty categories of Heidegger.
Historical factors do not explain, however, how Adorno's theory expresses
the checkmating of the historical movement by an unavoidable absence
of the connecting link which must unite with praxis, nor how this absence
becomes a *theory-immanent* fact which points to the inadequacy of the
critical appropriation of the real, antagonistic totality. To move beyond
Critical Theory it is necessary to proceed in accordance with the critique
of ideology and to grasp the weakness of the link with praxis as the
immanent limit of the theory itself. If one tries to cut through the haze
of general expressions to see how this limit is constituted, one finds that
it is not simply a matter of peculiarity of the thought of Adorno and
Horkheimer. Rather, it all goes back to the beginnings of "critical
Marxism," to Lukács's *History and Class Consciousness.* It derives from
the dialectical relationship between the abstract (quantitative) rationality
of "what remains" (of capitalist domination) and the bursting forth of
the qualitative dimension. Lukács solves the problem through a retransla-
tion of the relationship into a dialectic of the consciousness of an absolute
subject-object (the proletariat) which then becomes the guarantee of
historical development and of the inevitability of revolution. Critical

Theory categorically rejects this idealistic and Hegelianizing interpretation of Marxism, and confronts it with the *contingent character of the materialist dialectic*,[41] without being able to point to a positive solution.

The question remains unanswered. Not even the most recent Marxist interpretations have come close to a solution, mainly because they often settled for a "scientistic" or "theoretical" reduction of the concept of praxis by which the problem of class consciousness is eliminated. Consequently, some of the basic problems Critical Theory dealt with are still with us today, for example, the relationship between the blocking, the "self-structuring" of the historical process (described by Alfred Schmidt as the "freezing of the historical movement") and the bursting forth of the qualitative dimension. The reference made simply to the *form* of dialectic does not offer the solution, but rather obscures the problems inherent in this relationship which is connected with the entire question of revolutionary subjectivity. No solution can be forthcoming from a confrontation of the "immediate needs" of "human essence" with its "plundering" by capitalism. The outcome of the Marxian analysis of commodity fetishism is not a "rediscovery" of "estranged human subjectivity"[42] from under fetishistic objectivity but rather the unveiling of the fact that there are certain relations of production hidden behind commodity exchange. It is therefore necessary to start out by examining the *determinate* process of the capitalist socialization of labor to correctly pose the question of class consciousness, which is inseparable from the given material level of class composition.

The problem is far from being solved but, more importantly, its solution cannot remain purely philosophical (just as it cannot exhaust itself in the critical-philological restoration of texts). Nor can it come from the removal of the disciplinary boundaries that separate economics and philosophy, as some advocate. The solution to the problem cannot be a matter of the field's changing places with one another; this would mean nothing more than the traditional method of "syncretism." Rather, it is a matter of transcending both from the perspective of the critique of ideology.

A return of theory to historical praxis demands that theory allow its categories to become effective by means of subsuming theory itself under the new material created by the real totality and thereby recovering its analytical capacity. This, however, presupposes the *reappropriation of the critique of political economy* which is the sole means to "ascend" from the abstract to the concrete—to use the Marxian phrase. Any discussion of Critical Theory makes sense only if it examines thoroughly all the complex relationships at all levels of the economic analysis, so that the discussion does not remain purely historical or cultural historical.

338 Foundations of the Frankfurt School of Social Research

Notes

1. *Zeitschrift für Sozialforschung* (hereafter *ZfS*) 3 (1934):228.
2. *ZfS* (1932):8–27.
3. Weber's expression is not employed by chance. Pollock explicitly refers to it in the essay "State Capitalism," *ZfS* 9 (1941):200n.
4. To correctly pose the theoretical problem of planned economy, Horkheimer himself referred to the necessity of linking up "with the great experience which mankind is presently undergoing with planned economic efforts." P. 228.
5. Henryk Grossmann, *Das Akkumulations- und Zusammenbruchsgesetz des kapitalistischen Systems* (Leipzig, 1929). Reprinted Frankfurt: Neue Kritik, 1970.
6. Friedrich Pollock, "Bemerkungen zur Wirtschaftskrise," *ZfS* 2 (1933):350.
7. "Die gegenwärtige Lage des Kapitalismus," *ZfS* 1 (1932):8–27.
8. Ibid., p. 16.
9. Ibid., p. 15.
10. Ibid., p. 17.
11. Ibid., p. 19ff.
12. Ibid., p. 27.
13. Max Horkheimer, "Bemerkungen über Wissenschaft und Krise," *ZfS* 1 (1932):4.
14. Ibid., p. 7.
15. Ibid., p. 325ff.
16. Karl Marx, *Theories of Surplus Value* (Moscow: Progress, 1968), pt. 2, p. 509.
17. Cf. *Capital* (New York: International, 1967), vol. 1, sec. 7, vol. 3, sec. 15, where crisis theory takes the form of a theory of cycles.
18. Cf. M.J. Tugan-Baranowsky, *Studien zur Theorie und Geschichte der Handelskrisen in England* (Jena: G. Fischer, 1901), and *Modern Socialism in Its Historical Development,* trans. M.I. Redmount (New York: Russel & Russel, 1966); R. Hilferding, *Das Finanzkapital* (Vienna: Volksbuchhandlung, 1927); V.I. Lenin, "What the Friends of the People Are and How They Fight the Social-Democrats," in *Collected Works,* vol. 1 (Moscow: Foreign Languages, 1960), pp. 129–332.
19. Paul Sweezy, *The Theory of Capitalist Development* (New York: Monthly Review Press, 1968), p. 180.
20. Cf. Pollock, "Bemerkungen zur Wirtschaftskrise," p. 338.
21. Ibid., p. 348.
22. Ibid., p. 349.
23. Under the pseudonym "Kurt Baumann" in *ZfS* 2 (1933):79–103.
24. Pollock, "Bemerkungen zur Wirtschaftskrise," p. 353.
25. Pollock, "State Capitalism," passim.
26. Cf. the essay on Marx's money theory in *Grünberg's Archiv* 13 (1928):193–209, where the theses contained in the dissertation are taken up again ("Die Geldtheorie von Karl Marx" [Frankfurt, March 1923], unpublished).
27. Pollock, "State Capitalism," p. 217.

28. This does not mean that I subscribe to the subsumption of Critical Theory under the concept of the "idealistic reaction to science" with which some authors believe they have disposed of it.
29. Herbert Marcuse, *Negations,* trans. Jeremy Shapiro (Boston: Beacon, 1969), pp. 18–19.
30. Friedrich Pollock, *Automation* (Frankfurt: Europäische Verlagsanstalt, 1964), pp. 247–48.
31. Theodor W. Adorno et al. *The Positivist Dispute in German Sociology* (London: Heinemann, 1976), p. 42.
32. Max Horkheimer and Theodor W. Adorno, *Sociologica II* (Frankfurt: Europäische Verlagsanstalt, 1962), p. 117.
33. Theodor Adorno, *Minima Moralia,* trans. E.F.N. Jephcott (London: NLB, 1974), pp. 150–51.
34. Max Horkheimer and Theodor W. Adorno, *Dialectic of Enlightenment,* trans. John Cumming (New York: Herder & Herder, 1972), p. 155.
35. Cf. Pollock, *Automation,* 249ff.
36. Georg Lukács, *History and Class Consciousness* (London: Merlin, 1971), pp. 88–89.
37. Theodor W. Adorno, "Was bedeutet Aufarbeitung der Vergangenheit?" in *Erziehung zur Mündigkeit: Vorträge und Gespräche mit Helmut Becker, 1959–1969,* ed. Gerd Kadelbach (Frankfurt: Suhrkamp, 1970), p. 13ff.
38. Lukács, p. 90; cf. Pollock, "State Capitalism," passim; idem, *Automation,* p. 291.
39. Theodor W. Adorno, *Negative Dialectics,* trans. E.B. Ashton (New York: Seabury, 1973), pp. 355–56.
40. Adorno, *Minima Moralia,* p. 15.
41. Jürgen Habermas, *Theorie und Praxis* (Neuwied and Berlin: Luchterhand, 1963), p. 322.
42. Lucio Colletti, *From Rousseau to Lenin* (London: NLB, 1972), p. 89.

Part Six
MARXISM

22
The Frankfurt School

Göran Therborn

Critical versus Traditional Theory

The denomination "Frankfurt School" was not chosen by the members, but has been applied to them by others. Members of the group prefer their work to take its name from what they regard as their theoretical program: Critical Theory. An examination of what they, and particularly Horkheimer, who coined the phrase, have meant by "Critical Theory" therefore serves as a convenient introduction to their work as a whole.

The dividing line between traditional theory and Critical Theory in Horkheimer's conception is determined by whether the theory assists in the process of social reproduction, or whether, on the contrary, it is subversive of it. Traditional theory is embedded in the specialized work processes by which the existing society reproduces itself. It "organizes experience on the basis of problems arising from the reproduction of life within present society."[1] In the prevailing division of labor, the personal views of the individual scientist and his efforts for a free science have as little real significance as the individual entrepreneur's view of free enterprise. Both are allotted determinate roles in the process of social reproduction: "The apparent independence of work processes which ought to derive their movement from the inner essence of their objects corresponds to the apparent freedom of the economic subjects, in bourgeois society. They think that they act according to their individual decisions, whereas, even in their most complex calculations, they are really only exponents of an obscure social mechanism" (*KT* 2, p. 146).

Critical Theory, on the other hand, was for Horkheimer an immanent critique of the existing society itself. For it was designed to bring the basic contradictions of capitalist society to consciousness, by placing itself outside the mechanisms of its reproduction and the limits of the prevailing division of labor. "There now exists a human attitude which takes the society itself as its object. It is not merely oriented towards the removal of particular abuses, for the latter appear to it as necessarily bound to the whole arrangement of the social structure. Although this attitude has arisen out of the social structure, it is no concern either of its conscious intention or of its objective significance that anything in this structure should function any better than it does" (*KT* 2, pp. 155ff.). The intentions of this critical attitude "go beyond the prevailing social praxis" (*KT* 2, p. 158). Critical Theory is primarily a *prise de position (Haltung)*, and only secondarily a theory of a specific type: "On the whole, its opposition to the traditional concept of theory derives from a difference of subjects rather than one of objects. The facts as they arise from work in society are not so external to the bearers of this attitude as they are to the academic [*Gelehrte*], or to the members of the other professions, who all think as little academics" (ibid.). The critical theorist is "the theoretician whose only concern is to accelerate a development which should lead to a society without exploitation."[2]

Hence the content of Critical Theory was essentially indeterminate: "There are no general criteria for critical theory as a whole, for such criteria always depend on a repetition of events and thus on a self-reproducing totality. . . . Despite all its insights into individual steps and the congruence of its elements with those of the most advanced traditional theories, Critical Theory has no specific instance for itself other than its inherent interest in the supersession of class domination."[3] The only properties of Critical Theory are a political position and a place in the history of philosophy seen as a reflection of social development: "The categorical judgement is typical of pre-bourgeois society: That is how it is, man cannot change at all. The hypothetical and disjunctive forms of judgement belong especially to the bourgeois world: This effect may occur under certain conditions, it is either like this or otherwise. Critical Theory explains: It must not be like this, men could alter being, the conditions for doing so already exist" (*KT* 2, p. 175n.).

The Inheritance of Classical Idealism

This sociological radicalism has definite consequences for the logical structure of Critical Theory. For Horkheimer, the difference between traditional theory and Critical Theory is that they embody two different "modes of cognition" (*Erkenntnisweisen*). Traditional theory's mode of cognition derives from and is applied in the specialized sciences, particularly the natural sciences.

The axioms of traditional theory define general concepts within which all facts in the field must be conceived. . . . In between, there is a hierarchy of genera and species, between which there are generally appropriate relations of subordination. The facts are individual cases, examples or embodiments of the genera. There are no temporal differences between the units of the system. . . . Individual genera may be added to the system or other changes made, but this is not normally conceived in the sense that the determinations are necessarily too rigid and must prove inadequate where the relation to the object or the object itself changes without thereby losing its identity. Rather, changes are treated as omissions in our earlier knowledge or as the replacement of individual parts of the object. . . . Discursive logic, or the logic of the intellect [*Verstand*], even conceives living development in this way. It is unable to conceive the fact that man changes and yet remains identical with himself [*KT* 2, pp. 172 ff.].

Critical Theory, on the other hand, starts from a view of man as the subject or creator of history, and compares the existing objectifications of human activity with man's inherent possibilities. "The Critical Theory of society, on the contrary, has as its object men as the producers of all their historical life forms" (*KT* 2, p. 192). "In the formation of its categories and in all phases of its procedure, Critical Theory quite consciously pursues an interest in a rational organization of human activity which it has set itself to elucidate and legitimize. For it is not just concerned with goals as they have been prescribed by the existing life forms, but with men and all their possibilities" (*KT* 2, p. 193).

With this view of man and society, Critical Theory explicitly announces its concordance with German idealism from Kant onwards, and claims to represent the preservation not only of the heritage of German idealism, but also of philosophy *tout court*, with its roots in Plato and Aristotle. Indeed, Critical Theory's conception of truth is also that of classical philosophy. Horkheimer asserted the objectivity of truth, in opposition to all the relativist currents of the 1930s: "According to [Critical Theory], only one truth exists, and the positive predicates of honesty and consistency, of rationality, of the search for peace, freedom and happiness, are not to be discussed in the same sense as other theories and practices" (*KT* 2, p. 171). Truth is objective in the metaphysical sense of being inherent in the essence of human reality, however dismal the latter may appear, "for the goal of a rational society, which today, of course, only appears to arise in the imagination, is really invested in every man" (*KT* 2, p. 199). In this way Critical Theory was able to present itself as an inherent part of the historical process and of the struggle for a free society. But this "political" stand was no different from the ethical aims of the whole tradition of rational philosophy. As Horkheimer put it in *The Eclipse of Reason*, written during the war, "the philosophical systems of objective reason implied the conviction that an all-embracing or fundamental structure of being could be discovered and a conception of human destination derived from it. They understood science, when worthy of this name, as an implementation of such reflection or speculation."[4]

Thus, when examined from the epistemological point of view, the difference between critical and traditional theory turns out to be the difference between classical philosophy and modern science. Critical Theory's epistemological basis is a metaphysical humanism.

What is the effect of this epistemology where the science of economics is concerned? What is Critical Theory's conception of the Marxist critique of political economy? The step from classical philosophical speculation to Marxism is simply to put idealism back "on its feet." Classical idealism "treats the activity which emerges in the given material as spiritual. . . . For the materialist conception, on the contrary, every fundamental activity is a matter of social labor" (*KT* 2, p. 193). As an "implementation" of humanist speculation, Critical Theory (i.e. for the Frankfurt School, Marxism) is a unique existential judgment on man's life in capitalist society. The Marxist critique is thus conceived as a negation of economic concepts, above all of the concept of just or equal exchange, which the Frankfurt School regards as the key concept of bourgeois economics, just as exchange is the central principle of the bourgeois economy. "Unlike the operation of modern specialized science [*Fachwissenschaft*], the critical theory of society remains philosophical even as a critique of economics: Its content is formed by the inversion of the concepts which govern the economy into their opposites: fair exchange into widening social injustice, the free economy into the domination of monopoly, productive labor into the consolidation of relations which restrict production, the maintenance of the life of the society into the immiseration of the people" (*KT* 2, p. 195). But this radical philosophical critique has a paradoxical result. Since it is philosophical and does not directly intervene in scientific discourse, it cannot create any new scientific concepts. It certainly transcends bourgeois economics, but it leaves its system of concepts intact. Critical Theory sees bourgeois economics as ahistorical, but not as incorrect or unscientific. "The critical theory of society begins with an idea of simple commodity exchange defined by relatively general concepts; it then shows that, assuming all the available knowledge, and *without transgressing the principles of the exchange economy as represented by scientific political economy,* this exchange economy must, in the present of men and things (which of course changes under its influence), necessarily lead to a sharpening of the social oppositions which drive toward wars and revolutions in the present epoch" (*KT* 2, pp. 174 ff— my italics). The very radicalism of this interpretation of Marxism drastically limits its effects: The gaze of this philosophy on economics fulfills Wittgenstein's prescription. It leaves everything as it is.

Reduction to Philosophy

In another sense, according to this programmatic text, Critical Theory is more the intellectual aspect of a political practice than a specific theory. The critical theorist's "vocation is the struggle to which his thought belongs, not thought as something independent, to be divided from this struggle" (*KT* 2, p. 165). Horkheimer's programmatic statement links Critical Theory, as a mode of cognition, to the proletariat. "Those viewpoints which [Critical Theory] takes as the goal of human activity for historical analysis, and above all the idea of a rational social organization corresponding to the general will [*Allgemeinheit*], are immanent in human labor, without being present to individuals or in public opinion in a correct form. It is the property of a specific interest to experience and perceive these tendencies. Marx and Engels's theory claims that this will happen in the proletariat." As the last sentence suggests, however, Horkheimer is not sure. "But in this society, the situation of the proletariat does not provide any guarantee of correct knowledge, either. . . . The differentiation of its social structure which is fostered from above, and the opposition between personal and class interests which is only overcome at the best of times, prevent this consciousness from acquiring immediate validity" (*KT* 2, p. 162). Horkheimer then went on to explain the relationship between the critical theorist and the proletariat in the following terms:

> If we regard the theoretician and his specific activity alongside the oppressed class as a dynamic unity, such that his representation of the social contradictions appears not just as an expression of the concrete historical situation, but rather as a stimulating, transforming factor in it, then his function emerges clearly. The course of the conflict between the advanced parts of the class and the individuals who express the truth about them, and then the conflict between these most advanced parts together with their theoreticians and the rest of the class, should be understood as a process of mutual interaction in which consciousness unfolds with its liberating and propulsive, disciplinary and aggressive powers [*KT* 2, p. 164].

Note that the relationship is not present simply as one between the theoretician and the proletariat, but also as one between the theoretician and the "most advanced parts" of the class on the one hand, and the rest of the class on the other. A few lines earlier, the expression "advanced part" is equated with "a party or its leadership." In the main, however, Horkheimer's focus is on Critical Theory, not on a party. There is only one other reference to organization in Horkheimer's program, and that is equally abstract: "Something of the freedom and spontaneity of the future appears in the organization and community of those in struggle, despite all the discipline based on the need to prevail. Where the unity of discipline and spontaneity has vanished, the movement is transformed into a concern of its own bureaucracy, a drama which is already part of the repertory of recent history" (*KT* 2, pp. 166 ff.).

Thus Critical Theory's conception of politics also ends in a paradox. On the one hand, it presents itself as a mere component of a political practice; on the other, it lacks any specific political anchorage. This is not just a description of its historical situation after the victory of Nazism in Germany, but a rigorous consequence of Frankfurt School theory. The overpoliticization of theory leads logically to the substitution of theory as a surrogate for politics—an *Ersatzpolitik*.

So far our analysis has been confined almost exclusively to a single essay by Horkheimer outlining the differences between traditional theory and Critical Theory. Nevertheless, two important conclusions have already emerged. Horkheimer argues that Marxism, or Critical Theory, is a completely new kind of theory; yet on closer inspection it becomes clear that the radical break is not with classical philosophy, whose heritage, on the contrary, it claims, but with science. Moreover, it does not propose to replace existing science with a new science, i.e., it refuses to enter the scientific arena, but denounces science from outside, from the realm of philosophy. The paradoxical result is that bourgeois science is retained, the only change being a philosophical (or even ethical) minus sign in front of its categories. Similarly, Critical Theory associates itself with the struggle of the oppressed against capitalist class rule, but it is unable to situate this association in the politial arena. It remains outside denouncing bourgeois class politics from the philosophical sphere. Horkheimer's critical theory involves *a double reduction of science and politics to philosophy.*

Backdrop: Rationalization and Reification

What was this philosophy which could thus be substituted for both science and politics in a revolutionary stance? The theory outlined in Horkheimer's program and developed by the Frankfurt School from the 1930s to the present was by no means a completely original intellectual formation. It was rather an extreme development of the most philosophically self-conscious form of Marxism available to the Frankfurt theorists—the philosophy of the young Lukács and Korsch, which was itself a development of a whole trend of nineteenth- and twentieth-century German sociological thought represented most completely by

Max Weber's work. The central concern of this tradition was that of capitalist rationalization.

The original conceptualization of this problem in Germany was made in 1887 when Ferdinand Tönnies published *Gemeinschaft und Gesellschaft* (Community and Society). The distinction which constituted the title was the contrast between the intimate personal relations of family and neighborhood in rural preindustrial and precapitalist society, and the impersonal contractual relations between men in urban, commercial, and industrial society. The rationalization implied by *Gesellschaft* relations subsequently became the master concept of all Max Weber's work. For Weber, it was an inevitable destiny of Western society since the adoption of Judeo-Christian religion in the West. It meant the *Entzauberung* (disenchantment) of the Western world, its liberation from magic, tradition, and affectivity, and the development of instrumental rationality, calculation, and control. Weber traced this development in religion—the Reformation; in the political sphere—bureaucracy; and in the economy—the capitalist firm and the "spirit of capitalism."

In his *History and Class Consciousness* (1923), the young Lukács linked Weber's "rationalization" with Marx's conception of the "fetishism of commodities," which he generalized into the concept of reification—the reduction of human relations to relations between things. Reification was a feature not of modern society in general but of a particular type of modern society dominated by market exchange: capitalist society. The vertex of reification was the labor market, where the free laborer, the proletarian, is forced to treat his living activity, his labor, as a thing. Hence the proletariat, the class most oppressed by capitalism, was the negation of capitalist society, and the force which could realize the philosophical critique of reification by a socialist revolution. The proletariat was the legitimate heir to German idealist philosophy, and revolutionary politics was the only means to make the divided and reified world whole and human.

This tradition, especially as represented by Lukács, had two important consequences for the subsequent development of the Frankfurt School. The first concerned its attitude to science, particularly the natural sciences; the second, its attitude to history and historical and social knowledge. The rise of the natural sciences was also part of the process Weber called "rationalization," and one of the crucial problems of German idealism (using the term in the widest sense) during the latter half of the nineteenth century was therefore its relationship to science. In academic culture, the question concerned the relations between the natural and cultural sciences. Historians, philosophers of history, and sociologists in the idealist tradition, all insisted on a sharp distinction between them, both in the character of their object and in their method.

Paradoxically, the Marxism which developed in Western Europe after World War I and the October Revolution faced the same problems, since it saw itself as the heir to classical German idealism. But these problems were also relevant to it for directly political reasons. Both classical social democratic Marxism and revisionism had been permeated with a strong commitment to science, interpreted in a positivist and evolutionist sense, and with indifference and hostility, respectively, to Hegelian philosophy.

The revolutionary intellectuals of Western Europe in the 1920s, steeped in the Hegelian tradition, carried on the earlier fight of German historicism for a conception of social and historical theory different from the natural sciences. And just as Weber saw science as a moment in the process of rationalization, so Lukács regarded it as an aspect of reification, when applied to the human sphere. Immutable scientific laws of society were the expression of a world in which human relations had become things beyond human control, and the separation of different scientific disciplines revealed a specialization which destroyed the totality and historicity of human existence. For both Lukács and Korsch, the conception of Marxism as a strict science and the abandonment of the Hegelian dialectic were also directly connected with the political treachery of social democracy. They therefore regarded their reintroduction of Hegelianism into Marxist discourse as a reaffirmation of its revolutionary vocation.

In the early 1930s, the position on the natural sciences adopted by the Frankfurt School, and particularly by Horkheimer, was much the same as that outlined in Lukács's *History and Class Consciousness.* Lukács's critique of science was aimed at the contemplative position which he claimed it implied. To regard society as governed by scientific laws, was, according to Lukács, to take a reflective attitude to it, instead of intervening actively to change it and thereby transcend its laws. The social democrats had oscillated between contemplation of an inevitable evolution to socialism and moralistic exhortation of the proletariat. In both, the unity of theory and practice had been broken. The Frankfurt School took up this critique, but as it was almost completely isolated from the working-class movement, the unification of theory and practice was broken de facto—especially after the victory of fascism in 1933. Its critique of scientism therefore moves steadily away from the problem of its consequences for those who are to change capitalist society to the problem of its consequences for those who have to live in a still existing capitalist system. The emphasis is no longer on science as *contemplation* so much as on science as *domination*. In 1932, Horkheimer wrote:

In the Marxist theory of society, science is numbered among the human forces of production. . . . Scientific knowledge shares the fate of productive forces and means of production of other kinds: The extent of their application is in grave contrast both to the level of their development and the real needs of men. . . . Insofar as an attempt to found present society as eternity took over from the interest in a better society, which still dominated the Enlightenment, a restrictive and disorganizing moment entered science. A method oriented toward being and not toward becoming corresponded to the tendency to see the given form of society as a mechanism of equal and self-repeating process.[5]

By 1944, Horkheimer and Adorno were arguing: "Bacon exactly caught the spirit of the science that came after him. The happy marriage he imagined between the human intellect and the nature of things is a patriarchal one: The intellect which defeats superstition must command a disenchanted nature. Knowledge, which is power, knows no limits, either in the enslavement of creation or in its docile submission to the masters of the world."[6] The importance of this change for the political ideas of the Frankfurt School is discussed in the section on fascism below.

Theory as Self-Knowledge of the Object

A second influence of the historicist tradition on the Frankfurt School affected its view of history, and its characteristic form was that of a return to Hegel. Lukács had already stated this project in *History and Class Consciousness*. "The fact that historical materialism is profoundly akin to Hegel's philosophy is clearly expressed in the function of the theory as the *self-knowledge of reality*."[7] Horkheimer's program for Critical Theory states that this theory "constructs the unfolding picture of the whole, the existential judgement contained in history" (*KT* 2, p. 187). It is "a struggle inherent in reality that by itself calls for a specific mode of behavior."[8] The basic conception of history which unerlies this epistemology can be seen in a quotation from Marcuse: "When historical content enters into the dialectical concept and detemines methodologically its development and function, dialectical thought attains the concreteness which links the structure of thought to that of reality. Logical truth becomes historical truth. The ontological tension between essence and appearance, between 'is' and 'ought,' becomes historical tension, and the inner negativity of the object-world is understood as the work of the historical subject—man in his struggle with nature and society" (*ODM*, p. 11).

History is viewed as one all-embracing process, in which a historical subject realizes itself. This subject is no longer Hegel's Idea, but man. "The goal of a rational society . . . is really invested in every man" (*KT* 2, p. 199). This goal cannot be realized in the present society which is characterized, on the contrary, by its negation—the reification of human relations and the alienation of man. But in spite of this, human beings still maintain a will and a struggle for a rational organization of society, and it is through this will and this struggle, inherent in man and human existence, that man can discover the fact that human goals are negated in the prevailing conditions. Thus a knowledge of society becomes at the same time a judgement or evaluation of it. In this way, man and social reality (created by man) reach self-knowledge.

The reader will have noted that it is this historicist speculation which has in recent years constituted a primary target of Althusser and his followers. What effects does it have on the social theory of the Frankfurt School? The following list does not claim to be exhaustive, but it provides a starting point for analysis.

1. It means that for humanist historicism, the term *social totality* is something other than a scientific concept. In social science, the expression is used in a structural sense. To be able to explain a social fact, one must take into account the network of relationships of which it is a part, the structure which determines the place of that social fact and its mode of functioning. Marxism is a social science in this sense, and it was by this procedure, for instance, that Marx showed that it is not the consumers and their needs and wishes which direct the capitalist economy.[9] In a historicist perspective, however, the totality becomes the totality of humanity's generically determined (*gattungs-bestimmt*) history at a given moment. To grasp the totality then becomes to comprehend the existing reality from the standpoint of man's goal, a rational society.

2. There is no room in the historicist conception of history for social totalities as structures of irreducible complexity, or for a discontinuous development of those complex structures. Society is always reducible to its creator-subject, and history is the continuous unfolding of this subject. At every given point in time, society is a unique manifestation of man. This means that the concept of a mode of production, which in any classical reading of Marx is the central concept of historical materialism, plays at most a quite subordinate role. Capitalism is thus seen not as one mode of production among others, but as a completely unique moment in the history (or more strictly speaking, in the reified prehistory) of man. Here the Frankfurt School appeals explicitly to the treatment of capitalism in classical German historicism, as expressed, for example, by Max Weber: "Such a historical concept,

however, since it refers to a phenomenon significant for its unique individuality, cannot be defined according to the formula *genus proximum, differentia specifica,* but *it must be gradually put together out of the individual parts* which are taken from historical reality to make it up."[10] Etienne Balibar has convincingly proved that the Marxist conception of capitalism is, on the contrary, constructed in precisely the way which Weber declares impossible.[11] Nevertheless, Weber's conception has been hailed by Adorno as a third alternative between positivism and idealism.[12] This historicist conception of the social totality has prevented the Frankfurt School from making the contribution to historical materialism which would seem to be implied in its program of social research.

3. Critical Theory sees itself as humanity's self-knowledge. Therefore it cannot and must not have a structure which is (formally) logical and systematic. Such a systematization would mean that men systematized themselves, divided themselves up among the boxes of abstract categories. "The formalization of reason is only the intellectual expression of the mechanized mode of production" (*DA*, p. 126). Formal logic is an expression of "the indifference to the individual" (*DA*, p. 238).

4. In a historicist interpretation, the scientific specificity of Marx's critique of political economy disappears. That critique is either regarded as a philosophical critique (Horkheimer) or an examination of political economy from the standpoint of the totality of social being (Marcuse), but not as a scientific operation. This is quite clearly different from Marx's own conception of his work and of epistemology in general. In this context, Marx distinguished between four levels of thought: the economic subjects' immediate view of themselves and of the economy, special ideologies or speculative systems based on these immediate views, past science (above all, Ricardo's work, which Marx regarded as a science, but one which his own critique had superseded), and lastly positive science (Marx's own theory).[13]

5. The main effect of this historicist conception of knowledge is its view of capitalism, which is, of course, the present whose self-knowledge Critical Theory claims to represent. "In the course of history, men attain a knowledge of their action and thereby grasp the contradiction in their existence" (*KT* 2, p. 161). In capitalism this contradiction is absolute; capitalism is a negation of humanity. Hence for Critical Theory, all the institutions of capitalist society become expressions of a contradictory inner essence. Several options are then open to the historicist. The critical theorists could have taken as their starting point Marx's treatment of the concept of the commodity in *Capital,* and interpreted reification as the essential meaning of capitalism. This, of course, was Lukács's option: "One could say that the chapter in *Capital* on the fetishism of commodities . . . contains hidden in it the whole of historical materialism, the whole of the proletariat's

knowledge of itself as knowledge of capitalist society."[14] Or they could have started from the concept of labor and human activity, seeing capitalism above all in terms of alienation. This option is characteristic of all those who base themselves on Marx's *1884 Manuscripts*.[15] Horkheimer and Adorno have chosen a third path—to regard exchange as the fundamental relation of capitalism. In this version, capitalism is the negation of just and equal exchange, producing increasing social injustice and the polarizations of power and oppression, wealth and poverty which go with it (*KT* 2, p. 173 ff.). All these options say something true and important about capitalism, and they give an ideological judgment of it which can be used in the struggle to destroy it and replace it with a socialist society. But the tasks of Marxists are not confined to the ideological struggle, and from the point of view of science as a guide to political action all these variants have to be refuted. They substitute for real history a construction derived from a philosophy of history, the history of man's alienation or reification or—in Frankfurt vocabulary—the dialectic of enlightenment. In the science of history, capitalism is a specific mode of production, characterized by a specific combination of forces and relations of production. This mode of production both sets the stage for the class struggle and is its object. Without a scientific analysis of the mode of production and social formation, no coherent class strategy can be developed by which to overthrow it. The Frankfurt School not only does not provide Marxism with any instrument to assist in the construction of this strategy, it denounces all such instruments *as such*.

Fascism as the Truth of Liberalism

As we have seen, a typical feature of the Frankfurt School's historicist ideology is the reduction of the complexity of the capitalist social formation to an essence which is then both expressed and masked by the different phenomenal forms which the essence takes in concrete historical existence. As history unfolds, the essence is more and more revealed. This ideological conception acquired great political importance when the Frankfurt School turned to the analysis of fascism.

Efforts to explain the roots of fascism were a major preoccupation of all antifascist intellectuals in the 1930s and during the war. Many of these interpretations focused not on economic and political problems, but on ideological and cultural factors. It is remarkable that not only are these cultural explanations divided into two diametrically opposed camps where their interpretation of fascist culture is concerned, but also each of these camps contains both revolutionary and counterrevolutionary ideologists. To one of these camps, fascism was essentially an irrational phenomenon, a revolt against reason. To the other, on the contrary, it was the triumph of manipulative rationality. To the first camp belong both Karl Popper, with *The Open Society and Its Enemies*, and the later Georg Lukács in *Die Zerstörung der Vernunft* (The Destruction of Reason). The Frankfurt School emphatically belongs to the second group, where it finds its reactionary counterpart in figures like Friedrich von Hayek. But within this basic framework, the Frankfurt School's theory of fascism has not remained static. The year 1939 provides a convenient divide between two distinct phases in this development.

In the first period, the Frankfurt School view of the roots of fascism contains two main themes with sources in Marxism and psychoanalysis[16] respectively. On the economic level, fascism is explained as the replacement of competitive capitalism by monopoly and as the seizure of power by the monopoly capitalists to deal with the economic and political crisis of capitalism. In his vivid essay "The Struggle against Liberalism in the Totalitarian View of the State," Marcuse shows that fascist attacks on liberalism notwithstanding, these two ideologies and political systems represent two different stages of the same type of society, to which they both belong: respectively, monopoly capitalism, and competitive capitalism. Marcuse first points out that the attacks on the bourgeoisie, i.e. on the profit motive, in fascist ideology are directed against the capitalists of competitive capitalism. The "merchant" (*Händler*) is reviled, while homage is paid to the "gifted economic leader" (*Wirtschaftsführer*).[17] According to Marcuse, fascism finds its most important springboards in "the naturalistic interpretation of society and the liberalist rationalism that ends in irrationalism. Both believe in "natural," eternal laws of society. The liberal rationalization of the economy and society is essentially private, relating to the rational practice of the single individual; it lacks any rational determination of social goals. It therefore comes to an end when an economic crisis breaks through its supposed harmony of interests. At this point, liberal theory has to turn to irrational justifications of the existing system" (*KG* 1, p. 31; *N*, pp. 17–18).

The second theme in the first phase of the Frankfurt School's explanation of fascism is the precedent for fascist moralism provided by antisensual bourgeois morality in general, with its condemnation of hedonism and happiness in favor of "virtue."[18] This hostility to pleasure emerges paradoxically in what Marcuse called "affirmative culture," in which happiness and the spirit are split away from the material world into a separate, purely spiritual realm called *Kultur*. "By affirmative culture is meant that culture of the bourgeois epoch which led in the course of its own development to the segregation from civilization of the mental and spiritual world as an independent realm of value that is also considered superior to civilization. Its decisive characteristic is the assertion of a universally obligatory, eternally better and more valuable world that must be unconditionally affirmed: a world essentially different from the factual world of the daily struggle for existence, yet realizable by every individual for himself "from within" without any transformation of the state of fact" (*KG* 1, p. 63; *N*, p. 95). In the prefascist period this culture could be characterized as an internalization (*Verinnerlichung*), but "during the most recent period of affirmative culture, this abstract internal community (abstract because it left the real antagonisms untouched) has turned into an equally abstract external community. The individual is inserted into a false collectivity (race, folk, blood, and soil)" (*KG* 1, p. 93; *N*, p. 125).

Apart from culture in general, a crucial element in fascism, according to the Frankfurt School, was the psychology of the individual citizen which made fascist oppression possible, the so-called authoritarian personality. The authoritarian personality, too, was for the Frankfurt School a creation of the classical bourgeois epoch. In the huge collective volume *Studien über Autorität und Familie* (Studies in Authority and the Family), whose principal contributions were written by Fromm, Horkheimer, and Marcuse, the Frankfurt School examined the way in which the family functions as a mechanism to preserve the existing society, and, more specifically, the way in which the bourgeois family functions as an inculcator of authoritarianism.

In 1939, the Spanish Republic was defeated, Molotov and Ribbentrop signed the Nazi-Soviet pact, and World War II broke out. This was the decisive crisis for the intellectual Left of the 1930s. Its effect on the Frankfurt School was at first registered only in a practical retreat from politics, not a modification of theory. Hence the content of its theory of fascism changed very little, but its themes were more sharply expressed. This is well represented by Horkheimer's essay *The Jews and Europe*, which was completed in the very first days of September of that year.[19] Horkheimer argues that the present crisis, far from bringing Marxism into question, vindicates its analyses of the power relations, monopolistic tendencies, and eruption of crises in capitalist society. "He who does not want to speak about capitalism should also be silent about fascism" (*JE*, p. 115). "The [Marxist] theory destroyed the myth of a harmony of interests; it presented the liberal economic process as the reproduction of relations of domination by means of free contracts which are enforced by the inequality of property. The mediation has now been removed. Fascism is the truth of modern society, which this theory had grasped from the beginning" (*JE*, p. 116).

Logic as Domination

But the retreat from politics, even of the abstract type available to the Frankfurt School in the 1930s, eventually directly affected the theory, too, and as part of the theory, the theory of fascism. This is seen at its clearest in Horkheimer and Adorno's *Dialektik der Aufklärung* (Dialectic of Enlightenment), written during the war. Horkheimer and Adorno ask: "Why, instead of entering into a truly human condition, does humanity sink into a new kind of barbarism?" Here a comparison can be made with Popper's *Open Society and Its Enemies* and Von Hayek's *The Road to Serfdom*. These last two authors put the blame on socialism and the labor movement: Popper, because Marxism had allegedly substituted historicism and utopianism for "piecemeal social engineering"; Hayek, because socialism had introduced the ideas of planning and state intervention into the paradise of competitive capitalism. Horkheimer and Adorno's answer to the question is, of course, quite different. For them, fascism is the self-destruction of the liberal Enlightenment. Fascism is not just the truth of liberalism in the sense that it nakedly reveals the real inequalities and oppression inherent in the apparently free exchange in the capitalist market. Fascism is the truth of the whole aim of the bourgeois Enlightenment from Bacon on to liberate man from the fetters of superstition. The main offender is not the market and the relations of production, but the natural sciences and their empiricist counterpart in epistemology. The whole meaning of science and logic is brought into question:

> For many years now we have noted that the great discoveries of modern scientific organization [*Betrieb*] have been made at the cost of an accelerating decline in theoretical culture, but we still believe that we ought to follow this organization insofar as our contribution was limited primarily to the critique or continuation of specialized theories. It was at least designed to stick thematically to the traditional disciplines, to sociology, psychology, and epistemology. The fragments which we have brought together here, however, indicate that we have to renounce that confidence. A careful watch and examination of the scientific tradition, particularly where positivist censors have consigned it to oblivion as useless ballast, forms a moment of knowledge, but in the contemporary collapse of bourgeois civilization, not only the organization, but even the meaning of science has come into question [*DA*, p. 5].

Horkheimer's program for a critical theory still maintained the Lukácsian position on science: It was contemplative, as opposed to a commitment to fundamental social change. In *Dialectic of the Enlighten-*

ment, however, the focus is wholly on science as an instrument of domination.[20] Now natural science and Bacon's empiricist theory of knowledge are the main targets: "What men want to learn from nature is how to use it in order to dominate it and men completely." "The Enlightenment's attitude to things is the same as the dictator's to men. They know them in so far as they can manipulate them" (*DA,* pp. 14, 20). Logic as such is contaminated because of its indifference to the qualitative and to the individually unique. It is directly linked to the capitalist rationalization of labor. "The indifference to the individual which is expressed in logic draws the consequences of the economic process" (*DA,* p. 238). Fascism has granted science its full honors, freeing it from all moral considerations. "The totalitarian order . . . invests calculating thinking with all its rights and upholds science as such" (*DA,* p. 106).

Moreover, the form in which *Dialectic of Enlightenment* is written takes this critique of logic and science into account. It is a collection of philosophical fragments (Adorno's *Minima Moralia,* written at the same time, is similarly a collection of aphorisms). Its theme is the inner contradictions of the Enlightenment, defined as the "disenchantment [*Entzauberung*] of the world," and the self-destruction these contradictions bring about.[21] An allegory for this dialectic can be found in the twelfth book of the *Odyssey,* where Ulysses' ship has to pass by the sirens, whose immensely beautiful song leads men to lose themselves in the past. Ulysses avoids this danger in two ways. He has one solution for his sailors: He blocks their ears with wax. "The worker must look straight ahead, lively and concentrated, ignoring everything that happens on either side." The other solution is for himself, the landowner, he has himself bound to the mast. He can thus enjoy the sirens' song because he has made their temptation a merely contemplative object, an art, and the greater the temptation, the harder he makes his men bind him, like the later bourgeois who refuses himself happiness more and more obstinately, the nearer he comes to it through the growth in his power (*DA,* p. 47 ff.). The theme is then pursued in Kant, de Sade, and Nietzsche, to show that "the subjugation of everything natural to the autocratic subject reaches its acme in the domination of the blindly objective, of the natural" (*DA,* p. 10). The authors also follow the development of the Enlightenment into commercial culture and mass communications: "Enlightenment as mass deception."

The most directly political analyses in the book are found in seven theses on anti-Semitism. The seventh is the most remarkable. It was added after the war amidst the general euphoria over the defeat of fascism. Precisely at this moment, Horkheimer and Adorno argue that fascism and anti-Semitism have been preserved in the very structure of the existing party politics. The tone of this thesis is set by the first sentences: "But there are no more anti-Semites. The last ones were liberals who wanted to voice their anti-liberal opinions" (*DA*, p. 235). The preservation of anti-Semitism is then illustrated by a reality of the U.S. political system, the "ticket" (e.g. the Nixon-Agnew ticket). "Anti-Semitic judgement has always been an index of stereotyped thought. Today the stereotype is all that remains. People still choose, but only between totalities. Anti-Semitic psychology has been largely replaced by a mere yes to the fascist ticket, to the list of the slogans of quarrelsome heavy industry" (*DA*, p. 236). The ticket mentality is part of the all-pervasive process of the negation of individuality. Even progressive parties are directly attacked on these grounds. "In any case, the basis of the development which leads to ticket thought is the universal reduction of all specific energies to a single, equal, and abstract form of labor, from the battlefield to the film studio. But the transition from such conditions to a more human situation cannot take place, because the same thing happens to the good as to the bad. Freedom on the progressive ticket is as external to the structure of power politics, to which progressive decisions inevitably amount, as hostility to Jews is to the chemical trust" (*DA*, p. 243).[22]

This treatment of fascism reveals very clearly the limits of historicism. An interpretation of fascism as the essence behind the phenomena, as the "truth of" modern (capitalist) society, can never achieve the central aim of Marxist analysis, what Lenin called the "concrete analysis of a concrete situation." However deep its roots lay in the structure of monopoly capitalism, fascism was a special type of monopoly capitalist state which arose in a specific historical conjuncture.[23] In failing to recognize this, the Frankfurt School took up the positions adopted by the Comintern in the so-called Third Period, after the Sixth Conference of 1928: Fascism was seen as an inevitable and culminating phase of capitalism. For all its virtuosity, Frankfurt School explanations of fascism were thus ultimately an example of theoretical impotence. The theme of *Dialectic of Enlightenment* is the self-destruction of bourgeois reason; but this theory itself is a case of the self-destruction of intellectual radicalism. It is precisely the radicalism of the authors' rejection of bourgeois society and culture which wrests the weapons of socialist theory (science) from their hands, forcing them to retreat into speculative philosophical fragments.

The reduction of science to philosophy is thus revealed in this test case of Frankfurt School theory as doubly mystificatory. The direct condemnation of the logic of the sciences as responsible for fascism makes it impossible to develop a conjunctural theory of fascism which would have helped to fight it more effectively. The retreat from Marxist scientific concepts into a philosophical (ideological) critique of capitalist society then covers up for the lack of a theory of it.

The Political Collapse of Horkheimer

The second reduction characteristic of the Frankfurt School, as we have seen, is that of politics to philosophy. An examination of this entails an analysis of the school's attitude to political practice. In this too there is an evolution, but it is further complicated by the political divergences of the school in the postwar years. As we have seen, their initial position, as represented in Horkheimer's programmatic text of 1937, was similar to that of Lukács's. The proletariat was still regarded as the agent of revolution, and the aim of politics was the unity of philosophy and the proletariat in a realized proletarian class consciousness. However, in the late 1930s it was impossible to sustain the young Lukács's belief in the immediacy of this revolutionary unification.[24]

After the signing of the Nazi-Soviet pact in 1939, this initial skepticism deepened. The bleak political situation induced a retreat from politics, but no immediate capitulation. "Nothing is to be hoped for from the alliances of the great powers. No trust can be put in the collapse of the totalitarian economy. . . . It is completely naive to call from outside for the German workers to rise. He who can only play at politics should keep away from it. Confusion has become so general that truth has all the more practical value the less it meddles with any intended practice" (*JE*, p. 135). Horkheimer recalls the Jews' steadfast rejection of the worship of false gods: "A lack of respect for an existing authority which extends even to God is the religion of those who, in the Europe of the Iron Heel, continue to devote their lives to the preparation for a better one" (*JE*, p. 136). Of anticommunism, at this stage, there was not a word.

The postwar political position of Horkheimer and Adorno, by contrast, has had three aspects: the maintenance of critical theory as a pure theory; the retreat from politics into exclusive individualism; and academic integration. However, in none of their later works is either Critical Theory or its relationship to Marx and Engels repudiated.[25] In his *Negative Dialektik*, Adorno even openly scorns the idealist exploitation of the "young Marx" on the grounds that to center Critical Theory on the concept of reification only serves to make it idealistically acceptable to the ruling consciousness.[26] They have also maintained a firm dividing line between their positions and those of conservative *Kulturkritik*.[27]

In Horkheimer's program, Critical Theory was defined as part of the political practice of the oppressed classes. From the mid-1940s, Critical

Theory was located elsewhere, in the individual mind. The whole tenor of Horkheimer's and Adorno's works in this period is characterized by the conviction that the only place where anything is still possible in the totalitarian world is the "individual sphere," where the task is to resist the intruding cruelty of the "administered world." This is well expressed by Adorno in the preface to *Minima Moralia* (1951): "In view of the totalitarian unanimity which cries out for the eradication of difference directly as meaning, some of the liberating social forces may even temporarily come together in the sphere of the individual. Critical Theory can reside in the latter without a bad conscience."[28] Horkheimer added a decade later: "Our hope rests in the work to ensure that in the beginning of a world period dominated by blocks of administered men, a few will be found who offer up some resistance, like the sacrifices of history, to whom belongs the founder of Christianity" (*TA*, p. 19). This religious solution has at times taken a Jewish form, too.[29]

The academic integration of the West German wing of the Frankfurt School is best represented by *The Authoritarian Personality*, published in 1950, with Adorno as its senior author and Horkheimer as director of the entire research project (entitled *Studies in Prejudice*). Here the stress on individual psychology becomes a complete capitulation to bourgeois social psychology in theory, method, and political conclusions. Horkheimer says in his preface: "It may strike the reader that we have placed undue stress upon the personal and the psychological rather than upon the social aspects of prejudice. That is not due to a personal preference for psychological analysis, nor to a failure to see that the cause of irrational hostility is in the last instance to be found in social frustration and injustice. Our aim is not merely to describe prejudice but to explain it in order to help its eradication. . . . *Eradication means re-education*, scientifically planned on the basis of understanding scientifically arrived at. And education in a strict sense is by its nature personal and psychological."[30] In the last thesis on anti-Semitism in *Dialectic of Enlightenment,* anti-Semitism was embedded in the very core of the modern political system, both East and West. Here it has suddenly become something which can be done away with by personal education, presumably by the Adenauer government or the Western occupation authorities in Germany. It is profoundly symbolic that Adorno calls the consciously antiauthoritarian personality type "the genuine liberal."[31] This is a long way from the thesis that fascism is the truth of liberalism and the anti-Semite the liberal who wants to voice his antiliberal opinion.

The effect of the combined factors of formal preservation of the theory, exclusive individualization, and academic integration is a cumulative mystification. The formula here provides a legitimation for a purely ideological radicalism smugly installed in the cosy academic institution, without even an indirect relationship to politics as experienced by the masses, but still cultivating a Critical Theory going back to an interpretation of Marx.

This development has also been accompanied by a retreat from the resolute rejection of anticommunism in 1937 and even in 1939. *Dialectic of Enlightenment* already implies that the choice between the Soviet Union and the United States is one between two equal evils, two totalitarian "tickets," and in the Cold War period, Horkheimer and Adorno committed themselves further to the West against the East. Horkheimer has repeatedly declared his commitment to the "most civilized" or "European" states, against the threatening "totalitarian world," in which are included not only the Communist states but the "backward countries" with their "exaggerated nationalisms" (*TA*, p. 23). According to the former director of *Studies in Prejudice*, not only should Kaiser Wilhelm II's warning of the "menace of the yellow race . . . be taken very seriously today," but "it is perhaps more urgent than it appears," though "it is indeed not the only threat" to Europe.[32]

Marcuse: Integrity and Contradiction

Marcuse's political evolution has been a polar contrast, and his political record is exemplary. But it does not necessarily imply a deep gulf between the theoretical structure of his thought and that of the other members of the school. An ideological perspective is characteristically liable and can be made to fit many political positions.[33] However, one important theoretical difference can be detected even in 1937. This concerned the relation between philosophy and Marxism as a theory of society. This difference is discernible in the discussion of Horkheimer's program which followed its publication in the *Zeitschrift für Sozialforschung* under the title "Philosophy and Critical Theory." Horkheimer argued that "the critical theory of society . . . remains philosophical even as a critique of economics." This is because Critical Theory is something more than a specialized economic discipline, it is a theory and a judgment of the whole of human existence. For Marcuse, however, this transcendence of specialized economics is contained in a critical theory of society as such, which is the successor to classical philosophy. "Philosophy thus appears within the economic concepts of materialist theory, each of which is more than an economic concept of the sort employed by the academic discipline of economics. It is more due to the theory's claim to explain the totality of man and his world in terms of his social being. Yet it would be false on that account to reduce these concepts to philosophical ones. To the contrary, the philosophical contents relevant to the theory are to be deduced from the economic structure" (*KG* 1, p. 102; *N*, pp. 134–35). This conception of the relationship between Critical Theory and philosophy explains the subtitle of *Reason and Revolution* (*Hegel and the Rise of Social Theory*). "If there was to be any progress beyond this philosophy, it had to be an advance beyond philosophy itself and, at the same time, beyond the social and political order to which philosophy had tied its fate."[34] In 1948, Marcuse reaffirmed this attachment to Marxism as a social theory which rejects philosophy in a critique of Sartre's *L'Être et le néant*. "One step more [from Hegel's philosophy] toward concretization would have meant a transgression beyond philosophy itself. Such transgression occurred in the opposition to Hegel's philosophy. . . . But neither Kierkegaard nor Marx wrote existential philosophy. When they came to grips with concrete existence, they abandoned and repudiated philosophy. . . . For Marx, the conception of '*réalité humaine*' is the critique of political economy and the theory of socialist revolution" (*KG* 2, p. 83; *Philosophy and Phenomenological Research* 7 [March 1948]:335).

But these intellectual differences should not be taken too far. Marcuse's most famous work, *One-Dimensional Man*, is firmly in the Frankfurt tradition and shares its theoretical faults, particularly the self-destructive intellectual hyperrationalism which characterized *Dialectic of Enlightenment*. As Marcuse explains in the preface to the republication in 1965 of his essays from the 1930s: "Thought in contradiction must become more negative and more utopian in opposition to the status quo. This seems to me to be the imperative of the current situation in relation to my theoretical essays of the 1930s" (*KG* 1, p. 16; *N*, p. xx). But as realized in *One-Dimensional Man*, this project reveals at its center a massive contradiction. The book is conceived as a picture of industrial society or "the most highly developed contemporary societies," whereas in fact it is a highly conjunctural work, defined by the situation in the United States in the 1950s and early 1960s, before the internal effects of the Vietnamese War had made themselves felt, before the student movement and the rise of working-class resistance, and before the visible disintegration of U.S. supremacy over Western Europe and Japan.[35] Marcuse's weakness is not his failure to see these future tendencies, but the fact that his analysis provides no concepts by means of which he might have discovered them. As Marcuse himself says, "the critical theory of society possesses no concepts which could bridge the gap between the present and its future" (*ODM*, p. 14). Moreover, instead of using a Marxist analysis of modern monopoly capitalism, Marcuse relies on such works as Berle's and Means's *The Modern Corporation and Private Property,* William H. Whyte's *The Organization Man,* and the writings of Vance Packard. The crucial argument about the integration of the working class is characteristically sustained by reference to academic American sociology. Once again, the radicalism of the critique has left its ideologial object untouched.

One-Dimensional Man represents a step backwards for Marcuse vis-à-vis his attitudes to technology, to philosophy, and to classical bourgeois culture. In *Soviet Marxism* he upheld the Marxist notion of the "essentially neutral character" of technology and made it one of the cornerstones of his analysis of Soviet society; the change from a nationalized economy to a socialized one is a political revolution entailing the dismantling of the repressive state and the installation of control from below.[36] In *One-Dimensional Man,* the opposite view prevails: "The traditional notion of the 'neutrality' of technology can no longer be maintained. . . . The technological society is a system of domination which operates already in the concept and construction of techniques" (*ODM,* p. 14). Second, the conception of philosophy and its role in *One-Dimensional Man* contains a repudiation, though more implicit, of Marcuse's earlier positions. Instead of asserting the need to replace philosophy with a Marxist theory of society, *One-Dimensional Man* sets out to defend and maintain philosophy in the classical idealist sense, with concepts antagonistic to the prevailing discourse. This reversal is perhaps most clearly expressed in the following sentence, where instead of replacing philosophy with social theory and politics, he suggests that the problem is to replace politics with philosophy: "In the totalitarian era, the therapeutic task of philosophy would be a political task. . . . Then politics would appear in philosophy, not as a special discipline or object of analysis, nor as a special political philosophy, but as the intent of its concepts to comprehend the unmutilated reality" (*ODM,* p. 156). Third, the concept of "affirmative culture" discussed in the 1937 article mentioned above, the sublimated bourgeois culture in which the values denied by bourgeois society in everyday life are affirmed in the sphere of high culture, is replaced by the concept of "repressive desublimation." Here we are dealing with a change in the object of analysis, from one type of bourgeois society to another, and in this sense the concept of repressive desublimation is an important and fruitful tool of analysis. But in another paradox of intellectual hyperradicalism, what was once condemned as "affirmative culture" is now hailed as a culture of negation, denouncing the poverty of society (*ODM,* p. 58 ff.). In *One-Dimensional Man,* a critique which sets out to refute the very structure of logic and science bases its social analyses on pseudoliberal journalism and academic sociology, and a critique which does not even find Marxism negative enough turns the affirmative bourgeois culture into a negative one.[37]

The Negation of the Negation

One-Dimensional Man is thus, of all Marcuse's works, the closest to the mainstream of the Frankfurt School. Yet it is also the book that has had the most political influence, more probably, than anything else produced by the school in all its forty years of existence. Despite its pessimism, this book has become one of the standard texts of the student revolts of the late 1960s. But before examining the link between the views of the Frankfurt School and the recent student revolt, we must examine the concepts which underlie these political positions. The most important one arises directly from the hyperradicalism of the school's critique of capitalist society. Critical Theory rejects any positive presence in capitalist society (such as the proletariat) and seeks the purest negation, *the negation of the negation*, as the essence of revolution. This Hegelian notion of revolutionary change has played a central and disastrous role in Frankfurt thought. In their search for the absolute negation of the prevailing theoretical and ideological discourse, the thinkers of the Frankfurt School feel forced to go outside both science, concrete social analysis, and formal logic. Horkheimer's 1937 program for a critical theory tried to find an Archimedean point outside society to uproot itself from the process of social reproduction. In the 1940s, Horkheimer and Adorno considered it necessary to go even further, formulating their social critique only in philosophical fragments, because any continuous discourse was bound to lapse into positivity. The search for an absolute negation of the negation is also the rationale for Marcuse's retreat from Marxism in *One-Dimensional Man*: "An attempt to recapture the critical intent of these categories (society, class, individual, etc.), and to understand how the intent was cancelled by the social reality appears from the outset to be regression from a theory joined with historical practice to abstract, speculative thought; from the critique of political economy to philosophy. This ideological character of the critique results from the fact that the analysis is forced to proceed from a position 'outside' the positive as well as the negative, the productive as well as the destructive tendencies in society" (*ODM*, p. 12 ff.).

This attempt by the theory to pull itself up by its own bootstraps does not make it more revolutionary, but rather more philosophical. The same attitude can be detected in the denial that the economic class struggle can play a revolutionary role in the developed capitalist countries.[38] The historical experience of revolutions shows that they have not been sustained by the absolute negativity of the revolutionaries' demands, but by the determination with which concrete immediate demands have been urged in particular historical situations. Practical revolutionaries—Rosa Luxemburg as well as Lenin—have therefore always stressed the dialectical link between the various types of class struggle. None of them bothered to look for the absolute negation. On the contrary, Lenin's theory of revolution has two key moments. One is the building up of an organized revolutionary force and leadership. The other is the emergence of a revolutionary situation. This is characterized by a fusion of different contradictions such that the question of state power is put on the immediate agenda. The revolutionary situation can be ushered in by the most diverse and apparently banal causes, including even a parliamentary crisis. The conception of the revolutionary situation as a fusion of different contradictions is not an ad hoc explanation, but follows logically from the analysis of society as a complex social formation with mutually irreducible elements.[39] We have already seen that, far from conceiving society as a complex structure, historicist theories of society look for an inner essence revealed in all its parts. If this essence is oppressive, the source for a transformation cannot be found inside society, for all its manifestations share the oppressive nature of the essence. The agent of transformation can only be an external negating subject. The first historicist versions of Marxism thought that this external negating subject was the proletariat, thrust out of capitalist society as the object of all its oppressions, incarnating the capitalist negation of humanity. Both Lukács's *History and Class Consciousness* and Horkheimer's *Traditional and Critical Theory* contain this conception of the working class. But the proletariat no longer seems "absolutely" miserable and excluded in the so-called welfare state. The only groups who could still be so described are racial minorities and other outcasts. That is why, in his later works, Marcuse had tried to penetrate deeper into other human needs than economic ones, for he claims that the latter have now become means of integration and oppression. He has therefore turned his attention to the "biological dimension," to vital instinctive drives, to "erotic" needs in the broad sense of the term. In doing so he has found a new negating subject in the student movement and its refusal of the performance principle, its rejection of an economy based on exchange and competition, and its practice of sexual liberation.

But was the role of the proletariat in Marx's theory ever that of an absolute negation of capitalist society? On the one hand, Marx says explicitly that the social polarization resulting from the immiseration of the working class is crucial to the proletarian revolution (though this need not necessarily take the form of a strictly literal economic pauperization). On the other hand, Marx characterizes the epochal crisis of capitalism by a structural rather than a simply political contradiction, a contradiction between the social character of the productive forces and the private character of the relations of production. In this context, "productive forces" refers to the organizational-technical conditions under which production proceeds—handicrafts, manufacture, machine industry, and automated industry are different levels of the productive forces. These productive forces, which come into contradiction with the private mode of their appropriation, include the increasing use of science, developed communications, a high educational level, and an internalized discipline in the work force. Their effects on the working class are not immiseration but rather the provision of greater facilities for organization and a greater capacity to replace the capitalist regimentation of production by social appropriation and working-class control from below. There is always a social polarization between the working class and the bourgeoisie which arises directly from the fact of exploitation. This is intensified by economic crises induced by the contradiction between the productive forces and relations of production; a revolutionary situation then makes it explosive. Hence Marxist theory does not need a conception of the proletariat as the incarnation of the negation of human existence. A revolutionary situation is a function of the complex development of the social formation, whose different contradictions suddenly fuse in a "ruptural unity," not of the simple degree of wealth or poverty of the proletariat.[40]

The Marxist concept of the contradiction between the social character of the productive forces and the private character of the relations of production has never been incorporated into historicist interpretations of Marx in a way which preserves the objective character of both aspects of this contradiction as structures of the capitalist mode of production. For the young Lukács, the "decisive weight" is attached to whether "'the greatest force of production' in the capitalist order of production, the proletariat, experiences the crisis as a mere object of the decision or as its subject."[41] Here the analysis of the structural preconditions for revolution has been spirited away, reducing the forces of production to the proletariat. This makes the concept itself superfluous: All that matters is the proletariat and its degree of insight into its historical mission, its relationship to class consciousness. The Frankfurt School, on the other hand, has used the concept of the productive forces in another way. They are seen as representing the objective possibility of a new and better society. "This idea is distinguished from abstract utopia by the proof of its real possibility given by the present level of human productive forces" (*KT* 2, p. 168). The productive forces are not part of a *structural* contradiction, a contradiction between social and private *systems*, which affects class relationships, but are seen as the stage of human evolution which now enables the negating subject to abolish poverty and misery from the human condition.[42] It is in this sense that the productive forces are neutral, a raw material of potentiality. This neutrality is later denied: from a raw material of potentiality, technology becomes a means of oppression. But in neither case are the forces of production seen in their Marxist structural context. Rather, the analysis slips away from any positive identification of the structures of the capitalist social formation, or of the forces within it capable of transforming that social formation; from Marxist science and politics to philosophy as ersatz science and ersatz politics. Even when apparently anchored in the social structure, the negating subject was a philosophical concept. As Révai long ago pointed out in a review of *History and Class Consciousness*, the "assigned proletarian class consciousness" was merely substituted by Lukács for the Hegelian *Geist*.[43] In the Frankfurt School, this reduction of politics to philosophy has come directly out into the open.

Conclusion

The thought of the school has evolved, and marked divergences between its members have appeared in the years since the war. Nevertheless, there is a persistent underlying structure. This takes the form of a *double reduction* of *science* and of *politics* to philosophy. The specificity of Marxism as a theory of social formations and its autonomy as a guide to political action are thereby simultaneously abolished. This first reduction is clearly revealed by the Frankfurt School's theory of fascism, in which a philosophical critique of capitalism replaces a scientific conjunctural analysis of the nature of the fascist state. The second reduction appears in the conception of the revolutionary agent as a negating subject, which cannot be located in social reality and therefore eventually has to be confined to philosophy, conceived as social reality's opposite.

Since its inception, the Frankfurt School has probably produced more work and covered a wider variety of subjects (many of which could not be dealt with here) than any other comparable group of theorists. Yet as we have seen, the perspective underlying its thought has central and fatal weaknesses. What general verdict can we make of its historical achievement?

The theorists of the Frankfurt School were members of an academic intelligentsia with a high bourgeois background. They came to intellectual maturity in a period of international defeat for the working class, and were cut off from the proletariat of their own country by the Nazi counterrevolution. Like all members of the bourgeoisie, their initiation into a revolutionary position came about through a *revulsion* against capitalist oppression and capitalist ideology's hypocritical denial of that oppression. This revulsion took the form of a direct denunciation of all the nostrums of bourgeois ideology, particularly the economic ideology of free and equal exchange. But just as they adopted these positions, the capitalist system in their country suddenly took on a political form of unparalleled monstrosity with the Nazi seizure of power. This political machine was also a direct threat to themselves and their families. Understandably, fascism became a Medusa's head for the Frankfurt School. The result was that the initial attitude of revulsion was *frozen*, instead of developing into a scientific analysis and participation in revolutionary political practice. Sober political analysis seemed morally impossible; an objective scientific description of Nazism seemed to condone it because it did not condemn it violently in every sentence: In the dark ages, "a smooth forehead betokens/a hard heart" (Brecht).[44] When, to the surprise of most of the school, the monster was destroyed and Nazism was defeated, this attitude had become too fixed for them to make the step from philosophical revulsion to science and politics.

To this day, Frankfurt School thought has never moved from a reflection on its theorists' revulsion from capitalism to a theory of the object of that revulsion and a political practice to transform it. It has therefore been able to develop a powerful and well-articulated anticapitalist ideology, and this must be numbered among its achievements. It has helped to recapture that dimension of Marx's thought which deals with the qualitative aspects of work and human relations in capitalist society. As one of the school's severest critics, Lucio Colletti, has emphasized, neither the Second International nor the Comintern preserved this dimension. The decisive innovator here was Lukács, but the Frankfurt School has played an almost equally pioneering role, along with Wilhelm Reich, in enriching these ideas by adding a psychoanalytic dimension to them. It has also achieved a series of often brilliant and incisive critiques of bourgeois culture—Adorno's greatest contribution.[45]

Notes

1. Max Horkheimer, "Philosophie und kritische Theorie," *ZfS* (1937); reprinted in *KT* 2, p. 192.
2. Quoted from the original version in *ZfS* 3 (1937):274. In the republished version (*KT* 2, p. 170), "injustice" (*Unrecht*) has been substituted for "exploitation" (*Ausbautung*), and "only" (*einzig*) has been omitted.

3. Quoted from the original version, p. 292. In the republished version (*KT* 2, p. 190), "social injustice" has been substituted for "class domination" (*Klassenherrschaft*).
4. Max Horkheimer, *The Eclipse of Reason* (New York: Oxford University Press, 1947), p. 12. Cf. the chapters on one-dimensional thought in Herbert Marcuse. *One-Dimensional-Man* (Boston: Beacon, 1964). Hereafter this book will be referred to as *ODM*. Page references are to the London paperback edition of 1968.
5. Max Horkheimer, "Bemerkungen über Wissenschaft und Krise," *KT* 1, pp. 1–3.
6. Max Horkheimer and Theodor W. Adorno, *Dialektik der Aufklärung* (Amsterdam: Querido, 1947), p. 14. Hereafter this book will be referred to as *DA*. This position produces the characteristic idea that nature is not something to be mastered by man, as it appears in most Western thought from the Greeks onward, but something that should be regarded as a "garden," "which can grow while making human beings grow." See Marcuse, *Eros and Civilization* (Boston: Beacon, 1955). Some writers have argued that this idea is the defining feature of the school, but as we have seen, it was not present in Frankfurt thinking from the start. Moreover, it is shared by their archenemy, Heidegger. See "Brief über den 'Humanismus,' " in *Platons Lehre von der Wahrheit* (Bern: A. Francke, 1947).
7. Georg Lukács, *Werke*, vol. 2 (Neuwied and Berlin: Luchterhand, 1968), p. 188.
8. Horkheimer, *The Eclipse of Reason,* p. 11.
9. Karl Marx, *Grundrisse der Kritik der politischen Ökonomie* (Berlin: Dietz, 1953), p. 10ff.
10. Max Weber, *The Protestant Ethic and the Spirit of Capitalism* (London: Allen & Unwin, 1967), p. 47.
11. E. Balibar, "Sur les concepts fondamentaux du matérialisme historique," in Louis Althusser and Etienne Balibar, *Lire le Capital* (Paris: Libraire François Maspero, 1968), vol. 2.
12. Theodor W. Adorno, *Negative Dialektik* (Frankfurt: Suhrkamp, 1966), p. 165ff.
13. Marx's most succint formulation of this epistemology is perhaps to be found in *Theories of Surplus Value* (Moscow: Progress, 1968), vol. 3, esp. ch. on vulgar economics. Cf. Marx-Engels, *Werke* (Berlin: Dietz, 1965), vol. 26:3, esp. p. 445.
14. Lukács, p. 354.
15. Marcuse was among the first in the revolutionary camp to attach importance to the alienation of labor. See his "Über die philosophischen Grundlagen des wirtschaftswissenschaftlichen Arbeitsbegriffs" (1933), in *KG* 2.
16. Freudian psychoanalysis and metapsychology have been of great importance for Frankfurt theory. A psychoanalytic criticism of civilization as a repression of basic human instincts was thereby added to the Marxist critique of capitalist civilization. The core members of the group have refused to attenuate "the uneasiness [*Unbehagen*] in culture," the conflict between society and human instinct, by sociologizing the latter, and Adorno and Marcuse have directly attacked the neo-Freudian revisionists, including their former colleague, Erich Fromm, for doing so. See Theodor W. Adorno, "Sociology and Psychology," *New Left Review* 46, 47 (1967–68); and esp.

Marcuse, *Eros and Civilization*. But they give Freudian theory a historical character by distinguishing a reality principle specific to capitalist society, the performance principle. This approach both sharpens the indictment of capitalist society and radicalizes its negation, which is associated with a realm "beyond the reality principle," i.e. beyond the performance principle. The precondition for this is such a high level of the productive forces that labor can be abolished. Unlike Reich, sexual liberation in the genital sense is not the psychoanalytical aim of Frankfurt theory so much as the investment of all human activity with libidinous energy.

17. Marcuse, "Der Kampf gegen den Liberalismus in der totalitaren Staatsauffassung," *KG* 1, p. 25; *N,* pp. 11–12.

18. See Marcuse; Max Horkheimer, "Egoismus und Freiheitsbewegung," *ZfS* (1936 ff).

19. Max Horkheimer, "Die Juden und Europa," *ZfS* (1939) (hereafter referred to as *JE*). Characteristically, this resolute affirmation of the author's commitment to Marxism has been omitted from *KT*. However wild this article may be theoretically, it should be remembered that at this time, renegades like James Burnham were beginning to concoct the idea of the "managerial revolution."

20. Cf. *ODM*, esp. ch. 6.

21. This concept closely corresponds to Max Weber's notion of rationalization, whose initial manifestation was the absence or progressive elimination of magic from Western religion, starting with Mosaic Judaism, and from Western culture generally.

22. Hence it is possible to argue that all capitalist societies today are fascist still. This notion has pervaded much recent student thinking, especially in Germany, where it is embodied in the concept of *"Spätkapitalismus"* (late capitalism).

23. See Quintin Hoare, "What Is Fascism?," *New Left Review* 20 (Summer 1963).

24. See above.

25. See for example Max Horkheimer, "Theismus-Atheismus," in *Zeugnisse* (a festschrift for Adorno [Frankfurt 1963]), hereafter referred to as *TA*; his preface to *KT*; Adorno's *Negative Dialektik*.

26. Adorno, *Negative Dialektik*, p. 189.

27. See for instance Adorno's *Prismen* (Frankfurt: Suhrkamp, 1963). Translated as *Prisms* (London: Neville Spearman, 1967).

28. Theodor W. Adorno, *Minima Moralia* (Frankfurt: Suhrkamp, 1951), p. 11.

29. See the interview with Horkheimer in *Der Spiegel* (January 5, 1970).

30. *The Authoritarian Personality* (New York: Harper & Row, 1950), p. vii. The reader may feel that, after criticizing the Frankfurt School for its rejection of science, I am ungrateful in rejecting this apparent appeal to a policy "scientifically arrived at." But an appeal to science does not ensure scientificity. Here it is the bourgeois ideology of social psychology which is meant. This is another case of the paradox of Frankfurt hyperradicalism: the categories denounced philosophically have slipped back into academic discourse unscathed.

31. Ibid., p. 781.

32. Max Horkheimer, "On the Concept of Freedom," *Diogenes* (no. 53, 1966).

33. Habermas's suggestion that his political stand is due to an activism inherent in his Heideggerian formation need not be taken very seriously. Cf. Habermas (ed.), *Antworten auf Marcuse* (Frankfurt: Suhrkamp, 1968), p. 12.

34. Herbert Marcuse, *Reason and Revolution* (New York: Oxford University Press, 1941), p. 257.

35. For the effects of the Vietnamese war, see my "From Petrograd to Saigon," *New Left Review* 48 (1968); for the new tendencies of U.S. capitalism, see Ernest Mandel, "Where Is America Going," *New Left Review* 54 (1969), and "The Laws of Uneven Development," *New Left Review* 59 (1970).

36. Herbert Marcuse, *Soviet Marxism* (New York: Columbia University Press, 1958), pp. 160–91.

37. These critical remarks should not obliterate the differences between *One-Dimensional Man* and the postwar works of Horkheimer and Adorno. The former is still an attempt at a concrete social analysis with a direct bearing on politics.

38. Herbert Marcuse, *An Essay on Liberation* (Boston: Beacon, 1969), chs. 3, 4. This is still asserted despite the fact that the economic class struggle has been crucial to the militant working-class struggles of Italy and France in the last few years, and has also played a not insignificant role in the Scandinavian countries, which certainly cannot be dismissed as "more backward capitalist countries."

39. Lenin's theory of revolution is most clearly elaborated in his *Letters from Afar* and *"Left-Wing" Communism: An Infantile Disorder.* The incompatibility of his theory with any kind of historicism has been demonstrated by Louis Althusser in his essay "Contradiction and Overdetermination," in *For Marx* (London: Allen Lane, Penguin Press, 1969).

40. The line of reasoning very summarily outlined here suggests that a careful analysis of the place and implications of the concepts of productive forces and revolutionary situation in Marxist-Leninist theory is a more promising way to tackle the problem than to rely textually on the *Grundrisse* drafts, comparing them with *Capital,* as in Martin Nicolaus's otherwise important essay "The Unknown Marx," *New Left Review* 48 (1968).

41. Lukács, p. 241.

42. See Max Horkheimer's essay "Geschichte und Psychologie," where the structural condition is replaced by "the opposition between the growing powers of men and the social structure." *KT* 1, p. 17.

43. József Révai, review of *Geschichte und Klassenbewusstsein, Archiv für die Geschichte des Sozialismus und der Arbeiterbewegung* 11 (1925):227–36.

44. *An die Nachgeborenen.*

45. This essay has been mainly focused on the work of Horkheimer, chronologically and substantively the "founder" of the Frankfurt School, with some discussion of the separate itinerary of Marcuse. Comparatively little space has been devoted to Adorno. While Adorno's contribution to the main methodological and philosophical themes of the school seems to have been secondary, his specific applications of them are often the most dazzling exercises within the collective oeuvre—perhaps because his chosen fields of music and literature more properly permit a strictly "critical" analysis—criticism—than social formations or political systems.

References

KT Max Horkheimer, *Kritische Theorie,* 2 vols. Frankfurt: S. Fischer, 1968.
KG Herbert Marcuse, *Kultur und Gesellschaft*, 2 vols. Frankfurt: Suhrkamp, 1965.
N Herbert Marcuse, *Negations*. Boston: Beacon, 1968.
ZfS *Zeitschrift für Sozialforschung*

23

From Hegel to Marcuse

Lucio Colletti

Here the points to keep clear are as follows. First, the interpretation of Hegelian Reason as mere subjective *raison,* the reason of the empirical individual, rather than the Christian Logos. *Ergo*—as on the Left and especially in Bruno Bauer—a reading of Hegel along the lines of subjective idealism (Fichte). Reason is the *Ich,* the ego, the mass, etc.; hence the interpretation of the Hegelian realization of the Christian logos as a political program through which to realize "ideals," what reason prescribes for men. (The fundamental principle of Hegel's system, says Marcuse, is that "that which men believe to be true and good, should be realized in the effective organization of their social and individual life." Compare instead Marx's letter to Ruge of September 1843: "We shall not confront the world in a doctrinaire fashion with a new principle—here is the truth, kneel here!")

Second, the insertion of the Hegelian motif of the *destruction of the finite* into this liberal-radical idea of revolution (lacking in the entire interpretive tradition, except perhaps in Stirner and Bakunin); but while in Hegel this motif is linked to transsubstantiation or the immanentization of God, lacking any theological significance, in Marcuse it tends to acquire the literal or ordinary meaning.

Hence the antithesis which is central to *Reason and Revolution* and also to *One-Dimensional Man;*[1] the opposition between "positive thought" and "negative thought." The first corresponds to the intellect, i.e. to the principle of noncontradiction as a (materialist) principle of common sense and science. The second corresponds to dialectical and philosophical "reason." Positive thought is that which recognizes the existence of the world, the authority and reality of facts; vice versa, negative thought is that thought which denies facts. The finite outside the infinite has no true reality. The truth of the finite is its ideality. (Hegel said that "the proposition that the finite is ideal constitutes idealism.") Facts, insofar as they are external to and different from thought, and therefore insofar as they constitute the opposite of reason, are not reality but nontruth. Truth is the realization of reason; it is the idea or philosophy translated into reality. Marcuse writes: "According to Hegel the facts by themselves possess no authority. . . . Everything that is given must find a justification before reason, which consists of the reality of Man and nature's possibilities."

The opposites of Hegel are Hume and Kant. Marcuse writes:

> If Hume was to be accepted, the claim of reason to organize reality had to be rejected. For, as we have seen, this claim was based upon reason's faculty to attain truths, the validity of which was not derived from experience and which could, in fact, stand against experience. . . . This conclusion of the empiricist investigations did more than undermine metaphysics. It confined men within the limits of "the given," within the existing order of things and events. . . . The result was not only scepticism but conformism. The empiricist restriction of human nature to the knowledge of "the given" removed the desire both to transcend the given and to despair about it. In Hegel, on the other hand, the realization of reason is not a fact but a task. The form in which the objects immediately appear is not yet their true form. What is simply given is at first negative, other than its real potentialities. It becomes true only in the process of overcoming this negativity, so that the birth of the truth requires the death of the given state of being. Hegel's optimism is based upon a destructive conception of the given. All forms are seized by the dissolving movement of reason which cancels and alters them until they are adequate to their notion.

> Hegel's philosophy is, therefore, a negative philosophy. . . . It is originally motivated by the conviction that the given facts that appear to common sense as the positive index of truth are in reality the negation of truth, so that truth can only be established by their destruction.[2]

A formidable example of the heterogenesis of ends! The old spiritualist contempt for the finite and the terrestrial world reemerges as a philosophy of revolution, or rather of revolt. It is not a fight against particular sociohistorical institutions (such as profit, monopoly, or even socialist bureaucracy); it is a fight against objects and things. We are crushed by the oppressive power of facts. We suffocate in the slavery of recognizing that things exist. "They are there, grotesque, stubborn, gigantic, and . . . I am in the midst of Things, which cannot be given names. Alone, wordless, defenceless, they surround me, under me, behind me, above me. They demand nothing, they don't impose themselves, they are there."[3] Before this spectacle of things, indignation grabs us by the throat and becomes Nausea. We may easily compare it with the roots of a tree. "I was sitting, slightly bent, my head bowed, alone in front of that black, knotty mass, which was utterly crude and frightened me." Here is the absurdity which cries vengeance to the sky: "soft, monstrous masses, in disorder—naked, with a frightening, obscene nakedness." The absurdity is not that Roquentin should be pursuing his wretched little petty-bourgeois *débauche* in the public parks, while a Daladier or even a Laval is in power. The absurdity lies in the roots of the tree. "Absurdity was not an idea in my head, or the sound of a voice, but that long-dead snake at my feet, that wooden snake. Snake or claw or root or vulture's talon, it doesn't matter. And without formulating anything clearly, I understood that I had found the key to Existence, the key to my Nauseas, to my own Life."[4]

The manifesto of this destruction of things—which is what Marcuse too means by "revolution"—he himself points out in Hegel's writings. Emancipation from the slavery of facts coincides with the night and nothingness, which Hegel discusses in an early text, *The Difference between Fichte's and Schelling's Systems of Philosophy:* "Here in his first philosophical writings," Marcuse reveals, "Hegel intentionally emphasizes the negative function of reason: its destruction of the fixed and secure world of common sense and understanding. The absolute is referred to as 'Night' and 'Nothing' in order to contrast it with the clearly defined objects of everyday life. Reason signifies the absolute annihilation of the common sense world."[5]

Here we are dealing with familiar romantic themes. *The Difference . . .* is full of echoes of Schelling. But since Marcuse descends from Heidegger, perhaps we can see this celebration of Night and Nothingness (precisely where we were accustomed to expect the "sun of the future") as an echo of *Was ist Metaphysik?* Heidegger is a master of the *Nichtung.* And if even *Nichtung* is not *Vernichtung* nor *Verneinung,*[6] this philosophical "revolution" is hardly clear. It not only locates "authentic" and no longer "estranged" existence "in the clear night of Nothing," but as if this were not enough, prey to some pedantic fury, it insists on specifying that "Nothing itself annuls."

The Idealist Reaction against Science

The true direction of Marcuse's position lies in the so-called critique of science. The opposition of "positive thought" and "negative thought," of "intellect" and "reason," of noncontradiction and dialectical contradiction, is above all else the opposition of science and philosophy. For Hegel, says Marcuse, "the distinction between intellect and reason is the same as that between common sense and speculative thinking, between undialectical reflection and dialectical knowledge. The operations of the intellect yield the usual type of thinking that prevails in everyday life as well as in science."[7]

This Hegelian and romantic critique of the "intellect" reemerged precisely at the turn of the century, with the so-called idealist reaction against science.[8] The two tendencies meet and coincide, as Croce saw well, in their critical-negative aspect. In *Logic as the Science of the Pure Concept,* he comments on Bergson's critique of science:

> All these criticisms directed against the sciences do not sound new to the ears of those acquainted with the criticisms of Jacobi, of Schelling, of Novalis and of other romantics, and particularly with Hegel's marvellous criticism of the abstract (i.e. empirical and mathematical) intellect. This runs through all his books from *The Phenomenology of Mind* to *The Science of Logic,* and is enriched with examples in the observations to the paragraphs of *The Philosophy of Nature.*[9]

It is not possible here to describe all the variations on this "idealist reaction" against science. *Entsteht die Wissenschaft vergeht das Denken*[10] (science is born, thinking departs). Let it pass as far as Heidegger is concerned, since he no longer deceives anyone. But this same commodity is today sold on the Left. Horkheimer and Adorno:

> Science itself has no consciousness of itself; it is a tool. But the enlightenment is the philosophy which identified truth with scientific system. The attempt to establish this identity which Kant undertook, still with philosophical intentions, led to concepts which made no sense scientifically. The concept of the self-understanding of science conflicts with the concept of science itself. . . . With the sanctioning—achieved as a result by Kant—of the scientific system as the form of truth, thought set the seal on its own nullity, because science is technical performance, no less remote from reflecting upon its own ends than other types of labour under pressure of the system.[11]

This critique of science is immediately presented as a critique of society too. The scientific intellect is the form of thought which prevails in practice and in everyday life. The *Allgemeingültigkeit* of science, i.e. the universality of its statements, is identical with the impersonality and anonymity of social life. These developments are already present *in nuce* in Bergson. Our intellect, says *Creative Evolution,* is a function which is "essentially practical, made to present to us things and states rather than changes and acts." But things and states are only views, taken by our mind, of becoming. There are no things, there are only actions. Therefore, if "the thing results from a solidification performed by our intellect, and there are never any things other than those that the intellect has thus constituted,"[12] this means that the natural world, which science presents to us as reality, is in fact only an artifact. Matter is a creation of the intellect, things are the crystals in which form takes and coagulates our vocation to *objectify*, to "solidify" the world in order to act on it practically and transform it.

In addition to this original solidarity of science and materialism, there is the solidarity of materialism and society, of science and communal life. We objectify to act on the world, but this objectification is also a means toward intersubjective communication. Authentic or personal existence and social or impersonal existence result in two diverse subjects, one "fundamental" and the other "superficial" and "fictitious"; "two different selves, one of which is, as it were, the external projection of the other, its spatial and, so to speak, social representation." The spatialization or materialization of reality, says Bergson, is already an opening to social life.

> The greater part of the time we live outside ourselves, hardly perceiving anything of ourselves but our own ghost, a colourless shadow which pure duration projects into homogenous space. Hence our life unfolds in space rather than in time; we live for the external world rather than for ourselves[13]. . . . This intuition of a homogeneous milieu enables us to externalize our concepts in relation to one another, reveals to us the objectivity of things, and thus, in two ways, on one hand by getting everything ready for language, and on the other by showing us an external world, quite distinct from ourselves, in the perception of which all minds have a common share, foreshadows and prepares the way for social life.[14]

All the essentials are here in embryo: science as objectification or reification, and society as estranged and alienated existence.

It is impossible to discuss the elaboration and development these themes underwent at the hands of the various currents of irrationalism and German vitalism. Here I can only indicate the decisive "turn" that was signalled by Lukács's famous book in 1923. As the author himself recognized in a self-critical declaration in September 1962[15] and later in the introduction to the English edition of *History and Class Consciousness,* it is based on a move from the theory of alienation (fetishism or reification) elaborted by Marx to that of Hegel. The analysis of capitalist fetishism is expounded in this work in the terminology of the Hegelian critique of the materialism of the scientific intellect and common sense. That is, the "fetish" is not capital or commodities but natural objects external to thought. The division which capital introduces between the laborer and the objective conditions of labor is replaced by the distinction which the "intellect" introduced between subject and object, with the consequence, as Lukács himself has since observed, that a "socio-historical problem is thus transformed into an ontological problem." Capitalist reification becomes the product of the materialist intellect and of science, whose analytical vision of reality is denounced as "positivistic and bourgeois." Meanwhile the proletariat is equated with philosophical Reason, i.e. with that reason which unifies or "totalizes" (as they say nowadays) what the intellect and common sense spend all their time distinguishing.

The most important consequence of this shift was that by confusing Marx with Hegel, *History and Class Consciousness* presented the obscurantist contents of the idealist critique of science in the "revolutionary" form of a critique of bourgeois society. Emerging from the school of Rickert and Lask, and influenced to no small extent by the vitalist Simmel's *Philosophy of Money* (the German Bergson), Lukács ended up, in this work, by inscribing Marxism itself in the arc of the idealist reaction against science inaugurated at the turn of the century, whose remote presuppositions lie, as we have seen, precisely in the Hegelian critique of the "intellect."

The "fetish" is the natural object investigated by science. "Reification" or, as Bergson said, *le chosisme*, is the product of the scientific intellect that chops and breaks up (the famous *morcelage*) the fluid and "living" unity of the real into the "fictitious" outlines of the objects that have to be used for practical-technical action. Alienation, in short, is science, technology. After absorbing these themes, Lukács broadcast them in his turn, enriched with fresh appeal. The old repugnance of philosophical spiritualism toward production, technology, and science, in a word, the horror of machines, was now cloaked by the fascination of the critique of modern bourgeois society.

The kernel of Marcuse's philosophy is here. Oppression is science. "Reification" is to recognize that things exist outside ourselves. The dialectic of the "here and now"—i.e. the dialectic of the scepticism of antiquity—with which Hegel, at the beginning of the *Phenomenology*, destroys sensory certainty in the existence of external objects, appears to him as the emancipation of man himself.

> The first three sections of the *Phenomenology* are a critique of positivism and, even more, of "reification". . . . We borrow the term "reification" from the Marxist theory, where it denotes the fact that all relations between men in the world of capitalism appear as relations between things. Hegel hit upon the same fact within the dimension of philosophy. Common sense and traditional scientific thought take the world as a totality of things, more or less existing *per se*, and seek the truth in objects that are taken to be independent of the knowing subject. This is more than an epistemological attitude; it is as pervasive as the practice of men and leads them

to accept the feeling that they are secure only in knowing and handling objective facts.[16]

The conseqence of Marcuse's argument is an indiscriminate indictment of science and technology, or, to use Marcuse's expression, of "industrial society." If we examine it closely, the argument is the same as that which had already formed the basis for Husserl's *Krisis* (not to mention Horkheimer and Adorno's attacks on Bacon and Galileo). It has also been the theme which in recent decades has nourished all the publicity about the so-called crisis of civilization (for example Jaspers's *Vom Ursprung und Ziel der Geschichte*). The "evil" is not a determinate organization of society, a certain system of *social relations*, but rather industry, technology, and science. It is not capital but machinery as such. Marcuse, let no one be mistaken, is the product of that very tradition which today fears him so much.

Conclusion

In *One-Dimensional Man* there is a short section, where the author takes his distance from Marx, which can provide our concluding point. Marcuse writes:

> The classical Marxian theory envisages the transition from capitalism to socialism as a political revolution: the proletariat destroys the *political* apparatus of capitalism but retains the *technological* apparatus, subjecting it to socialization. There is continuity in the revolution: technological rationality, freed from irrational restrictions and destruction, sustains and consummates itself in the new society.[17]

Marcuse does not agree with this analysis because he believes that the roots of today's evil lie precisely in the technological apparatus as such. But he is right to locate here the basis of Marx's entire thought.

Capitalist development is the development of modern industry. Under capitalism this growth of modern industry is inseparable, according to Marx, from a series of seriously negative phenomena: exploitation, wage labor, the formation of the "industrial reserve army," etc. But nevertheless, says Marx, under this cover capitalism prepares the conditions for the liberation of man: an enormous increase in the productivity of labor (even though in the form of the "intensification" of exploitation of labor power); the eradication of local and national boundaries and the unification of the world (even though in the form of a world market); the socialization of man, i.e. his unification with the species (although by means of the formation of the factory proletariat). The *Manifesto* states:

> The bourgeoisie has through its exploitation of the world market given a cosmopolitan character to production and consumption in every country. To the great chagrin of Reactionists, it has drawn from under the feet of industry the national ground on which it stood. . . . In place of seclusion and self-sufficiency, we have intercourse in every direction, universal interdependence of nations.

The meaning of this passage is summarized by Marx in the following formulas: contradiction between modern productive forces and the capitalist envelope in which they have developed; between the social nature of industrial production and the still private mode of capitalist appropriation.

The use and abuse of these formulas have rendered them meaningless. But beneath the veneer of time it is not difficult to recognize in them two important points. The first is that Marx does not deduce the nature and quality of the forces concerned in the transformation and liberation of modern society from a mere ideal of philosophic Reason (which is, anyway, always the reason or ideal of X or Y) but from a scientific analysis of modern society itself. This means, therefore, not from an a priori evasion of the object under examination (the so-called destruction of the finite) but from the individualization of the role of the working class in the modern productive process. (Marx wrote to Ruge: "We do not anticipate the world dogmatically, but rather wish to find the new world through criticism of the old. Until now the philosophers had the solution to all riddles in their desks, and the stupid outside world simply had to open its mouth so that the roasted pigeons of absolute science might fly into it.") This means that the "solution" is not deduced from any external *deus ex machina*, but that one appeals for it to *real* historical forces, internal to that society itself. The second is that precisely this function in the modern productive process makes the working class (from the mere manual laborer to the engineer) the historical agent through which the new society can inherit the essentials of the old: the modern productive forces developed in its bosom—science, technology, industry, the critical spirit, and the experimental style of life.

For Marx, and Marcuse is right this time, "there is continuity in the revolution." I would say that the difference between revolution as a real historical act and the Promethean attempt of the Great Refusal is all here. The revolution is an act of real life; it is born from history and has the consciousness to give rise once again to real historical conditions. It is the liberation of forces accumulated by historical development. It is the recuperation, at a higher level, of all that humanity has seized in the course of its history; seized from nature and seized from the irrational suggestions of myth.

Marcuse's Great Refusal, on the other hand, is defined precisely by its ahistoricity. It is a *total negation* of the existing. Having diagnosed that "technology is the major vehicle of reification," he can only seek liberation either before history or after it. In either case, outside the bounds of common sense. "Terror and civilization are inseparable;" "the growth of culture has taken place under the sign of the hangman;" "we cannot abandon terror and conserve civilization."[18] These are aphorisms of Horkheimer and Adorno which help us understand Marcuse's Great Refusal.

A barely cultivated literary taste would soon desire to turn elsewhere. A barely expert reader would recognize immediately their origin in Heidegger. ("Der Mensch irrt. Die Irre, durch die der Mensch geht, ist nichts.")[19] Yet we must make allowances for them. These are the last "flowers of evil" of the old spiritualism and of its impotent desire to destroy things: the swan song of two old gentlemen, slightly nihilistic and *demodés*, in conflict with history.

Postscript on Marcuse

For Marcuse, alienation and fetishism are not the product of wage labor, of the world or commodities, and capital. The "evil" for him is not a determinate organization of society, a certain system of *social relations*, but rather industry, technology, and science. It is not capital but machinery as such. *One-Dimensional Man* is entirely prisoner to this old assertion. The book is brilliant and contains a series of minute and honest observations. But when the substance is examined it is easy to see that it is not an indictment of capital but of technology. Marcuse, who rebels against "integrated thinking," does not realize that he is arguing like the most integrated of bourgeois sociologists. For him there is no difference between capitalism and socialism; what he fights is industrial society, "industry" without class connotations, industry in itself. Not machinery insofar as it is *capital*, not the capitalist employment of machinery, but machinery plain and simple.

In his analysis of the Industrial Revolution in the chapter of *Capital* entitled "Machinery and Heavy Industry," Marx frequently underlines the bourgeois economists' identification of machinery and capital.

> Since, therefore, machinery *considered alone* shortens the hours of labour, but, when in the service of capital, lengthens them; since in itself it lightens labour, but when employed by capital heightens the intensity of labour; since in itself it is a victory of man over the forces of Nature, but in the hands of capital, makes man the slave of those forces; since in itself it

increases the wealth of the producers, but in the hands of capital, makes them paupers—for all these reasons and others besides, says the bourgeois economist without more ado, the *treatment of machinery itself* makes it as clear as noonday that all these contradictions are a mere *semblance* of the reality, and that, as a matter of fact, they have neither an *actual* nor a *theoretical* existence. Thus he saves himself from all further puzzling of the brain, and what is more, implicitly declares his opponent to be stupid enough to contend against, not *the capitalistic employment of machinery,* but *machinery itself.*[20]

Here Marx is aiming at the position of bourgeois apologetics. In this case, the identification of capital with machinery allows the determinate historical contradictions derived from the capitalist employment of machinery to be spirited away, i.e. to be presented as mere appearances. On the other hand, it allows the positive advantage and qualification of machinery as such—i.e. the increase in the productivity of labor—to appear as a merit of capital itself. Marcuse's position, which is certainly not that of the economists, nevertheless repeats its operations, but in the opposite sense. Marcuse equates machinery and capital, not to attribute to the latter the advantages of the former, but rather to impute to machinery the enslavement and oppression of the laborer for which in fact capital is responsible. In the first case, the result is the apologetic approach of *Vulgärökonomie.* In the second case, it is the so-called romantic critique of bourgeois society—i.e. a critique of the present, not in the name of the future but in the name of, and inspired by, nostalgia for the past. For the economist, whoever wants modern productive forces, i.e. machinery and modern industry, must also want capitalist *relations of production.* (As Marx writes: "No doubt he is far from denying that temporary inconvenience may result from the capitalist use of machinery. But where is the medal without its reverse? Any employment of machinery, except by capital, is to him an impossibility. Exploitation of the workman by the machine is therefore, with him, identical with exploitation of the machine by the workman.")[21] For Marcuse, on the contrary, whoever does not want exploitation, or rather (given that for Marcuse, in the final analysis, exploitation does not exist), whoever does not want integration, must return to patriarchal conditions of life, or even perhaps to feudalism—a subject upon which our author expatiates like any high-thinking social prophet. Taken to its extreme, Marcuse's approach leads to that cult of primitivism and barbarism which the abstract spiritualism of the bourgeois intellectual so easily turns into. His perspective, like that of Horkheimer and Adorno, is one of Luddism, as Lukács recognized: "If we say that manipulation has arisen as a consequence of technological development, then to fight manipulation we must transform ourselves into some kind of Luddites fighting technical development" (see *Gespräche mit Georg Lukács* [Hamburg, 1969]).

This reference to the romantic critique of bourgeois society may seem amazing. This is an adversary about which we never think. In reality, there is not just Marxism on the one hand and bourgeois-capitalist ideology on the other; the game is more complex and has three players. No less than against bourgeois ideology, Marxism fights against "the romantic conception that," says Marx in his *Grundrisse,* "will accompany the former as its legitimate antithesis until its dying day."

Obviously Marcuse is not Carlyle or Sismondi. But he is neither of these, apart from a series of obvious reasons, also because of the subtly apologetic implications of his entire argument. The concept of industrial society, the idea of industry without class connotations, or industry "in and for itself" that he shares with bourgeois sociology (see for example Dahrendorf), is to defer involuntarily to the great corporations. Industry and technology are oppressors everywhere, in Russia no less than in America. "Soviets plus electrification" (Lenin) is an empty illusion. If we wish to escape oppression it is pointless to attempt socialism. The remedy that Marcuse proposes is in keeping with the gravamen of his analysis. It is enough for us all to oppose the system with the "Great Refusal" and set sail together, perhaps, for Tahiti.

I am not criticizing Marcuse in the name of the ideology of the Soviet bureaucratic caste. Nevertheless, in the case of this author our judgment cannot be anything but severe. Marcuse is a critic of Marx of long standing, and the bases of his criticism (see for example *Soviet Marxism* [London, 1958]) are derived from the old social democratic revisionism. His attribution to Marx of the theory of "absolute immiseration" and the theory of "collapse" are derived from Bernstein (see pp. 22–28). The theory of "ultraimperialism" which he uses again and again to illustrate how neocapitalism is capable of anything, is derived from Kautsky (p. 33ff.). His whole argument, from beginning to end, is an attempt to show that Marx has been surpassed! And the more general and vague the contents of his analysis, the more resolute Marcuse's conclusions. The Marxian theory of the proletarian revolution has been surpassed; "the Marxist notion of the organic composition of capital" has been surpassed; and "with it the theory of the creation of surplus value."[22]

The first book by Marcuse that I read was *Reason and Revolution* in the second American edition (New York, 1965). The book contained a supplementary chapter which was not reproduced in the recent Italian edition. If this chapter were translated today many ambiguities would disappear and Marcuse would be seen for what he is, a fierce critic of Marx and socialism. Moreover, the concluding pages of *One-Dimensional*

Man appear even more significant as to the point of view from which he conducts his criticism. Here Marcuse acclaims "the interior space of the private sphere"; he invokes "that isolation in which the individual, left to himself, can think and demand and find"; he acclaims the "private sphere" as the only one which "can give significance to freedom and independence of thought." How can we fail to recognize in this the old liberal rhetoric?

Notes

1. Herbert Marcuse, *One-Dimensional Man* (Boston: Beacon, 1964), chs. 5, 6.
2. Herbert Marcuse, *Reason and Revolution* (New York: Oxford University Press, 1941), pp. 26–27.
3. Jean-Paul Sartre, *Nausea* (London: H. Hamilton, 1965), p. 180.
4. Ibid., pp. 181–83.
5. Marcuse, *Reason and Revolution*, p. 48.
6. Martin Heidegger, *Was ist Metaphysik?* (Frankfurt: V. Klostermann, 1949), p. 31.
7. Marcuse, *Reason and Revolution*, p. 44.
8. This expression, "the idealistic reaction against science," was originally used in a positive sense by Aliotta in his book of 1912. It has rightly been reproposed—but with the meaning of a regressive phenomenon—by F. Lombardi in *Il senso della storia* (Florence: G.S. Sansoni, 1964), p. 165ff.
9. Benedetto Croce, *Logic as the Science of the Pure Concept* (London: Macmillan, 1917), p. 556.
10. Martin Heidegger, *Über den Humanismus* (Frankfurt: V. Klostermann, 1949), p. 39.
11. Max Horkheimer and Theodor W. Adorno, *Dialektik der Aufklärung* (Amsterdam: Querido, 1947), p. 104.
12. Henri Bergson, *Creative Evolution,* trans. A. Mitchell (New York: H. Holt, 1911), pp. 261–62.
13. Henri Bergson, *Time and Free Will (Essai sur les données immédiates de la conséquence),* trans. F.L. Pogson (London: Allen & Unwin, 1910), p. 231. First French edition 1888.
14. Ibid., p. 236.
15. In I. Fetscher, *Der Marxismus,* vol. 1 (Munich: Piper, 1962).
16. Marcuse, *Reason and Revolution*, p. 112.
17. Marcuse, *One-Dimensional Man*, p. 22.
18. Horkheimer and Adorno, *Dialektik der Aufklärung*, p. 256.
19. Martin Heidegger, *Vom Wesen der Wahrheit* (Frankfurt: V. Klostermann, 1949), p. 22. On the same page, the notion of history as error.
20. Marx, *Capital* (New York: International, 1967), vol. 1, p. 441 (my italics).
21. Ibid., pp. 441–42.
22. Marcuse, *One-Dimensional Man,* p. 28.

24
Understanding Marcuse

Lucien Goldmann

It is not easy to connect in just a few pages with one of the most complex figures of contemporary thought. And it is even harder when one tries to account for the resounding echo struck by Marcuse's ideas in the thinking of students all over the world—particularly since the relation of the young to Marcuse is based on a misunderstanding.

But let us begin by sketching, if only roughly, Marcuse's place in contemporary philosophy. A disciple of Martin Heidegger, Marcuse's first work, *Hegels Ontologie und die Grundlegung einer Theorie der Geschichtlichkeit,* in which he traced Heidegger's origins, quickly won him an academic reputation. Later he moved toward a Marxism which was at the same time Hegelian and Heideggerian, and published a series of philosophical papers in *Die Gesellschaft,* the theoretical organ of German social democracy. His position brought him close philosophically to Lukács and Karl Korsch, both of whom were, however, more committed politically and more radical. (Lukács was a Communist, and Korsch, at first a Communist, later joined the leftist opposition.) Marcuse became the third leading figure in what was called at that time "European Marxism."

Here we must pause for a moment. Heidegger, Hegel, Marx—the juxtaposition of these names seems strange in the light of the philosophical history in the last forty years. It is much less so if one returns to the original texts and the intellectual climate of 1928–32. Existential philosophy had its intellectual origins in Lukács's *Soul and Form,* which appeared in 1911; and on the basis of this book, a dialogue developed between two thinkers who, although unequal in intellectual force, would each play an important role in the thought of the first half of the twentieth century—Georg Lukács and Ernst Bloch.

As he moves from the existential, tragic, and Kantian position of *Soul and Form,* through the Hegelianism of the *Theory of the Novel,* toward the Marxist philosophy of history in *History and Class Consciousness,* Lukács is unshakable in his demand for clarity and rigor, with the criticism that this implies of all forms of false consciousness and ideology.

Against this position, Bloch unflaggingly defends human and intellectual values, and especially the creative historical function of a kind of thought which goes beyond the scientific and positivistic—utopianism. Bloch is asking whether a hope which conceives itself and is philosophically if not literally founded in a future radically different from the present, a future which men must create by their actions—whether such a hope is negative ideology or positive, false or historically creative. Though a bit schematic, this description provides the essence of the argument carried on in a series of works which are particularly important in the history of European thought.

In sum, on the one hand we have Lukács's *Soul and Form, Theory of the Novel,* and *History and Class Consciousness,* teeming with concrete analyses and totally reevaluating philosophy and the social sciences; on the other hand, Bloch's more poetic and speculative *Spirit of Utopia,* and the simpler and more popular *Thomas Münzer: Theologian of Utopia.* University sociology will be influenced by the two through Karl Mannheim's *Ideology and Utopia,* and especially by Lukács, through the first part of Heidegger's *Sein und Zeit.* Most academically trained readers read *Sein und Zeit* in a completely different way and did not see the relation. It was left to Sartre in *Being and Nothingness* to read in Heidegger things that are not there (the theory of the transindividual subject and of the team), but which are at the roots of the work, that is to say, in Lukács. In the same way, at a much deeper level, Marcuse, beginning in 1928, finds Heidegger's Hegelian and Marxist origins (which were in fact mediated through Lukács).

If I remember the *Die Gesellschaft* articles correctly, (though I have not read them for twenty years), there was still an important difference between Marcuse and Lukács. Heidegger, developing a dualist philosophy of history, radically separated ontology from the ontic, philosophy from the positivist sciences (and also the authentic from the inauthentic, the elite from the mass, and so on). A monist, faithful in this respect to Hegel and Marx, Lukács refused any such separations. While radically criticizing not only any positivism, any concept of science in the indicative mood, but all metaphysics, all philosophical theory which was conceptually closed and separated from action and from totality, Lukács called for a philosophical science and a scientific philosophy (not even conceiving that one could develop on a purely conceptual level a Marxist ontology of history). Each of these positions was internally coherent and defensible.

Marcuse's articles had a curious and ultimately significant characteristic: They were written on a conceptual and philosophical level, beyond concrete historical analysis—on the plane where any philosophy of the concept, from Plato, to Descartes, to Kant, is situated. It was a Heideggerian leftover within the system that was no longer Heideggerian, but a leftover which, given the Marxist position he had adopted, led Marcuse's thought back at least in this respect to a more conceptual theoretical philosophy, with which Marx, Lukács, and Heidegger actually had broken.

The second important phase (1933–41) in Marcuse's evolution is his membership in the Frankfurt School to which, basically, he still belongs. At that time, it was made up of the three principal figures who continue to represent it today—Horkheimer, Adorno, and Marcuse; along with Walter Benjamin, who died during the war, and Erich Fromm and Leo Löwenthal, who both later left the group. In France, its principal activity was the publication of a magazine called *Zeitschrift für Sozialforschung*, and a book on authority and the family. In the United States they put out a theoretical work signed by both Horkheimer and Adorno, *Dialektik der Aufklärung* (Dialectic of Enlightenment), centered on the dialectic between progressive concreteness and the abstractions of classical rationalistic philosophy that lent themselves to oppression.

Marcuse's articles in this period (some of which have just been republished), though written in a different style—and in any case more clearly—deal with the same problem. Horkheimer and Adorno concentrated on those elements of liberal rationalism which imperceptibly laid the ground for the abrupt shift to totalitarianism in the most advanced industrial countries and for the compliance of the middle class, particularly in Germany; and Marcuse also attempted to show that this acceptance of oppression and exploitation on the part of the middle class is inherent in idealist philosophy. But far more than the other thinkers of the school, Marcuse emphasized the critical character of idealist philosophy, its demand for rationality, for happiness, which despite reactionary distortions is preserved from its heroic period, mainly from the Renaissance. These promises and demands, he suggests, have been adopted by revolutionary ideology, by materialism and "critical philosophy"—a term by which, given the prudent tone of the journal, Marcuse means Marxism.

In sum, a difference of accent within a unified school. At most, one can say that Marcuse ties that negative criticism which will become more and more a characteristic of the Frankfurt School to a demand for radical change, at the risk—which seems to him to be the price of continuing the true philosophic tradition—of placing himself at least partially in the domain of utopian thought.

But suddenly, with Hitler's victory and the development of Stalinism in Russia, passages appear which show a removal from what—as a way of designating certain political and philosophical strains in the radical tradition—has been conventionally called "dialectic" thought. It was one of the central ideas of dialectical thought, particularly that of Marx and Lukács, that instead of counterposing abstract moral or utopian ideas to reality, one should try to understand their birth within the real world. Against those who attributed to him a moral and normative position, Marx insisted that his program expressed the vision of a genuine social force within capitalist society, the proletariat. And even if (as seems more and more to have been the case) Marx's specific analysis was incorrect, the notion that any valid idea must be the expression of a group consciousness within society, which means *the partial or total identity of the subject and the object of thought*, remained the pivot of dialectical thought. We read in Marcuse's "Philosophy and Critical Theory," an article published in 1937:

> But what if the evolution foreseen by Critical Theory dosen't take place, if the forces which should bring about change are repulsed and seem to be beaten? To the extent that the truth of the theory itself is not weakened by the fact, it can be seen in a new light, illuminating new aspects of its subject. Many facets of the theory thus take on a different weight, giving it more distinctly the character of a critical theory. . . .
>
> Like philosophy, Critical Theory is opposed to any justice which accepts reality as it is, to any complacent positivism; but, contrary to philosophy, it develops its goals only on the basis of the actual tendencies of the social process. Thus it does not fear being reproached as utopian, as ideas of new orders customarily are. If truth is not realizable within the existing social order it will always appear utopian to that order. Such a transcendence doesn't speak against its truth, but for it. For a long time, the utopian element has been the only progressive element in philosophy; hence constructs of a better State, of the greatest possible pleasure, of perfect happiness, of eternal peace, etc. . . . The stubbornness born of a partisanship to the defence of truth against all appearances has been replaced today in philosophy by extravagance [*Schrullenhaftigkeit*] and unlimited opportunism. Critical Theory remains faithful to such stubbornness in so far as it is a real quality of philosophical thought. The current situation displays it even more conspicuously; retreat has come at a moment when economic conditions for the transformation had been realized.

I have quoted this long passage because it indicates clearly the effect of the victory of National Socialism and Stalinism on the evolution of Marcuse's thought (and probably on that of the entire Frankfurt School). The defeat of progressive forces may have rendered official philosophy completely reactionary, but it brought Critical Theory back to Utopia, from a going beyond philosophy to progressive positions within philosophy.

Did Marcuse and the Frankfurt School go over to Ernst Bloch's position? Not completely, because Bloch continued to develop an optimistic utopianism while Marcuse, Horkheimer, and Adorno applied themselves to the criticism of existing social reality and the cultural life, while pointing out the retrograde aspects of the rationalism of earlier periods. Without denying the existence of a connection between Bloch's position and that of the Frankfurt group, one could formulate their not inconsiderable differences schematically as the opposition between optimistic utopianism and a critical pessimism, if it is understood that Bloch's utopia implies critique of the existing as well, and that the realistic criticism of the Frankfurt School involves (and, in Marcuse, always will) the idea of a future society free from oppression and radically different from the present order.

Both positions were opposed to that so-called dialectical thought which history had already proven wrong. Only a few partisans of what is now called "institutional Marxism" defended that lying and oppressive ideology. There can be no question in that period of the intellectual superiority of the Frankfurt School over the dogmatic mouthings of the orthodox Marxists. The few critical Marxists shut themselves off in historical or aesthetic analyses, or, like Erich Fromm, moved toward "revisionist" psychoanalysis; and the situation was to remain unchanged until the work of several Italian thinkers and the early studies of the self-taught Serge Mallet, among others.

But back to Marcuse, whose *Reason and Revolution: Hegel and the Rise of Social Theory* was published in 1941. For a long time, *Reason and Revolution* was considered the representative work of progressive Hegelianism, a sort of counterpoint to the conservative Hegelianism represented by Kojève's *Introduction to the Study of Hegel*, and by Eric Weil; and I confess that I myself read it then that way. But on reading it today, one can see that it is not truly dialectical: It uses Hegel and a Hegelian language to return to a Kantian and Fichtean position, brought up to date and radicalized, and in some respects close to Sartre. Though *Reason and Revolution* may be radical and critical, nowhere does it contain the idea of the identity of subject and object, of reason and reality, fundamental to the belief that the only valid and realizable goals are those discoverable within the real tendencies of the social process. When Hegelian terms appear, they are used to signify a moral, Kantian desire to incarnate the subject in the object and create a society responsive to the rational aspirations of the individual, or at least to a reason which is at the same time individual and universal.

Stemming from this, Marcuse is separated from the dialectical position at two important points. The absence of an empirical and transcendental subject *within* society as a basis for reason poses the problem of reason's empirical or transcendental character. And just as it did for seventeenth-

and eighteenth-century rationalism, the absence of an *internal* progressive force created for Marcuse the problem of an external one. On neither of these points are Marcuse's texts completely unequivocal. It does seem clear, however, that the need for coherence has forced him to the idea of an individual subject (even to an intelligible or transcendental one) and to the idea of a dictatorship (albeit transitional and pedagogical) of philosophers and wise men. In an article published in 1948, Marcuse criticized *Being and Nothingness* for its confusion between the ontological and the empirical conceptions of the individual subject, without questioning the idea of a subject as such. And in 1965 he added a paragraph subscribing to the views of Sartre, who had become the theoretician of a "radical conversion" and a "morality of liberation."

Similarly, in a 1954 afterword to *Reason and Revolution*, he made the same point: "The Marxist idea of the proletariat as the absolute negation of capitalist society brings together in *one* concept the historical relation between the realization of liberty and its necessary conditions. In a rigorous sense liberation *supposes* liberty; it cannot be realized unless it is the work of free individuals and is carried forward by them—by individuals free of need and free of interests of domination and oppression." He ends with the following lines: "The idea of another form of reason and liberty, such as had been envisioned as much by Idealism as by Dialectical Materialism, again appears utopian; but the triumph of the repressive forces which oppose progress doesn't diminish the truth of this utopia. The total mobilization of society against definitive liberation of the individual, which constitutes the historical content of the present period, shows to what point the possibility of this realization is real."

On the question of the conditions of transformation one idea recurs in Marcuse's writing:

> The frustrations and deflections of the satisfaction demanded by the general will need not necessarily be somber and inhuman, nor need reason necessarily be authoritarian. Nevertheless, the question remains: how can civilization create freedom without being prevented from doing so, given that an absence of freedom has become an element and indeed the nucleus of the psychic apparatus? And if this is not the case, who has the right to establish and impose objective scales of value?

> From Plato to Rousseau, the idea of an educational dictatorship exercised by those who are generally thought to have acquired a knowledge of the true good is the only answer. This answer has been forgotten. Since then, knowledge concerning the creation of a humane existence for all men has no longer been limited to a privileged elite, the facts have become too evident, and the individual consciousness would understand them without difficulty if it were not methodically prevented and turned aside from doing so (*Eros and Civilization*).

Though characteristically ambivalent, the passage is coherent. The educational dictatorship is the only honest solution. If it has been forgotten it is not because knowledge is not accessible to all, but because in modern society it is accessible only to rational consciousness and not to empirical consciousness, which is kept from the truth by social repression. The only thing we can count on is the educational dictatorship of the philosophers, even though it is only temporary and transitional.

Thus Marcuse arrives at a position both opposed and related to Heidegger's. Opposed, because Heidegger's reactionary theory of elites reserved the consciousness of Being for the philosopher, the poet, and the statesman, who were radically opposed to the inauthentic mass (the study of which is for sociology and positivist psychology)—a theory which was a philosophical justification for a permanent dictatorship of leaders and elites. Marcuse's progressive philosophy maintained the accessibility of liberty and universal knowledge to all men, and opposed the very idea of an elite. Still, there are similarities. For, in contrast to Marx's and Lukács's monism, which brought together in a single concept the relation between freedom and necessity, Marcuse arrived at a radical version of Heidegger's dualism. Marcuse's rested on a sharp but not dialectical opposition between oppression and liberty, the existing and the ideal, the empirical and the rational, the given and the utopian—a duality which despite his democratic spirit forced him to entertain the idea of a dictatorship of the wise.

The postwar period was one of profound disappointment for humanists and "critical thinkers." For, instead of the new society free of oppression and exploitation which the struggle against fascism had led them to expect, what they saw developing in the West was an extension of the old system in the form of corporate capitalism and a consumer society. It is not surprising, therefore, to see that Marcuse and the Frankfurt School have not had to modify their critical attitudes toward existing society; in fact, they reinforced them, pointing out that there has been a growing gap between the humanistic hopes animating the cultural life of the West and its social realities. (Adorno's work has been most important here, even if one disagrees with him, and has played a constructive role, particularly among German intellectuals and students.)

It is true that postwar Western society was essentially different from both pre–World War I liberal society and German fascism; and to maintain a critial position in this period, to refuse to accept a social order in which, in contrast to the earlier liberal era, living standards were rising and, in contrast to fascism, freedom of expression and parliamentary rule were reestablished—in sum, to understand this situation, a new social analysis was required. This Marcuse accomplished in *Eros and*

Civilization and *One-Dimensional Man,* two complementary works which
have profoundly influenced contemporary thought. To summarize briefly,
Eros and Civilization deals with the relations between society and
individual aspirations. Through Freud, Marcuse, like the rest of the
Frankfurt School, came to the fundamental conflict between instinctual
drives (the libido and the death wish) and social organization, which
must repress them in the name of the reality principle. In Freud, the
antagonism had an "essential" and ahistorical meaning; Marcuse, as a
sociologist and philosopher of culture, gives it historical dimension,
without, however—like Fromm—minimizing the opposition between
man's basic desires and social repressiveness.

For Marcuse, the concrete form of the reality principle in contemporary
society is the principle of productivity. He goes on to distinguish between
the repression which is necessary at any time to maintain a rational
society, and the actual repression that supports the oppressive social
structure. Thus he arrives at a concept of surplus repression, which is
measured by the difference between necessary and actual repression; and
he demonstrates that while the extraordinary productivity of contemporary
society has reduced necessary repression to a minimum, the structure
of corporate capitalism and consumer society has greatly increased actual
repression. Hence surplus repression has grown considerably, affecting
not only the possibilities of liberation in which Marcuse is primarily
interested, but also our understanding of past societies.

One-Dimensional Man argues that capitalism and consumer society
represent a threat to culture and the development of personality. From
Pascal through Kant, Hegel, and Marx, dialectical philosophy had defined
man by the double dimension of his adaptation and his transcendence
of reality, that is, by the real and the possible. And earlier philosophy,
based on reason, had also led to the transcendence of reality. Transcendence
is rooted in Western culture. But, now, as Marcuse demonstrates quite
brilliantly, we have for the first time a stratified society, which, by raising
the standard of living and manipulating men's minds, makes people
more adaptable and reduces the drive toward transcendence. Thus creativity as well as human liberty are threatened by the monster of social
planning: We have one-dimensional man, well paid, comfortable, knowing
only how to execute other people's decisions, and consume.

One cannot overestimate the importance of *Eros and Civilization* and
One-Dimensional Man, the first works to formulate the program of the
opposition which, despite Marcuse's pessimism, was *in reality* developing
in the advanced industrial societies. Traditional socialist thought spoke
mainly in the name of the suffering masses, and only incidentally in the
name of freedom and equality. By continuing to press economic demands,

which corporate capitalism was actually satisfying, the Left was beginning to find itself in a false position; it was becoming more dogmatic, more ideological, and more artificial. Marcuse's achievement—despite one's disagreements with him—was to formulate the contemporary problem. He was first to account for the growing discontent all over the world. To be sure, it had been voiced in avant-garde literature and in the other arts, but they had been treated with contempt by positivist sociologists, who, like Dahrendorf, spoke ironically of "cultural criticism" or the "bohemian literature of St. Germain-des-Prés," until it became evident that their own enormous apparatus of analysis and research had missed the fundamental tensions of the society they were designed to study.

Marcuse's thought demanded as a transitional factor a force outside consumer society, and this led him occasionally to refer to the idea of a dictatorship of the philosophers (which perhaps explains the fact that, according to several witnesses, he once in a lecture defended the role of the universities). But Marcuse did relate other forces alienated from the consumer society—the Third World, American Blacks, and bohemians— to his central idea of philosophers as the agents of historical change.

As for the controversy between Marcuse and psychoanalytical and Marxist revisionism, Adorno and Marcuse had been for a long period on a much higher level, not only than academic sociology and literary criticism, but also than official Marxism. But Fromm's more recent work in psychoanalysis, and that of a few Italian theoreticians and of Serge Mallet in sociology, who abandoned the letter of Freudian and Marxist theories to preserve their spirit, is of a still different order. I am not competent to judge the differences between Marcuse and Fromm. It seems evident, however, that Freud had no idea of forces for the adaptation of the individual to society or vice versa. Thus one cannot go along with Marcuse when he lumps together all attempts to adjust the individual to the social system, whether critical or not.

Similarly, one has to question Marcuse's attitude toward what is currently known as Marxist revisionism. There is an essential difference between the accommodation to existing society on the part of a whole sector of thought which still calls itself socialist, and the doctrine of "revolutionary reformism," associated with Serge Mallet and André Gorz. Discarding such outworn ideas as the pauperization of the working class, the proletariat as the universal revolutionary class, the necessity of a political revolution as a condition for any economic transformation, and even the idea of the dictatorship of the proletariat in Western societies, the "revolutionary reformists" insist on the development of a new working class. But even this is a concession to the tradition because it involves workers in advanced branches of production and a growing number of specialists who might be expected to reject corporate capitalism and demand an economic democracy based on the management of businesses and social institutions. Here too Marcuse refused to admit the existence of differences between the two kinds of revisionism and lumped them together as ideologies of integration into existing society.

Finally, if one tries to relate Marcuse to the positivist and conservative theories of academic sociology, one sees that just as in his relation to Heidegger, there is both a radical opposition and a certain agreement. Raymond Aron's and Daniel Bell's "end of ideologies" is conservative and apologetic, as is Riesman's theory of "the disappearance of internal radar," despite his superior mind. Against these optimists, Marcuse has warned us of the one-dimensional man's threat to both culture and liberty, and has pointed to a transcendental reason which condemns consumer society in the name of human dignity and freedom. He saw what was coming where the Arons and the Bells saw only hope. But having said this, it is still true that they all—Aron, Marcuse, Bell, Riesman—share the mistaken belief that Western society has been so stabilized that no serious opposition can be found within it.

The events of May and June 1968 in France quickly refuted this analysis and revealed that the transition from monopolistic capitalist society to the corporate capitalist society of the postwar period was much more complex than it appeared to Marcuse. Roughly (these ideas, which I can present here only schematically, will be the subject of a separate study), there were two phases of prewar capitalism: liberal capitalism and the monopolistic capitalism of trusts, what I have called "crisis Capitalism." In the one, there was partial, liberal regulation of the market and philosophic individualism, rationalism, and empiricism. In the other, there was no regulation of the market, social and economic crises, and existential philosophy. The *third* phase of Western capitalism—which sociologists have variously labeled consumer society, mass society, technocratic society, corporate capitalism—emerged from the second industrial revolution and the mechanisms of economic self-regulation designed to replace the liberal regulation of the market which had been virtually abolished by industrial monopolization. These technical and economic transformations took place within traditional legal and political social relations, which had been modified in a deeply authoritarian and managerial way. And modification without legal and institutional change was possible because it was accepted by a generation, mostly over forty, who felt it satisfied its most important need, that for greater income and security.

But the realization of those objectives, taken for granted by a new generation, would sooner or later make the authoritarian managerial relations which arose from the exclusive need to augment productivity seem less and less rational. The richer a society, the more important are culture, liberty, and personal authenticity, as against sheer efficiency and production of goods. In addition, a new class, the strata of skilled workers, technicians, and specialists, would become dissatisfied with the one-dimensional role of well-paid executors. To make decisions more democratic they would demand that social relations be geared to the new technical and economic structure of society. They would ask for self-management—and a term which before May 1969 was known only to a small number of intellectuals and students, became in a few weeks a slogan of all salaried workers in France. At that point it became evident that what had appeared to theoreticians as a period of stabilization and equilibrium was only a phase in the adjustment of Western industrial societies to the second industrial revolution, and that it had been superseded.

The concrete forms of these first symptoms of opposition still have to be analyzed, particularly the split, characteristic of all social upheavals that open the way for a new era, between the consciousness and the actual behavior of the actors. Why did these upheavals manifest themselves first among students, and why were they so intense and widespread in France? Again, I cannot go into all this here. But I should mention in passing one process ignored by positivist sociology: the transformation of the function and nature of the French university.

Liberal society was marked by a duality in social relations: It was authoritarian, almost monarchical in business, and democratic and egalitarian in the market, as well as in the economic, political, legal, and cultural spheres within the dominant class. Its authoritarian structure, however, extended beyond the factory to other institutions, and, mainly in the middle layers of society, to the family. The independent burgher was head of both factory and family. This meant that in liberal society the transition between childhood and adulthood was difficult: As children, future "directors" had to obey the father (and later the schoolmaster as well); as adults, they had to be egalitarian, democratic, and critical in their relations with their peers. Their adult role was authoritarian only in the sense that it involved the exercise of responsibility and authority, and not that of obedience within their profession or business. To effect the shift, the university, reserved for the sons of the managerial class, was called upon to inculcate the critical spirit and independence of judgment, and to ensure the progression from obedience to autonomy, from submissiveness to responsibility and equality. To fulfill these functions, the university had to be largely liberal and critical.

In the transition to postwar corporate capitalism, the extension of managerialism and authoritarianism had an odd effect on society as a whole. The state, virtually separated from the economy during the liberal phase, now became the most important economic agent. In place of the opposition between the authoritarian organization of production and the democratic organization of social and political life characteristic of liberalism, a closer relation between the state and the economy developed, encouraged by the intervention of the state in the economy and the compliance of people whose standard of living had been rising. Hence formal constraints or institutional change were almost superfluous. The natural evolution toward a technocratic society widened the gap between the technocrats who make decisions and the specialists and technicians who execute them.

The old independent burghers have also been gradually replaced by the new intermediate salaried classes—what Mallet calls "the new working class"—made up of more or less qualified specialists living at least at the level of the old directors, but no longer having the same status or responsibilities. These new specialists are busy executing as well as they can decisions made elsewhere, in which they have no hand. As a result, the structure of family life has been affected: These intermediate salaried classes are not prepared by their professional and social life to assume the familial authority of the old independent burghers. This explains in part why the growth of hierarchic and authoritarian social relations in modern society has been accomplished by an increasing liberalization of family life in the intermediate layers of society, and a decline in parental authority, particularly that of the father.

In this situation, the function of the university has been completely reversed. Now it must effect a transition from a liberal family structure. It must convert young people accustomed to a relatively high degree of independence into specialists ready to serve as executors in an economic and social hierarchy. The old critical and liberal university has been slowly and imperceptibly transformed into an authoritarian institution nurturing a mandarin class. The transformation was facilitated by the enormous growth of its student body, made possible by the new affluence and by the university's Napoleonic structure, which up to this point had been counterbalanced by its function, but which now lent itself admirably to the new demands of a technocratic society. Yet the university proved inadequate as a preparation for the new society. For when each field is too big for one man, and often researchers, assistants, and advanced students are superior to their professors, the only way to cope is to replace authority with teamwork among researchers and teachers.

The transformation of the French univeristy (which to my knowledge has not been noted by academic sociologists) does not itself account for the student revolt. Many factors were responsible, which I cannot go into here. Marcuse, like other sociologists, must have been surprised by the revolts of the Blacks in the United States and the student movements, which he had neither foreseen nor inspired. Nevertheless, these movements, which were mainly cultural and moral and only partly and in certain countries economic, had found their most complete theoretical formulation in his works. As early as 1965, Marcuse declared his sympathies in the famous piece "Repressive Tolerance," at the conclusion of which he stated that no educator, no intellectual, could justifiably condemn those who took the risks of a violent revolt against established oppression. Later, faced with the movements of May and June 1968 in France, he indicated in a lecture at the colloquium of Korcula a turn toward optimism, referring to an essay he was writing to be called "Beyond One-Dimensional Man." But he also emphasized once again the need for a radical transformation, and insisted on the danger of being satisfied with partial changes. Ernst Bloch, who was present, immediately hailed Marcuse's support of Bloch's own optimistic utopianism, which Marcuse, with some reservations, confirmed.

Let me end this essay with an anecdote from a discussion which took place in May at a colloquium organized by UNESCO to celebrate the centenary of the publication of *Das Kapital*. Marcuse had just read a characteristically distinguished paper. Four members of the colloquium then reproached him for his pessimism and his radical critique. A Communist philosopher explained that all was fine in his party and in the working class; a Soviet economist delivered an apology for the Soviet Union; an English participant let it be known that everything was going very well in Red China; finally a professor from the University of Paris sang the praises of Western society.

At that point I asked for the floor to note that all these critics of Marcuse proved he was right, since they revealed how well they were integrated into some oppressive and reified part of the contemporary world, while at that very moment, in Paris and in other great cities of Europe and the world, millions of students were demonstrating by their acclaim of Marcuse and by their own acts, that if his criticism of modern society was often justified, if it had given a theoretical dimension to their movement, he was nevertheless essentially wrong in his pessimism, in his theory of one-dimensional man, and in his belief that there were no forces of revolt and renewal in consumer society.

25

The Limits of Praxis
in Critical Theory

Wolf Heydebrand and Beverly Burris

The Frankfurt School of Critical Theory was and is a diverse intellectual phenomenon which has ranged over many fields, many decades, and two continents. It has thus defied easy categorization and has stimulated prodigious amounts of commentary. The present paper will make no attempt at comprehensiveness, but will rather attempt to illuminate one narrow but integral aspect of the ongoing Frankfurt School tradition: its approach to the question of praxis, to concrete political efforts aimed at individual and social emancipation and transformation. We will focus in particular on the work of Jürgen Habermas, a contemporary Critical Theorist working to extend the tradition of Critical Theory to the current sociopolitical situation so as to stress its relevance for our troubled times.

The Frankfurt School crystallized largely in response to the limitations of economistic and deterministic varieties of Marxism, with their objectivistic theories of revolution. Critical Theory, on the other hand, was to restore to Marxism the fullness of the dialectic of subjectivity and objectivity by incorporating psychology, aesthetics, and the critique of ideology so as to explore both the preconditions and fetters of praxis. Thus from the beginning the Frankfurt School was concerned with developing a theory of praxis. The corollary contradiction was the fact that all their theoretical work on this question was developed in isolation from concrete political activity. The Frankfurt School rigorously maintained autonomy from any political groups or parties, as well as from concrete political action of any kind. Here we will explore the various aspects of the Frankfurt School's approach to praxis with the aim of assessing them and their relation to this autonomy from actual praxis.

Theory as Praxis

The predominant approach the Frankfurt School took to the question of the relationship between theory and praxis was to conceive of theory,

401

and especially critique and negation, as an integral component of viable praxis. The precise delineation of this relationship varied among the different members of the school, and also changed over time. For instance, in 1935 Horkheimer conceived of theoretical clarification as clearly distinct from and subordinated to praxis: "Truth is a moment in correct praxis; he who identifies it with success leaps over history and becomes an apologist for the dominant reality" (1935:345). For the early Horkheimer, theory could expose and analyze societal contradictions, but only praxis could overcome these contradictions. However, Horkheimer also defended the autonomy of Critical Theory in "Traditional and Critical Theory" in a quasi-Kantian manner; a certain distance from the irrationality of social reality is a necessary precondition of critique, historical relativization, and theoretical innovation: "Critical theory is not concerned only with goals already imposed by existent ways of life, but with men [sic] and all their potentialities" (1976:223).

This emphasis on autonomous theoretical practice was even more marked in Marcuse's *Reason and Revolution*: "The concrete conditions for realizing the truth may vary, but the truth remains the same and theory remains its ultimate guardian. Theory will preserve the truth even if revolutionary practice deviates from its proper path. Practice follows truth, not vice versa" (1960:322). By 1941, the world political situation was such as to justify a certain pessimism concerning the potential for revolutionary praxis, making a retreat into autonomous Critical Theory seem warranted. This trend toward pessimism regarding the possibility for concrete political action, initially engendered by fascism and Stalinism, was to lead to a reliance on the life of the mind as a refuge for authentic praxis, a reliance which was to become even more marked in the postwar years in America; America in the 1950s was equally antithetical to praxis.

If, as Jay contends, fantasy and the idea of praxis were "the two cardinal expressions of Critical Theory's refusal to eternalize the present and shut off the possibility of a transformed future" (1973:78), the later Frankfurt School increasingly came to emphasize fantasy and autonomous thought, as the possibilities of embodying their theoretical vision through revolutionary praxis came to seem increasingly slim. To the later Frankfurt School, especially Marcuse, reality seemed more and more "one-dimensional," to be rejected in its entirety, rather than viewed as embodying contradictions which might be overcome. Existing leftist political tendencies seemed as depressing as politics in general, and the school's own empirical findings concerning the authoritarian personality structure of workers made traditional Marxism seem naive in its optimism concerning the revolutionary potential of the proletariat. Instrumentalism and positivism were fast becoming hegemonic; the only alternative for Critical Theorists was theoretical negation and autonomous speculation. Adorno, for instance, combatted positivism by defending speculation as "thought which renounces its own narrowness" (1976:5), pointing out that "the prohibition of fantasy is all too compatible with societal statics" (1976:51). Praxis was increasingly seen as a capitulation to the instrumentalism and positivism which the "negative dialectic of the enlightenment" had brought about.

Art as Praxis

As yet another alternative to instrumentalism and positivism, some members of the Frankfurt School turned to art, literature, and music as forms of aesthetic praxis. These aesthetic forms had the capacity to reveal societal contradictions while preserving the *promesse de bonheur* which their transcendence would imply. For Adorno, aesthetics was far more than a theory of art; it concerned the very nature of the subject-object relationship. Art, and especially music for Adorno, preserved the non-identity of the subject with objective reality, expressing instead a non-alienated relationship of creative praxis. As Buck-Morss puts it: "Adorno found a structural convergence between Schönberg's music's inner logic and a Marxist critical understanding of the reality of contemporary society" (1977:23). By listening to authentic music or observing authentic art, the subject would experience not passive contemplation but an original and activist relation to the world.

Adorno, of course, realized that authentic aesthetic forms were becoming increasingly rare, and that "fetishistic" and regressive forms of artistic appropriation were becoming the norm as individuality was progressively eroded. For Adorno, the only valid response was to preserve the autonomy of authentic aesthetic form:

> Today, every phenomenon of culture, even if a model of integrity, is liable to be suffocated in the cultivation of kitsch. Yet paradoxically, in the same epoch it is to works of art that has fallen the burden of wordlessly asserting what is barred to politics. . . . This is not a time for political art, but politics has migrated into autonomous art, and nowhere more so than where it seems to be politically dead [1974:318].

In this regard, he diametrically opposed Lukács and Brecht in defending authentic art as an autonomous realm of praxis which would change consciousness by its very aesthetic form, and need not have political content to have political validity. Here he is perhaps reflecting Nietzsche (a not inconsiderable influence on the Frankfurt School in general and Adorno in particular), who said: "Art must insist on interpretations that are germane to its essence. . . . This world can be justified only as an aesthetic phenomenon" (1956:143).

Marcuse, like Adorno, was seeking to refute more orthodox Marxist aestheticians by focussing on the form rather than the content of art and by stressing the autonomy of art from the prevailing sociohistorical situation. However, for Marcuse, it was the more psychological dimensions of aesthetic experience that were politically salient. True art and literature release the subject's repressed subjectivity and eroticism by transcending societal determination so as to express the "beautiful image of liberation" (1977:6). Art evokes another "reality principle," one which is more liberated and committed to eros, to pleasure and the life instincts. Art expresses a "concrete, universal humanity" which points toward the emergence of human species being: community, freedom, and liberation. Art is therefore a productive force qualitatively different from labor, and one that can achieve political relevance only by virtue of its autonomy from social and political imperatives: "The autonomy of art contains the categorical imperative: 'Things must change' " (1977:13).

Thus the Frankfurt School combined an ongoing concern about the relation between theory and praxis with an increasingly pronounced pessimism concerning the possibilities of concrete political action. Their early emphasis on societal contradictions, which can be revealed theoretically and artistically but only fully transcended through praxis, became transformed into a view of society as one-dimensional, instrumental, and highly impervious to change. As Adorno put it, paraphrasing Hegel: "The whole is the untrue." In such a world, theory and aesthetics can preserve the *promesse de bonheur*, the "beautiful image of liberation," but only to the extent that they are autonomous from social reality and its hegemonic ideology. The "culture industry" and positivistic tendencies both within Marxism and in non-Marxist social science are seen as increasingly salient threats to this requisite autonomy. In the perverse dialectic of the enlightenment, people dominated nature, but were in turn subject to the unleashed forces of domination so that praxis became all but impossible. Existing political efforts are seen as inevitably instrumental, as exacerbating oppression rather than pointing toward liberation. Thus, as Adorno disparagingly said of the student unrest of the sixties, which the Frankfurt School had unwittingly helped to inspire: "When I made my theoretical model I could not have guessed that people would try to realize it with Molotov cocktails" (1969:204).

Habermas's Conceptions of Praxis

The work of Jürgen Habermas reflects both continuities and discontinuities with the Frankfurt School tradition. Like the original members of the school, Habermas has been intent on supplementing orthodox Marxism's overemphasis on production by examining other productive forces and more subjective dimensions. In addition, he has contributed to the Frankfurt School project of criticizing instrumental rationality in all its forms and attempting to delineate an expanded conception of a more substantive rationality. Like the original Frankfurt School, Habermas has turned to psychoanalysis and culture as crucially important in forging neo-Marxist theories of subjectivity and substantive rationality. Finally, like the earlier Critical Theorists, Habermas has stressed the transformed nature of the economy under state capitalism: The ways in which the expanded role of the state and of science and technology have led to fundamental changes in the nature of capitalism, changes which have important implications for both theory and praxis.

Habermas also differs from the original Frankfurt School in several important respects. He has explored different dimensions of psychoanalysis and culture, being, for instance, more intent on examining the psychoanalytic method in order to broaden dialectics to include greater subjectivity. Moreover, he has gone beyond the Frankfurt School's emphasis on high culture to recapture a more anthropological sense of culture as life style and as forms of interaction and intersubjectivity. Most importantly, his approach is directly antithetical to the pessimism of the original Frankfurt School. He has discovered the contradictions in state-regulated capitalism, and a potential legitimation crisis, as opposed to one-dimensional domination and hegemony. More than any other Critical Theorist, Habermas has been concerned with the question of mediating the theory/praxis dichotomy so as to begin to realize the new and democratic forms of interaction which are the prerequisites of substantive rationality and a liberated society.

Throughout his work Habermas has been concerned with the question of praxis. In *Theory and Practice* he poses the question: "How, within a political situation, can we obtain clarification of what is practically necessary and at the same time objectively possible?" (1973:44). He makes the distinction between practical and technical interests to emphasize the insufficiency of functional rationality, of mere technical considerations, to constitute liberating praxis. In technocratic society there is an escalating scale of continually expanded technical control over nature and a continually refined administration of human beings and their relations to each other by means of social organization. . . . The social potential of science is reduced to the powers of technical control—its potential for enlightened action is no longer considered. The empirical, analytical sciences produce technical recommendations, but they furnish no answer to practical questions [1973:254].

In contrast to the earlier members of the Frankfurt School, Habermas does not reject positivism and empirical science or technology as inherently oppressive. Scientific understanding and technical expertise are important components of Habermas's conception of praxis. However, technical interests become ideological when they purport to be the only approach to social reality so as to imply the irrelevance of political debate and practical decision making.

In his search for a model of emancipatory praxis which would incorporate science without being technocratic, Habermas turned to psychoanalysis. The psychoanalytic model goes beyond empirical science in two important ways: It is practical because of its concern with meaning, and it is critical because it has emancipatory intent. Psychoanalysis involves a "depth hermeneutics" of distorted human activity, a decoding of the manifest content so as to reveal the latent content and meaning of neurotic behavior and dreams. And central to this process of depth hermeneutics is the necessity of grasping "not only the meaning of a . . . distorted text, but the *meaning of the text distortion itself*" (1968:220). To understand the meaning of the text distortion involves analysis of the past history of the individual and scientific self-reflection. Finally, psychoanalysis is inherently emancipatory in its intent, since it is oriented toward freeing the subject from the irrationality of neurotic behavior so as to allow him to act freely and consciously.

Habermas views this psychoanalytic model of depth hermeneutics with emancipatory intent as potentially applicable to social institutions and as a potential model of praxis. Social institutions are often as irrational and counterproductive as neuroses: "The same configurations that drive the individual to neurosis move society to establish institutions. . . . Like the repetition compulsion from within, institutional compulsion from without brings about a relatively rigid reproduction of uniform behavior that is removed from criticism" (1968:276). As in psychoanalysis, the task of a depth hermeneutics of society is to provide this critical dimension by penetrating the manifest content, the reified appearance of institutions, in order to reveal the repressed fantasies and needs of society. Depth understanding of the irrational and unnecessary oppressiveness of social institutions is the first step toward their transformation.

To continue his exploration of the prerequisites of praxis, Habermas turned to a more intensive analysis of intersubjective interaction and communication. Here he utilizes his distinction between work and interaction as two aspects of praxis: "I do not mind at all calling both phenomena work and interaction praxis. Nor do I deny that normally instrumental action is embedded in communicative action. But I see no reason why we should not adequately analyze a complex" (1973:158–59). Moreover, under technocracy, work and interaction are increasingly separated and relegated to different spheres of life. According to Habermas, Marx overemphasized work as being overly dominant in the work/interaction dialectic, and ignored the relatively autonomous sphere of interaction. In order to supplement Marx's analysis of political economy and refute the earlier Frankfurt School's pessimism concerning one-dimensional instrumentalism, Habermas in his more recent work has increasingly turned to an analysis of intersubjective interaction and communication as crucial components of democratic decision making and collective praxis, as a universal pragmatics.

In analyzing the political dimensions of communication, Habermas focuses on the systematic distortions caused by power relationships which pervert attempts at communication, as well as on the depoliticization of the public sphere under technocracy. The context for democratic discussion of political issues is all too often lacking, and when communication does occur, it is usually systematically distorted by "relations of power surreptitiously incorporated in the symbolic structures of the systems of speech and action" (1973:12). However, Habermas is optimistic about the capacity of communicative competence to begin to transcend these limitations on communication. Communicative competence is distinct from linguistic competence in that it involves the mastery of social norms of communication rather than formal linguistic rules. Communicative consensus rests on four separate validity claims: that the utterance be comprehensible, that its propositional content be true, that the intentions of the speaker be manifest, and that the utterance be appropriate to the social context. Communicative competence is therefore "the ability of a speaker oriented to mutual understanding to embed a well-formed sentence in relations to reality" (1979:29). The immediate and manifest aim of communicative competence is understanding and consensus; however, according to Habermas, communicative competence also anticipates the "ideal speech situation," which is a communicative situation that is not systematically distorted, but in which "there is no other compulsion but the compulsion of argumentation itself" (Bernstein 1978:212). Communicative competence is thus an important first step of praxis for Habermas, for not only does it facilitate discussion of political issues, it also directs the communicating actors toward liberation from constraints on interaction:

> No matter how the intersubjectivity of mutual understanding may be deformed, the design of an ideal speech situation is necessarily implied in the structure of potential speech, since all speech, even intentional deception, is oriented toward the idea of truth [and understanding]. . . . In so far as we master the means for the construction of the ideal speech situation, we can conceive the ideas of truth, freedom, and justice, which interpenetrate each other, although of course only as ideas. On the strength of communicative competence alone, however, and independent of the empirical structures of the social system to which we belong, we are quite unable to realize the ideal speech situation, we can only anticipate it [1970b:144].

Habermas has not been very concerned with elucidating the further stages of praxis which would allow for the realization of the ideal speech situation. One reason for this reluctance might be the historically specific and varied nature of concrete political situations; Habermas has been concerned with developing a universal pragmatics, whereas concrete political action tends to be more particularistic. However, Habermas has addressed the general question of the relationship between theory and praxis. In his 1971 introduction to *Theory and Practice*, he implies that to some extent communicative interaction mediates between the two, but also assumes such interaction to be a component of praxis. In the final analysis, the constraints of action must be bracketed so that theoretical discussion will be unencumbered:

> Discourse . . . is a form of communication in which the participants do not exchange information, do not direct or carry out action, nor do they have or communicate experiences; instead they search for arguments or offer justifications. Discourse therefore requires the virtualization of constraints on action. This is intended to render inoperative all motives except solely that of a cooperative readiness to arrive at an understanding. . . . Solely the structure of this peculiarly unreal form of communication guarantees the possibility of attaining a consensus discursively which can gain recognition as rational [1973:18–19].

And yet, would such an "unreal" consensus, based merely on a discursive imperative and untainted by information, action, or experience, be very meaningful? Habermas is attempting to argue against the facile and mechanical unification of theory and praxis into an instrumental politics ("theory . . . can by no means legitimize a fortiori the risky decisions of strategic action" [1973:33]), but at the risk of dichotomizing the two.

At times Habermas does seem to approach a more dialectical theory of the interrelationship between theory, discourse, and action. Certainly he is clear in refuting a Leninist approach to praxis in favor of a more democratic one:

> Decisions for the political struggle cannot at the outset be justified theo-
> retically and then be carried out organizationally. The sole possible jus-
> tification at this level is consensus, aimed at in practical discourse, among
> the participants, who, in the consciousness of their common interests and
> their knowledge of the circumstances, are the only ones who can know
> what risks they are willing to undergo, and with what expectations [1973:33].

However, in general Habermas gives priority to theory and to "discourse that is free of experience and unencumbered by action" (1973:21), and avoids, whenever possible, the "risky decisions of strategic action." He is arguing for a somewhat ambiguous relative autonomy of theory and theoretical discussion from praxis.

Yet with his emphasis on communication and interaction, Habermas has taken an important first step toward grounding Critical Theory and making it into a "universal pragmatics." Moreover, he has made valuable efforts to reveal the political in what appears as the personal, and has raised the critical question of how to begin to approximate democratic structures of interaction in the face of increasingly technocratic structures of control. Despite these valuable contributions, Habermas is still some distance from achieving an adequate conception of praxis.

Critique of Habermas's Conceptions of Praxis

The notion of limits of praxis in the title of our paper was intended to acknowledge the considerable achievement of Critical Theory in bridging subjectivism and objectivism in sociological theory and in transcending both in the direction of articulating the idea of emancipatory interests and practical intent. Critical social science provides a theoretical meth-odology that goes beyond the controversy of methodological individualism versus holism and of value neutrality versus ideological engagement, a theoretical framework that seeks to establish a connection between knowl-edge and interest, between social theory and social policy. But while critique, self-reflection, emancipatory interest, and practical intent may all be seen as elements or moments of praxis, they are not the same as praxis, and especially not the same as Marx's notion of praxis which emerged from his critique of both Hegel and Feuerbach. To be sure, insofar as the Frankfurt School intellectuals "saw themselves," as Oscar

Negt put it, "not as the avant-garde of [the historical-substantive forces of reflection], but as their conscience, the standard criticism of them as lacking praxis misses the mark and loses sight of their concept of the relationship between theory and *praxis*" (1978:77). However, what is at stake here is not their actual praxis, but their concept and vision of praxis.

In contrast to the Frankfurt School's dominant versions of praxis as theory, aesthetic praxis, critique, and self-reflection, Marx's notion in the "Theses on Feuerbach" (1967:400), the "German Ideology" (1967:403ff.), and the *Grundrisse* (1973) refers to praxis as human, sensuous, critical, practical, and revolutionary activity. As is well known, the concept includes different dimensions of activity, such as productive activity, creative activity (e.g. art, play, fantasy), symbolic activity (e.g. speech, communication, and interpretation), and cooperative activity (e.g. inter-action, collective action, and organization). The primary thrust of the concept of praxis is toward processes of transformation and self-trans-formation, an emphasis which distinguishes it from the concept of action and, of course, from mere behavior.

We have already indicated that Adorno and Marcuse had a highly developed notion of aesthetic praxis, a notion that was curiously absent in the earlier work of Habermas and has only very recently reappeared in the form of "aesthetic rationality" as a sphere separate from both technical-instrumental rationality and moral-practical rationality. Haber-mas's early work on the idea of praxis is grounded in a special interpretation of Hegel's *Philosophy of Mind* (Habermas 1973:142). Paradoxically, this interpretation results in the decomposition of the Marxian concept of praxis into a dualistic construct of work and interaction, or *techne* and praxis. "A reduction of interaction to labor or derivation of labor from interaction is not possible," Habermas (ibid.:159) argues. Habermas claims that

> Marx does not actually explicate the interrelationship of interaction and labor, but instead, under the unspecific title of social praxis, reduces the one to the other, namely: communicative action to instrumental action. Just as in the *Jena Philosophy of Spirit* the use of tools mediates between the laboring subject and the natural objects, so for Marx instrumental action, the reproductive activity which regulates the material interchange of the human species with its natural environment, becomes the paradigm for the generation of all the categories: everything is resolved into the self-movement of production [ibid.:168–69].

Thus in Habermas's interpretation, Marx's concept of praxis is reduced to work or technical-instrumental activity, while Habermas proposes to restore to the discourse on praxis the "lost" second dimension, namely interaction or practical (substantive) rationality.

Habermas is correct in saying that there is "no reason why we should not adequately analyze a complex," although it is somewhat confusing when the term *praxis* refers at one time to the whole complex and at other times to only part of the complex. However, a more problematic question is whether we are talking about the analysis of a complex concept such as praxis, or whether the analysis is guided by a transcendental philosophical interest in "a priori categorial distinctions" (Bernstein 1978:223) which dissolve the complex and reduce it to a dualistic construct such as work and interaction. As Bernstein remarks, Habermas's "typical strategy in criticizing previous thinkers is to show that they confuse categorially distinct levels of action . . . the validity of these criticisms is itself dependent on the acceptance of Habermas's categorial distinctions. The tables can be turned on Habermas by arguing that he seeks to introduce hard and fast distinctions where there is really only continuity" (ibid.: 220–21).

Similarly, the very distinction between theory and praxis, between reason and commitment, and between enlightenment and liberation (Habermas 1973:177, 253, 268) presupposes a separation of praxis from theory. Moreover, it relegates praxis either to a form of technical instrumentalism and pragmatism or to an irrational decisionism (ibid.: 265), or else to the notion of nontheoretical, blind, mindless activity. In short, the dualistic separation has the hierarchical effect of putting theory ahead of praxis. It reduces praxis to what Habermas himself, in his critique of the student movement of the 1960s, labeled "infantilism," "compulsive action," "delusion," "verbal masturbation," and action for the sake of "short-term narcissistic gratifications" (Negt 1968:12, 15). Once theory is analytically separated from the notion of praxis, it must be added back into it, leading to constructs such as the "unity of theory and practice," "theoretical presuppositions of praxis" (ibid.:15), action as demanding orientation (Habermas 1973:265), or "committed reason" (ibid.: 268). Technical and substantive rationality are distinguished only to be reunited under special conditions. On the "proper distinction between these two forms [of rationality]," Habermas states, "depends the relation of theory and praxis in a scientific civilization" (ibid.).

We can see now that the analytical decomposition of the concept of praxis leads to the establishment of its partial aspects as separate and relatively autonomous spheres, a theoretical result which reduces praxis from a dialectical category to a dualistic and neoidealistic construct. Habermas shares this fateful analytical ambition with Althusser, Popper, and more recently, Giddens. Althusser (1976) separates economic, political, and ideological practices from each other and assigns them to separate, "relatively autonomous" regions within a given social formation. Ideological practice is forced into the theoretically blindest role: Ideology is merely "lived experience"; in other words, the category of experience is given a relatively low ontological status. Scientific and theoretical practice are altogether outside the social formation and therefore are kept distinct from everyday life, history, and social praxis.

Similarly, Popper (1982) distinguishes between three separate spheres of reality or "worlds": World I, that of physical states and historial events; World II, the realm of subjective interpretation and experience; and World III, objective knowledge produced by critical rationalism. Giddens (1979) proposes to analyze action in terms of three levels of consciousness: practical consciousness, discursive consciousness, and unconscious sources of cognition and action. In all these categorical distinctions, the taxonomic impulse tends to crowd out or displace the dialectical core of Marx's concept of praxis.

We have already seen Habermas's attempts to apply the psychoanalytic paradigm, with its primacy of interaction and interpretation, to the question of collective self-transformation. But as Oscar Negt and others have pointed out in a collection of essays entitled "The Left Responds to Jürgen Habermas" (Negt 1968), such a transfer of models from therapy to political praxis is not without its problems. Political praxis is constituted in the unity of enlightenment and action. The unity of communicative and instrumental activity is a conception which Habermas (1973:36) rejects with the almost tautological statement: "The autonomy of theory and enlightenment . . . is required for the sake of the independence of political action."

We are arguing here that the ultimate form of nonalienated praxis is constituted in individual and collective self-transformation, self-organization, and self-determination. This form of organized "doing" is not adequately theorized by Habermas inasmuch as his vision of political emancipation remains at the level of discussion, interaction, communicative action, critique, undistorted communication, massive-collective enlightenment, and consensus formation, all under the imperative of affective neutrality and, more importantly, of the continued split between state and civil society, general and private interest, public and private sphere. Habermas's analysis remains at the level of political emancipation as visualized by the young Hegelians, and does not take the last step toward human emancipation proposed by Marx in "The Jewish Question." As Marx put it: "Political emancipation is indeed a great step forward. It is not, to be sure, the final form of universal human emancipation, but it is the final form within the prevailing order of things. It is obvious that we are here talking about actual, practical emancipation" (Marx 1967:227). Habermas does not go beyond his critique of the bourgeois public sphere to a positive conceptualization and discussion of the "proletarian sphere," a task continued by one of his former close associates (Negt 1976; Negt and Kluge 1972). This proletarian public sphere, according to Negt (1978:77) is a sphere of "autonomous class politics" in which "subjective interests and needs, experiences and ideological inversions are articulated and assume physical force."

In sum, Habermas does not adequately address the need for new forms of self-organization, in contrast to consensus formation, as the central problem of democratic political praxis today. Instead, Habermas lingers at the threshold of a theory of praxis which Critical Theory always claimed and pointed to, but never quite entered and developed. In response to his many critics, Habermas continues to insist that "we must distinguish between the level of theoretical discourse and the organization of processes of enlightenment in which the theory is applied" (1973:31). Thus, "decisions for the political struggle cannot at the outset be justified theoretically and then carried out organizationally" (ibid.: 33). But it is clear that under such restrictions on praxis, no political struggle is possible or legitimate for Habermas. His conclusion is that "organizational questions are not primary things," a telling retreat from the issue of practical emancipation. The result is a "self-intimidating" preoccupation with theoretical analysis (Negt 1968), a preoccupation that tends to result in political and practical paralysis. "Massive and collective enlightenment" was counterposed by Habermas to the "pseudorevolution" of the New Left. The "politicization of the public sphere" is demanded, yet it is to be achieved through interaction and communication alone. Habermas's vision is rich in colorful circumscriptions and creative ambiguities and, above all, rich in abstraction and generalization. But it is meager and bloodless when it comes to the concrete determinations of collective praxis or the strategies of defense and offense within a new public sphere of self-determination and communal self-organization.

Most importantly, Habermas does not give full ontological credit to the category of experience, i.e. of individual and collective experience in which the past appears as something to be transcended and the future as something to be desired. Communication and interaction do not fully capture the dimension of human experience. As Negt argues: "It is essential to continue reflecting on *how* scientific organizational forms of experience and the modes of experience that occur in proletarian daily life . . . are and must be linked with one another in order to further organization and the collective unfolding of the individual's social possibilities and needs" (1978:79; see also Negt and Kluge 1972, ch. 1).

Experience constitutes the dialectical unity of being and consciousness, especially in the context of historical space and time, or, more accurately, in the context of *durée*. As E.P. Thompson put it in his *The Poverty of Theory* (1978:7,8):

> Experience [is] a category which, however imperfect it may be, is indispensable to the historian, since it comprises the mental and emotional response, whether of an individual or a social group, to many interrelated events or to many repetitions of the same kind of event. . . . We cannot conceive of any form of social being independently of its organizing concepts and expectations, nor could a social being reproduce itself for a day without thought. What we mean is that changes take place within social being, which give rise to changed experience, and this experience is determining in the sense that it exerts pressures upon existent social consciousness, proposes new questions, and affords much of the material which the more elaborated intellectual exercises are about.

Conclusion

We have attempted to delineate, in broad strokes, the origins and career of the concept of praxis in Critical Theory. We saw that in the early formulations of Horkheimer and Marcuse, praxis moved from the "critical awareness" of the contradictions of capitalist society to the "theoretical negation" of that society as a totality. Later, the conception of art as praxis led to a theory of the structural convergence of art and critical-activist experience, and to the notions of aesthetic experience, fantasy, play, and spontaneity as potentially liberating forces. We then examined the continuities and discontinuities of Habermas's concept of praxis with those of the earlier Frankfurt School tradition, focusing particularly on the emancipatory methodology of the psychoanalytic model, the distinction between work and interaction as constituting two separate dimensions of praxis, the dialectic of enlightened will and self-conscious potential within the arena of the public sphere and, finally, the notions of communicative competence and the ideal speech situation.

In evaluating these transformations and specifications of the concept of praxis within the framework of Critical Theory, it may be useful to adopt a critical perspective in the sense of locating these different conceptions of praxis in their specific historical context and relevance. We indicated that the careful distance of Critical Theorists from political engagement and praxis has its understandable origins in a variety of specific historical and political circumstances: in the Stalinist deformations of Marxism, in the overpowering presence of German fascism and anti-Semitism, and in the alienating and isolating effects of post–World War

II America in which the "New Sociology" of C. Wright Mills and the sociological critique of mass society could barely establish themselves. In still another historical context, the painful confrontation between Critical Theory and the New Left student movement left the exasperated and frustrated Habermas with the conviction that "there can be no meaningful theory which, per se, and regardless of the circumstances, obligates one to militancy" (1973:32).

From a more integrative perspective, one could interpret Habermas's reduction of the Marxist concept of praxis to productive activity and to the labor process as a deliberate theoretical strategy of relating praxis to different stages or levels in the development of human historical societies. Thus praxis as control over nature, as technical rationality, can be seen to recede in importance as its methods are technically established and its outcomes institutionalized. By contrast, praxis as moral-practical rationality, as the self-organization of social and political forces, and as a problem of democratization under late capitalism and early state socialism may be an urgent challenge of the present. This latter form of praxis is still evolving, although we have tried to show that it was never, for Marx, excluded from the generic concept of praxis, and that the dichotomy of instrumental and expressive forms is an unnecessary, dualistic restriction of the concept. Furthermore, play, experimentation, artistic activity, and sensual experience are all forms of praxis which are only artificially, i.e., culturally and ideologically, separated from work and productive activity. Thus it does correctly express a certain state of affairs to say that now, in advanced capitalist society, there is a separation between work and interaction. But to say that, is already a description and a performance of critical theorizing, i.e., it is not inherent in the Marxian concept of praxis which provides the basis for the critique in the first place.

If we remember that Critical Theory, in Horkheimer's and Marcuse's formulation, is a two-level structure, that is, both a theoretical reproduction of society and a metatheoretical reflection on that reproduction itself, it will not come as a surprise that the line between the two theoretical levels is occasionally blurred. In its effort to reflect on the historical and ideological limitations of traditional sociological theory, Critical Theory itself often falls prey to the reproductive tendency of positivist theorizing. As Negt (1978:79) points out: "Critical theory posed this problem [of the dialectical relationship between theory and praxis, subject and object, theoretical and empirical analysis] but was not capable of solving it because critical theory contained elements which tended toward a reversion to traditional theory in its very origins. . . . Critical theory originally conceived itself as the intellectual side of the real revolutionary emancipation process. The fact that it did not build a material base of power, may be rooted in the unfavorable circumstances of a historical situation, but at the same time it affected its truth content."

Critical Theory, especially under the influence of Habermas, has taken important steps in transcending subjectivism and objectivism and, by doing so, transcending the problem of reductionism and that of value neutrality in the social sciences. But the last step from critique to praxis which would contain all the previous ones, yet transcend them, is still missing. As a result, the theory of praxis is still in its beginnings. A curious absence in Habermas's work is any kind of reflection on the effort of Jean-Paul Sartre to develop just such a theory of praxis, particularly the notions of the project, the "progressive-regressive method," and the idea of praxis as process and historical totalization (1968). Similarly, one cannot help but wonder to what extent Pierre Bourdieu's *Outline of a Theory of Practice* (1977) was written in the spirit of a Critical Theory that sought to overcome subjectivism and objectivism, especially insofar as it addresses itself to the "dialectic of internalization of externality and the externalization of internality" (p. 72) or the "dialectic of objectification and embodiment" (p. 87). But then, it may simply be asking too much to expect Critical Theorists to take account of each others' work, display a little communicative competence, and cooperate with each other.

The remaining problem for all of them is to theorize a notion of praxis as overcoming dualism, as the transcendence of alienation in its myriad forms, and as the method of reconciliation in practical terms. Thus understood, praxis is the process of emergent, collective self-determination, a form of practical, sensuous activity based on the fullest development of human needs and powers, the struggle for undistorted and unrestricted communication between autonomous individual activity and collective life forms. Finally, and concretely stated, praxis is the overcoming of socially generated inequalities and ideologically legitimated dualities, be they master and slave, intellectual and manual, rich and poor, male and female, Black and White, old and young, normal and deviant.

References

Adorno, Theodor W. 1969. "Keine Angst vor dem Elfenbeinturm." *Der Spiegel* 23 (May 5):204–8.
———. 1973. *Negative Dialectics.* New York: Seabury.
———. 1974. "Commitment." *New Left Review* (December):75–89.
Adorno, Theodor W., et al., eds. 1976. "Introduction." In *The Positivist Dispute in German Sociology.* New York: Harper & Row.

Althusser, Louis. 1976. *Essays in Self-Criticism*. London: New Left Books.
Bernstein, Richard. 1978. *The Restructuring of Social and Political Theory*. Philadelphia: University of Pennsylvania Press.
Bourdieu, Pierre. 1977. *Outline of a Theory of Practice*. Cambridge: University of Cambridge Press.
Buck-Morss, Susan. 1977. *The Origin of Negative Dialectics*. New York: Free Press.
Giddens, Anthony. 1979. *Central Problems in Social Theory*. Berkeley: University of California Press.
Habermas, Jürgen. 1968. *Knowledge and Human Interest*. Boston: Beacon.
———. 1970a. *Toward a Rational Society*. Boston: Beacon.
———. 1970b. "Toward a Theory of Communicative Competence." In H. Dreitzel, ed. *Recent Sociology*, vol. 2. New York: Macmillan.
———. 1973. *Theory and Practice*. Boston: Beacon.
———. 1975. *Legitimation Crisis*. Boston: Beacon.
———. 1979. *Communication and the Evolution of Society*. Boston: Beacon.
Horkheimer, Max. 1935. "Zum Problem der Wahrheit." *Zeitschrift für Sozialforschung* 1 (no. 3).
———. 1974. *Eclipse of Reason*. New York: Seabury.
———. 1976. "Traditional and Critical Theory." In P. Connerton, ed. *Critical Sociology*. New York: Penguin.
Jay, Martin E. 1973. *The Dialectical Imagination*. Boston: Little, Brown.
Marcuse, Herbert. 1960. *Reason and Revolution*. Boston: Beacon.
———. 1969. "Repressive Tolerance." In R.P. Wolff et al., *A Critique of Pure Tolerance*. Boston: Beacon.
———. 1977. *The Aesthetic Dimension*. Boston: Beacon.
Marx, Karl. 1967. *Writings of the Young Marx on Philosophy and Society*. Ed. L.D. Easton and K.H. Guddat. New York: Doubleday.
———. 1973. *Grundrisse*. Ed. M. Nicolaus. London: Penguin.
Negt, Oscar, ed. 1968. *Die Linke antwortet Jürgen Habermas*. Frankfurt: Europäische Verlagsanstalt.
———. 1976. *Keine Demokratie ohne Sozialismus: Über den Zusammenhang von Politik, Geschichte und Moral*. Frankfurt: Suhrkamp.
———. 1978. "Mass Media: Tools of Domination or Instruments of Liberation?" *New German Critique* (Spring):61–80.
Negt, Oscar, and Kluge, Alexander. 1972. *Öffentlichkeit und Erfahrung: Zur Organisationsanalyse von bürgerlicher und proletarischer Öffentlichkeit*. Frankfurt: Suhrkamp.
Nietzsche, Friedrich. 1956. *The Birth of Tragedy and the Genealogy of Morals*. Garden City, N. Y.: Doubleday.
Popper, Karl. 1972. *Objective Knowledge: An Evolutionary Approach*. Oxford: Oxford University Press.
Sartre, Jean-Paul. 1968. *Search for a Method*. New York: Vintage.
Thompson, E.P. 1978. *The Poverty of Theory and Other Essays*. New York: Monthly Review Press.

About the Contributors

Ehrhard Bahr is professor of German at the University of California at Los Angeles. He is the author of numerous studies on significant figures in German literary history, among them on Kafka, Lessing, and Goethe. He is the author of *Georg Lukács* (1970) in German, and of *Georg Lukács* (1972) in English together with Ruth G. Kunzer.

Beverly Burris is teaching sociology at Trinity University, Texas. He is the author of *No Room at the Top: Underemployment and Alienation in the Corporation.*

Lucio Colletti is professor of philosophy at the University of Rome, Italy. His first published works were on Heidegger, Jaspers, and Dewey's logic. His most recent works are *From Rousseau to Lenin* and *Marxism and Hegel.* He has also written numerous articles on the same subjects which were translated into German, English, and French.

Ferenc Fehér is a member of the so-called Budapest School. He has now settled in Australia with his wife, Ágnes Heller, and is presently a Fellow at Canberra University. He is a frequent contributor to the journals *New German Critique* and *Telos.*

Franco Ferrarotti is professor of sociology at Rome University. He has been a visiting scholar at Columbia University, Boston University, and the Center for Advanced Studies in the Behavioral Sciences at Palo Alto. He was at one time member of the Italian Parliament as an independent deputy. He is editor of the journal *La Critica Sociologica.* His English-language publications are: *Toward a Social Production of the Sacred* (1976), *An Alternative Sociology* (1979), and *Max Weber and the Destiny of Reason* (1982). He is the author of more than fifteen books in Italian.

Lucien Goldmann was professor of sociology and literature at the Sorbonne in Paris until his death. He served also as director of the Centre des Recherches de Sociologie de la Littérature, Brussels. He is considered to have established the sociology of literature as a distinct field of inquiry. He wrote extensively on Lukács (*Lukács et Heidegger*). Among his books which were translated into English are: *The Hidden God* and *Human Sciences and Philosophy.*

Jürgen Habermas until recently was director of the Max Planck Institute in Starnberg, West Germany. Previously he was assistant to Adorno (1956–59) and professor of philosophy and sociology at the University of Frankfurt am Main (1964–71). Most of his numerous books have been translated into English; they include *Toward a Rational Society, Knowledge and Human Interest, Legitimation Crisis,* and *Theory and Practice.* His magnum opus is *Theorie des kommunikativen Handelns* (two volumes).

István Hermann was a student of Lukács at the University of Budapest where he is now professor of aesthetics and philosophy. He is also a member of the Hungarian Academy of Sciences. He is the author of over ten books in Hungarian. His intellectual biography of Lukács, *Die Gedankenwelt von Georg Lukács* (1978) was published also in German. He is now working on a Lukács biography.

Wolf Heydebrand is professor of sociology at New York University. He has taught at the University of Chicago and at Washington and Columbia universities. In 1953–54 he was research assistant to both Max Horkheimer and Theodor W. Adorno at the University of Frankfurt. He is the author of *Hospital Bureaucracy,* editor of *Comparative Organizations,* and has contributed many scholarly articles on organizations and Marxist theory, among others.

Peter Uwe Hohendahl is professor of German and comparative literature at Cornell University. He received his Ph.D. from the University of Hamburg and taught previously at Washington University and Pennsylvania State University. He is the author of several books on German expressionism and on the European novel, and has edited books on East German literature and on German nobility. His latest work is *Institution of Criticism,* published in 1982 by Cornell University Press.

Leszek Kolakowski was previously professor of the history of philosophy at the University of Warsaw, Poland. He is now a Fellow of All Souls College, Oxford, and has been a visiting professor at the universities of Montreal, Yale, and California, Berkeley. He is the author of over twelve books, the latest of which is *Religion* (1982), and of *Main Currents of Marxism* (1978, 3 volumes).

Hans Jürgen Krahl was a student of Theodor W. Adorno at the University of Frankfurt and one of the leaders of the student movement in Germany in the 1960s. He died young in an automobile accident. He was considered one of the most promising young scholars produced by the Frankfurt School.

Reinhard Kreckel is professor of sociology at the University of Nuremberg at Erlangen, Germany. Previously he taught at the University of Aberdeen, Scotland, and was also Visiting Theodor-Heuss-Professor of Sociology at the New School for Social Research (1979). He is the author of *Soziologische Erkenntnis und Geschichte* (1972) and *Soziologisches Denken* (1975), and the editor of other works.

Arnold Künzli is professor of political science and philosophy at the University of Basel, Switzerland. From 1946 to 1955 he was a foreign correspondent of major Swiss newspapers and also editor of the Basel-based *National-Zeitung.* He has published a *Marx-Psychobiographie* (1966), *Über Marx hinaus: Beiträge zur Ideologiekritik,* and *Aufklärung und Dialektik.*

Edith Kurzweil is associate professor of sociology, Rutgers University, Newark, and the graduate faculty in New Brunswick. She is also executive editor of *Partisan Review.* Her book *The Age of Structuralism: Lévi-Strauss to Foucault* was published in 1980 by Columbia University Press. She is also the editor of two other books and of numerous scholarly articles.

Michael Landmann was professor emeritus of philosophy and anthropology, Free University, Berlin. He was teaching philosophy and classics at the University of Haifa, Israel until his recent death. He is the author of some 20 books and over 150 articles in German. His English-language publications include *Philosophical Anthropology, Alienatory Reason,* and *The Reform of the Hebrew Alphabet.*

Paul F. Lazarsfeld was professor of sociology at Columbia University until his death. Born and educated in Vienna, he came to the United States in 1934, bringing with him the idea of the Viennese type of complex market studies combined with statistical data. His association with Columbia University as lecturer and director of the Office of Radio Research began in 1939; it later developed into the Bureau of Applied Social Research. He authored many seminal works such as *Main Trends in Sociology,* and was coauthor or editor of others, such as *The Language of Social Research* (with Morris Rosenberg).

Michael Löwy is presently with the Centre National de Recherche Scientifique, Paris, and teaching sociology at the Université de Paris. He is the author of several books in French, among which one has been published in English, *From Romanticism to Bolshevism: Lukács's Political Evolution, 1909–1929.* The same study has been translated into Spanish,

Italian, Greek, and Portuguese. He is also the author of numerous scholarly articles.

Heinz Lubasz is presently professor of history at the University of Essex, England. Previously he has taught at Brandeis University. He is the author of *Revolutions in Modern European History* and of numerous scholarly articles.

Georg Lukács, who died in 1971 at the age of eighty-six, has been regarded by many as the most original and important Marxist thinker of the twentieth century. Many of his seminal works have been translated into English: *Soul and Form, Theory of the Novel, History and Class Consciousness,* and *The Destruction of Reason.* His 2-volume *Aesthetics,* from which the excerpts have been taken, appeared only in Hungarian and German.

Joseph B. Maier is professor emeritus of sociology, Rutgers University. He was associated with the Institute of Social Research from the mid-1930s until the death of Max Horkheimer, first as Horkheimer's student and later as his assistant and friend. He is the author of *On Hegel's Critique of Kant* (1939) and *Politics of Change in Latin America,* and of numerous articles on the Frankfurt School and on Vico. As one of the literary executors of the Horkheimer estate, he is preparing—together with Alfred Schmidt—a selected correspondence of Max Horkheimer.

Judith Marcus, coeditor of the volume, has taught German and sociology at the universities of Illinois, Kansas, at SUNY at Geneseo, and at the Graduate Faculty of the New School for Social Research. She is the author of *Thomas Mann und Georg Lukács* (1982), soon to be published in English by the University of Massachusetts Press. She has published on Thomas Mann, Lukács, intellectual history, and Eastern Europe.

Giacomo Marramao is professor of political economy at the University of Salerno, Italy. He is the author of several books on political economy in Italian, and of many scholarly articles.

Karl R. Popper is regarded by many as the greatest living philosopher of science. From 1937 to 1945 he taught philosophy at the University of New Zealand. Since 1946 he has been residing in England where he became a professor of logic and scientific method at the London School of Economics. He is the author of a number of seminal works such as *The Open Society and Its Enemies, The Logic of Scientific Discovery,* and *The Poverty of Historicism.*

Alfred Schmidt is professor of philosophy and sociology at the University of Frankfurt am Main. His first book, *Der Begriff der Natur in der Lehre von Marx*, was hailed in 1962 as one of the most important new philosophical interpretations of Marx. Among his many books are *Zur Idee der kritischen Theorie, Die Kritische Theorie als Geschichtsphilosophie*, and *Drei Studien über Materialismus*. He is the editor of Max Horkheimer's *Kritische Theorie* in two volumes. He is now working— together with Joseph B. Maier—on a selected correspondence of Max Horkheimer.

Zoltán Tar, coeditor of the volume and author of the introduction, is the author of *The Frankfurt School: The Critical Theories of Max Horkheimer and Theodor W. Adorno* (1977). He wrote numerous articles and reviews of Weber, Lukács, Mannheim, the Frankfurt theorists, on Marxism, Critical Theory, and Eastern European affairs. He has been a 1981–82 National Endowment for the Humanities Fellow and a 1982–83 Fulbright Fellow for the forthcoming "Selected Correspondence of the Young Georg Lukács" (Columbia University Press).

Göran Therborn is reader in sociology at the University of Lund, Sweden. Among his books are *Critique and Revolution* and *Science, Class and Society*. He is a frequent contributor to the *New Left Review*, among others.

Index